Basic Family Therapy
Second Edition

Also by Philip Barker

Basic Child Psychiatry
Fourth Edition
0 00 ,383318 6

Forthcoming titles

Basic Forensic Psychiatry
Malcolm Faulk
0 00 383347 X

Basic Adolescent Psychiatry
Derek Steinberg
0 00 383232 5

Behaviour Disorders and Mental Retardation
John Corbett and Chris Oliver
0 00 383301 1

Interprofessional Consultation
Derek Steinberg
0 00 383348 8

Basic Family Therapy
Second Edition

Philip Barker
MB, BS, FRCP(Ed), FRCPsych, FRCP(C), DPM, DCH

COLLINS
8 Grafton Street, London W1

Collins Professional and Technical Books
William Collins Sons & Co. Ltd
8 Grafton Street, London W1X 3LA

First published in Great Britain by
Collins Professional and Technical Books 1986

British Library Cataloguing in Publication Data
Barker, Philip 1929–
   Basic family therapy.—2nd ed.
   1. Family psychotherapy
   I. Title
   616.89′156   RC488.5

ISBN 0–00–383159–0

Typeset by V & M Graphics Ltd, Aylesbury, Bucks
Printed and bound in Great Britain by
Mackays of Chatham, Kent

This book is dedicated to the world's deprived and unhappy children, and their parents; and to those who strive to help families to a better life.

Contents

Foreword

Quentin Rae-Grant, MB, ChB, DPM, FRCPsych, FRCP(C)

Professor and Head of Child Psychiatry and Professor of Behavioural Science, University of Toronto; Psychiatrist in Chief, The Hospital for Sick Children, Toronto.

The task of preparing a basic text in a sprawling clinical area is akin to the challenge that faces the gardener in a neglected and untrimmed thicket. In both the growth is luxurious and uncontrolled. In both it is difficult to see the basic shape because of a proliferation that is erratic and exuberant. With both a topiary emerges which may be truer to the original intention but undoubtedly loses some of the rich, errant limbs of adventure. The task is clearly a challenging and a rewarding one. To cut too much threatens the very existence; to cut too little leaves an amorphous product, verdant but without form or purpose.

In this book Professor Philip Barker, a British-trained and Canadian practising Child and Family Psychiatrist, performs exactly this task for the field of family therapy. This field is notable for its growth over the last thirty years, for the vigour with which it has produced ideas, and for the rapidity with which these ideas have been accepted. It is also characterized by the variety of seemingly different opinions and schools within a general practice that puts the family rather than the individual as the issue of prime concern. While many of these differences are differences of metaphor rather than of substance, they do represent for people coming anew to the field of family therapy a dazzling and confusing array of contradictory opinions and practices.

The field of family therapy began its career with trenchant criticisms of the absence of validation of individual therapy. It now stands in a position where it can be equally and, because of its earlier accusations, even more validly accused of similarly being defenceless in this present era that requires rigorous scientific proof.

New treatments, as Laties and Weiss observed in the nineteen-forties, go through the cycle of panacea, poison and pedestrian remedy. The period of panacea is that of enthusiasm for the new, the necessary evangelical zeal, and the unfortunately exaggerated claims of which the field of mental health has seen far too many in the past. The period of poison is ushered in by reports of complications, negative reactions, disappointment with the earlier enthusiastic claims, and a negative feeling almost in inverse relationship to the positive feeling that preceded it. Most treatments finally settle somewhere between the two extremes, acquiring a place alongside other treatments, integrating with other treatments, and with indications for and against their use in particular situations.

Because this book is clearly and analytically written, it also affords a view of where the field of family therapy lies today. Clearly it has been a fertile and prolific field in its brief thirty-year existence. It has attracted and mostly retained original and creative minds. It has flourished in the field of practice. It started from the attraction for the unorthodox. Along the way it has developed its own orthodoxy or, more properly, orthodoxies. Thus there is a thinly veiled contempt for insight and more cheer for getting the family to do something and then to control this active change process. Theories and concepts abound, sometimes radically different, sometimes different only in the terms they use. There is a rich clinical literature of experience, personal style, and preferred selection of concepts. Such is the desire to share these clinical gems that it has become the spectator sport of the therapies – the video as well as the group is watching or even intervening.

Yet much remains unclear. Despite several runs at the problem, even Barker seems unable to synthesize definitive indications for the choice of family therapy as the preferred mode of treatment. Treatment chosen (and this is true for many of the psychotherapies) still tells more about the therapist than the recipients and their needs.

Even more striking is the lack of concern, except from a very few, for the value of family therapy practised along with other modalities and how these can augment each other. Medication is alluded to in passing albeit reluctantly, again reflecting accurately the thinking in the field.

In research in family therapy, the yet unaccepted challenge is to substitute product for process, to measure change by change in function in everyday life rather than intrafamilial alterations. To illustrate – the success of family treatment of sexual abuse of children can be measured not by the alterations of the family dynamics that may take place, but by whether or not the abuse of the child ceases. Family therapy faces the challenge to substantiate its theories and their derived hypotheses in a rigorous, scientific way, and to weed out the extraneous, the irrelevant, or the overlapping. It faces the need to compare and contrast various types of family therapy for various conditions and in combination with other therapies, so that prescriptions may move from the elegantly idiosyncratic to validated preferred methods.

The analogy with the gardener continues to be valid, particularly with this publication by Philip Barker. His *Basic Child Psychiatry*, also published by Collins Professional and Technical Books has gone through several editions. It is regarded as an excellent distillate of that field and a valuable document both to people at the beginning of their careers and to those with a continuing interest in updating their skills. This edition of *Basic Family Therapy* is like the plant that has been pruned for the third or fourth time. The terseness which prevailed in the first volume is equally present; the style has been refined and combines great clarity and crispness with a flow and readability which makes this a pleasure to peruse. The form and shape of this field have been evolving between the two editions of this book. The field itself has acquired a certain maturity and a greater degree of coherence from at least some of the divergent schools. There is more centrality in the basic opinions. These are reflected in the greater confidence with which Philip Barker can state certain of the accepted principles in this area of practice.

Most introductory texts are so geared towards basic information that they run the risk of boring their reader. Professor Barker's book is the opposite. It uses sophistication to create a synthesis that is cogent as well as clear. The bushes have indeed been well trimmed on this second occasion.

In a field as rapidly changing as family therapy, a periodic update of basic texts is a requirement. Professor Barker has addressed his by now finely honed talents to do this, and to do it in an exemplary fashion. It is once again a pleasure as well as an education to read this important addition to the field.

Introduction

This new edition of *Basic Family Therapy*, like the first, is designed to provide a clear, easily-read and readily understandable introduction to the subject. A basic, eclectic survey of the field may be needed even more now than it was four years ago when the first edition appeared, for there has been an explosive growth in the family therapy literature since then. The wealth of journal articles, books, videotapes and workshops, by therapists of every persuasion, can easily intimidate the newcomer to the field.

The proliferation of literature makes the task of writing a concise but comprehensive account of the subject more difficult than it was four years ago. So many new techniques and theoretical ideas have been described and proposed that it is hard to deal adequately with, or even to mention, all of them. On the other hand, there has been some coming together of family therapists of different schools during the 1980s, and it seems that the contemporary therapist is increasingly using techniques and ideas drawn from a wide range of sources.

There is much new information in this edition, and I have also rearranged the contents. Almost all the text is either new or rewritten. I have tried to emphasize the basics of the subject rather than go too deeply into its more exotic and complex aspects. I believe, however, that one of the most important features of any introductory book is the assistance it gives readers in obtaining further information. I have therefore greatly increased the number of references to the literature, so that readers will readily be able to obtain further information on any aspect of family therapy they wish to study in more depth. If a book such as this is to be kept to a reasonable size, many aspects of family therapy must, perforce, be dealt with in quite a cursory fashion, but the reader will quickly be able to discover where to read more about structural therapy, or expressed emotion in families, or the use of paradoxical methods – or any other topic mentioned.

Whilst I have aimed to present an eclectic view of family therapy, I have also offered the reader a model of therapy which I have myself found useful. I believe this is a good starting point for those learning family therapy, whether or not they come to it after having become expert in other types of psychotherapy. This model may also serve as an illustration of how existing ideas from a variety of family therapy schools may be brought together and built into a coherent approach to family problems.

Where there is no acknowledgement to anyone else, the cases quoted are from my own practice, with the exception of the story of Fay, described in Chapter 10. This family was treated by my colleague, Karen Rempel, and her account appears also in my book *Using Metaphors in Psychotherapy* (1985). I have altered the names and other details that might identify families mentioned, while taking care not to change the essential features of their cases.

Finally, I must emphasize that you cannot learn family therapy from a book. There is no substitute for well supervised clinical practice, and I do not intend this as a family therapy cookbook. But clinical work must be complemented by reading, and the well rounded therapist should have a wide knowledge of the literature in the field, though not necessarily a detailed knowledge of all aspects of it. It is to fill such a need that I have written this book.

Philip Barker

Acknowledgments

Many people have helped me with this book. Foremost among these are my colleagues in the Mental Health Programme at Alberta Children's Hospital, especially Karen Rempel, a creative and painstaking therapist and a continual inspiration to me. I have learned from many other therapists over the years, and it is impossible to name them all, but I owe a special debt of gratitude to Duane Bishop, now at Brown University and Butler Hospital, Rhode Island. He provided me with supervision and teaching of a high order, starting shortly after I came to Canada in 1975. Among the other colleagues who have helped broaden my knowledge of and develop my skills in family therapy are Erica Schneider, formerly of the Parent and Child Centre, Birmingham, UK; Barbara Dydyk, of Thistletown Regional Centre in Toronto; and Karl Tomm and Evan Imber-Black (formerly Coppersmith), of the University of Calgary.

Evan Imber Black also commented helpfully on drafts of the early chapters of the book. My wife Heather, daughter Lorna, and prospective son-in-law Janok all read drafts of the manuscript and made many suggestions for improving the text. They often helped me express my ideas more concisely and clearly. Without their help the book would surely read less well.

I also received massive help in this book's preparation from Barbara Hatt, librarian at Alberta Children's Hospital. She has been indefatigable, efficient and always courteous in dealing with my requests – they must sometimes have seemed more like demands – for literature and information about literature. Without her help the book would certainly have been a less useful reference source. Richard Miles, my editor, has been his usual courteous and helpful self, and I have also received invaluable input from Shelley Reinhardt of Oxford University Press, New York.

I am delighted, too, that this edition is being co-published in the USA by Oxford University Press.

Despite all the help I have received from others, responsibility for the book, and the imperfections it no doubt has, is solely mine.

Chapter 1

The Development of Family Therapy

Family therapy takes the family group as the unit for study and treatment. Most other types of psychotherapy focus on the individual, and concentrate on 'intrapsychic' or behavioural processes. This individual approach has its limitations; in the treatment of juvenile delinquents, for example, the 'medico-psychological model' – the basis of which is the consideration and treatment of the individual – has not proved effective. Research has emphasized rather the 'power of the contemporary environment' (Clarke, 1985).

Family therapists tend to see the problems of individuals in the context of this environment, especially the family. They concentrate on interpersonal processes, rather than on problems within the minds of the individuals in the families they treat. We might think of them as traffic engineers whose job it is to see that vehicles travel smoothly on highways. Therapists with an 'intrapsychic' orientation would correspond to mechanics, whose concern is the internal workings of vehicles. There are differences, though, because mechanics repair cars one at a time, whereas individuals are sometimes treated in groups, even though the focus is on their individual problems; and the boundaries of families are more distinct than those of highway traffic systems.

The two approaches to psychotherapy – individual and family – are complementary. Thus healthy members make healthy family groups more probable, just as reliable vehicles help ensure smooth traffic flows. Similarly a well-functioning family system helps the development and adjustment of the family members, just as traffic runs more smoothly in a well-designed and efficient road system than in a poor system.

Despite their complementary functions and related aims, family therapy, and therapy designed to help individuals change, require different skills and training. The theoretical systems on which they are based are also different. In the same way, traffic engineers require skills and training different from those needed by mechanics.

The early years of family therapy

Family therapy developed after the Second World War. Although the importance of the families of psychiatric patients was previously recognized by some psychiatrists, their response was often to remove the patients from their families in order to ensure recovery in a setting away from the possible adverse effects of their family environments.

Freud, whose influence was considerable in the pre-war years, believed that his patients' neurotic problems dated back to unhealthy childhood interactions with their parents; he therefore aimed to isolate them from their families. The problems his patients had in their relationships with their parents were dealt with in the context of the 'transference relationship' – that is, a relationship which developed between patient and therapist and which represented that between patient and parent. It was in this context that neurotic conflicts were resolved. Family therapy thus represents the reverse of the way Freud sought to help his patients; this probably helps explain why the family approach was a relative latecomer among psychiatric therapies.

Yet psychoanalytically trained therapists were among the first to consider the family approach to psychiatric disorders. Notable among these pioneers was Nathan Ackerman. The publication of his book *The Psychodynamics of Family Life* (1958) marked an important point in the development of family therapy. It is clear from what Ackerman says in this book that he came to family therapy from psychoanalysis. He discusses the merits of the family approach to the treatment of emotional disorders, but also makes references to psychoanalysis and the use of individual psychotherapy.

Ackerman (1958) pointed out that while psychiatrists had 'acquired adeptness in the retrospective study of mental illness, in the minute examination of family histories ... they [had] not yet cultivated an equivalent skill in the study of family process here and now' (page 89). He went on to say that, by acquiring skills in working with whole family groups, we would come to have 'a new dimension to our insights into mental illness as an ongoing process that changes with time and the conditions of group adaptation.' This prophecy now seems to be in the process of being fulfilled, but by a whole range of mental health disciplines, not just psychiatry.

The year before Ackerman's book appeared Christian Midelfort (1957) published *The Family in Psychotherapy*. While Midelfort writes that 'the family ... must be viewed as the unit for treatment', the book is really about the use of relatives in the care of psychiatric patients. Midelfort seems to have realized the importance of the family and involved family members in the treatment of psychiatric patients much more than had been usual; but like many others who followed him, he was unable immediately to make the conceptual leap necessary in order to regard the family as the patient.

Ackerman, too, took time to change his way of thinking. Considerable development is evident in his second book *Treating the Troubled Family* (1966a). This is indeed a book about the treatment of 'the family as an organic whole'. It is a major pioneering treatise which addresses all the main issues pertinent to the treatment of families. It also contains clinical examples, covering 'treating husband and wife', 'child-oriented intervention', 'rescuing the scapegoat', and 'the return to reality' – in which the treatment of a family with a schizophrenic member is described.

Ackerman was not the sole pioneer of family therapy. According to Nichols (1984), John Elderkin Bell 'may have been the first family therapist'. Bell, however, did not publish descriptions of his work until the early 1960s (Bell, 1961; 1962), and his book *Family Therapy* did not appear until 1975.

Several other groups of researchers and therapists were also active in the USA in the 1950s, most of them concerned with the investigation and/or treatment of schizophrenics and their families. In 1952 Gregory Bateson obtained a grant to study communication and its different levels; he was joined in 1953 by Jay Haley and John Weakland and, later in the year, by a psychiatrist, William Fry. In 1954 the group obtained another grant which led to the setting up of the 'Project for the Study of Schizophrenia'. Don Jackson joined this group as a consultant and as the supervisor of psychotherapy with schizophrenics. The work of this group has had a profound influence on the thinking of many family therapists. Bateson and his colleagues introduced the concept of the 'double-bind', which they considered an important feature of the communication occurring in the families of schizophrenics. It is discussed in a later section.

The Mental Research Institute (MRI) was founded by Don Jackson, in Palo Alto, in 1959. Although Jackson acted as consultant to the Bateson group, the MRI was separate. The staff of the Institute were also notable pioneers in our field and the MRI continues to this day, whereas Bateson's group disbanded in 1962.

Theodore Lidz, another pioneer, began studying the families of schizophrenic patients at Johns Hopkins Hospital, Baltimore in 1941, and later published a survey of fifty families (Lidz and Lidz, 1949). He noted a high prevalence of broken homes and seriously disturbed family relationships. In the early 1950s he moved to Yale University where he proceeded to study sixteen families, each containing a schizophrenic member, over periods of time ranging from six months to several years. He introduced the concepts of *schism*, the division of the family into two antagonistic and competing groups; and *skew*, whereby one partner in the marriage dominates the family to a striking degree, as a result of serious personality disorder in at least one of the partners.

Lyman Wynne, another important figure, started to study the families of schizophrenics shortly after he joined the staff of the National Institute of Mental Health in 1952. In 1972 he became Professor in the Department of Psychiatry at the University of Rochester, New York, but continued to study schizophrenic families until his recent retirement. He introduced the concepts of *pseudo-mutuality* and *pseudo-hostility*.

Pseudo-mutuality (Wynne et al, 1958) arises when an individual feels the need for a relationship with someone – perhaps because of failure in other relationships or, in a child, because of painful earlier experiences of separation anxiety. A person who becomes involved in a pseudo-mutual relationship tries to maintain the idea or feeling that he or she is meeting the needs of the other person – in other words that there is a mutually complementary relationship. Thus those involved in pseudo-mutual relationships are predominantly concerned with fitting together at the expense of their respective identities. Genuine mutuality, by contrast, thrives upon divergence. The partners in the relationship take pleasure in each other's growth. Each has a real wish that the other develop and achieve fulfilment of desires and expectations. In pseudo-mutuality there is dedication only to the sense of reciprocal fulfilment, not to its actuality.

Pseudo-hostility (Wynne, 1961), like pseudo-mutuality, is a surface phenomenon only. The apparent emotional relationship, in this case hostility, is a substitute for a true, intimate relationship, which is absent.

Wynne and his colleagues came to the conclusion that the families of 'potential schizophrenics' are characterized by pseudo-mutuality and consequently have rigid, unchanging role structures which they cling to as essential; the attempt by a family member to become more independent is a matter for concern and is resisted.

Wynne et al (1958) also introduced the idea of the 'rubber fence'. This is a flexible psychological boundary to the family, one that keeps individual family members confined within the family role structure, so that the children do not have normal and necessary experiences with people outside the family. Instead there is a continual effort to maintain the family as a self-sufficient social system. The boundaries of the family system move, if necessary, like a rubber fence so that members cannot leave psychologically, even though the feelings and ideas acceptable within the family may constantly shift (Singer and Wynne, 1965).

Carl Whitaker, a psychoanalytically trained psychiatrist, had started to experiment with the treatment of family groups before he took up the Chair of Psychiatry at Emory University, Atlanta in 1946. Together with John Warkentin and Thomas Malone, who moved to Atlanta with him, he continued this work, developing his own distinctive approach to family therapy. Nichols (1984) describes Whitaker as 'strong-willed and colorful ... dynamic and irreverent'. He organized a series of conferences on family therapy, promoting the exchange of views, ideas and techniques among many of the early family therapists. After resigning his university appointment in 1955, he continued in practice in Atlanta until 1965, developing his own, highly personal approach to therapy (Whitaker, 1958). This is discussed further in Chapter 3.

Ivan Boszormenyi-Nagy, another psychoanalyst turned family therapist, founded the Eastern Pennsylvania Psychiatric Institute in Philadelphia in 1957. This became a major centre for the study of families. With his colleagues, James Framo, David Rubenstein, Geraldine Spark and Gerald Zuk, Boszormenyi-Nagy developed an approach to family therapy which paid particular attention to the multi-generational aspects of family therapy. Like Whitaker, Boszormenyi-Nagy and his colleagues made extensive use of co-therapy, the practice of having two therapists in the room with the family being treated. Boszormenyi-Nagy (1965) edited the book *Intensive Family Therapy*, which contained a variety of contributions surveying much of the contemporary family therapy scene.

Two other important early pioneers were Murray Bowen and the British psychiatrist Ronald Laing, both of whom started to study the families of schizophrenics in the mid-fifties. Bowen (1960) developed the concept of schizophrenia as a process requiring three generations to develop. Typically, he said, the grandparents were 'relatively mature but their combined immaturities were acquired by one child who was most attached to the mother' (Bowen, 1960, page 354). When such a child married an equally immature spouse the same process was repeated in the next generation. The result was one child who was very immature while the others were much more mature. Bowen believed that such a child is liable to develop schizophrenia in an attempt to adapt to the demands of growing up.

Bowen (1960) also noted considerable emotional distance or 'emotional divorce' between the parents of schizophrenic patients. He noted that these parents had difficulty with questions of domination and submission and often could not make decisions. They thus tended to avoid responsibility. Parental conflict had usually started within the first few days or weeks of marriage.

Out of such situations Bowen and his colleagues saw the schizophrenic disorder arising. Despite consciously wishing their child to grow and develop normally, the parents were unable to avoid doing things to keep the child in a helpless position – a kind of 'double-bind' situation. Bowen saw the mother–child relationships as being the crucial ones. In adolescence the subject changes from helpless child to poorly functioning young adult to helpless patient. The psychosis is related to a disruption of the symbiotic attachment of mother and child, together with 'a collapse of the long-term independent father–mother–patient triad' (Bowen, 1960, page 368). Bowen's formulation offers the prospect of helping these families by means of family therapy, which he considers to be a more effective and quicker procedure than individual therapy – though still a long and difficult one.

Laing also studied the families of schizophrenics, starting in the 1950s. His findings concerning the first eleven patients and their families were reported by Laing and Esterson (1964) and his ideas were also set out in a chapter entitled 'Mystification, confusion and conflict' (Laing, 1965). He places great emphasis on the concept of *mystification*. The term can be used both to describe the *act* of mystification and the *state* of mystification. The state of mystification is one of being befuddled and clouded. The mystified person feels masked from situations and finds them obscure. The act of mystification is what is done by others to bring about this state in a person. The person may or may not be aware of being befuddled, and so may not *feel* mystified.

Laing considers that some mystification occurs in everyday life. People sometimes deny the experience of others and replace it with their own. A mother may use a 'straight' way of telling her son to go to bed saying, for example, that it is bedtime or that it is her function to determine when he should go to bed; or she may use a 'mystifying' way saying, for example, 'I'm sure you feel tired, darling, and want to go to bed, don't you?' Here a command is dressed up as an expression of solicitude and concern. It attributes to the child feelings, such as fatigue, which he may not have. Laing believes that mystification is especially powerful when one person appears to have the right to determine the experience of another.

Laing (1965, pages 347-48) quotes the case of a fifteen-year-old who, over a short period of time, started to behave in a more autonomous way. She became quieter, no longer shared her thoughts and feelings with her mother, wanted to be by herself, began to take a great interest in boys, became disobedient and truculent, started to smoke and ceased to believe in God. Her mother did not like these changes in her daughter and felt they must be caused by either illness or 'evil'. As the process continued the daughter began to feel sick and to feel bad. She began to ask her mother, whom she still trusted, to forgive her for her badness. Meanwhile, the mother continued to complain of those normal developmental features which first caused her to feel concerned about her daughter, while making no complaints about the delusional and other psychotic symptoms the girl later developed.

Mystification, as illustrated by this case, is thus a means whereby one person tries to control another. The person who is trying to achieve control does not use direct means, but instead attributes opinions, feelings or values to the other person. An example is to be found in the following quotation from Laing (1965, pages 349-50):

> *Mother*: I don't blame you for talking that way. I know you don't really mean it.
> *Daughter*: But I do mean it.
> *Mother*: Now, dear, I know you don't. You can't help yourself.
> *Daughter*: I can help myself.
> *Mother*: No, dear, I know you can't because you're ill. If I thought for a moment you weren't ill, I would be furious with you.

Laing links his concept of mystification with the ideas of Wynne and Lidz. He considers that it functions to maintain stereotyped roles at the expense of reality, rather as pseudo-mutuality and pseudo-hostility do. It also serves to fit other people into a set mould as described by Lidz et al (1958). The parents are impervious to their children's emotional needs and instead preserve their own integration by maintaining 'their rigid preoccupation about who they are and who they ought to be, who their children are and ought to be, and the nature of the situation that characterizes family life' (page 351). The imperviousness to children's needs and the masking of disturbing situations in the family, both of which are described by Lidz and his colleagues, are common concomitants of mystification.

Laing (1965) also refers to Searles' (1959) description of six ways 'to drive the other person crazy'. Searles was another early student of the families of schizophrenics, and Laing points out that all six of the processes Searles describes are mystifying – involving, as they do, things which undermine the other person's confidence in his or her own emotional reactions and perception of reality.

The six ways are:

1. Repeatedly drawing attention to areas of the subject's personality of which the subject is unaware.

2. Stimulating the person sexually in situations in which sexual gratification would have disastrous consequences.
3. Exposing the person to stimulation and frustration, either simultaneously or in a rapidly alternating pattern.
4. Relating to the person simultaneously at levels which are unrelated, for example sexually and intellectually.
5. Switching 'emotional wavelengths' while discussing the same topic, for example talking in a humorous way and a serious way about the same thing.
6. Switching from one topic to another while maintaining the same 'emotional wavelength', for example talking about a matter of life and death in the same vein as a trivial matter.

The sixties

Most of the pioneers mentioned above continued their work with families in the 1960s, although Bateson, who was never a family therapist, left the field early in the 1960s to study communication among animals. He worked at the Oceanographic Institute in Hawaii until his death in 1980. The pioneers were joined by many new entrants to the family therapy field. We will review first the continuing work of the pioneers, and then consider the contributions of some of the new entrants.

Jackson, at MRI, continued to develop his methods of treating families. Although he had psychoanalytical training, increasingly he concentrated on the study and treatment of inter-personal processes, rather than individual psychopathology. He introduced the term 'behavioural (or communicational) redundancy', to describe the way family members, and others in ongoing relationships, develop repetitive patterns of interaction – patterns which therapy must sometimes assist in altering if the changes that clients seek are to occur. He also wrote about such concepts as homeostatic mechanisms – the means whereby families maintain a relatively constant way of functioning – complementarity/symmetry, 'quid pro quo' processes and, of course, the double-bind. He also distinguished between families' 'norms' – rules which are not overtly acknowledged, but can be observed when the functioning of families is studied; 'values' – rules which are consciously acknowledged; and 'homeostatic mechanisms', which are rules about how the family's norms and values are to be applied. These 'rules about rules' he dubbed *metarules*.

Jackson's work appeared in a number of papers, some of them written with John Weakland (Jackson and Weakland, 1959, 1961; Jackson, 1961; Jackson, 1965). Jackson was also co-author, with Paul Watzlawick and

Janet Beavin, colleagues at MRI, of *Pragmatics of Human Communication* (Watzlawick et al, 1967), an important book which set out much of what had been discovered at the MRI concerning human communication, especially in families. Jackson died in 1968.

Jay Haley, an original member of Bateson's group, also made major contributions to the growth of family therapy during the 1960s, as indeed he has continued to do ever since. He was much influenced by the work of Milton Erickson, about which he later wrote in the book *Uncommon Therapy: The Psychiatric Techniques of Milton H. Erickson* (Haley, 1973). *Strategies of Psychotherapy* (Haley, 1963) set out Haley's early position, and a series of books and articles have since traced his development as one of the most continuingly creative of the fathers of family therapy (Haley, 1967; 1976; 1980; 1984).

Haley developed a directive approach to therapy with families. He also stressed the importance of the hierarchical structure of the family, seeing many family problems as due to confused or dysfunctional hierarchies. Similarly he emphasizes the importance of the therapist being in charge of the treatment, rather than allowing the family members to take over. Like many family therapists, Haley has never held the attainment of insight by clients in high regard; for him, the main need is to get the family to *do* something – something that will help them change their habitual, but dysfunctional, ways of interacting. This key aspect of strategic therapy, is discussed further in Chapter 10.

For Bowen, the 1960s seem to have been a time of personal re-examination and exploration of his own family relationships. But first he expanded the range of his clinical work, so that he treated the families of children with problems other than schizophrenia. In doing so he discovered that many of the processes which he and others had observed in the families of schizophrenics were also to be found in other families. Bowen also described what he called the *undifferentiated ego mass*, observing that in many families with problems, members often seemed to lack separate identities (Bowen, 1961).

In the mid-sixties Bowen experienced an emotional crisis. He came to understand this as being related to unresolved issues in his own family which, as it turned out, were not in his current nuclear family, but in his family of origin. His problems concerned the process of *triangulation*, a concept that has played a large part in the thinking of family therapists. Triangulation occurs when a third member is drawn into the transactions going on between two people – often a marital couple. Instead of communicating directly with each other the couple commun-icate through the 'triangulated' third person, who may be a child. Thus one spouse may voice complaints about the other to a child, who is then faced with the problem of whose side to take, or whether to take either parent's side, and indeed how to react generally. This may result in the child becoming unduly anxious, or acting in an antisocial way, or developing other problems. At the same time, the issues with which the parents are faced remain unresolved.

Apparently, such unresolved problems existed in Bowen's family of origin. Eventually Bowen returned to his family in Pennsylvania and managed to 'detriangulate' himself, a process which he described in a paper published anonymously (Anonymous, 1972), though it was not long before its authorship became apparent. This paper is included in the volume *Family Therapy in Clinical Practice* (Bowen, 1978), which brings together all of Bowen's major publications.

By the end of the 1960s Bowen had developed his own ways of working with families. While his theory and method have not changed much since then, he no longer treats the families of schizophrenic patients but rather applies his concepts to the many other problems with which families come for therapy. His approach is discussed further in Chapter 3.

Ackerman continued as a leader of the family therapy movement throughout the 1960s. In 1961, with Jackson, he co-founded *Family Process*, the first journal to be devoted to family therapy, and one which is still pre-eminent in the field. Haley was the journal's first editor, a position he held until 1969.

Ackerman wrote *Treating the Troubled Family* (1966a) and made many other important contributions to the family therapy literature (Ackerman, 1961; 1966b; 1970a; 1970b; 1970c). He died in 1971, but is commemorated in the name of the Ackerman Institute in New York City.

Throughout the 1960s Wynne and Boszormenyi-Nagy continued their work at, respectively, the National Institute of Mental Health (NIMH) and the Eastern Pennsylvania Psychiatric Institute. Bowen, however, left his position as chief of family research at NIMH, Wynne replacing him in this role. All three continued to work along lines similar to those they had pursued in the 1950s. The year 1965 saw the publication of *Intensive Family Therapy*, edited by Boszormenyi-Nagy and Framo.

In 1966 and the early part of 1967 the Committee on the Family of the Group for the Advancement of Psychiatry distributed questionnaires to over 500 people thought to be interested in or practising family therapy (Group for the Advancement of Psychiatry, 1970). One of the questions asked of the respondents was which theorists in the field of family therapy had most influenced their work. An analysis of the first 127 replies produced the following names, in order of the frequency with which they were mentioned: Virginia Satir, Ackerman, Jackson, Haley,

Bowen, Wynne, Bateson and John E. Bell. This is probably a fairly accurate listing of the most influential early workers in the field. Of them we have yet to mention, Satir.

Virginia Satir, a charismatic and enormously talented therapist with a forceful personality and strong views, joined Jackson shortly after he founded MRI. Her book *Conjoint Family Therapy* (1967) has influenced many therapists. She places special emphasis on the communication of feelings in families and, more than many other family therapists, she is also interested in the personality and development of the individuals in a family and the psychodynamic processes behind their behaviour. Satir was particularly interested in how people select their mates, and the effects on this process of their self-esteem. This is referred to further in Chapter 3.

A major figure to emerge in the United States during the 1960s was that of Salvador Minuchin. A native of Argentina, and a psycho-analytically trained psychiatrist, he went to work with young delin-quents at the Wiltwyck School for Boys in New York City. He soon realized the limitations of current methods of treating these young people and their families – mostly urban slum families. Along with a group of colleagues, he developed methods of working with them. His innovative approach, published jointly with four colleagues in the book *Families of the Slums* (Minuchin et al, 1967), was probably responsible for his being offered the directorship of the Philadelphia Child Guidance Clinic. Under his direction, this was transformed from being a traditional child guidance clinic into one of the world's foremost family therapy centres; it also moved from an old, rather run-down building into the magnificent structure, adjacent to the equally fine Philadelphia Children's Hospital, which it occupies today. But that story belongs to the seventies.

Minuchin was also largely responsible for the development of the structural school of family therapy. This has been a major contribution to the development of our field. Minuchin and other structural therapists are particularly interested in how families are organized in sections, or subsystems, and in the boundaries between these parts; also in the boundaries between the family unit being studied and the wider community. Therapists using this model see family problems as related to their structure. There may be a structure which does not permit satis-factory functioning, for example a lack of an appropriate boundary between the parental and the child subsystems. The structural approach is already evident in *Families of the Slums* (Minuchin et al, 1967), but was set out in perhaps its classic form in *Families and Family Therapy* (Minuchin, 1974). It is described more fully in Chapter 4.

Another of Minuchin's important contributions to family therapy was his advocacy of the use of the one-way observation screen. Until the advent of family therapy, therapists rarely watched each other work; even therapists in training limited themselves to reporting to their supervisors what they believed had happened during their therapy sessions. Family therapists have opened up the process, both by the common practice of having observers watch and listen through one-way observation screens, and by the use of videotapes which enable therapy to be reviewed, if necessary, repeatedly. Minuchin played an important part in this development.

Although family therapy developed primarily in the United States there were, even in the 1960s, important developments elsewhere. A 'family psychiatric unit' was established at the Tavistock Clinic, London, in the late 1940s. Under the direction of Henry Dicks (1963; 1967), the staff of this unit worked mainly with marital couples who were having problems in their relationships. Another British pioneer of family therapy was Robin Skynner, who made two noteworthy contributions to the family therapy literature before the 1970s (Skynner, 1969a; 1969b).

In Germany family therapy had made enough progress that Horst Richter could, by 1970, publish his book *Patient Familie*. This was later translated into English and published as *The Family as Patient* (Richter, 1974). The Italian onslaught did not come until the 1970s.

In Montreal, Canada, Nathan Epstein led the 'family research group' at the Department of Psychiatry of the Jewish General Hospital, in collaboration with the McGill University Human Development Study. This led to the development of one of the earlier systems for describing the functioning of families, the 'Family Categories Schema' (Epstein et al, 1968).

The seventies

Family therapy came of age in the decade of the seventies. It was increasingly accepted, at least in some form, in most major psychiatric centres. Family therapists also began to address themselves to a wider range of disorders; there was less emphasis on schizophrenics and their families, though these were still studied and treated, especially in certain centres. Indeed, it is ironic that despite the early work with schizophrenics, family therapy has probably found less application in the treatment of psychotic subjects and their families than it has in the therapy of other clinical problems.

Most of the centres in which family therapy had been developed, practised and taught in the 1960s continued their work into the 1970s, but they were joined by many new ones. Following Ackerman's death in 1971 the Family Institute, which he had founded in 1960, was renamed the Ackerman Institute, and it has continued to this day as a centre of excellence. Donald Bloch became its director and remained so throughout the decade. Lynn Hoffman and Peggy Papp were notable members of the staff of the Institute during the 1970s. Papp (1977) edited *Family Therapy: Full Length Case Studies*, an interesting book which presented the work of twelve prominent family therapists, including herself; each contributed an account of the treatment of a family. The book provides a fascinating snapshot of family therapy in the 1970s, and effectively illustrates the wide diversity of approaches used by therapists at that time. Hoffman (1981) wrote *Foundations of Family Therapy*, which surveyed comprehensively the state of family therapy as the seventies came to an end.

The Philadelphia Child Guidance Clinic, under Salvador Minuchin's leadership, became one of the world's leading family therapy centres during the seventies. *Families and Family Therapy* (Minuchin 1974), which deserves to be called a classic, became the standard textbook for those wanting to learn the 'structural' approach to family therapy. The Child Guidance Clinic was closely associated with the Children's Hospital of Philadelphia, and this facilitated the joint study of children with psychosomatic disorders and their families. This led to the book *Psychosomatic Families: Anorexia Nervosa in Context* (1978), which Minuchin wrote with Bernice Rosman and Lester Baker. The work of Minuchin and his colleagues on psychosomatic problems was important in defining some of the links between disorders of family systems and the mainstream of medicine.

Haley spent several years at the Philadelphia Child Guidance Clinic before going to Washington, DC where, with his wife, Cloe Madanes, he founded the Family Institute of Washington, DC. Also established in Washington, DC, by Murray Bowen, was the Georgetown Family Center, which teaches Bowen's brand of family systems theory.

The Center for Family Learning was founded in 1973 by Philip Guerin, a former student of Bowen's. It is located in New Rochelle, New York, and is one of the many family therapy training centres to emerge during the seventies. Guerin (1976) was also editor and part-author of *Family Therapy: Theory and Practice*, another of the steadily rising flood of books on family therapy.

The Family Institute of Westchester was founded in 1977 and is located in Mount Vernon, New York. It has on its staff a number of teachers who formerly worked at the Center for Family Learning. It is currently directed by Elizabeth Carter who, with Monica McGoldrick, another member of the staff, edited and in part wrote the book *The*

Family Life Cycle (Carter and McGoldric, 1980). The Institute has an excellent reputation as a teaching centre, combining an extended family systems approach with elements of structural and strategic therapy.

During the 1970s, and since then, Murray Bowen continued to refine his theory, renaming the 'undifferentiated family ego mass' the 'nuclear family emotional system'. He also ceased treating the families of schizophrenics, applying his methods instead to a wider range of problems, not usually involving a psychotic family member. Wynne, on the other hand, continued to study schizophrenics and their families and built up a highly productive team of researchers at the University of Rochester (Wynne et al, 1978). He and his colleagues also addressed the important issue of the relative 'invulnerability' of some children by studying the 'presence of healthy communication patterns and other aspects of healthy family functioning that may coexist with disturbed family relationships and, indeed, that may reduce the risk of severe psychopathology and promote healthy or even superior functioning in the offspring' (Wynne et al, 1982). In his therapy Wynne came to combine a systemic approach with the use of strategic and psychoeducational methods.

In Canada, Epstein and his colleagues made the Department of Psychiatry at McMaster University, Hamilton, Ontario an important centre for the practice and teaching of family therapy. With his colleagues Duane Bishop and Sol Levin Epstein (1978), developed, from the Family Categories Schema, the McMaster Model of Family Functioning, and later, the McMaster Model of Family Therapy. Also in Canada, at the University of Calgary, Karl Tomm (1980) developed a programme which combined cybernetic concepts with systems thinking. Subsequently Tomm, like many other family therapists, came to be heavily influenced by the Milan group of therapists.

The seventies also saw important developments in Europe, especially Italy and Great Britain. In Milan, Mara Selvini Palazzoli played the major role in setting up the Institute for Family Study. This was founded in 1967 but had its main impact in the 1970s. Palazzoli was one of four psychoanalytically trained psychiatrists who became the 'Milan Group'. The others were Gianfranco Cecchin, Giulana Prata and Luigi Boscolo. They were much influenced by the work of the Palo Alto therapists, especially Bateson and Watzlawick and his colleagues. They seem to have seen many severely disturbed families and were struck by the fact that these families came for help, yet seemed determined to defeat the attempts of their therapists to help them change their way of functioning. They proposed the term 'families in schizophrenic transaction' for these families and described them and their treatment in the book *Paradox and Counterparadox* (Palazzoli et al, 1978a; the book was originally published in Italian in 1975).

The Milan group made important contributions to family therapy in the 1970s, including the understanding they gave us of the severely disturbed families they described in their book. These contributions included: their techniques of 'circular interviewing' and 'triadic questioning', whereby the therapist asks a third family member about what goes on between two others; their concept of developing hypotheses about the functioning of a family in advance of the interview and then devising questions to test the hypotheses; and a generally more highly 'systemic' way of looking at families.

In Rome, Maurizio Andolphi started working with families early in the 1970s, and in 1974 he founded the Italian Society for Family Therapy. By 1979 he was able to publish an excellent systems-based book *Family Therapy: An Interactional Approach*. In this Andolphi, apparently successfully, sets out to apply the 'theories and clinical experiences that have been developed in the United States' to the Italian context. From his work it seems that family systems and their problems are much the same worldwide – or at least in the western world.

In Britain, Skynner continued to work with families and in 1976 published his book *One Flesh: Separate Persons* (published in the USA as *Systems of Family and Marital Psychotherapy*). This provided a comprehensive view of the state of family therapy as seen by a British psychiatrist trained in the Kleinian school of therapy. Important work was also being done during the seventies at the Family Institute in Cardiff, Wales. The first director of this Institute, Sue Walrond-Skinner (1976), published *Family Therapy: The Treatment of Natural Systems*, a book which was addressed primarily to social workers. Brian Cade and Emilia Dowling were among the other members of the staff of this Institute who were responsible for placing it in the forefront of family work in Britain. Walrond-Skinner (1979) also edited the book *Family and Marital Psychotherapy*, which contains contributions by eleven British family therapists and gives quite a wide-ranging view of the British family therapy scene as the seventies drew to a close.

In Britain another pioneer of the family approach to psychiatric problems was John Howells, a child psychiatrist turned family therapist, who founded the Institute of Family Psychiatry in Ipswich. Howells has tended to pursue a lone course, developing his own methods and training programmes, with particular emphasis on 'vector therapy', a treatment designed to alter the emotional forces in families. His approach has not been widely adopted, and he has also marked it out from others by insisting on calling it 'family psychiatry', rather than 'family therapy'.

To complete this brief review of family therapy in the 1970s one further name needs to be mentioned, that of Milton Erickson. Erickson was not a family therapist; he was an unconventional, but creative psychiatrist who made much use of hypnosis in his practice of psychotherapy. He studied hypnotic phenomena throughout his long career and published many books and articles on hypnotherapy. He founded the American Society of Clinical Hypnosis and was the first editor of the *American Journal of Clinical Hypnosis*. He greatly influenced Haley, who studied with him, and wrote *Uncommon Therapy: The Psychiatric Techniques of Milton H. Erickson* (Haley, 1973), a fascinating description of how Erickson worked.

Erickson's importance in the development of family therapy is due to his interest in the interpersonal processes in which his patients were engaged, and his use of strategic methods of treatment. Traditional psychodynamic psychotherapy explores and aims to resolve the repressed conflicts of individuals. This model is of limited value in dealing with family systems. The objective of the family therapist is rather to get the family members to *do* something different – to interact with each other in a different way – and this was how Erickson approached many of the clinical problems with which he was con-fronted. Moreover he found, as family therapists have too, that telling people what to do does not always work. Instead indirect – or 'strategic' – methods, including paradoxical ones, may be needed.

The recently published *Conversations with Milton H. Erickson, MD*, Volumes II and III (Haley, 1985a; 1985b) consist of transcriptions of conversations between Erickson and, in most cases, Jay Haley and John Weakland, though on a few occasions Gregory Bateson was present also. These took place in the 1950s and early 1960s and make it clear that Erickson had by that time developed many innovative, strategic ways of helping families change. Erickson's influence on the mainstream of family therapy has mainly been indirect, however. He himself wrote little on the subject and his innovative ideas were spread mainly by those who studied with him, notably Haley and Jackson.

The seventies also saw an explosive development of family therapy literature. Some of the many books written during the decade have been mentioned. Many new journals joined *Family Process* and journals were established in Britain, Australia and Canada, as well as in the USA. The principal family therapy journals are listed in Appendix A.

The eighties

This book is written as the 1980s are still unfolding; even the early years of the decade are too close to be seen in perspective, but a *rapprochement* appears to be developing between the different schools of family therapy. Many of the pioneers were charismatic characters with strongly held views, and in family therapy's early days it was hard to discern a body of knowledge which all, or even most, therapists would accept. I believe this situation is changing. Extreme views seem to be giving way to those occupying the middle ground. Therapists of particular schools are increasingly using the concepts, theoretical ideas and techniques of other schools. It is becoming possible to write an 'eclectic' book on family therapy, drawing on ideas developed in different centres around the world. Indeed the first (1981) edition of this book was an attempt to do this – something which has become easier since then.

It now seems that family therapy has established a secure place among methods of psychiatric treatment. The systemic approach to human problems has proved itself to be valuable. The history of family therapy to date provides ample evidence that considering and modifying the interactions of people, by whatever means, can be a valuable way of treating a variety of problems. Until the family approach was tried and studied psychiatry was too much concerned with individuals and too little with their ecological contexts. This imbalance is being put right; sometimes particular therapists have gone overboard in one direction or the other, but we are probably now nearer to an appropriate balance than we have ever been before.

The systemic approach also seems to be spreading to fields other than family therapy. Its importance in family medicine was recognized by the establishment of the journal *Family Systems Medicine* in 1983, under the editorship of Donald Bloch. A systemic approach to the practice of family medicine is also explored in the book *On Diagnosis: A Systemic Approach* by Michael Glenn (1984), a family practitioner. Nursing is another discipline which is recognizing the importance of looking at people in the context of their social (especially family) systems. Evidence of this was the appearance of the book *Nurses and Families* by Lorraine Wright and Maureen Leahey (1984). This looks at how nursing care may be – indeed probably should usually be – family focused.

Summary

Family therapy has developed since the Second World War as a new way of dealing with the human problems which were previously dealt with by one of the various forms of individual psychotherapy. It is based on a new conceptualization of how these problems come to exist. Formerly they were thought to be mainly the result of intrapsychic processes – or individual 'psychopathology' – which was believed often to have its roots in early childhood experiences. The family approach, by contrast, is based on the belief that these problems are related to the current interactions taking place between the individuals in the family and, sometimes, between these individuals and other social systems. They are understood as having their cause in people's present social systems, rather than in their past histories.

Family therapy started in the late 1940s and the 1950s in a small number of centres in the USA. Initially these were mainly concerned with schizophrenic patients and their families. Subsequent years have seen the spread of family therapy throughout the western world, and its application to the full gamut of psychiatric disorders. In its early days family therapy was divided quite sharply into schools of thought and practice, these often being led by charismatic therapists with strongly held views. A process of assimilation of the different schools is now occurring, and a common body of knowledge concerning the field is emerging. The systemic approach to problems is also beginning to influence other sections of the helping professions, for example family medical practice and nursing.

This chapter has outlined the development of family therapy, with more emphasis on its earlier stages than its more recent ones; the latter will receive mention in later chapters. Although many important names have as yet gone unmentioned, including those of prominent contemporary therapists, they will be featured in later chapters.

Chapter 2

Healthy Families and Their Development

We live in a pluralistic society in which it is hard to define a 'typical' or even a 'normal' family. Yet there are certain criteria we can apply to determine the health of a family. The most important is the extent to which the family provides for the needs – material, emotional and spiritual – of its members. Even this, fairly basic, criterion is open to interpretation, however, since it is hard to decide when the needs of family members are being adequately met; indeed, any cut-off point must inevitably be arbitrary.

The complex issues raised when we try to define a 'normal' family were addressed by authors of various theoretical persuasions in the book *Normal Family Processes* (Walsh, 1982). In the opening chapter Froma Walsh, the book's editor, discusses criteria for normality. She distinguishes families which function asymptomatically, those that function optimally, and those that function in a way which is statistically average. Another possibility is to define normality in terms of the processes occurring in the family. She says of these:

> Basic processes involve the integration, maintenance, and growth of the family unit, in relation to both individual and social systems. What is normal – either typical or optimal – is defined in temporal and social contexts, and it varies with the different internal and external demands that require adaptation over the course of the family life cycle. (Walsh, 1982, page 6)

In western society, particularly since the industrial revolution, there has been a tendency to regard the 'nuclear' family – husband, wife and children – as 'normal', but over recent decades this view has become progressively less tenable. Writing over 10 years ago Keller (1974) stated that the 'ideal' family of married husband and wife with dependent children, 'living in a household of their own, provided for by the husband's earnings as the main breadwinner and emotionally united by the wife's exclusive concentration on the home', accounted for no more than one third of the families in the United States. The proportion of such families has continued to decrease since then, as divorce rates have risen and more married women with children have obtained work outside the home.

Walsh, in 1982, pointed out that the United States divorce rate had doubled since 1965, leading to a situation in which one third of marriages were likely to end in divorce. (Similar figures apply to Britain and other countries in western Europe.) More children than ever before are reared throughout childhood by one parent, and fewer are nowadays adopted or admitted to institutions. On the other hand, the proportion of blended, stepfamily units is increasing.

There have been similarly marked changes in the number of women in the workforce. In the USA the number of such women grew by 173 per cent between 1947 and 1980, whereas the number of working men increased by only 43 per cent; by 1980 there were 45.6 million working women in the US (Bianchi and Spain, 1983; Duvall and Miller, 1985). A similar trend is evident in Britain where in 1984 working women comprised nearly 11 million out of a total working population of 27 million.

As will become clearer in later chapters there are many theoretical models available for use in assessing families, and thus in deciding whether they are 'normal'. The factors which any particular therapist will regard as important will depend to some extent upon that therapist's orientation. An integration of the various points of view has not yet occurred, but attempts have been made, for example, by Barnhill (1979) and Fleck (1980).

Barnhill suggested that healthy families can be distinguished from dysfunctional ones on the basis of the following eight dimensions, which he grouped under four 'basic family themes', as follows:

I. Identity Processes
   1. Individuation versus enmeshment.
   2. Mutuality versus isolation.
II. Change
   3. Flexibility versus rigidity.
   4. Stability versus disorganization.
III. Information Processing
   5. Clear versus unclear or distorted perceptions.
   6. Clear versus unclear roles or role conflict.
IV. Role Structuring
   7. Role reciprocity versus unclear or conflictual roles.

8. Clear versus diffuse or breached intergenerational boundaries.

In therapy, any one or more of these issues may need to be addressed. They are seen by Barnhill (1979) as interdependent, change in one often promoting change in others.

Fleck (1980) suggested five parameters of family functioning that should be considered. These are:

1. *Leadership*: this is a result of the parents' personalities, the characteristics of the marital coalition, the complementarity of the parental roles, and the parents' use of power – that is, their methods of discipline.
2. *Family boundaries*: this covers ego boundaries, generation boundaries, and family–community boundaries.
3. *Affectivity*: important in this parameter are interpersonal intimacy, the equivalence of family triads, family members' tolerance of each others' feelings, and unit emotionality.
4. *Communication*: relevant here are the responsiveness of family members to each other, the extent to which verbal and non-verbal communications are consistent, the ways in which family members express themselves, the clarity of the form and syntax of their talk, and the nature of members' abstract and metaphorical thinking.
5. *Task/goal performance*: this covers the nurturance given to members by the family, the ways in which the children master the process of separation from the family, behaviour control and guidance, the nature of family members' peer relationships and the guidance they are given in these, leisure activities, how the family copes with crises, and the adjustment of members after they leave the family of origin.

Skynner has also discussed 'the healthy family', in the opening chapter of the book, *Family Therapy: Complementary Frameworks of Theory and Practice* (Bentovim et al, 1982). In the following chapter Bentovim and four colleagues present differing views of a family considered healthy, based on the viewing of videotape recordings of the family carrying out various tasks. Interviews with two families that considered themselves normal are also presented in *Families and Family Therapy* (Minuchin, 1974).

Schlesinger (1979, page 8) defined the following types of families in Canada, and the classification is probably applicable to the western world generally:

(a) The nuclear family, consisting of husband, wife and children.
(b) Childless couples, consisting of husband and wife.
(c) One-parent families, made up of widows, widowers, divorced persons, separated and deserted spouses and non-married mothers.

(d) Adopted families, consisting of husband and wife and adopted children.

(e) Reconstituted families, consisting of second marriages or 'blended families'. There are eight possible types of reconstituted family:

  (i)   divorced man–single woman
  (ii)   divorced man–widowed woman
  (iii) divorced man–divorced woman
  (iv)   single man–widowed woman
  (v)   single man–divorced woman
  (vi)   widowed man–single woman
  (vii) widowed man–widowed woman
  (viii) widowed man–divorced woman

The range of reconstituted families is actually greater than this list implies because many variations are possible, depending on whether children are brought into the marriage by one or other partner, or both partners, and on the parenthood of these children. In addition there may be children of the 'reconstituted' union.

(f) Communal families, which may consist of a group of families, or a group of families with children and some single adults.

Homosexual couples and families should probably be added to the above categories.

These are not only the main social groupings within which people may live; they are also the units with which family therapists must work. For each category there is presumably a range of 'normal' functioning.

Ethnic variations

In assessing and understanding families, as well as in offering them treatment, it is important to take into account the considerable ethnic variations between them. What is normal in one ethnic group may not be so in another; it can be tempting for therapists, especially those just starting to work with families, to expect that all families will have norms and values similar to their own. This, however, often leads to problems in engaging families in therapy, and consequent therapeutic failure. A good working knowledge of the ethnic variations to be found in the population with which one is working is therefore important.

McGoldrick (1982) has reviewed the relationship between ethnicity and family therapy. She points out that ethnicity is 'deeply tied to the family' and is transmitted by means of the family. She makes the point also that family therapists in the past have tended to pay too little attention to the cultural influences on families. Yet any therapist from a white Anglo-Saxon background who, like myself, has been faced with West Indian and Asian immigrant families in Britain, or North American native families in Canada, knows that their cultural norms are very different from those of white middle-class families, and that therapy, if it is to be successful, must take these differences into account.

McGoldrick's article is the opening chapter of the book *Ethnicity and Family Therapy* (McGoldrick et al, 1982), in which various authors review features of family life in a wide range of cultures. Included are Native American, Black, Afro-American, West Indian, Mexican, Puerto Rican, Cuban, Asian, French Canadian, German, Greek, Iranian, Irish, Italian, Jewish, Polish, Portuguese, Norwegian and British cultures; there are also chapters dealing with various 'special issues', such as a description of intervention in a Vietnamese refugee family and therapy with families in cultural transition. The book is useful because it illustrates how varied family functioning can be, and how important ethnic variations are, but it concerns itself mainly with the situation of the various groups as immigrants into the USA. There are, moreover, many variations within the cultures described, so that such a book can be no more than a guide to working with the different ethnic groups.

The functions of families

The criteria proposed by Barnhill (1979), Fleck (1980) and others are ways of assessing how well a family is functioning. But what are the functions that a family should perform? The most obvious ones are reproduction and the raising of children. The family also has an economic function; it must be able to provide at least the basic necessities of life for its members.

Western society depends upon families to rear and socialize children. It helps in the process by providing schools, which socialize as well as educate, and sometimes other institutions – youth groups, boy scouts, girl guides, church groups, summer camps and so on – which supplement what the family does. Western society also waits in the wings for families to run into trouble. Thus it provides social service agencies to assist families, or to take over the care of children when families are considered unable to carry out their functions in rearing children satisfactorily; it also provides financial and material help, though on widely varying scales, to needy families.

In the past many of the functions now carried out by society's agencies were performed by the extended family. This consisted of a kinship network of grandparents, uncles, aunts, adult siblings, cousins and other relatives. Sometimes people unrelated by blood but living in the same social network participated also. Nowadays a smaller role is generally played by the extended family and the neighbourhood community, especially in urban societies and above all in large cities. Thus the nuclear family, that is parent or parents and their children, is faced with a bigger task to perform than it used to have. The reasons for this change are complex. The movement, since the start of the industrial revolution, from a rural society to an urban one is a major factor. Another is the increased ease with which people can travel long distances to seek education and work. Children are nowadays liable to obtain jobs in places far from their families of origin.

These changes are not universal, of course. In western society today there are still villages, small towns and rural areas in which extended family networks continue to function well; even in the cities some extended family networks exist. These, however, are often families which have recently migrated to the cities, and as the generations succeed each other there is a tendency for such families to become more 'nuclear'. In many parts of the world the extended family continues to play a major role, though with much variation from culture to culture.

The traditional western view of the purposes of the family is perhaps set out as well in the Church of England's *Book of Common Prayer* (1662) as it is anywhere. According to this book, matrimony was ordained for three reasons. The first was for the 'procreation of children, to be brought up in the fear and nurture of the Lord and to the praise of His Holy Name'. This is a way of describing the purpose we have been discussing – raising children and teaching them society's ways and values. Secondly, matrimony was to be a 'remedy against sin, and to avoid fornication'. In other words, marriage was seen as a legitimate context for the expression of mankind's sexuality. Thirdly, marriage was ordained 'for the mutual society, help and comfort that the one ought to have for the other, both in prosperity and adversity'.

In marrying couples who had passed the age at which they could be expected to have children the priest was permitted to omit the first of the above reasons. Nowadays, with efficient methods of contraception readily available, an increasingly large number of couples of childbearing age are choosing not to have children. The main purposes of such families are therefore presumably to provide 'mutual society, help and comfort', and a context for the maintenance of a satisfying sexual relationship for the partners.

Family therapists are concerned with all forms of family life, whether traditional or not. All of these probably aim, explicitly or implicitly, to provide for some or all of the functions envisaged by the compilers of the English prayer book, but they set about achieving these aims in different ways. Attitudes towards sex and its expression have changed greatly over the years, and continue to do so. The easy availability of effective methods of birth control is certainly a factor which has led to a more permissive attitude, in many sections of society, towards sexual activity among young people. Many people nowadays regard premarital sex as quite acceptable; much the same applies to the increasingly common practice of unmarried couples living together. The family therapist must be sensitive to the standards and the moral and cultural values of the families coming for treatment; these must be accepted even though they may differ from the therapist's.

Courtship

The courtship of a man and a woman is a preliminary to the development of a family. The courting partners each bring to the relationship their value systems, their temperamental and personal characteristics and their capacities to love and enter into a giving, sharing relationship. Each partner has needs and looks to the other to meet them, usually without being consciously aware of these needs.

Young people often enter into a courtship relationship on the basis of feelings of mutual sexual attraction. This is not always the case, however, since some relationships develop primarily out of companionship and mutual interests. The element of romantic love is often strong, though, and in contemporary western society tends to be reinforced by the mass media, popular music and the youth culture generally. To all this is often added the projection by one member of the courting couple on to the other of those characteristics that will meet the one member's emotional needs. This is the state of being 'in love'; the 'loved' partner is not viewed realistically, but instead is endowed by the other partner with whatever characteristics that person needs him or her to have. The courtship should last long enough for each partner to discover whether the other one does actually meet his or her emotional needs. Sometimes marriage or parenthood, or both, are entered into before this process is complete. This is obviously a risky situation.

Many courtships are entered into, only to be abandoned when the partners realize that they do not suit each other. Eventually, though, a couple decide to commit themselves to each other, and it is still usual to formalize this by going through a marriage ceremony.

Family development

Duval's book *Marriage and Family Development*, now in its sixth edition and with a co-author (Duvall and Miller, 1985) has long been a standard reference source on family development. It divides family development into eight stages. These are:

1. Married couples without children.
2. Childbearing families, in which the oldest child is less than 30 months of age.
3. Families with pre-school children, in which the oldest child is from 2½ to 6 years of age.
4. Families with schoolchildren, with the oldest child between 6 and 13 years of age.
5. Families with teenagers, with the oldest child between 13 and 20.
6. Families launching young adults, starting with the first child's departure from the home and ending when the last one goes.
7. Middle-aged parents, from the 'empty nest' to retirement.
8. The stage of ageing family members, the period from retirement to death.

For family therapists, a useful way of dividing the family life cycle into stages is that proposed by McGoldrick and Carter (1982). These authors take the view that 'the central underlying process to be negotiated is the expansion, contraction and realignment of the relationship system to support the entry, exit, and development of family members in a functional way' (page 175). They also point out that the ever greater diversity of family life means that, 'It is becoming increasingly difficult to determine what family life cycle patterns are "normal" ... often a cause of great stress for family members, who have few models for the passages they are going through' (page 167). The family is a system passing through time, in a social context which is also changing – examples of this being the falling birth rate, the increasing life expectancy, and the rising divorce and remarriage rates.

The first of McGoldrick and Carter's stages is that of the *unattached young adult*, a person who is between families, and who should have accepted separation from his or her family of origin. Such a person should achieve a sense of self differentiated from the family of origin, and also the capacity to develop intimate relations with peers, as well as finding a suitable place in the workforce.

The next stage in family development, according to this scheme, is the *joining of families through marriage* – which nowadays is not always legally formalized. This process involves commitment of the two partners to each other, so that a new marital system is formed and the appropriate adjustments are made in the couple's relationships with their extended families and friends.

The third stage is that of the *family with young children*. The arrival of children necessitates great changes in the family system. To the marital system is added a new parental system. The new generation must be accepted into the family and there is a further change in the family's relationships with the extended family. The role of grandparent can be a significant and important one.

Stage 4, the next one, is that of the *family with adolescents*. During this stage there should be a gradual but substantial change in parent–child relationships, so that the children become increasingly independent; for a time they may move in and out of the family system, the boundaries of which become increasingly flexible. At the same time parents begin to address their attention once again to marital as opposed to parental issues, and sometimes also to career issues; wives who have stayed at home to rear their children may return to the workforce or seek new social activities.

Stage 5 is that of *launching children and moving on*. This is almost a new stage, since until about a generation ago most parents were engaged in raising their children throughout their active adult lives. The low birth rate and the long life span of most adults have now changed this, and it can lead to difficulties. During this stage there may be many exits and entries of family members, as the younger generation leaves, and the parents' parents tend to become frail or ill, and thus dependent upon *their* children. As the children are launched into the world and become independent adults, a new type of relationship is needed, based on adult-to-adult equality. Then, as the children marry and have children, the role of grandparent develops. The children of the family require to come to terms with their in-laws, and may at this period also have to deal with illness or death in the older generations.

The final stage in McGoldrick and Carter's scheme is that of *the family in later life*. The parental generation has become the grandparental generation, and the grandparents may be on their own; they may need to acquire new interests and a new social circle. At the same time the middle generation plays a more central role in the family, perhaps looking after the older one rather than the reverse, while making room for, and using, the wisdom and experience of the older generation. This is also a time when illness and death in the older generation are common, affecting spouses, siblings and peers.

This scheme bears many resemblances to that proposed by Haley (1973), based on his study of the work of Milton Erickson. His scheme comprises the following stages:

1. The courtship period.
2. Marriage and its consequences.

3. Childbirth and dealing with the young.
4. Middle marriage.
5. Weaning parents from children.
6. Retirement and old age.

A further valuable source of information is *The Family Life Cycle*, edited by Elizabeth Carter and Monica McGoldrick (1980). This has chapters on the various stages of the family life cycle, written by different authors, and chapters dealing with the implications for family development of such events as death and serious illness, separation, divorce and forming a remarried family. Among the other subjects covered are variations in the family life cycle seen in 'multiproblem poor families', and cultural variations, as exemplified by the Mexican–American family. In the final chapter, Friedman (1980) discusses the family aspects of the rites of passage through which are celebrated various stages of development, notably funerals, weddings and puberty rites; he also considers three other 'nodal points' which nowadays have become important in the development of many families, namely divorce, retirement, and geographical uprooting.

Variations in family development

Family development is subject to many variations, some of which are discussed in *The Family Life Cycle* (Carter and McGoldrick, 1980). These may be caused by the death of family members, divorce or separation, the late birth of a child or children after the others have grown up, or the bringing of new children from another family into a reconstituted family. Chronic illness, financial setbacks, migration, natural disasters, military service, war, and many other circumstances have their effects, great or small, upon families and how they develop. No model of family development can take account of all such possibilities, but therapists need to be aware of them and deal with them appropriately.

Therapy sometimes involves helping families deal with the effects of adverse circumstances, but on other occasions it may be better to assist them to obtain help elsewhere. Thus it may be better, at least initially, to refer a family facing severe financial difficulties to a credit counselling agency, rather than offering therapy aimed at altering its transactional patterns; or a family containing a member with a chronic disabling illness, for example cystic fibrosis, might be put in touch with a self-help group such as the local Cystic Fibrosis Association. Such actions may assist both a family's development and its current functioning. They may be sufficient to help the family deal satisfactorily with its problems, or they may be an aid to therapy conducted directly with the family group.

The clinical importance of family developmental stages

Every family that presents for treatment needs to be looked at from two points of view. One concerns the structure and way of functioning of the family, topics that are dealt with in later chapters. The other concerns the family's developmental stage. Many of the clinical problems of families are best viewed as difficulties in making the transition from one developmental stage to the next. When this is the case the therapist needs to consider how the developmental process can be freed or assisted. Are there any road blocks – either in the family's social context, or within the family itself – which can be removed by any means available to the therapist?

Barnhill and Longo (1978), using Duvall's stages of family development, defined nine *transition points* which have to be negotiated as the family passes from stage to stage. These are:

0–1 Commitment of the couple to each other.
1–2 Developing new parental roles, as husband and wife become mother and father.
2–3 Accepting the new personality, as the child grows up.
3–4 Introducing the child to institutions outside the family, such as school, church, scouts, guides, sports groups and so on.
4–5 Accepting adolescence, with the changed roles associated with this, and the parents' need to come to terms with the rapid social and sexual changes occurring in their son or daughter.
5–6 Allowing the child to experiment with independence in late adolescence and early adulthood.
6–7 Preparations to launch, the term used by Barnhill and Longo for the process whereby the parents come to accept their child's independent adult role, including starting his or her own family.
7–8 Letting go – facing each other again, when child-rearing is finished and the couple face each other as husband and wife alone again.
9–10 Accepting retirement and/or old age, with the changed lifestyle involved.

Barnhill and Longo (1978) go on to discuss the use of these concepts in therapy. They apply the psychodynamic ideas of fixation and regression to the process of family development, and especially the various transitions listed above. So just as an individual's development may be fixated at a particular stage – that is to say it has failed to proceed beyond that stage at a time when it normally would have done so – so may a family fail to make one or more of the needed transitions. In addition a family may regress, that is go back to an earlier transition point, usually when faced with some stress. Barnhill and Longo also use the concept of 'partial fixation', when a family life cycle transition has not been made successfully, although a partial and even superficially satisfactory adjustment has been made. Such an adjustment is precarious, however.

The same authors go on to illustrate the use of the concept of transition points in the treatment of families in crisis. They believe that when a family life cycle transition has not been successfully accomplished, families are especially susceptible to stress. The careful consideration of a family's developmental stage, and of the transition points it has successfully passed, should probably be a part of the assessment of any family coming for therapy. Therapy will often focus on these issues too.

Optimal family functioning

While it is impossible to define a 'normal' family, it is helpful to have a concept of 'optimal' family functioning. Many therapists, understandably, like to offer families more than the resolution of the particular problems for which they have come seeking help. In doing this, the model of 'optimal family process' described by Kirschner and Kirschner (1986) in Chapter 2 of their book *Comprehensive Family Therapy* is valuable.

In defining optimal functioning, the Kirschners consider the marital transactions, the rearing transactions and the independent transactions – the functioning of the individual family members in their own activities, be they vocational, educational, social or recreational. In two-parent families, the marital transactions are the foundation on which everything else rests. The marital couple first need to meet each other's needs.

> As reparental figures for each other, each spouse can provide inputs that were lacking in the partner's family of origin. A spouse may program the other for self-confidence and success through suggestions and directives regarding productive behaviours. Education, modeling, confrontation, validation, encouragement, and inspiration may also be provided ... (Kirschner and Kirschner, 1986, page 30)

If the marital relationship is a poor one, the foundations for a successful, well-functioning family unit are lacking, or at least are shaky. It is hard for a couple who do not get along well together to function well as a parental team. An important part of the assessment of a family, therefore, is the assessment of the quality of the marital relationship; how to do this will be discussed later. The essential question, though, is whether the marital partners get satisfaction out of their relationship; they should nurture, affirm and support each other, and the relationship should be one of mutual trust and respect. Elements of romance and intimacy are involved in this, and the couple need also to have effective ways of recognizing and resolving conflict.

Many families are nowadays headed by single parents. Such parents need to perform the same tasks as couples, but are required to find the support they need elsewhere than in the marital relationship. An important part of the process of working with one-parent families is identifying the sources of support, and the social network, available to such families, and involving them, directly or indirectly, in the treatment process. In many cases the estranged parent of the children is important in this regard.

The *rearing system* comprises the way the parental couple work together to rear and care for their children. The parents should be agreed on the principles to be used in doing this, and the care provided according to these principles should meet the needs of their children and foster their healthy development. It is the transactions or the network of relationships between the parents and the children, and those between the children, that largely determine how the children develop.

Finally, the therapist should consider the relationships that exist between the members of the family and the wider community of which the family is a part. In the terminology of 'comprehensive family therapy' these are the *independent transactions*. In an optimally functioning family these enable family members to function autonomously outside the family. A successful outcome of child-rearing is one which produces children who are able to do this.

Summary

Families vary greatly in their composition, and healthy family functioning can take many forms. Precisely which features are regarded as important in assessing whether family functioning is normal depends to some extent upon the theoretical orientation of the therapist making the assessment. The cultural values of families, and their ethnic backgrounds, are also relevant factors.

There is also a predictable series of stages families must go through as they are formed, bear and rear children, and then launch the children into the world. Consideration of the stage which a family that presents for treatment has reached, and whether it is having or has had difficulty surmounting a particular family developmental hurdle, is an important part of the family therapist's task.

The concept of 'optimal family functioning' is helpful; it is concerned not just with the problems a family may present, but also with whether the needs of the marital couple, and the children, are being met as well as they might be. A family should both meet the current emotional and psychological needs of all its members, and prepare the children for an autonomous existence in the wider world into which it will, at the appropriate time, launch them.

Chapter 3

Some Basic Theoretical Concepts

As therapists came to look upon families, rather than individuals, as the basic units they were treating, they found that they needed new theoretical schemes upon which to base their work. Those which had been developed for use with individuals, and which had served therapists well in individual therapy, were much less useful in work with family groups. Theories were needed of how *families* function, what may go wrong with their functioning, and how they may be helped to change. This is not to say that the psychological and biological processes occurring in individuals are irrelevant. To return to the automotive analogy we used in Chapter 1, traffic engineering should take account of the size, speed, acceleration and reliability of the vehicles that will be using the road system; yet a study simply of individual vehicles and how they function would not be a satisfactory basis for designing a road system in which traffic can flow freely. The study of vehicles alone would tell us no more than the study of individual chessmen would tell us of the game of chess.

It *is* possible to look at the psychological and emotional functioning of individual family members, and by this means to gain some understanding of how family members relate to each other. The intelligence levels, personality types, emotional states and mental defence mechanisms used by each member can be studied, and family patterns of defences may be observed. However, while all these points have their relevance, consideration of them alone still treats the family as a group of individuals. It does not tell us anything very much about the family as an entity in itself.

So the family therapist needs a way of conceptualizing the functioning of the family group, as distinct from understanding its members. In attempting to meet this need, family therapists have pressed into use ideas derived from such theoretical schemes as general systems theory, cybernetics, learning theory, communications theory and theories about the relative functioning of the right and left cerebral hemispheres.

Theories derived from individual and group psychotherapy

Before considering the new theoretical models family therapists have used, we will briefly review the application to family work of older theories, developed for use with individuals.

(A) Psychodynamic theory

Many of the early family therapists relied heavily on psychodynamic theory in their work with families. Ackerman (1956) introduced the idea of 'interlocking pathology', arguing that the psychopathology of the different members of a family fitted together to produce the family system the therapist encountered. Bowen's concept of the 'undifferentiated ego mass', discussed in Chapter 1, is another example of the application to families of ideas derived from the study of the psychopathology of individuals. Satir, too, in her book *Conjoint Family Therapy* (1967), concerned herself with the relationship between individual psychopathology and family dynamics. In her second chapter, entitled 'Low self-esteem and mate selection', she explored how people whose views of themselves are poor depend on what others think of them. They come to present a 'false self' to the world, rather as Winnicott (1960) defined the term; this false self is designed to give people the impression they want them to have and is based on identifications. Such people, Satir says, are liable to marry each other. Each partner is deceived by the psychological defences of the other – that is by the false self the other presents to the world. At the same time each has fears of disappointment and difficulty in trusting others, including their respective mates, which can lead to serious marital difficulties.

While many other leading family therapists came into the field with psychoanalytic training – for example Lidz, Wynne, Minuchin, Dicks, Boszormenyi-Nagy, Skynner and Epstein – according to Nichols (1984, page 223) they 'traded in their ideas about depth psychology for those of systems theory'. How far such therapists have used their understanding of individual psychodynamic processes to facilitate their work with families it is hard to say. Consideration of the psychopathology of individuals is, however, evident, for example in the work of Dicks (1967) and Skynner (1976). Psychodynamic theory does not, however, seek to explain the workings of family systems.

(B) Group therapy

Much group psychotherapy is based on psychoanalytic principles. The aim is to help the members of the group gain insight through the process of group interaction; the therapist's role is principally that of facilitator and, sometimes, interpreter of what is happening between the group members. While family members can certainly learn things of value to each other in a 'group therapy' setting, the situation is quite different from that which exists when a group of unrelated strangers starts to meet – the context in which most group therapy methods have been developed. The long shared history of family members, their established – and often shared – psychological defences, and their set attitudes towards each other may make it hard for them to engage in the process of interaction and confrontation which is the essence of most group therapy. It is likely that instead the family will simply re-enact the same scenarios that are characteristic of its usual way of functioning - unless the therapist does something active to change this, which is not typical of most forms of group therapy.

Other theories which have been used in therapy with families

(A) Cybernetics

Cybernetics is a term that was introduced by Weiner (1948) to describe regulatory systems that operate by means of feedback loops. This process requires a receptor of some sort, a central mechanism and an effector. These are connected to form a feedback loop. A good example is a thermostatically controlled central heating system. The thermostat is the receptor; it constantly measures the temperature in the space that has to be heated. It is connected to a central mechanism, the furnace. The system is set up so that when the temperature drops to a certain level, the furnace is switched on and heat is distributed, via the effector channels, to the area to be heated. When the temperature rises to another predetermined level, the reverse process occurs and the furnace is shut off. This process provides an illustration of 'homeostasis' – the tendency of systems, or at least some of them, to maintain themselves in a fixed, steady state.

Quite early in the development of family therapy some of the ideas of cybernetics were adopted by therapists trying to understand the fixed, but dysfunctional, processes occurring in many of the families they saw. The difficulties many families experienced when faced with the need to make changes was 'explained' by saying that the homeostatic mechanisms in the system tended to maintain the status quo, rather than permit needed changes to occur. Whether introducing a concept such as homeostasis really *explains* anything, rather than simply describing a process, is open to question.

A development of cybernetics is *control theory* (McFarland, 1971). This considers not only feedback mechanisms, but also 'feedforward' control. This latter type of regulatory activity is governed by factors which are independent of the results of the activity. Feedforward processes include the deliberate, conscious planning designed to reach a future goal. An example given by Tomm (1980) is the planning of certain families who send their children to private schools in order to have them attain particular educational or social goals. The accomplishment of these goals will not lead to any modification of the original plan.

Feedback may be either positive or negative. If it is positive it is 'deviation amplifying', and if negative 'deviation minimizing'. Positive feedback often operates within a certain range, while negative feedback comes into play at the limits of the range, as with a couple who get progressively more angry with each other until a certain maximum intensity is reached, but who stop short of physical violence, or at least of murder! Thus in families there are often periods of positive feedback regulation which are limited by negative feedback. A change in the relationship between those involved implies that there is also a change in the regulatory limits of the control system.

Cybernetics presents a superficially attractive model for understanding some of the phenomena we observe in families, but it is far from being an adequate theory of family functioning. The addition of McFarland's (1971) control theory ideas strengthens it somewhat, but many questions remain; for example, it is not clear how people decide to make the plans which lead to 'feedforward' processes. What determines that people are going to make the deliberate, conscious plans which can lead to 'feedforward' processes?

Tomm (1980) described a model of therapy, which he dubbed the 'Calgary model' and which paid particular attention to cybernetic regulatory mechanisms. This was a systems-based model and it took into account such factors as interpersonal and subsystem boundaries, attachments and coalitions, control mechanisms, family rules, collective beliefs and goals. Stress was, however, placed on the control mechanisms within the family. These were illustrated by circular pattern diagrams (CPDs). These illustrate the repetitive, stable and self-regulating interaction patterns within families. An example is given in Figure 1. Tomm points out that the control mechanisms operate through multiple channels, largely non-verbal.

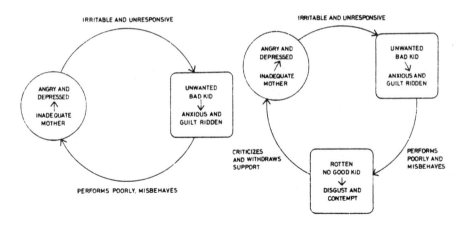

Figure 1. Dyadic and triadic parent–child patterns (Reproduced with permission from 'Towards a cybernetic-systems approach to family therapy at the University of Calgary' in Freeman D. S., ed. (1980) *Perspectives on Family Therapy*, Toronto: Butterworth).

CPDs can be of value in therapy in that they facilitate circular rather than linear thinking in the therapist; they can also direct the attention of the therapist to parts of a circular pattern which may not be immediately obvious. Linear thinking (the distinction of which from circular thinking is discussed in the next section) may present problems because it tends to mobilize feedforward mechanisms and may fail to make use of the 'constructive potential of negative feedback'.

The ideas of cybernetics and control theory, then, have contributed to the development of an epistemology for work with families, but they are far from being adequate for this purpose. Tomm (1981; 1984a; 1984b) himself has gone on to develop a more systemic approach to family therapy, influenced largely by the work of the Milan group (Palazzoli et al, 1978a).

(B) Systems theory and its application to family therapy
General systems theory was proposed by von Bertalanffy as a general theory of the organization of parts into wholes. A system was defined by von Bertalanffy (1968, page 55) as 'a complex of interacting elements'. Hall and Fagan (1956) worded the same concept slightly differently. They defined a system as 'a set of objects together with the relationships between the objects and between their attributes'. These definitions place no limits on what the 'parts' or 'objects' may be. They may thus be living or non-living. The theory is designed to cover physical phenomena and machines as well as biological systems.

Von Bertalannfy (1968) distinguished *open* from *closed* systems. Closed systems are those in which there is no interaction with the surrounding environment, as in a chemical or physical reaction in a closed container. Such systems obey rules different from those obeyed by open systems. Closed systems, for instance, show *entropy*, the tendency to reach the simplest, least ordered possible state from whatever may be the starting situation. Thus if two gases which do not react chemically with each other are introduced into a closed container, the result will be a diffuse complete mixing of the two. Once this process is complete the system is said to be in a state of *equilibrium.*

Open systems such as families, by contrast, do not show entropy. Instead there is a steady inflow and outflow of relevant material across the boundary of the system. If the characteristics of the boundary remain the same and the outside environment is also unchanged, a *steady state* is reached. The environment of most open systems is, however, liable to change. There may also be alterations in the characteristics of the boundary. These properties of open systems make change and evolution possible.

Systems theory as developed by von Bertalanffy and others consists of a complex of mathematical propositions about the properties of systems. Although family therapists have made much use of the basic concepts of the theory, they have not used the mathematical models. This is no doubt mainly because the phenomena with which they deal cannot readily, if at all, be reduced to mathematical terms. The term *systems thinking* (Beckett, 1973) is probably a better one than systems *theory*, at the present stage of the development of our subject. The importance of systems theory to family therapy lies in the ideas and concepts it has brought to the field. These include the following:

(a) Families (and other social groups) are systems having properties which are more than the sum of the properties of their parts.
(b) The operation of such systems is governed by certain general rules.
(c) Every system has a boundary, the properties of which are important in understanding how the system works.
(d) The boundaries are semi-permeable; that is to say some things can pass through them while others cannot. Moreover it is sometimes found that certain material can pass one way but not the other.
(e) Family systems tend to reach a relatively, but not totally, steady state. Growth and evolution are possible, indeed usual. Change can occur, or be stimulated, in various ways.
(f) Communication and feedback mechanisms between the parts of a system are important in the functioning of the system.

(g) Events such as the behaviour of individuals in a family are better understood as examples of *circular causality*, rather than as being based on *linear causality*.

(h) Family systems, like other open systems, appear to have a purpose.

(j) Systems are made up of *subsystems* and themselves are parts of larger *suprasystems*.

Some characteristics of systems

Systems theory, or at least systems thinking (that is the use of von Bertalanffy's (1968) ideas without also using the mathematical models he proposed) has more to offer family therapy than cybernetics, which is mainly concerned with feedback mechanisms. The idea of *circular causality* as opposed to *linear causality* as a basis for understanding the processes occurring in families is, however, common to both. Linear causality describes the process whereby one event causes another. Thus when it starts to rain a man may put up his umbrella. But putting up an umbrella is not generally believed to have any part in causing it to rain. This is a case of linear causality because event A (the onset on rain) is seen as the cause of event B (the umbrella being put up), while event B does not affect event A.

Circular causality is the term used for the situation that exists when event B does affect A. Thus if person A tells another person B to do something, and that person does it, this in turn will affect the behaviour of person A – who, for example, may then be more likely to ask B to perform the task again when the need arises.

A slightly more complex example of circular causation was afforded by a family containing a boy who was anxious about going to school. His mother, too, was worried and she turned to her husband who failed to give her any reassurance or support. Instead he spoke angrily to his son for not going to school. This made the boy more anxious still, and this was followed by a further increase in the mother's anxiety. Her son's school refusal worsened and she turned with greater force to her husband who got even more angry with the boy, and so the circular process continued. So who was 'causing' the problem? Indeed what was the problem? Was it the mother's anxiety, which was communicated to both father and son? Was it the boy's school refusal? Was it the father's unsympathetic and angry behaviour towards the boy and his failure to support his wife? To the systemic therapist the problem is none of these things; to such a therapist the problem lies in the family system as a whole. A circular process is occurring and it is the system that must be addressed in therapy, not any one person, nor even any one dyadic interaction.

An important concept derived from systems theory is that of the relationship between systems, subsystems and suprasystems. All living systems are composed of subsystems (Figure 2). So if a family is the system under study, it will be found to consist of various individuals or groups of individuals which function as subsystems. Examples are parental, marital and child subsystems; there may also be boy and girl subsystems, or subsystems consisting of older and younger children. Such subsystems have their subsystems too; an individual human being is also made up of various systems, whether physical (renal, cardiovascular, nervous and so on) or psychological (ego, id, superego).

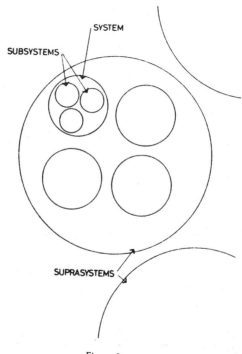

Figure 2.

Suprasystems to which families may belong include the extended family, the village, the neighbourhood, the tribe, a church community and so on. These in turn are part of larger suprasystems, until we get to nations, groups of nations and planet Earth itself. The Earth, of course, is but part of a still larger celestial system.

The system upon which family therapists usually concentrate is, of course, the family. Family therapists are interested also in the subsystems and, usually, the suprasystems of the families they are treating.

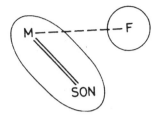

Figure 3.

There may be problems in a family's subsystem pattern. Figure 3 illustrates a pattern which is often associated with problems. The diagram represents over-close involvement (or 'enmeshment') of mother and son and underinvolvement of the parents with each other. The two subsystems are circled. A more satisfactory situation would probably be that shown in Figure 4. Many other, more complicated, subsystem patterns are possible, indeed common.

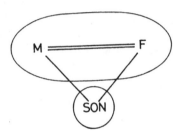

Figure 4.

Every system has a *boundary*, which marks it off from its surroundings. Living systems have readily identifiable physical boundaries, consisting of skin, mucous membranes, the bark of trees and so forth. The boundaries of emotional and psychological systems are not visible in the same way, but they are equally important. They control emotional interchanges, closeness and joint actions. The boundary between one subsystem and another is characterized by restricted emotional interchange, compared with that between individuals within the one subsystem. Similar considerations apply to the boundaries between systems and their suprasystems.

Some families have relatively impervious boundaries, so that they are quite isolated from the social environment in which they exist. Others have quite highly permeable boundaries and so may be unduly susceptible to events and changes in their wider social environment. The boundaries of all open systems are, in some degree, semi-permeable; that is they allow some things to pass through and prevent others from doing so (see Figure 5). By this means the integrity of the system and its distinctness from the surrounding environment are maintained.

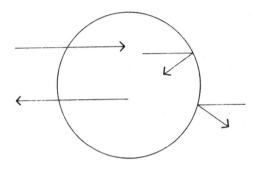

Figure 5.

Subsystems, of course, have boundaries too. Work on subsystem boundaries is often an important part of family therapy, particularly when a structural approach is being used. If the situation in Figure 3 were to be tackled using a structural approach, a clearer boundary would need to be established between mother and son and a closer relationship between mother and father would be required, so that a situation such as that depicted in Figure 4 could be achieved; in this situation there are clear boundaries around each of the two subsystems – that made up of the parents and that comprising the son.

Skynner (1974) discussed the role and importance of boundaries, not only in families, but also in professional groups such as the staffs of schools or of hospital units. These, too, are systems with properties similar to those of other living systems. Boundaries are largely defined by the communication that occurs across them, though much of the communication is non-verbal and is concerned with emotional issues rather than cognitive ones. The ideas behind structural therapy, which above all else deals with boundary issues, and those of communication theory (discussed below) thus have much in common.

Feedback. Systems thinking takes in the ideas about feedback which form the basis of cybernetics, but it goes further; the systemic therapist considers not just the feedback processes that are occurring, but also the processes whereby change occurs in the family system. Referring to the 'recursive loops' which are characteristic of living systems, Hoffman (1981, page 339) says that these loops 'are never totally closed, since there is always space for new information. Each cycle comes round to a new position, sometimes so minutely different from the previous one as to be imperceptible, but sometimes representing a major shift'. Family therapy is, in part at least, a matter of promoting this process.

Equifinality. Equifinality is the ability of open systems to maintain the same steady state with differing inputs. The chemistry of the body is a good example. The concentration of most electrolytes and other chemical compounds remains within narrow limits regardless of dietary intake. This is because of regulatory mechanisms involving the kidneys, lungs and other organs. Similarly families tend to have their set method of functioning, regardless of what is happening around them, or what information or stimulation is coming in from outside. Although the principle of equifinality seems to have relevance to the way families function, the term is not nowadays much used in the family therapy literature.

(C) Learning theory
Much, perhaps most, human behaviour is learned (the rest is biologically, and mostly genetically, determined). It is therefore important to consider how learning theory may be applied in family therapy.

Respondent conditioning changes behaviour by altering the circumstances leading up to it. Pavlov's classical experiments with dogs are examples of this type of conditioning; by pairing the ringing of a bell with the presentation of food, the dogs were conditioned to salivate simply when the bell was rung.

Operant conditioning changes behaviour by altering the circumstances following it. Thus if a person touches something hot and gets burned, that person is less likely to touch the same thing again. Similarly the way family members respond to each other does determine, at least in some considerable measure, how they behave. For example, if a girl is told to leave the table and forfeit the rest of her meal whenever she misbehaves, it is quite likely she will modify her future behaviour so that she can enjoy her meals in their entirety. Indeed all the rewards and punishments which parents give their children are designed to bring about changes in the children's behaviour.

When learning theory is to be applied clinically to families, their behaviour patterns are first carefully studied. A plan is then worked out to alter the 'contingencies' (or circumstances) believed to be controlling the behaviour. This usually involves direct intervention in the family to change the patterns of responses which are causing concern.

Wahler (1976) pointed out the similarities between the ideas of 'non-behaviouristic family therapists' who regard the family as 'a structured system of interbehaving people', and those of many who use learning theory in treating families, that is behavioural family therapists. Thus deviant behaviour is seen by many behaviour therapists as a result of feedback processes in the interactions of family members; it is regarded as an understandable, even inevitable, response to the contingencies presented by the system – these contingencies being the circumstances that govern the behaviour. This point of view leads therapists to look for reinforcing and discriminating stimuli from other family members which may result in the 'disturbed' behaviour of a particular member. This does not necessarily mean that the other members are *causing* the behaviour of the identified patient; that person's behaviour is also part of, probably, a number of feedback loops and so may equally be seen as causing the behaviour of the others.

Wahler (1976) also considered the possibility of the operation of larger cybernetic systems. The 'contingency pattern' of one parent interacting with a child may, he suggested, depend partly on the cues and reinforcers provided to that parent by the other one, and vice versa. Moreover similar processes may occur throughout the family. Wahler goes on to describe the 'positive reinforcer trap' and the 'negative reinforcer trap'. In the former, one or more family members find the identified patient's behaviour reinforcing and in turn provide reinforcers for it. Thus a mother may find a 'clinging' child's behaviour reinforcing and so may, in her turn, reinforce that behaviour by cuddling or otherwise indulging the child; this will then increase the clinging behaviour. Such a process may ultimately lead to refusal to leave the mother's side and so, for example, to the development of school refusal. When the family seeks help for this problem, they may be quite unaware of the underlying difficulties.

The negative reinforcer trap is said by Wahler (1976) to be the most common process involved in the development of deviant child behaviour. Giving in to tantrums is an excellent example of the process. A small boy in a supermarket wants one of the chocolate bars off the shelf and screams when he sees them. His mother does not want him to have any chocolate but, perhaps to quieten him or avoid embarrassment (though behaviour therapists tend not to be too concerned about motives), lets him have the chocolate bar. The screaming, which to the mother is an aversive stimulus, ceases temporarily; but the child has received reinforcement for his behaviour. So too has the mother, since the screaming has stopped. This sequence of events can easily lead to escalation of such behaviours by both partners in the interaction, and the process can become generalized to other situations. Eventually the child may come to be regarded as having a severe behaviour disorder.

Most writers, including Wahler (1976) and Werry (1979), agree that so far behavioural family therapists have concentrated on two-person (or dyadic), or at most three-person (triadic) models of interaction. Werry considers that they have had spectacular success in these endeavours and in the application of scientific method to their work. They have also been notable for their attempts to measure relevant behaviour precisely. He suggests that one reason why they have not extended their efforts to take in the whole family lies in the success of their work so far, but another reason is probably the greater complexity of work with larger groups. Nichols (1984) puts it more strongly. Commenting that behaviourists hardly ever treat whole families, but instead 'bring in only those subsystems they consider central to the targeted behaviours', he says that 'failure to include – or even consider – whole families in treatment may be disastrous. A therapeutic program to reduce a son's aggressiveness towards his mother can hardly succeed if the father wants an aggressive son, or if the father's anger toward his wife is not more directly addressed' (page 338).

Learning theory provides us with a series of techniques, which can be very effective, to deal with pathological interactions between family members. In its present stage of development it deals best with dyads: it can therefore be very useful in the treatment of marital problems, and Jacobson and Margolin (1979) discuss its use in this area of work quite extensively.

Behavioural techniques in marital therapy were also reviewed by Patterson and his colleagues (1976). Although they found the scientific status of the work unsatisfactory (though probably no more so than that of much family therapy), it does appear that many marital relationship problems are characterized by the use by each partner of aversive stimuli to control the other's behaviour. Thus when a husband disapproves of his wife's behaviour he may speak harshly to her or shout angrily at her. This may be followed by a temporary cessation of the behaviour. The wife, however, may retaliate in a similar way when he does something she dislikes. Over time, as they become accustomed to shouting at each other, the intensity of the shouting may increase. Thus although they may be successful in controlling the undesired behaviour in the short term, aversive behaviours tend to be ineffective in the longer term. Instead a situation of chronic conflict may develop. Eventually this may cause the partners to avoid each other.

(D) Communications theory

The communication processes occurring in families have long interested family therapists. This has led many of them to develop theories about human communication, and to explore how it may be modified when this seems to be needed. Since the pioneer work of Bateson, referred to in Chapter 1, further work in this area has been carried out at the Mental Research Institute, from which have come a series of important publications.

In *Pragmatics of Human Communication*, Paul Watzlawick, Janet Beavin and D. Jackson (1967) made a major contribution to the understanding of communication in families. These authors first defined three aspects of human communication: syntax, semantics and pragmatics.

Syntax refers to the conventions used when words are put together in sentences and paragraphs to express meaning; it comprises the grammatical rules of the language. *Semantics* is concerned with the meanings of words; it deals with the principles that govern the relationship between words or sentences and their meaning, the clarity of language and its use in particular situations. While the meanings of words may be defined in a dictionary, in practice people do not always stick to such definitions. In many families (and other settings) there are private languages and shared systems of communication which it is helpful for the therapist to understand.

Pragmatics is the study of the behavioural effects of communication; these are related as much, or perhaps even more, to the non-verbal behaviour of those involved and to the context of the communication as they are to the semantic content of what is said. It is well known that non-verbal cues, as well as the context of a communication, can convey, for example, that something is being said as a joke, or a threat, or an apology, and so on.

Watzlawick and his colleagues (1967) proposed some 'tentative axioms of communication'. They considered that these properties of communication had 'fundamental interpersonal implications', and they have certainly been used as the basis for much work done by many family therapists. They include the following points:

(a) *It is impossible not to communicate.* All behaviour occurring when one person is in the presence of another carries some sort of message. There is no opposite of behaviour, no 'non-behaviour'; so there can be no 'non-communicating'. A man sitting silently ignoring everyone around him is communicating, at the very least, that he does not want to speak to those around him. Depending on the context, and how far it would normally be socially appropriate to speak under the circumstances, he may be communicating a great deal more also. Moreover communication is much more than just what is said; it takes in posture, gesture and tone of voice, as well as context.

(b) *Communication has relationship aspects, as well as content.* Communications do not just give information; they also define the relationships between those communicating. Thus the statements, 'I wonder if you would mind shutting the door?' and 'How many more times do I have to tell you to shut that damned door?' are both requests to the person addressed to close the door, but the relationship defined is clearly different. Often the same sentence, spoken in a different way, can imply a different relationship. Compare 'I *think* you're wrong' with 'I think you're *wrong*'.

(c) *Punctuation is an important feature of communication.* In a series of interactions it is not always clear what is stimulus and what response. Thus a wife may nag because her husband comes home late, while the husband comes home late because his wife nags. Each may thus consider the other the 'cause' of the conflict; how it is perceived depends on how the sequence of behaviours is punctuated and each partner may punctuate it differently, and thus come to consider the other to be at fault. In such situations a major problem may be the inability of the marital pair to discuss the question of the punctuation of such processes – that is to 'metacommunicate' (or communicate about the communication) on the issue.

(d) *Communication may be divided into digital and analogic varieties.* In digital communication messages are coded into spoken or written words. The meaning of the messages is clear from the nature and ordering of the words, as in sentences such as, 'John is entering the theatre' or, 'The show starts at 8.00 pm'. In such sentences facts are being communicated by the use of the verbal code.

Analogic communication includes all non-verbal communication, such as gesture, body and limb postures, facial expression, tone of voice and the 'sequence, rhythm and cadence of the words themselves'. It also takes in poetry, music, painting and other forms of artistic expression. Other modes of analogic communication are caresses, blows, kisses, hugs and other forms of contact. In addition the way people dress, use make-up, and generally present themselves carry their own analogic messages. All are very relevant in family therapy, an important part of which is understanding the communication that is occurring between the family members. 'Fats' Waller, the jazz musician and singer, summed up the difference between digital and analogic communication in one of his records many years ago, with the phrase, 'Tain't what you say, it's the way that you say it'.

The distinction between these two types of communication is taken up further by Watzlawick (1978) in his book *The Language of Change.* Here he discusses the evidence that digital and analogic communication are associated primarily with, respectively, the left and the right cerebral hemispheres. While this may be something of an oversimplification, increasing evidence to support this idea has become available in recent years.

(e) *Symmetrical and complementary interaction.* Any relationship between two people – or between two groups of people – may be, in varying degrees, symmetrical or complementary. When an interaction is described as symmetrical this implies that the participants are on an equal footing. Complementary interaction occurs on the basis of inequality; examples are many doctor–patient, penitent–confessor and servant–master interactions. In these examples the complementary relationship conforms to the customs of the culture. Marital couples and other pairs of people may relate and communicate in complementary or symmetrical fashion though, of course, there are differing degrees of both.

The McMaster Model of Family Functioning (Epstein et al, 1978) also considers, as one of the parameters to be assessed, the nature of communication within families. These authors concern themselves mainly with verbal, rather than non-verbal, communication. They consider that this may be sufficient or insufficient; clear or masked; and direct or indirect. Thus some relationships get into difficulty because too little information is communicated; others because the messages are unclear; and yet others because messages are sent via third parties, with the avoidance of confrontation and the risk that the message will be distorted en route.

When one person addresses a communication to another, the latter may respond in one of three ways. The first is *acceptance* of the communication: the person responds to the question or remark in an appropriate way. The second is *rejection*: the person addressed does not reply but may continue reading, listening to something else or looking out of the window. This is still communication, of course, but it is less direct and clear. The third, and probably most pathological, is *disconfirmation*. This is the giving of offhand, disinterested, illogical, irrelevant or contradictory replies; such replies may be delivered in a bored, laconic or sarcastic way. The person replying is, by means of the reply, labelling the original speaker as a person of no account. Politicians sometimes reply to awkward questions in this way; sometimes they even resort to gibberish, another form of disconfirmation. Symptoms may also be used for communication, as when a person who is being addressed resorts to sleepiness, deafness or frail health as a reason for not responding in a positive way.

(f) Finally, communication may be *paradoxical*. Watzlawick et al (1967) defined a paradoxical communication as a 'contradiction that follows correct deduction from consistent premises'. Examples of paradoxical remarks are, 'I am lying' or 'I will visit you unexpectedly this evening'. The logical fallacy of such statements was pointed out by Whitehead and Russell (1910) in their 'theory of logical types'. This states that anything that involves all of a collection cannot be one of the collection. In the same way we cannot deal with language and metalanguage as if they were of one class. Thus the statement 'I am lying' is both a statement and a statement about the statement (that is a metastatement). It is therefore meaningless. The same applies to the remark 'I will visit you unexpectedly this evening'. To say that I will visit you is fine, but to say that the visit will be unexpected is a communication at a different level in the language hierarchy. It could only be logically stated by someone observing the events from outside the interaction.

Haley sees relationships as involving struggles for power, and he asserts that, 'When one person communicates a message to another he is manoeuvring to define a relationship' (Haley, 1963, page 4). According to Haley (1976, page 103), 'When a child has temper tantrums and refuses to do what his mother says, this situation can be described as an unclear hierarchy.' Hierarchy, Haley says, is present in every group of people who have a history and a future together. Creatures of any sort who are organized together make up a status, or power, ladder. Confused hierarchical arrangements, as exemplified by the above mother–child communication sequence, tend to be associated with symptoms. A hierarchy may be confused or ambiguous, or there may be a coalition between members at different levels.

The *sequence* of communications is related to the hierarchy. Thus if A repeatedly tells B to do something, and B does it, B is probably lower in the hierarchy than A. If this represents an inappropriate hierarchy and a manifestation of a pathological situation associated with symptoms, a goal of therapy would probably be to change the sequence of events or, in other words, change the hierarchy or power structure. This, incidentally, cannot usually be done simply by providing the family members with insight into their situation; more creative and often indirect methods tend to be needed.

Other useful concepts

(A) Epistemology
Epistemology is a term which has been much used by family therapists in recent years. It refers to the theory on which knowledge is based; that is, it represents the underlying assumptions which people make when they seek to understand something. The search for new theoretical

models for use in the treatment of families has thus involved the development of new epistemologies, though whether the use of the term has been helpful is a different question. Its use owes much to Gregory Bateson (see, for example, Bateson, 1978) who was keenly aware of the importance of the rules we use for making sense out of the world.

Family therapy has certainly needed new rules – different from those which have traditionally been used to understand individuals. It is probably this fact that has led to the use of the term 'the new epistemology' by some therapists. It is, however, misleading because it suggests that a specific, new, generally accepted way of thinking about and understanding families has emerged and been adopted, at least by avant garde therapists in the field. No doubt many therapists are using new epistemologies, but the process seems to me an evolutionary one; there is no one 'new epistemology', but rather a variety of new epistemologies being tried out and reported on by various therapists. Nevertheless, we have not reached a consensus on the matter.

Lynn Hoffman (1981) ends her book *Foundations of Family Therapy* with a thoughtful chapter entitled 'Toward a new epistemology'. She points out that there has been a shift from the study of homeostatic mechanisms, that is those processes that promote stability in systems, to a concern about how change occurs. She, too, seems to foresee a continuing evolution of new ideas and thus of new epistemologies as the study and treatment of families develops.

(B) Coherence

Coherence, as the term is used by Dell (1982), refers to one of the concepts that have emerged as part of the quest for new epistemologies by those who work with families. Dell uses 'coherence' as a sort of shorthand term for 'organized coherent system'. He defines it as follows:

> Coherence simply implies a congruent interdependence in functioning whereby all aspects of the system fit together. It would seem to be adequate for describing the behaviour of a system-being-itself without inadvertently implying anything more than that. (Dell, 1982, page 31)

Dell makes a strong case for the abandonment of the concept of homeostasis. He says that homeostasis is 'an imperfectly defined explanatory notion'. Indeed he goes on to criticize many of the other concepts and terms which have become associated with various schools of family therapy. He writes:

> In fact, the family therapy field is awash with such notions: family rules, resistance, therapeutic paradox, hierarchy, negative feedback, perverse triangle, and so on. All of those are imperfectly defined

explanatory notions that hang in the air. There is a desperate need for some fundamentals that can begin to explain the data of family interaction, psychopathology, and therapeutic intervention. (Dell, 1982, page 38)

Dell's objection to the use of the term 'homeostasis' is that it suggests a process – 'homeostasis' – which prevents change occurring in the system. But he believes there is no such specific thing as homeostasis. It is just an 'imperfectly defined explanatory notion'. He believes we should simply accept systems as they are. He sides with the view of the noted Chilean zoologist, Humberto Maturana (1978), who asserts that everything is 'structure determined'.

That means that individuals behave out of their coherence; they can behave in no other way. Control is impossible. Their coherence determines how they will behave, and no amount of determined attempts to control them will ever change that fact. Moreover, an individual's coherence specifies his reaction to the other's attempts to control him. The coherence will, in most cases, 'respond' in a different way than was intended by the attempt to control. You can lead a horse to water, but you cannot make it drink. Each successive attempt to make the horse drink results in the coherence (which is the horse) doing whatever it does under *that* particular perturbation. The coherence always determines. The best that can be achieved is for the owner of the horse to discover the perturbation to which the coherence (which is the horse) 'responds' with drinking behaviour. (Dell, 1982, page 37)

Dell is but one of a number of therapists, and other students of family systems, who are putting forward ideas about how we can better understand families and help them overcome the problems with which they come to us. His views are by no means generally accepted; indeed they were published in an issue of *Family Process* which also contained two other articles suggesting new ways of viewing families and the processes going on in them (Keeney and Sprenkle, 1982; Allman, 1982). All three were subject to criticism in a later issue of the journal (Coyne et al, 1982; Wilder, 1982; Watzlawick, 1982; Whitaker, 1982).

Dell's article was the least criticized of the three, and I have found it the most helpful. It defined therapy as a matter of discovering what particular inputs (or 'perturbations') produce the changes required in those coming for therapy. It *is* true, I believe, that the concept of homeostasis is not particularly helpful. The same probably applies to 'resistance'; it is generally better to regard the failure of a family or an individual to respond to a therapeutic intervention (that is, a 'perturbation') as due to the selection by the therapist of the wrong perturbation for those particular circumstances, rather than just labelling the family or individual 'resistant'. Dell's theories do not, however, address the issue of how a therapist is to determine which 'perturbation' is likely to result in the desired response. This is the very essence of therapy, of course, and will be the subject of most of the rest of this book.

(C) Our two brains and first and second order change
Another concept which many therapists have found useful concerns the different functions the two cerebral hemispheres are thought to have. Family therapists have long been aware that many of those who come to them with problems do not respond to straightforward injunctions about how they should modify their behaviour in order to rid themselves of their problems. At first sight this seems surprising. Why should it be? The main reason seems to be that much of what we do is determined not by our conscious, rational minds, but by our emotions, deep-rooted attitudes and habitual ways of reacting and behaving.

Watzlawick (1978), in his book *The Language of Change*, addressed the question of how change occurs in psychotherapy. He distinguishes first order change from second order change – an important distinction which is generally recognized by family therapists. First order change is simply the result of a conscious decision by one or more of those concerned to do something differently – for example, to try harder to accomplish a task. Second order change involves a change in attitude, or a reframing of a situation, so that things are perceived differently. It goes beyond the application of logical, rational measures to something much less logical, like laughing at one's earlier attempts to try harder, or even employing a totally paradoxical approach (Barker, 1981).

According to Watzlawick (1978) the two cerebral hemispheres have different functions. Each also has its own language, corresponding to the digital and analogic languages mentioned above:

> The one, in which, for instance, this sentence is itself expressed, is objective, definitional, cerebral, logical, analytic; it is the language of reason, of science, explanation, and interpretation, and therefore the language of most schools of psychotherapy. The other, in which the preceding example is expressed [the example being a passage, rather poetic in style, from Kafka's *An Imperial Message*], is much more difficult to define – precisely because it is not the language of definition. We might call it the language of imagery, of metaphor, of *pars pro toto*, perhaps of symbols, but certainly of synthesis and totality, and not of analytical discussion. (Watzlawick, 1978, pages 14-15)

Watzlawick goes on to suggest that the second of the two 'languages' is more effective in producing the kind of changes which psychotherapy aims to help people achieve. This language is believed to be the business primarily of the right cerebral hemisphere which 'tends to draw illogical conclusions based on clang associations and confusions of literal and metaphorical meanings, to use condensations, composite words and ambiguities, puns and other word games' (Watzlawick, 1978, page 24). The left hemisphere, on the other hand, deals with the direct, logical, rational communication of ideas.

Second order change, Watzlawick suggests, involves making contact with, and presumably producing changes in, the processes occurring in the right hemisphere. The left hemisphere may function as a sort of logical watchdog, guarding the right hemisphere against undue outside influence. It must therefore be bypassed. But how is this to be done? Watzlawick (1978) has a chapter (7), in which he describes methods of 'blocking the left hemisphere'. This often involves reframing the problem. Other ways of doing it include the use of paradox, metaphor and hypnosis, each of which may be effective when direct methods are not. How metaphor may do this is discussed further in *Using Metaphors in Psychotherapy* (Barker, 1985).

Assessing the value of new concepts and epistemologies

New theoretical ways of understanding families and the processes occurring in them are constantly being put forward. But how are we to evaluate them and decide which we should use in our clinical practice?

The ultimate test of any theory of change is whether it works when put into practice. It must also be stated clearly enough for therapists from different backgrounds to be able to understand it and make practical use of it. The three articles appearing in *Family Process* for March 1982 referred to above, all deal with theories of change. They are considered further in Chapter 16, where research in family therapy is discussed.

Summary

The history of family therapy has been characterized by the search for new theoretical schemes – sometimes referred to as new epistemologies – to aid in the study of the processes occurring in families. Theories derived from the study of individuals are of limited value when applied to family or other groups. Cybernetics, systems theory, control theory, learning theory and communications theory are among the models which have been pressed into use by therapists of various schools. All have proved useful, but none has been found to be entirely satisfactory.

One newly-emerged concept is that of coherence; the idea that families constitute 'organized coherent systems', determined by their structure. Therapy then consists of discovering what will perturb the organized system, or 'coherence', in a helpful way. Contemporary ideas about the respective functions of the left and right cerebral hemispheres may also be helpful in devising effective ways of promoting change. It seems likely, however, that family therapists will continue to use ideas from a variety of theoretical schemes, much as carpenters, electricians and other technicians carry around a variety of tools and pieces of equipment.

Chapter 4

Schools of Family Therapy

The work of the main pioneers of family therapy was outlined in Chapter 1. From this a number of schools of family therapy developed; in recent years, however, there has been a blurring of the distinctions between the schools, as therapists from different schools have shared their theories and methods of practice with each other. There is now much more in common than there used to be between schools that started with very different ideas. Nevertheless there are still a number of different approaches to the task of helping families make the changes they seek.

The differences between schools of therapy sometimes appear to be greater than they really are. Some of them are based very much on the work of particular therapists – Minuchin in the case of structural therapy, or Bowen in the case of the 'extended family systems' approach, for example. Sometimes what look like big differences in theoretical approaches prove to be, at least in part, features of the differing personalities of the, often charismatic, leaders of the field.

One of the earlier attempts at classification in our field was that of Beels and Ferber (1969). These authors classified therapists as 'conductors', 'reactor analysts' or 'systems purists'. *Conductors* take an active role in promoting what they consider to be healthier and more constructive methods of functioning in the families they treat. This implies that they have clear and firmly held views about how families can best function. They may, however, use a variety of techniques – forceful, subtle, tactful, persuasive or manipulative – to bring about change.

Reactor analysts believe that every family has the capacity to grow and change, as have the individual family members also. Therapy aims to free families to realize their potential rather than imposing the therapist's values and family style upon them. These therapists involve themselves in the emotional systems of families by reacting to their behaviour and examining their own emotional responses to the families' projections. The risk that the therapist will become overinvolved in the family can be diminished by the use of co-therapists, or by having one or more observers watching through a one-way observation screen.

Systems purists aim to change specific features of the family system by changing its 'rules' – the unwritten conventions that govern its behaviour. This usually involves work on system and subsystem boundaries and restructuring the alliances, coalitions and hierarchies in the family.

Foley (1974) classified therapists along two dimensions: one was concerned with how active a role the therapist played; the other with the extent to which the therapist took a systems or interpersonal approach, as opposed to an analytic or individually orientated one (Figure 6).

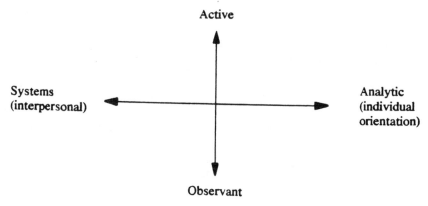

Figure 6. Analytic and systems introduction (Reproduced with permission from *An Introduction to Family Therapy*, Vincent Foley, 1974; New York: Grune Stratton).

As can be seen in Figure 6, each dimension is conceived as a continuum, at some point of which every therapist falls, though presumably therapists may vary their ways of working from time to time and with different families. There seems to have been a tendency, as family therapy has developed, for therapists to move to the left – that is towards a more systemic approach – and upwards – towards a more active role.

These two classifications are of therapists' styles rather than their theoretical beliefs, though Foley's horizontal dimension does touch on the latter. Goldenberg and Goldenberg (1980) distinguished four 'theoretical models of family interaction': family psychodynamic theory; family communications theory; structural family theory; and family behaviour theory. These are rather broad categories, and Nichols (1984) chose to divide family therapy into eight categories: psychoanalytic, group, experiential, behavioural, extended family systems, communications, strategic and structural varieties. The first four are attempts to use for families theoretical models designed to help understand and treat individuals; none of them is entirely satisfactory. Richter's (1974) description of 'family character neuroses' – he described the 'anxiety-neurotic family', the 'paranoid family' and the 'hysterical family' – was another attempt to use for families concepts derived from the study and treatment of individuals. As family therapy has developed, however, theoretical models which address family systems issues, rather than those relating to individuals, have increasingly gained popularity.

Psychodynamic family therapy

Although psychodynamic theory is used by many family therapists – though by some much more than by others – to help them understand what is happening in family groups, it is not easy to define a psychoanalytic school of family therapy, with its own specific treatment methods. It seems, though, that the main objective of the psychodynamic family therapist is to help the family members obtain insight into themselves and the way they react with each other. As in the psychoanalytic treatment of individuals, the family members are encouraged to 'free associate', that is to allow their thoughts to flow freely without conscious censorship, and to verbalize these thoughts. By comparison with family therapists of other schools, psychoanalytic therapists generally make fewer comments, ask fewer questions and intervene less actively. They usually refrain also from giving advice and from actively manipulating the families they treat.

Goldenberg and Goldenberg (1980) cite Ackerman as their example of a therapist 'influenced by psychodynamic theories', and his book *Treating the Troubled Family* (1966a) as illustrative of this method. They point out that:

> Ackerman, trained as a psychoanalyst, remained interested in each member's personality dynamics. However, also influenced by social psychology, he was impressed by how personality is shaped by specific social roles people are expected to play. (Goldenberg and Goldenberg, 1980, page 168)

Ackerman also put forward the idea of 'interlocking pathology', mentioned in the previous chapter. His position was described well by James Framo, who worked with Boszormenyi-Nagy – himself an analyst by training – in the early days of the Eastern Pennsylvania Psychiatric Institute.

> Departing from the conventional, simplistic view of symptoms as intrapsychic entities and as stemming from a central illness, it is the author's view that symptoms are formed, selected, faked, exchanged, maintained and reduced as a function of the relationship context in which they are naturally embedded. (Framo, 1972, page 127)

Good accounts of psychoanalytical approaches are provided by Dicks (1967) in the case of marital therapy, and by Skynner (1976) in his description of his work with families. As mentioned in Chapter 3, Murray Bowen and Virginia Satir are prominent among the many other therapists who have made use of psychoanalytical ideas in their work with families, though it would be inaccurate to describe either of them as psychoanalytical family therapists. Satir, however, is difficult to categorize, since she uses in a creative way ideas from a variety of sources, and this may be as good a place as any to say a little more about her approach.

Satir has paid much attention to the emotional needs of marital partners. It is clear that all marital partners have such needs, and that they hope – consciously or unconsciously – to have these needs met in marriage. As children come into the family they too have emotional needs, and their parents have needs which they hope to satisfy by having and rearing children. In her book *Peoplemaking*, Satir (1972) suggests a number of exercises with which people can work, without the help of a therapist, to improve their functioning and relationships. For Satir therapy is, above all, an exercise in maturation. Mature people, she says, are:

(a) Fully in charge of their own selves.
(b) Able to make decisions, based on accurate perceptions of self, others, and the social context.
(c) Able to acknowledge these choices and decisions as their own.
(d) Able to accept responsibility for their outcome.
(e) In touch with their own feelings.
(f) Able to communicate clearly with others.
(g) Able to accept others as different from themselves.
(h) Willing to see such differences as a chance to learn, not as threats.
   (Satir, 1972, page 91)

Satir's work is hard to summarize, and her approach, like that of every developing therapist, has changed over the years. Woods and Martin (1984), however, have provided an excellent brief review of it.

They distinguish four 'leading assumptions' with which they believe Satir nowadays works:

1. Underlying every behaviour is a reasonable or honorable motive. People are doing what they have learned to do and this is the best they can do in the circumstances.
2. Everyone is healable, and healing is inherent in the therapy process (Satir, 1982). Process, not content, is the important ingredient of effective therapy, but Satir's use of process is very personal. She does, however, model good communication, congruent behaviour and what Woods and Martin consider 'the primary prerequisite to change', namely risk-taking.
3. Mind and body are part of the same system. Physical vitality and emotional wellbeing are related. In therapy all avenues of access should be used. Satir identifies eight: physical, intellectual, emotional, sensual, interactional, contextual, nutritional, and spiritual (Satir, 1981).
4. Self-esteem and effective communication beget one another. A person's self-esteem 'affects choice of spouse, the nature of the marital relationship, the needs expressed in the parents' relationship to their children, responses to stress, abilities to cope, flexibility, abilities to deal with differences and ambiguity, and enhanced freedom to grow and flourish' (Woods and Martin, 1984, page 7). Satir emphasized in her earlier writings that self-esteem and the capacity to communicate effectively went together, and working on these things seems to be an important part of her method of therapy.

Some of Satir's other 'insights and assumptions' are also worth listing, since much therapeutic wisdom seems to be contained in them. They are:

(a) At some level of awareness a glimmer of hope is present among all who enter therapy (Satir, 1981).
(b) When people enter therapy the process of change has already begun – as evidenced by their taking the decision to come (Bandler et al, 1976).
(c) Those who display the most resistance have the least hope and the greatest fear (Satir, 1981).
(d) One cannot whimsically expect people to change their long-developed life support systems of defence (Satir, 1981).
(e) The meaning of a communication is the response it elicits (Bandler et al, 1976). This is a basic tenet of neurolinguistic programming, which is discussed further in Chapter 11.

(f) At some level of awareness people blame themselves first (Satir, 1981).

(g) There is no substitute in communication for clean, active, open sensory channels, so that you can always assess the response you are eliciting (Dilts and Green, 1982).

(h) Therapists' words are their weakest resource (Satir, 1981).

(i) Regardless of the importance of process, clients expect to deal with the content they perceive to be important.

The above material is summarized from the paper by Woods and Martin (1984, pages 6–8). These authors consider Satir to be 'in many respects...an educator'. She likes to define the goals of therapy, and is an expert in establishing rapport with her clients. These important topics are discussed in, respectively, Chapters 6 and 5.

To return to psychodynamic therapy it appears, *in summary*, that while psychodynamic concepts have undoubtedly contributed to our understanding of families, there is no well defined psychodynamic school of family therapy. Nichols (1984, page 223) summed up the situation well when he pointed out that when most psychoanalytically trained clinicians began treating families, they 'traded in their ideas about depth psychology for those of systems theory. The result was most often an eclectic mix of psychoanalytic and systems concepts, rather than a true integration.'

Behavioural family therapy

At the other end of the psychotherapeutic spectrum to psychoanalysis lies behaviour therapy, the theoretical ideas and practical techniques of which have also been used in treating family problems.

Behaviour therapists apply the laws of learning theory, which were summarized in Chapter 3, to the treatment of families; they work either by altering the circumstances leading up to a behaviour – 'respondent conditioning' – or those following one – 'operant conditioning'.

The behavioural family therapist starts by studying the family's behaviour patterns to determine the 'contingencies' (or circumstances) which appear to be controlling the problem behaviours. The resulting 'behavioural analysis' enables the therapist to develop a plan to alter these contingencies, often by direct intervention in the family.

Behavioural therapists tend to be more precise in their definition of problem behaviours and in their criteria for success, than are therapists of other schools. They often make numerical counts of such things as temper tantrums, compliance and non-compliance, arguments and other behaviours. Their primary objective is usually to increase the 'positive' behaviours, that is those that are desired, at the expense of the 'negative', or undesired ones. This is achieved by arranging things in the family so that desired behaviours are reinforced by being rewarded in some way. In addition, treatment programmes are sometimes set up so that the response to undesired behaviours is a form of 'punishment', this meaning any response which decreases the frequency or intensity of a behaviour, or both. On the whole, however, behaviour therapists prefer to reinforce desired behaviours rather than punish undesired ones. The latter are usually left to be extinguished by non-reinforcement or their replacement by incompatible, desired behaviours.

Since behavioural methods are most easily applied to dyads, they have been used quite widely in marital therapy. The bahavioural marital therapist is primarily concerned with teaching the couple to use 'positive' reinforcement in dealing with one another, rather than using 'negative' or aversive methods.

According to the behaviour exchange model, upon which much behavioural marital (and family) therapy is based, 'marital distress is viewed largely as a function of the *rate* of reinforcement (and/or punishment) directed by marital partners toward one another, and the *relationship* between each person's delivery of reinforcement and punishment' (Jacobson and Margolin, 1979, page 29). An important feature of behavioural marital therapy consists of increasing the positive exchanges between the partners, which is the subject of the first chapter of the book *Marital Therapy*, from which the above quotation is taken. This book is also an excellent source of additional information on behavioural methods of treating marital problems.

One of the foremost practitioners and researchers in the field of behavioural family therapy during the last two decades has been Gerald Patterson. He has worked not only with marital problems but also with families containing children with severe behaviour problems. A good example of his work is his description of the investigation and treatment of 27 'severely aggressive' boys (Patterson, 1976). The behavioural assessment of the interactions of these boys with their parents led to the identification of eight 'coercive behaviours'; these occurred significantly more often in the interactions of the aggressive boys than in those of a control group of 27 'non-problem' boys. The essence of the problem in these families was seen as consisting of reciprocal, and often escalating, aggressive attacks by the boys on other family members, and vice versa. As one side increased the vigour of its attack on the other, the latter might terminate his or her attack temporarily. But the use of 'high amplitude aggression' had been reinforced. In other words the interactions were examples of the 'negative reinforcer trap', described in Chapter 3.

When the functional analysis of what was happening was complete, an intervention plan was worked out and then implemented. It appeared that in these families there were high levels of coercive behaviour among all family members. In other words, everyone tried to get everyone else to do as they wished by the use of aggression of one sort or another. One person would make a coercive attack on another, who would then retaliate with aversive behaviour designed to terminate the attack. Over time the intensity of each behaviour increased so that the child's 'problem' behaviour worsened. These families thus provide an example of the operation of positive feedback.

Treatment was planned on the basis of the behavioural analysis. An approach designed to increase the 'parenting skills' of the parents was used. Parents were trained to do the following three things:

1. To observe the children's behaviours and keep records of them.
2. To use effective punishment, namely the withdrawal of whatever had been shown to reinforce the undesired behaviour.
3. To use effective reinforcers, both social and non-social, for 'pro-social' behaviours.

The parents all received at least one month's training. This included the use of the programmed text *Living with Families* (Patterson and Gullion, 1968) or *Families* (Patterson, 1971); instruction on how to define, track and record a series of specific target behaviours, both deviant and pro-social; and assignment to a parent training group in which they learned by modelling and role play. The parents also learned to construct contracts covering specific consequences to be applied in response to a list of problem behaviours which might occur at home and at school. A programme of behaviour management at school was also devised for use in the classroom.

The final stage of the process was the observation of the boys following periods of treatment. The measures of behaviour taken then were compared with baseline data obtained before treatment. In this particular study two-thirds to three-quarters of the boys, depending on the criteria used, showed major reductions in the levels of coercive behaviour, the changes being both clinically and statistically significant.

It will be clear, even from this brief account, that behavioural family therapists do not usually deal primarily with whole family systems; instead they intervene in families by working out and implementing plans to change the interactions between certain members, in fairly specific ways. Their hope is that this will lead to a permanent change for the better in the family situation generally – something which does indeed seem to occur in many cases.

Group therapy approaches

It is possible to approach the treatment of families in much the same way as unrelated groups of individuals are treated in group therapy. The extensive literature on group therapy, to which major contributions have been made by Dreikers (1951), Bennis and Shepard (1956), Bion (1961) and Foulkes (1975), among others, is devoted to the process whereby individuals with problems may help one another in group settings. It is the interaction between the group members which is seen as the main helpful feature of this form of treatment; the therapist's role is principally that of facilitator, and sometimes interpreter of what is happening between the group members.

Although many family therapists have used some of the approaches of group therapy, the one most identified with their use is J.E. Bell (1975). In an early paper Bell (1961) described how he interpreted the interactions between family members. 'Reflective' interpretations simply described what the therapist observed occurring between family members. 'Connective' interpretations pointed out links the therapist observed, or at least postulated, between the behaviours of different family members – perhaps a particular action or statement by one follows another particular action or statement by someone else. 'Reconstructive' interpretations link current behaviours with past experiences, and 'normative' interpretations aim to change family interactions by comparing them with more 'normal' ways of interacting, which may be characteristic of better functioning families.

While family members can certainly learn things of value from each other in a 'group therapy' setting, the situation is quite different from that which exists when a group of unrelated strangers starts to meet, as was explained in the previous chapter.

Although 'group family therapy' is one of the forms of family therapy listed and discussed by Nichols (1984), it is probably not nowadays distinguishable as a separate school. Group therapy is better seen as one of the elements which have contributed something of value to family therapy; observing the interactions between family members, and interpreting these to the family – a central feature of group therapy – can sometimes be useful and has been incorporated into the work of therapists of various schools.

Experiential family therapy

The term 'experiential' has been applied to the work of various therapists who, for the most part, downplay the value of theory in what they do; or at least their theory is often limited to the idea that it is possible to help families change by becoming involved in an intense interaction with them. Carl Whitaker and Walter Kempler are the best known practitioners of this form of therapy.

I find it hard to know how seriously to take some of Whitaker's statements about his work. Thus in an article entitled 'The Hindrance of Theory in Clinical Work', published in a section headed 'Theory' in Guerin's book *Family Therapy*, Whitaker (1976) states that 'theories are destructive' and that theory 'is the effort to make the unknowable knowable'. He even quotes the authority of the Bible – 'It's not given to man to see the face of God except through a glass darkly' (all these quotations are from page 154). If we are not to base our therapy upon theory, what then should we use? According to Whitaker (1976, page 163), the answer is:

> The accumulated and organized residue of experience, plus the freedom to allow the relationship to happen, to be who you are with the minimum of anticipatory set and maximum responsiveness to authenticity and to our own growth impulses...The therapist must develop the kind of power necessary to invade the family, and do battle with them. Simultaneously, he must develop the courage to be himself, and to share his own irrelevancies and free associations.

Kempler (1981), in his book *Experiential Psychotherapy Within Families*, starts one of his chapters with the sentence, 'Theorizing, if not theory, is treacherous' (page 45). For Kempler, it is the human encounter between therapist and client that is the stuff of therapy. The following passage from his book gives an idea of his approach:

> In this therapy, as the therapist I laugh and cry, I rage and sometimes even outrage. I sometimes do things usually assigned to those called patients. In an initial demonstration session, for example, I said vehemently to a wife who droned on morosely about her 20 years with ulcerative colitis, 'You make me sick. I feel that I'll vomit if you continue. Be quiet! I don't want to hear any more of this. I hate the way you use your colon to destroy yourself and everyone around you. I refuse to let you do this to me. Be quiet, if that is all you can say.' I actually felt disgusted, I looked disgusted. I couldn't stomach this woman, and I told her so ... When I discussed this session afterwards with colleagues who had witnessed the session, they assumed that this woman would not return. She not only returned, but she had

dramatically improved. She took heart from my expression. I had dared to challenge the power of this vengeful colon. Gradually she took back the power she had relinquished to her colon. At the moment I'd reacted in that initial session, I wasn't thinking that I was speaking to her colon. I was aware. I acted. (Kempler, 1981, pages 10-11)

It is the 'existential encounter' that is at the centre of this form of therapy (Kempler, 1981; Whitaker, 1976). The therapist must be a genuine person whose personal impact on the family stimulates therapeutic change. Experiential therapists subscribe to the view held by therapists of other schools – Haley is prominent among these – that insight is not what heals; it is rather what the client experiences in the therapy process that promotes change. Nevertheless, as Nichols (1984, page 291) points out, it is hard to be active without being interpretive and directive (as indeed Kempler was in the session he refers to in the quotation above), and 'even the best of those who practice in this tradition find it hard to resist telling people what they should be, rather than simply helping them find out who they are' (for example, see Napier and Whitaker, 1978).

Experiential family therapy is not currently a widely used method, and it is likely to remain the province of a few gifted, charismatic figures, like Whitaker, Kempler and Satir, whose approach owes much to this school.

Extended family systems therapy

Extended family systems approaches to family therapy, sometimes known as three-generational approaches (Anderson and Stewart, 1983), pay special attention to intergenerational issues and the wider family context. Murray Bowen, Ivan Boszormenyi-Nagy and James Framo are major proponents of this approach.

Bowen's early work on schizophrenia, and his concept of 'triangulation', have been mentioned in Chapter 1. Unlike the practitioners of experiential therapy, Bowen has for long been concerned with theory and he has developed quite a comprehensive theoretical basis for his work. He accepts the idea of the family as a system. Indeed he says it is a number of systems: a social system, a cultural system, a games system, a communication system and a biological system, among other possibilities (Bowen, 1978, page 169). For the purposes of therapy he regards a family as 'a combination of emotional and relationship systems'. The forces that motivate family systems are emotional and they are expressed through relationships.

Bowen's idea of the 'undifferentiated ego mass' has been mentioned in Chapter 1. More recently he has used, instead, the term 'nuclear family emotional system' (Bowen, 1976). The 'oneness' to which these terms refer may exist at any level of intensity; thus it may be very intense, scarcely perceptible, or anything in between. An extreme example of an undifferentiated ego mass is seen in the *folie à deux* phenomenon, in which psychotic thoughts, feelings and fantasies are shared by two people. An intense symbiotic relationship between a mother and her child is another example.

Bowen believes that many family problems arise because the family members have not differentiated themselves psychologically from their families of origin. It is indeed a commonplace to see families in which one, or perhaps both, parents are still much involved with their own parents, to the detriment of their relationship with their spouses. In other words these parents are still part of the 'ego mass' or 'emotional system' of their families of origin.

The number of people involved in Bowen's 'ego mass' varies. The whole nuclear family may be one undifferentiated ego mass, or one or more members may be excluded from it. In periods of stress additional members may be involved. One of Bowen's major therapeutic aims is to facilitate the differentiation of members from the ego mass, so that they become able to function independently and autonomously, for example as members of their own newly-created families. This process has similarities to Satir's (1967) concept of the maturation of family members being part of the family therapy process. There are indeed a number of resemblances between the views of Satir and Bowen, both of whom regard families as systems but who also look carefully at the functioning of the individuals in family systems.

Bowen's contributions to family therapy were brought together in the book *Family Therapy in Clinical Practice* (Bowen, 1978). The 'Bowen theory' is set out particularly clearly in one of the articles reprinted in this book (Bowen, 1976). Bowen sees therapy as being primarily a matter of having family members, especially the parents, discover and come to terms with their relationships with their parents, grandparents and extended families generally. It is their position in the extended family that is responsible for their functioning in their present family; if this is unsatisfactory it can be put right through their coming to an understanding of this situation. This may involve a 'voyage of discovery', that is to say paying a visit to the appropriate members of the extended family to clear up unfinished business.

Boszormenyi-Nagy and his colleague Geraldine Spark (1973) set out their views on the role of the extended family in the book *Invisible Loyalties: Reciprocity in Intergenerational Family Therapy*. They observed how patterns of relating are often passed on from generation to generation. Thus in one family there had for generations been violent deaths of women caused by the men with whom they had been sexually involved.

These authors believe that there are within families loyalties, or bonds, which transcend generations and physical distance and which are important in helping determine family behaviour. Like many other therapists they see families as open systems (as described in Chapter 3), but emphasize the importance of the family relationship structures. Emotional health depends on there being a balance between the repayment of the person's debt to the family of origin, on the one hand, and self-fulfilment on the other. In order to resolve these intergenerational issues Boszormenyi-Nagy and Spark often ask grandparents and other extended family members to attend some of the therapy sessions. During these sessions the intergenerational issues are the focus of therapeutic attention.

James Framo (1976; 1981), a former colleague of Boszormenyi-Nagy at the Eastern Pennsylvania Psychiatric Institute, also believes that family problems usually have their roots in the extended family system. He regards the relationships between parents and grandparents as important, and sees current problems with children as being due to attempts to deal with early conflicts in the families of origin. Children's problems are closely related to problems in the marital relationship, the nature and quality of which depends on the respective families of origin, and especially upon how far conflicts in those families have been resolved.

There are wide variations in how extended family systems therapists work with families. Many of them make use of the principles of systems theory, as set out in Chapter 3, applying these to the extended family rather than just to the nuclear family group. In addition, there is a tendency also to use psychodynamic concepts, as unresolved feelings and conflicts in the larger family groups are dealt with, something which is quite evident in the work of Boszormenyi-Nagy. What therapists of this school have in common, however, is a concern for the extended family system and its relationship to the problems which the family presents.

Approaches to family therapy using communications theory

Many therapists emphasize the importance of the communication processes in the families they treat. Foley (1974) divided communications theorists into three groups, according to the aspect of family communication they regard as most important. These aspects are:

- Communication and cognition
- Communication and power
- Communication and feeling

Communication and cognition
A leading proponent of this approach was the late Don Jackson, who worked with Watzlawick and his colleagues and made use of many of the ideas set out in *Pragmatics of Human Communication* (Watzlawick et al, 1967), discussed in Chapter 3. Jackson and his colleagues considered pathological modes of communication to be important in the genesis of schizophrenia, but it soon became clear that these communication patterns were not confined to the families of schizophrenics.

Those family therapists who pay particular attention to communication and its relationship to cognition concern themselves especially with helping family members clarify the meaning of the communications passing between them. They do not, however, *confine* themselves to the cognitive understanding of what is going on, and the distinction between them and those who emphasize communication and feeling is a fine one; indeed there is much overlap between the two.

Family therapists of this subschool get family members to check what the other members mean when they say things. In many families the message received is often not that which the would-be communicator intended to send. Examples of how communication may be clarified are to be found in the book *Changing with Families* (Bandler et al, 1976); methods of clarifying communication are also discussed further in Chapter 12.

Therapists of this school also pay particular attention to the punctuation (as discussed in Chapter 3) of the communication processes occurring in the family. Their aim is usually to make explicit the misunderstandings that have been a feature of the family's functioning. They are concerned also with the analogic, or non-verbal, communication that is taking place, since this can often negate the content of the verbal communication, or at least give it a different meaning.

Communication and power
Haley has probably been the family therapist who has most emphasized the relationship between communication and power. He said many years ago that, 'When one person communicates a message to another he is manoeuvring to define a relationship' (Haley 1963, page 4). His views were summarized in Chapter 3, and he applies them in therapy by seeking to re-order the hierarchy, or perhaps to create an appropriate one where none has existed. Parents *are* responsible for their children, and they do have the right, in fact the duty, to set limits on their

children's behaviour. They must also determine what part the children should play in the family's collective activities – for example in the performance of household chores. It is possible, of course, to carry this concept too far and to make excessive, heavy-handed demands on children, as well as to be too rigid and dogmatic in laying down rules. Moreover, as children grow up and become adolescents they become more equal, and can have a bigger, but always limited, share in family decision making.

This approach to therapy has much in common with strategic therapy, described below, in that the therapy process aims to change nature or even the position of the boundaries between the different subsystems in the family. In the practice of family therapy it is only too frequent to find children who ignore their parents' authority, or even order their parents around. The phenomenon of the 'parental child', who cares for younger children instead of the parents doing so, or who even looks after the parents, is also common. These situations may all be seen as ones in which the distribution of power in the family is inappropriate, so that one or usually more members find themselves in stressful or difficult positions and thus develop symptoms.

Communication and feeling

Of the pioneers of family therapy, Virginia Satir is probably the one who has placed the most emphasis on the communication of feelings. She has pointed out that all marital partners have emotional needs of one sort or another – needs they hope to have met in marriage (Satir, 1967), though they are not fully aware of these needs. As children come into the family *they* have their needs too, and the parents have needs which they hope to satisfy by having children. Satir believes that in the meeting of everyone's emotional needs, the communication of feeling is important; where it is unsatisfactory, the aim of therapy should be to improve it.

Satir's views on how marital partners may select each other were also referred to in Chapter 1. Other aspects of her work were discussed earlier in this chapter, in the section on psychodynamic family therapy.

Structural approaches

The structural approach to the assessment and treatment of families was developed primarily by Salvador Minuchin and his colleagues at the Philadelphia Child Guidance Clinic, during the 1970s. It is set out in a number of publications, including the books *Families and Family Therapy* (Minuchin, 1974), *Psychosomatic Families* (by Minuchin, with Bernice Rosman and Lester Baker as co-authors and Ronald Liebman as a contributor, 1978) and *Family Therapy Techniques* (by Minuchin and Charles Fishman, 1981). It makes use of many of the ideas derived from systems theory which were set out in Chapter 3.

Minuchin (1974) suggested that the following six aspects of a family's functioning should be assessed by the therapist planning structural treatment:

1. The family 'structure'. This consists of the arrangements which govern the transactions between family members.
2. The flexibility of the family's patterns of function, and its capacity for change.
3. The family's 'resonance', that is the extent to which family members are enmeshed with or disengaged from each other.
4. The family's life context. This is the suprasystem, or the family's sources of support and stress in the environment. The environment will normally include the extended family, neighbours, and the neighbourhood, work and school environments of family members.
5. The family's developmental stage, as discussed in Chapter 2.
6. The ways in which the identified patient's symptoms are used by the family and how they fit into its transactional patterns.

Structural family therapists are concerned with the subsystem patterns of families, and with the boundaries between the different subsystems as well as those between the family system and its wider environment, or 'ecological context'. The structural therapist starts by 'joining' the family, a process which is discussed further in Chapter 5. As a result of joining a family and participating for a time in its transactions, the therapist is able to observe certain aspects of its functioning. The principal ones are:

The boundaries. Who participates in particular transactions? Who is in and who is out of a particular transactional pattern, or of the total family transactional process? The answers to these questions define the family's subsystems and the boundaries between them.
Alignments. These comprise coalitions and alliances. A *coalition* occurs when two or more members join together against another member or members. An *alliance* is the joining together of two or more family members without regard to anyone else.
Power. Who is it that decides what is going to happen in the family?

'Enmeshment' and 'disengagement' are terms which relate to the type of boundaries which exist between family members, and between the subsystems in the family. When a relationship is described as enmeshed, this is another way of saying that the boundary between those whose relationship is being discussed is diffuse. This implies that the behaviour of one family member has an immediate and marked effect on those with whom that person is enmeshed. On the other hand, in a disengaged relationship the behaviour of one member of the family will have little effect on those family members from whom that member is disengaged. In such a case stresses affecting one member have little effect on the other family members.

'Alignment' concepts include those of stable coalition, triangulation and detouring. A *stable coalition* may be represented as follows:

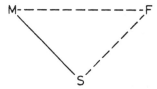

In this situation mother and son each count on the other for support against father.

In *triangulation*, problems between two family members are not worked out directly between these two people, but instead a third person is brought in and becomes part of the process. For example, father and mother might fight each other through use of the son, as illustrated in the following diagram:

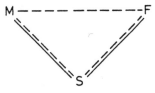

Detouring may be represented as follows:

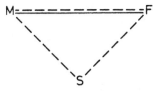

Here mother and father are not really getting along, but appear to do so, using the son to assist this appearance by either attacking him or protecting him. The feelings related to the conflict between the parents are expressed in the context of the interactions between parents and son, thus detouring the conflict.

The concepts of power, alignment and boundaries are not independent of each other. Rather than being separate dimensions they are abstractions which can help us in our understanding of families. Thus power may result from an alignment, as of mother and son in the first example above. In other families it derives, in appropriate degree, from the healthy alignment of the parents as they deal constructively with the task of rearing their children – a task which involves setting limits and working together to see that these are enforced.

The family structure must also be assessed according to the operation being studied. Thus when a family is discussing whether they should move to another city, the father may wish to go, while the mother may not. The son may then attack the father in support of mother. On the other hand, when the subject under discussion is whether they should go to watch a football match the son may be in coalition with the father – to go to the match – against the mother.

Before planning a structural intervention in a family it is helpful to have an idea of three other features of its functioning. The first is the *richness* or *paucity* of the functions available to it. Does it always operate in more or less the same way, or does it have available a variety of functions to suit different circumstances?

The second point to be considered is the family's *flexibility* or *rigidity*. How easily can it change its functioning when circumstances change, as for example when children are born into it, reach adolescence or leave it?

Finally there is the question of *coherence* or *incoherence* (a different use of the word 'coherence' from that of Dell (1982), discussed in Chapter 3). Coherence, as used in this context, is a measure of how drastic the changes in the family's functioning are when they do occur. While changes are often needed there should also be some coherence and continuity in the family's structure and way of functioning. The therapist must estimate the extent to which this is the case.

Having joined the family system and acquired an idea of its structure, the therapist must decide how far the identified patient's symptoms, or the problem with which the family is seeking help, are related to the family's way of functioning – that is, its structure. If these things appear to be related, intervention to alter the structure will be indicated.

Structural therapy techniques are among the most used family therapy procedures. They are discussed in more detail in Chapter 12, but they consist essentially of a variety of means of modifying, in one way or another, system and subsystem boundaries and altering the patterns of coalitions and alliances within families. Structural therapists usually address these issues directly, though much skill and fine clinical judgement are required in order to do this well. It seems that most successful structural therapists have, or develop, powerful but empathic personalities, so that they are able to persuade, cajole – even manipulate – families into making the needed alterations in their structure.

Strategic therapy

There are many forms of strategic therapy, but in all of them the therapist devises a strategy to solve the problems of the client or family. As Madanes (1981) puts it, 'The therapist sets clear goals, which always include solving the presenting problem. The emphasis is not on a method to be applied in all cases but on designing a strategy for each specific problem.' Perhaps this description could be improved by making the point that the goals are really set by the clients, though the therapist works with the clients to define them. (The setting of goals, an important issue in therapy, is discussed in Chapter 6.)

Strategic methods are indirect, and they are chiefly required when direct methods prove ineffective. Some people and some families will respond to direct injunctions; thus if, for example, you tell parents to set agreed limits to their children's behaviour and to work together to enforce these limits, some will do just that. In many families, however, such a straightforward approach is not effective, and something both more subtle, and indirect, is required.

Milton Erickson was exceedingly skilled at devising effective, economical, strategic ways of helping his patients achieve their objectives. A good, very readable account of his work is that of Haley (1973). Strategic therapy owes much to Erickson, though it is well to bear in mind that he often used direct methods. Indeed Hammond (1984), on the basis of interviews with colleagues who worked with Erickson when he was at the height of his powers, maintains that about eighty per cent of his therapy used direct rather than indirect methods.

Strategic methods include:

1. **Reframing**. This is the process whereby new meaning is given to a behaviour, a sequence of interactions, a relationship, or some other feature of the current situation. Bandler and Grinder (1982) distinguish *context reframing*, and *meaning* or *content reframing*. In context reframing a behaviour is redefined as useful in certain circumstances, though probably not in the particular ones in which it is currently manifest. The essence of context reframing, therefore, is identifying *where* a behaviour is useful.

In meaning or content reframing, the meaning of some event, behaviour or stimulus is changed. Bandler and Grinder (1982, pages 5-7) cite as an example the case of a woman who liked to have her carpets perfectly clean and smooth; whenever there were any footprints on them she became intensely upset. She was asked first to imagine that the carpets were perfectly clean, fluffy and unmarked, but it was then pointed out to her that this meant that her loved ones were nowhere around and she was quite alone. She was then asked, in the scene she was imagining, to put a few footprints in the carpet, 'and look at those footprints and know that the people you care most about in the world are nearby'. The footprints thus came to have a new meaning, and the woman became able to tolerate, perhaps even feel happy about, their presence.

2. **Paradox**. It appears, from the steadily increasing flood of reports and descriptions of the use of paradoxical methods in therapy (Frankl, 1939; 1960; 1965; Haley, 1976; Palazzoli et al, 1978a; Cade, 1979; Fisher et al, 1981; Barker, 1981), that more and more use is being made of such methods. In 1982, Weeks and L'Abate published the first book devoted exclusively to the subject, *Paradoxical Psychotherapy*.

There is nothing new about the use of paradox in human communication. Children in playgrounds who want to be chased and caught can be heard telling each other, 'You can't catch me'. In the Bible St Paul, in his letter to the Romans, writes of how the harder he tried to obey the Jewish law the less successful he was. His solution is not to try harder, but to stop trying and reframe the problem.

In family therapy, and in other forms of therapy in which the therapist takes responsibility for devising interventions which will enable clients to achieve their objectives, there are situations in which telling people to do the opposite of what might seem logical leads to a successful outcome. Paradoxical methods are discussed further in Chapter 10.

3. **Changing the sequences of interactions**. Prescribing the sequences in which things are to be done in families is not necessarily a strategic intervention, but it may be. If it addresses a problem directly it is not, but often quite small changes in the sequencing of events, which may appear unrelated to the presenting problems, can have extensive therapeutic repercussions. An example from Erickson's work, reported by Haley (1973), is discussed in Chapter 12.

4. **Metaphor**. Human beings have long used metaphorical methods to communicate ideas and information. Greek mythology, biblical parables and children's fairy tales are examples. Objects, relationships and activities can also have metaphorical meanings. When direct communications are ineffective, conveying the same message by means of a metaphor may succeed. Gordon (1978) discussed and described the setting up of full-length metaphorical stories as a major part of a therapeutic plan. In the book *Using Metaphors in Psychotherapy* (Barker,

1985) I have examined the use of metaphor in a wider range of clinical situations. The use of metaphor is discussed further in Chapter 10.

5. **Rituals**. Rituals are another way in which ideas can be communicated, points made and sequences of behaviour changed. Marriage and funeral ceremonies, birthday parties, and many rites of passage are everyday examples of human beings' use of rituals. Much use is made of them by the Milan group of therapists (Palazzoli et al, 1978b), as well as by other strategic therapists; their use in psychotherapy has been examined by van der Hart (1983) in the book *Rituals in Psychotherapy*. Rituals are also discussed further in Chapter 10.

6. **Other strategic devices.** Many other strategic interventions in families are possible. Palazzoli and her colleagues (1978a), for example, describe how therapists may declare their impotence without blaming anyone in the family, how they may take upon themselves the dilemma which the relationship between parents and child presents, and several other creative ways of approaching difficult therapeutic challenges.

Systemic family therapy

I have not, in this brief survey of schools of family therapy, distinguished a separate school of 'systemic' therapy, despite the fact that many family therapists describe themselves – usually accurately – as systemic therapists. Nowadays most family therapists look upon the family system as the entity they are treating, rather than any of the individuals in it. So most structural, strategic and extended family therapists, and many of those who emphasize communications theory, are systemic therapists. The term therefore has limited usefulness in defining a school of therapy.

The overlap between schools

Finally, a word of caution about labelling therapists as belonging to particular schools. An important feature of the last decade has been a coming together of therapists of different schools, and an increasing recognition that no one approach to treatment suits all families. Many therapists use ideas and techniques derived from a variety of schools. While it may be a good plan – indeed it is necessary – initially to learn one specific approach, it is equally necessary for therapists to broaden their skills and learn techniques derived from a variety of schools, as they grow and develop. Consequently it is hard to find therapists who are pure examples of any one school, and there has come to be much overlap between schools. Eclecticism, if based on a firm body of knowledge and a good repertoire of clinical skills, is a great virtue.

Summary

Family therapy developed in a variety of settings, and much of the early work was done by creative, charismatic individuals who brought their own ideas to a new field, often without much regard to what other therapists were doing in their work with families. This led to the development of a number of quite distinct schools of therapy, as well as to many styles of working with families. These styles often had as much, or more, to do with the personalities of the therapists concerned as with their theoretical approach to their work.

Early classifications of therapists tended to pay attention particularly to their styles of working, but more recently attention has been paid rather to the theoretical basis of the work therapists do, and to the origins of their theoretical ideas. Some of the concepts that have been used in work with families are based on ideas derived from the psychotherapy of individuals. These include much of the contribution of psychodynamic theory, group therapy and behaviour therapy – and probably also experiential therapy.

As family therapy developed it became clear that it required its own theoretical models. The chief ones that have emerged are models based on communications theory, extended family systems models and the structural and strategic models. But cross-fertilization between these schools of therapy is increasingly occurring, so that therapists are learning and using the concepts and techniques of more than one model, either blending them into a style uniquely their own, or having available a variety of approaches to suit the different needs of the various families they see. The schools of therapy discussed in this chapter are thus less often seen in 'pure culture', which seems a healthy development.

Chapter 5

Assessing Families

In order to assess families it is necessary to have a theoretical model of how families function and of the ways in which their functioning may go awry. Many such models exist and it is possible for the therapist to take concepts from several and develop a scheme for his or her own use. The therapist training in a school which uses a particular approach to assessing families should, of course, start by using that approach, but most therapists modify their practice as they gain experience, read more widely and have contact with therapists of other schools.

Models for the assessment of families

We will first consider some of the research-based models available for the assessment of families, namely the McMaster Model of Family Functioning (Epstein, Bishop and Levin, 1978), and the closely related Process Model of Family Functioning (Steinhauer, Santa-Barbara and Skinner, 1984); the structural model of Minuchin (1974); the triaxial scheme of Tseng and McDermott (1979); the circumplex model of Olson and his colleagues (1979); and the Beavers model (Beavers, 1981). We will then consider the process of obtaining the information needed to apply whatever model is being used to assess the family and plan treatment.

The McMaster model and the Process model have many points in common and will therefore be considered together.

The McMaster Model of Family Functioning

This model (Epstein et al, 1978) is a development of an unpublished model, the Family Categories Schema, originally devised in 1962. It has proved a useful way of looking at families, and is based on a systems approach to families, as set out in Chapter 3. It considers six aspects of family functioning:

1. Problem solving.
2. Communication.
3. Roles.
4. Affective responsiveness.
5. Affective involvement.
6. Behavioural control.

The scheme deals with the *current functioning* of the family, rather than its past development or present developmental stage.

The Process Model of Family Functioning

This model is also derived ultimately from the Family Categories Schema. As described by Steinhauer and his colleagues (1984), it considers family functioning along six dimensions, all but one of which are similar to categories in the McMaster model. They are:

1. Task accomplishment, which is similar to the McMaster model's problem solving.
2. Role performance.
3. Communication (including affective expression).
4. Affective involvement.
5. Control.
6. Values and norms.

Task accomplishment and problem solving
These functions are viewed in similar ways in each of the above two schemes. In both, the following processes are considered to be involved:

• Identifying the tasks to be accomplished.
• Exploring alternative approaches and selecting one.
• Taking action.
• Evaluating (or monitoring) results and making any necessary adjustments.

The McMaster model has an additional stage in the process of 'problem solving', namely that of communicating the existence of the problem to whoever needs to know about it.

Both models divide family tasks into basic, developmental, and crisis varieties. *Basic tasks* comprise such things as the provision of food, shelter, clothing and health care – the essentials for survival in society. *Developmental tasks* are those that must be performed to ensure the healthy development of members as the family life cycle unfolds. Thus the care needed to ensure the healthy development of an infant is quite different from that needed by an adolescent. The well-functioning family is sensitive to what its needs are and makes the necessary adjustments as it passes through the family life cycle.

Crisis tasks tax the family's skills and resources to the limit and sometimes beyond. They may consist of dealing with unexpected or unusual events such as the death of a family member, serious illness in the family, job loss, natural disaster, loss of the family home through fire or foreclosure, or migration from one culture to another. In some families, however, events which other families might deal with quite easily may precipitate a crisis – for example receiving a bad school report about a child, or discovering that a teenager has been shoplifting or is smoking marijuana. As the authors of the Process model put it, 'A family's capacity to accommodate to stress and avert potential crises is an excellent indicator of family resilience or health' (Steinhauer et al, 1984, page 79).

The McMaster model also distinguishes between *instrumental* and *affective* problems. The former comprise such things as the inadequate provision of food, shelter or clothing, or poor management of the family's finances. The latter are concerned with feelings, examples being serious hostility or distrust between family members.

Roles

Roles have been defined as 'prescribed and repetitive behaviours involving a set of reciprocal activities with other family members' (Steinhauer et al, 1984). Task accomplishment requires that there is a suitable allocation of roles and that the family members carry out the activities demanded by the roles allocated to them. Roles must be assigned, mutually agreed and enacted; they must also be integrated with one another. For satisfactory task accomplishment they must also cover all the things that need to be done. In most families many of the roles to be performed are not allocated in a formal way; they rather become habitual patterns of behaviour carried out by particular family members. Sometimes, however, it is necessary for family members to get together and agree upon who is going to do the shopping, clean the house, mow the lawn, feed the cat, or whatever needs to be done and is not being done.

The McMaster model distinguishes 'necessary' family functions – that is roles that must be performed for healthy family functioning – and 'other' family functions. Necessary functions include the provision of material resources; nurturance and support of family members and the sexual gratification of the marital partners; and life skill development and the maintenance and management of the family system. 'Life skills' refers to such matters as supporting children through school, helping adult members obtain and keep jobs, and assisting them in their personal development. 'Systems management and maintenance' refers to the provision of leadership in the family and to the process of decision making, maintaining the family's boundaries and establishing and maintaining its standards.

'Other' family functions are those unique to a particular family, such as 'scapegoating' or idealizing a family member. In the description of the Process model, roles are described as 'traditional' and 'idiosyncratic', the former covering similar ground to the 'necessary' family functions mentioned above, while idiosyncratic roles are often the expression of individual and family pathology. The authors of this model also cite the role of scapegoat as an idiosyncratic one. Role problems are discussed further in Chapter 9.

Communication
Communication is a dimension of family functioning considered by both the McMaster and Process models, as well as by the other models we shall consider. The authors of the McMaster model consider mainly verbal communication, not because they discount the importance of non-verbal communication, but because of the practical difficulties of measuring and collecting data on non-verbal content. The Process model does, however, consider non-verbal, or what they refer to as 'latent' content – which includes 'metacommunications' expressed by voice tone, facial expression, eye contact or its lack, body language and choice of words.

Critical aspects of communication, whether verbal or non-verbal, are the clarity, directness and sufficiency of communications sent by family members to each other, and the availability and openness of those to whom the communications are addressed. Communications may be affective (the expression of feeling), instrumental (related to the ongoing or needed activities of everyday life), or neither affective nor instrumental (for example, the discussion of political issues or opinions of works of art).

Clear, as opposed to masked, communications are generally desirable, since 'masked' – that is vague, disguised or ambiguous – ones increase the likelihood of confusion and distortion by the receiver, with resulting anxiety. It is also generally better if communications are sent directly from sender to receiver, rather than through a third person. When messages are sent indirectly they may be distorted, and in addition the third party involved may be placed in a difficult position, trapped between sender and receiver. Finally it is helpful for the therapist to discover whether sufficient information is being communicated between family members, or whether the family has a problem disseminating needed information among its members.

Affective involvement
Affective involvement is a matter of 'the degree and quality of family members' interest and concern for one another' (Steinhauer et al, 1984). Ideally a family will meet the emotional needs of all its members, until they reach a stage of development at which some of these needs are met by people outside the family group, as increasingly happens during normal adolescent development.

Both the McMaster and the Process models distinguish various *types* of affective involvement, as well as being concerned with the *degree* to which family members are involved with each other. The following types of involvement are listed in both schemes:

(a) Uninvolved (or lack of involvement, in the McMaster model). This implies that the family members live rather 'like strangers in a boarding house'; they are frequently alienated and unfulfilled.
(b) Interest (or involvement) devoid of feelings. In such families involvement of family members with one another seems to arise from a sense of duty, a need in one member to control another, or curiosity.
(c) Narcissistic involvement. Here one family member is involved with another in order to bolster his or her own feelings of self-worth, rather than because of real concern or care for the other person.
(d) Empathic involvement. This is based on a real understanding of the needs of those with whom the subject is involved, resulting in responses which meet those needs.
(e) Enmeshment. This term is used in the Process model, although the McMaster model has two categories which describe a similar concept: 'overinvolvement' and 'symbiotic involvement', the latter being seen only in seriously disturbed relationships.

According to Steinhauer and his colleagues (1984) the types of involvement, as set out in the list above, are related to the degree of involvement and its quality, which can be either nurturant or destructive – although, as with all these terms, we are not dealing with 'either/ or' situations, but with an infinite number of possible variations along various continua.

The McMaster scheme has a separate dimension called 'affective expression', but the Process model incorporates this into the 'affective involvement' dimension, since the former is simply the expression of the latter.

Control

This dimension of family functioning, as described in the Process model, is similar to that which is labelled 'behaviour control' in the McMaster model. It consists of the influence family members have on one another. The Process model distinguishes 'maintenance functioning' and 'adaptations of functioning'. In order that these can be accomplished, a means of controlling family members' behaviour is necessary.

Both the models we are considering recognize four basic styles of behaviour control, namely rigid, flexible, laissez-fair and chaotic. *Rigid control* is high on predictability but low on constructiveness and adaptability. It may work quite well for maintenance functioning – the performance of day-to-day tasks and roles – but is less successful in adapting to change, including the developmental tasks families must confront. Steinhauer and his colleagues (1984) point out that its punitive aspects tend to encourage subversion, passive–aggressive behaviour, power struggles and the displacement of anger outside the family.

Flexible styles of control are predictable but constructive, and can adapt appropriately to changed circumstances. In the words of Steinhauer and his co-authors (1984, page 83) it 'assists task accomplishment because its supportive and educational tone encourages family members to participate and to identify with the idfeals and rules of the family'.

Laissez-faire styles are fairly predictable but low on constructiveness. In 'laissez-faire' families 'anything goes'. Inertia and indecision are the watchwords, rather than organization and action. Task accomplishment tends to be poor and there are often problems of communication and role allocation. Children raised in these disorganized families are often insecure and attention-seeking in their behaviour, and display little impulse control or self-discipline. Entry to school, where conformity to certain standards of behaviour is expected, can be difficult for them.

Chaotic styles of control are low in both predictability and constructiveness. These styles are unpredictable, switching from rigid to flexible to laissez-faire, so that no one knows what to expect. Changes occur more according to the whim or mood of family members than on the basis of changes in the family's situation and needs. The instability and inconsistency which characterize these families usually result in poor functioning on the other parameters we have mentioned.

Values and norms

This is a dimension of family functioning which is not included in the McMaster model. The Process model, however, considers the family's moral and religious values, which are derived from a variety of social and psychological sources, and its norms, which are 'the sum total of what is/is not acceptable within that family'.

It is certainly helpful, perhaps even essential for successful therapy in many cases, for family therapists to understand the value systems of the families they see. Not only are there widely varying views on such things as abortion, the role of women in society, the existence of God, and whether it is acceptable to smoke marijuana, but families differ also on what may seem quite minor issues; these include such matters as whether children should have set bedtimes and when these should be, who should wash the dishes or iron the clothes, and just how much responsibility for household chores children of different ages should be given. Such apparently trivial things can be the focus of much tension and difficulty, especially when families disagree on them.

The structural approach to assessing families

The structural model of family functioning was described by Minuchin (1974) in his book *Families and Family Therapy*. It was also outlined in the section on structural approaches in the previous chapter. This explained the six aspects of family functioning which Minuchin suggests should be assessed by the therapist in planning treatment – the family's structure, flexibility, resonance, life context, and developmental stage, and the relationship of the identified patient's symptoms to the family's transactional patterns. It also set out the ways in which structural therapists understand family systems and subsystems, and their boundaries.

The structural therapist joins the family system, though without becoming involved to the extent of losing objectivity, and experiences its structure through participating in its transactions. Boundaries are delineated both by observation of the family's transactions, and by planned interventions – such as attempts to create boundaries between subsystems, or to break them down – the results of which are carefully noted.

The structural approach to understanding families was outlined in Chapter 4.

A triaxial scheme

Tseng and McDermott (1979) proposed a 'triaxial' classification of families with problems. This aims to identify three classes of problems:

1. Family development dysfunctions.
2. Family system dysfunction.
3. Family group dysfunction.

This scheme is quite complex and the original article should be carefully studied by anyone who is considering using it. In summary, the axes are divided up as follows:

Axis 1. Family development dysfunction

   A. *Developmental dysfunction*
      (i)   Primary family dysfunction: this is difficulty in establishing a satisfactory marital relationship.
      (ii) Childbearing family dysfunction: this occurs with the arrival of children.
      (iii) Childrearing family dysfunction: this is difficulty in accommodating to and rearing young children.
      (iv) Maturing family dysfunction: this is usually centred on problems of differentiation and issues of separation.
      (v)   Contracting family dysfunction.
   B. *Developmental complications and variations*
      (i)   Interrupted family: this applies when there is a family crisis associated with a separation or divorce.
      (ii) One parent family problems: these are related to the presence of only one parent in the family.
      (iii) Reconstructed family dysfunction: where there is a remarriage with children already present.
      (iv) Chronically unstable family: this is characterized by frequent moves, separations or divorces.

Axis 2. Family subsystem dysfunction

   A. *Spouse–system dysfunction*
      (i)   Complementary marital dysfunction.
      (ii) Conflicting marital dysfunction.
      (iii) Dependent marital dysfunction.
      (iv) Disengaged marital dysfunction.
      (v)   Incompatible marital dysfunction.
   B. *Parent–child subsystem dysfunction*
      (i)   Parent-related dysfunction.
      (ii) Child-related dysfunction.
      (iii) Parent–child interrelational dysfunction.

      (iv) Parent–child triangular dysfunction.
  C. *Sibling subsystem dysfunction*
Axis 3. Family group dysfunction
  A. *Structural–functional dysfunctions*
      (i)   Underperforming families.
      (ii)   Overstructured families.
      (iii) Pathologically integrated families.
      (iv) Emotionally detached families.
      (v)   Disorganized families.
  B. *Social coping dysfunctions*
      (i)   Socially isolated families.
      (ii)   Socially deviant families.
      (iii) Special-theme families (dominated by commonly shared themes, mysteries, secrets or cultural beliefs).

An interesting feature of this scheme is that it is multi-axial; that is to say, it defines a number of parameters or axes on which each family must be assessed. A multiaxial approach will almost certainly be necessary for the satisfactory assessment of families. This has been found to be needed in the classification of psychiatric disorders of children (Rutter et al, 1975) and is also used in the third edition of the *Diagnostic and Statistical Manual* (DSM-III) of the American Psychiatric Association (1980). Multiaxial classifications are based on the principle that there are a number of distinct aspects of any disorder which can be considered and classified separately, for example, clinical syndrome, the presence or absence of physical disease, intelligence level, and psycho-social stressors. Tseng and McDermott's triaxial scheme is a commend-able attempt to look at families in a similar way.

The circumplex model

Olson, Sprenkle and Russell (1979) described what they called a 'circumplex' model for the assessment of families, and later published a 'theoretical update' of it (Olson et al, 1983). From an extensive review of the literature they identified two aspects of family behaviour, cohesion and adaptability, which they believe are of fundamental importance.

Cohesion is a measure of the 'emotional bonding that family members have toward one another'. It is closely related to the enmeshment-disengagement continuum described by Minuchin (1974) and discussed in Chapter 4.

Family adaptability is a measure of how far the family permits change (referred to by these authors as morphogenesis), and how far it is characterized by stability (morphostasis). The satisfactory functioning of a marital dyad, or a larger family group, requires both an element of stability and the capacity to change, the two characteristics being suitably balanced. Cohesion, also, should fall somewhere in the middle ground, being neither too great nor too little. The authors point out, however, that precisely what is best will vary with the culture in which the family is living; in some cultures extremes on one or other continuum may be of value.

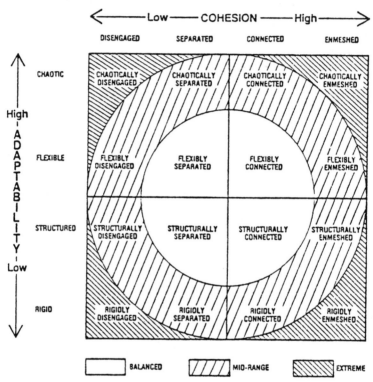

Figure 7. (Reproduced, with permission of the editor, from Olson, D. H. et al, 1983, *Family Process*, **22**, p. 71).

After assessment, families are rated on the two axes, for each of which there is a four point scale as follows:

	Cohesion	Family adaptability
High	Enmeshed	Chaotic
	Connected	Flexible
	Separated	Standard
Low	Disengaged	Rigid

Figure 7 illustrates how families can be grouped into sixteen possible types by using this scheme. The central area of the figure is the one in which most well-functioning families are expected to fall. The four extreme types, in the corners of the figure, are those most likely to be associated with family problems or problems in individual members.

The authors have also developed three assessment tools to assess family cohesion and adaptability. One of these is known as FACES II, an acronym for the second version of the Family Cohesion and Adaptability Evaluation Scales. This is a 30-item self-report scale that is claimed to have high reliability and validity (Olson et al, 1983). A different 'couple form' is available for couples without children. The authors point out also that the form is short enough to be completed twice by families, so that one response can consist of how the family perceives itself to be, and the other how it would like to be. They suggest, moreover, that it is possible that 'it is less important where the family falls in the circumplex model than how they feel about their levels of cohesion and adaptability'.

The circumplex model also recognizes a dimension of *family communication* (Olson et al, 1983). This is called a 'facilitating dimension', and is 'considered critical for facilitating couples and families to move on the two dimensions' – that is cohesion and adaptability.

The circumplex model has been subject to some empirical evaluation, and it seems that it is of real value (Sprenkle and Olson, 1978; Russell, 1979). Nevertheless some objections have been raised to certain aspects of it, particularly by Beavers and Voeller (1983), who have developed their own family model, which we will now briefly review.

The Beavers model

The Beavers model was described by its author in 1981. A later paper (Beavers and Voeller, 1983) compared it with the circumplex model, claiming that it had certain advantages over the latter. It has two axes. One is concerned with the 'stylistic quality of family interaction', which is classified as 'centripetal', 'mixed' or 'centrifugal'. The other is concerned with the:

> Structure, available information, and adaptive flexibility of the system. In systems terms, this may be called a negentropic continuum, since the more negentropic [the more flexible and adaptive], the more the family can negotiate, function and deal effectively with stressful situations. (Beavers and Voeller, 1983, page 89)

Figure 8 illustrates the Beavers model. It also illustrates the characteristics of families with varying degrees of functioning from 'severely

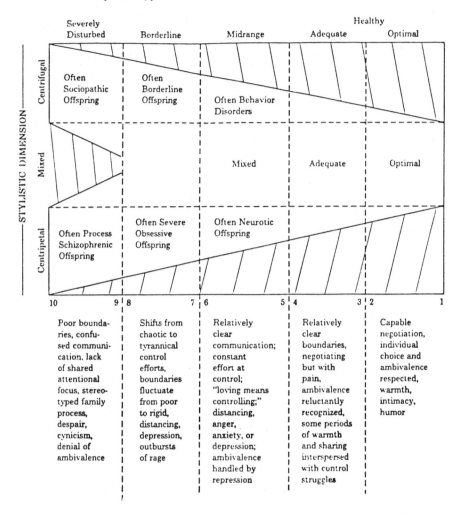

Autonomy: A continuous or infinite dimension, related to the family system's capacity to allow and encourage members to function competently in making choices, assuming responsibility for self, and negotiating with others.

Adaptability: A continuous or infinite dimension, related to the capacity of a family to function competently in effecting change and tolerating differentiation of members.

Centripetal/Centrifugal: A curvilinear, stylistic dimension with extreme styles associated with severely disturbed families and the most competent families avoiding either extreme.

Inflexibility: The inability to change. The most chaotic families are the most inflexible owing to their lack of a shared focus of attention.

Severely Disturbed: The lowest level of functioning along the adaptiveness continuum manifested by poorly defined subsystem boundaries and confusion owing to nonautonomous members having little tolerance for clear, responsible communication.

Borderline: A level of functioning between severely disturbed and midrange, manifested by persistent and ineffective efforts to rid the system of confusion by simplistic and often harsh efforts at control.

Midrange: Families that typically turn out sane but limited offspring, with relatively clear boundaries but continued expectations of controlling and being controlled.

Figure 8. (Reproduced, with kind permission of the editor, from Beavers, W. R. and Voeller, M. N., 1983, *Family Process,* **22,** p. 90).

disturbed' to 'optimal'. In the paper from which this figure is reproduced, Beavers and Voeller (1983) also provide fuller descriptions of severely disturbed, borderline, midrange, adequate and optimal families. Similar ground is covered in a contribution to the book *Normal Family Processes* (Beavers, 1982).

Beavers and Voeller (1983) assert that if autonomy is eliminated as an aspect of cohesion, what remains is essentially their centripetal/ centrifugal 'stylistic dimension'. They go on to maintain that:

> When adaptability is seen as an emerging, ever expansible capability to be placed on a continuum ranging from dysfunctional to optimal, we have a model that is clear, coherent, and capable of integrating family systems theory with developmental theory. (Beavers and Voeller, 1983, page 89)

These authors claim that the Beavers model conforms better to clinical reality than does the circumplex model; that it relates systems theory to developmental theory whereas the circumplex model does not do this; and that the circumplex model has 'logical defects' and does not (as theirs does) involve a 'scale of functional ability (adaptability) that reaches toward infinity'.

The reality is perhaps that there have been insufficient reports of the relative clinical usefulness of the two schemes for it to be clear which is the more useful. Both seem to have their merits, however, though neither is likely to represent the last word on the subject.

Practical aspects of the assessment of families

While the procedures therapists follow in assessing families depend in part upon their theoretical orientation, there are some widely accepted and generally applicable ways of approaching this task. This section will set these out, and provide a scheme which will enable novice therapists to approach newly referred families with confidence. It will, of course, be no substitute for supervised clinical practice, which must supplement any written account of family therapy if the student is to become proficient.

The assessment of a family may be described in stages. These may overlap or occur simultaneously. The stages are:

1. The initial contact.
2. Joining the family and establishing rapport.
3. Defining the desired outcome.
4. Reviewing the family's history, determining its present developmental stage and constructing a genogram.

5. Assessing the current functioning of the family.
6. Developing a diagnostic formulation.
7. Offering the family feedback and recommendations.
8. Arranging whatever further interviews, diagnostic procedures or referrals are recommended.
9. Informing a professional colleague who has referred a family of the results of the assessment, and of any recommendations arising from it, including any proposed treatment plans.

The initial contact

The initial contact may come from a member of the family that is seeking help, or it may come from a professional who wishes either to refer the family or to enquire whether the service you or your agency offers is appropriate. Enquiries from professional colleagues are usually easy to deal with. They most often come by telephone, but even if they arrive by letter or in the form of a telephone message, a phone conversation with the colleague is often helpful. If referral is being directly requested, it is a matter of collecting whatever relevant information the referring person has and telling that person when the family can be offered an appointment.

I ask those referring their patients or clients to do so in writing, giving whatever relevant information they have about the family. This helps avoid confusion and misunderstanding. It is also important that the therapist is clear, from the start, what part the referror wishes to have in the ongoing process of treatment; members of families in therapy may go, for example, to their family doctors to discuss some of the problems which treatment is addressing, or to ask for tranquillizers or other medication. This can have unfortunate results if the therapist and the family doctor are not in communication and working together. Therapy tends to go better when the therapist works closely with the person who referred the family, at least when that person has a continuing relationship with the family. This is usually easy to do when the referral comes from someone who regularly refers families to you, knows how you work and has collaborated with you on previous cases. In other cases you may have to work quite hard to establish this sort of relationship with the referror.

It is important to manage the initial contact with the family correctly. If the family has been referred by a colleague the members may already have been given most of the information they need about the services you provide. If not, or if the family is self-referred, they should be told how you operate, who should come to the first interview, how long the interview will take and generally what will happen when they arrive at the clinic or office. The question of payment may arise and, if fees are payable, it can be useful to explain them and to establish whether they are to be paid by a third party insurer or by the family. Many therapists like to make this initial contact themselves, but some leave it to a receptionist or secretary; this can work well if that person knows how you work, can discuss the above issues knowledgeably and has good skills in communicating over the telephone.

Many of those referred to programmes where family therapy is carried out do not realize why the therapist will want to see the whole family. Only in a minority of cases is it the family group as a whole that is referred or refers itself; often just one family member is seeking help or help is being sought on one member's behalf by other family members – as when parents seek help for a child; sometimes the problem is presented as a dyadic one, as when a marital couple, or a parent/child unit, present themselves. Most family therapists, however, like to start by seeing the whole family, which is usually defined as being all those living together in the household.

There are several points that explain why all family members should attend. The first is that problems of individual members can often be best understood in the context of the family of which they are a part; the second is that the behaviour of one family member inevitably has an effect on the other members; the third is that other family members can often be part of the solution of the problem. It is not usually a good idea to suggest that they are a part of the problem, even though that may be the case. It is generally quite easy to persuade parents that *they* are important to their children, but they are sometimes reluctant to bring children whom they consider to be well adjusted and problem-free; in that case the point can be made that the well-functioning children may have much to offer the problem child, in that they have acquired the skills to function well in the family – skills the identified patient may need to learn.

Joining the family and establishing rapport
Establishing rapport is a crucial process. It starts with the initial contact, it should be your primary objective in the first interview, perhaps the first several interviews, and it should continue throughout treatment. Rapport may be defined as a state of understanding, harmony and accord, though the understanding will be less than total; people who are in rapport with one another have a sympathetic relationship and each feels warmly towards the other. Psychotherapy probably fails more often because of the failure to establish rapport than for any other reason.

Establishing rapport has been given other names. Minuchin (1974) writes of 'joining' the family; and Karpel and Strauss (1983), in their book *Family Evaluation*, refer to 'building working alliances'. As rapport develops the participants become intensely involved with each other. Hypnotherapists have long recognized the importance of rapport, and know that failure to induce an hypnotic trance is due mainly, if not entirely, to the lack of sufficient rapport. Erickson and his colleagues, in their book on medical and dental hypnosis, described rapport as:

> ... that peculiar relationship, existing between subject and operator, wherein, since it [hypnosis] is a cooperative endeavour, the subject's attention is directed to the operator, and the operator's attention is directed to the subject. Hence, the subject tends to pay no attention to externals or the environmental situation. (Erickson et al, 1961, page 66)

When rapport is well developed the therapist can say almost anything, even quite outrageous things, to the clients without their becoming upset; even though the remarks could be construed as insulting, the clients will take them to have been meant jokingly, or at least not seriously.

So how is rapport to be achieved? There are both verbal and non-verbal techniques available and you should make use of both, although non-verbal techniques are probably more important.

The non-verbal communications the therapist offers a family start at the first contact, even if it is a telephone conversation, since one's tone of voice and manner of speaking convey powerful messages. A warm, friendly tone of voice, and a respectful, interested and accepting approach are important. When the family arrives it is best to greet them personally in the waiting room and to make the acquaintance briefly of each family member. I like to address them by name, if I know their names, and shake hands with each (except for very small children); if I do not know their names I ask for them as I greet them, at the same time telling the family who I am and expressing pleasure at their arrival. It is important, of course, to *appear* pleased to see the family, not just to say so.

Comfortable physical surroundings can assist in promoting rapport. It is helpful to have a pleasantly furnished room, well ventilated and unobtrusively lit, with comfortable chairs, paper tissues (in case of tears, which are not too uncommon in family therapy sessions) and ashtrays (since there are smokers in many families, and it does not help to ban smoking, even though the therapist may not like it). Yet the therapist's manner and behaviour are by far the most important factors, and excellent rapport can be established in prison cells, classrooms, public parks or on the beach.

The therapist's mode of dress carries its own message. People seeking therapy generally like their therapist to be respectably dressed and well groomed, though dress which is too formal can be off-putting to some – as can the white coats which doctors tend to wear in hospitals.

Most important of all is the therapist's behaviour. Rapport is promoted by matching or 'pacing' the behaviour of those with whom you wish to establish rapport. You can do this by matching your client's body posture and movements, respiratory rhythm, speed of talking, and voice tone and volume. You can also either 'mirror' or 'cross-match' their movements; mirroring is the moving of, say, your left arm or leg in response to similar movements of the client's right arm or leg. 'Cross-matching' occurs, for example, when the therapist's hand or finger is moved in rhythm with movements of the client's foot. Movements which may be matched include such things as crossing and uncrossing the legs, the tilting of the head to one side or the other, and leaning forward or settling back.

You do not need to match all the behaviours of those with whom you are establishing rapport. Matching should be done sensitively and unobtrusively; if it is, clients never become consciously aware of it. While it is not possible to match simultaneously the behaviours of all members of a family, you may observe common things about their behaviour which you can use. With families, though, it is usually more a matter of matching the behaviour of the different family members in turn, perhaps as you speak to each one. Of course many of the other behaviours I have mentioned are things you share with the whole family – your courteous manner, mode of dress and so forth.

The developers of 'neuro-linguistic programming' (NLP) have paid much attention to rapport-building processes. NLP was developed from the study of such highly effective communicators as Milton Erickson and Virginia Satir; it is designed to help those who study it to become more effective communicators. The above matching and mirroring devices are part of what the authors of the literature on NLP call 'pacing'. They write:

> When you pace someone – by communicating from the context of their model of the world – you become synchronized with their own internal processes. It is, in one sense, an explicit means to 'second guess' people or to 'read their minds', because you know how they will respond to your communications. This kind of synchrony can serve to reduce resistance between you and the people with whom you are communicating. The strongest form of synchrony is the continuous presentation of your communication in sequences which perfectly parallel the unconscious processes of the person you are

communicating with – such communication approaches the much desired goal of irresistibility. (Dilts et al, 1980, pages 116-7)

Your *verbal communications* can also assist or impede the development of rapport. The developers of NLP have also addressed the issue of how rapport can be facilitated by the right choice of words. They point out that rapport is helped by matching the predicates used by those with whom you wish to establish rapport (Bandler et al, 1976; Bandler and Grinder, 1979). A predicate is a word that says something descriptive about the subject of a sentence; predicates include verbs, adjectives and adverbs. Some people tend to use visual rather than auditory or feeling predicates – as, for example, in the phrases, 'I see what you mean', 'things are looking brighter', or 'that is a pretty hazy idea'.

Examples of the use of auditory predicates are, 'I hear what you're saying', 'that sounds terrible', or 'it was like music to my ears'. Sentences such as, 'I'm facing a lot of heavy problems,' 'that feels like a good idea', or 'that's a big weight off my shoulders', illustrate the use of 'kinesthetic' or feeling-type predicates. Rapport can be enhanced by matching your predicates with those of the person with whom you are in conversation. Of course most people use predicates of all three types – as well as some olfactory ('this business smells fishy to me') and gustatory ('it leaves a bad taste in my mouth') ones. The point is that most people have a preferred way of processing information, using mainly one or other of the three main sensory channels, and it can be helpful to note this and use it while you are establishing rapport. This is but another way of matching your communications with your clients' internal worlds.

In addition to matching predicates, it can be helpful to listen carefully to the vocabularies of the family members you are interviewing, noting the kinds of words and expressions they use; this will enable you to match not only the predicates they use, but also their vocabularies generally. My own experience is that few things impede the establishment of rapport as much as repeatedly using words and expressions with which those to whom you are speaking are unfamiliar. This is especially important when you are dealing with children, whose vocabulary is partly a function of age, but it applies also to adults. Thus the vocabulary of a university professor is likely to be different from that of an unskilled labourer who left school at the age of 15.

Other useful rapport-building devices include accepting family members' views of things without challenging them in the early stages of your contacts with them; adopting a 'one-down' position; and talking of experiences and interests you have in common with members of the family. The 'one-down' position can help in various circumstances.

Some people are convinced they are right, for example about the nature of their family's problems, and to confront them with a conflicting opinion may simply lead to an unproductive argument and symmetrical battle; others appear overawed or intimidated by the therapist. In either of these circumstances a one-down approach may help. It might consist simply of saying that you know little about the job a family member has and asking that person to explain something about it to you, or asking children to spell their names for you; or it could be a matter of declaring therapeutic impotence or defeat, or at least expressing doubts about the completeness of your understanding of the family or its situation, and offering interventions in a tentative, doubtful way.

Common experiences might be having lived in the city, county, province or state the family come from. I was once seeing a family at a time when I had a stiff and painful back; I mentioned this as I eased myself slowly into my chair, and it transpired that the mother in the family also had back problems. This at once gave us something in common to exchange a few words about. Common hobbies, sports and pastimes may be used in similar ways.

Defining the desired outcome
Like most other human endeavours, psychotherapy makes better progress if it has well-defined goals; indeed there is no way to define success if no desired outcome has been established. At the same time, therapy goals may be modified as treatment proceeds, and the family's potential for change becomes increasingly apparent. The defining of therapy goals is a matter of such importance that the next chapter is devoted to it.

Reviewing the family's history, determining its developmental stage and constructing a genogram
These tasks can conveniently be tackled together. Family therapists differ in the amount of information they routinely collect concerning a family's history, but it is helpful to have some understanding of how the family has come to be where it is. Much of this information can be gathered in the course of the construction of the genogram, of which more shortly.

A good way to approach the family's history is to start with the parents' births and childhoods. If the parents are initially reluctant to discuss their own histories, it may be helpful to preface these questions with an explanation; you may say that you are interested in how the present family came to be, and want to understand something of its background. The parents can then be asked where they were born and brought up, what their family lives were like when they were children, how they got along at school and what they did when they left school. As they answer these questions they will probably speak of their parents and siblings. They can next be asked how they met and courted, and then they may be invited to outline the course of the marriage so far.

It may be convenient to ask next about the births of the children, and the children's development to date. It is more than likely that by this stage of the interview the problems for which the family are seeking help will have emerged; indeed they may already have become clear when the treatment goals were defined. It will also probably now be clear what stage in its life cycle the family has reached; there may also have emerged evidence of any difficulty the family is having in surmounting one of the family transition points mentioned in Chapter 2.

A *genogram* (sometimes called a geneogram), or family map, is a useful adjunct in both assessment and treatment. Guerin and Pendagast (1976) drew attention to its value, and its use by family therapists seems to have been increasing since then. It gives a concise, graphic summary of a family's current composition. It should also show the extended family network, the ages of the family members, the dates of the parents' marriage, and of any divorces or separations; it indicates how all the family members are related and it can also show who is the identified patient – although I usually omit this information when I am engaging family members in constructing a genogram. The geographical locations of the family members can be indicated, as also can brief summaries of the salient points concerning each family member – for example occupation, school grade or year, health, and important points from individuals' past histories (illnesses, accidents, losses, incarcerations and so forth).

While some therapists prepare the genogram later using the information they have obtained from the family during sessions with them, I prefer to prepare it with the assistance of the family members during the first session or two – often the first one. Specimen genograms are shown in Figures 9 and 10. Figure 9 shows a relatively uncomplicated family situation. The oldest child is adopted, the maternal grandfather is dead, the paternal grandparents were divorced when the father was aged 9, the paternal grandfather remarried four years later and his second wife died in 1973.

Figure 10 shows a more complex family constellation. In this family the parents of the identified patient, Brad (distinguished by a double boundary), cohabited in a 'common law' relationship from 1965 to 1969, after which they got married. They separated in 1973 and were legally divorced in 1980. Carmen, Brad's mother, has since had a common law

The Brown Family - 1985

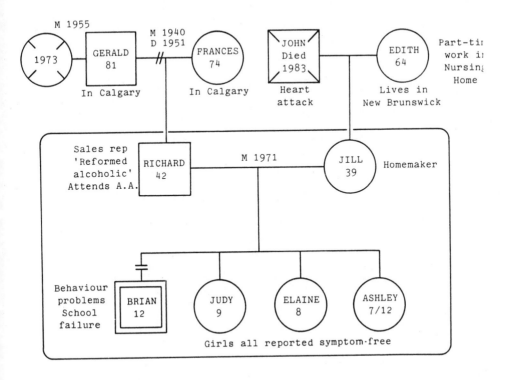

For interpretation of symbols see Figure 10

Figure 9.

relationship (with Eric) and is now married to Ken, with whom she lives with her two children by Eric and a 3-year-old by Ken. Brad and his father, Dave, live with Katrina and her 10-year-old daughter by her former husband, Len. She also had a previous pregnancy which ended in a miscarriage in 1974. Carmen is an only child and both her parents are dead; Dave is the fourth in a family of one girl and four boys.

A genogram can contain information about the health, behaviour, strengths or problems of the people shown in it. These points can be written beside the symbols representing the various family members. While such information is not an integral part of a genogram, I often find it helpful to include it.

The Green Family - 1985

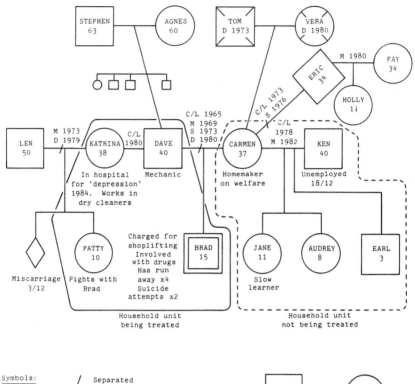

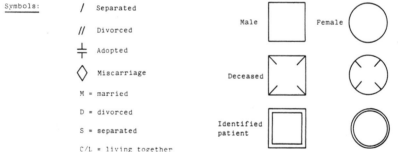

Figure 10.

I like to involve all family members in the preparation of the genogram, apart from those too young to understand the process. The establishment of rapport can often be advanced during this process, and much information about how the family functions is often obtained in addition to the facts which are recorded in the genogram.

Nichols (1984, pages 374–376) outlines how genograms may be developed, and a pioneer of their use was Bowen. His scheme, and the symbols he uses, are reproduced by Carter and McGoldrick (1980, page xxiii). The value of the genogram is also stressed by Holman (1983). She uses the development of the genogram as a means of getting the family to share information, and of encouraging the expression of feelings about the people and events that are discussed. She observes:

> Even reticent family members are generally willing to share abundant information and are often surprised to recognize that while they know much about some areas of the family history, they know little about other areas. As information is discussed, it often becomes clear that spouses are unfamiliar with information that it was assumed they knew (Holman, 1983, page 69).

The book *Genograms in Family Assessment* (McGoldrick and Gerson, 1985) also gives valuable and comprehensive information on the construction, interpretation and clinical uses of genograms, with many illustrations. It is the most comprehensive source of information on genograms available as this is written.

Heinl (1985) instructed subjects to draw their own genograms, and then visually analysed the results. He took the following into account:

- The global image of the genogram.
- The balance between paternal and maternal segments of the genogram.
- The (vertical) spacing between generations.
- The (horizontal) spacing within generations.
- The use of the symbols.
- The sequence in which the genogram was developed.

Heinl (1985, page 227) concluded that 'the visual features of a subject's genogram drawn by the subject himself may provide pointers towards transgenerational and individual psychodynamic issues and may therefore contribute to fruitful therapeutic work'.

Assessing the current functioning of the family

The main objective of the assessment process is to come to an understanding of the current functioning of the family. The previous stages have been necessary preliminaries; it is helpful to have some knowledge of the family's history and development, but it is crucial to understand how it is functioning in the present.

The therapist learns more about how a family functions from the experience of interacting with the family than from information obtained by asking family members about it. There are only two reliable ways of obtaining information about family relationships. One is to observe the interactions between family members; the other is to ask questions which bear on the relationships between the members, and study carefully the family's responses, both verbal and non-verbal. In order to obtain as much information as possible it is advisable to do both these things. A family, or indeed any other social group, cannot adequately describe how it functions. The formal organizational structure may be described, but this says little about how the different parts habitually interact and about the functioning of the system as a whole. The questions asked of family members are not, therefore, usually about *how* the family functions as a group or organization; instead they are designed to reveal this indirectly.

There are many ways of interviewing families; some direct, others, in varying degrees, indirect. An important contribution to the literature on family assessment was made by the Milan group of therapists in their paper entitled, 'Hypothesizing – circularity – neutrality: three guidelines for the conductor of the session' (Palazzoli et al, 1980). As the paper's title suggests, these authors recommend that the interviewer should first develop some *hypotheses* about the family system; one always knows something of a family, even before the first interview – for example its composition and the fact that it contains a rebellious child, an anorexic adolescent or a depressed adult. Whatever information *is* available is the basis of the hypothesis with which the therapist starts.

Palazzoli and her colleagues (1980, page 5) define a hypothesis as 'an unproved supposition tentatively accepted to provide a basis for further investigation, from which a verification or refutation can be obtained'. Having developed such suppositions the therapist then proceeds to test them. This is an active process in which the therapist asks a series of questions designed to explore the patterns of the family's relationships. The Milan authors believe that if the therapist were to behave in a passive fashion, that is as an observer rather than a mover, the family, 'conforming to its own linear hypothesis, would impose its own script, dedicated exclusively to the designation of who is "crazy" and who is "guilty", resulting in zero information for the therapist' (Palazzoli et al., 1980, page 5).

Hypotheses, the Milan group believe, must be systemic, that is, they must concern the family system as a whole. It is not enough to say that somebody may be depressed or anxious about something. This may be the case, of course, but to treat a family system successfully it is necessary to consider the *relationships* between the family members, and how these fit together to make up the family system as a whole.

This brings us to the concept of *circularity*. The Milan associates derived many of their ideas from the work of Gregory Bateson, and they quote the following passage of which he was co-author:

The same general truth – that all knowledge of external events is derived from the relationships between them – is recognizable in the fact that to achieve more accurate perception, a human being will always resort to change in the relationship between himself and the external object. If he is inspecting a rough spot on some surface by means of touch he moves his finger over the spot, thus creating a shower of neural impulses with definite sequential structure, from which he can derive the static shape and other characteristics of the thing investigated ... In this sense, our initial sensory data are always 'first derivatives', statements about *differences* which exist among external objects or statements about *changes* which occur either in them or in our relationship to them ... What we perceive easily is difference and change – difference is a relationship. (Ruesch and Bateson, 1968, page 173)

This way of thinking led the Milan group to develop their process of 'circular interviewing'. A 'Milan-style' interview is a circular process. The therapist responds to information the family gives about relationships by formulating more questions, to which the family then responds again, and so on. The questions are framed in a circular way too; their method is to ask one member of the family to describe the interactions or relationships between two others. Many of the questions concern differences between such things. This might better be called triadic interviewing, and is an example of triadic thinking.

Triadic theory – which is the idea that two people (or groups or even agencies) in conflict tend to involve a third person or group in the conflict – has been described as 'one of the cornerstones of many models of family therapy' (Coppersmith, 1985). Bowen's views on 'triangles', outlined in Chapter 1, and the concepts labelled alliances, coalitions and detouring, described in Chapter 4 as part of structural therapy's theoretical basis, are also examples of triadic thinking. The process of bringing in a third person is sometimes referred to as 'triangulation'.

Coppersmith (1985) points out that the ability to think in terms of triads (or triangles, which are essentially the same thing) is an important skill for the family therapist. It is the basis of the style of interviewing practised and advocated by Palazzoli and her colleagues (1980). The therapist is always thinking of the various triads in the family and how they function. The questions asked of a family member, or group of members, are often about differences between the behaviours or responses of two other members or groups of members; and the emphasis is on relationships between people rather than on the behaviour of individuals.

There are some other important practical points about interviewing families using the ideas of Palazzoli et al (1980):

(a) It is better to ask questions about specific behaviours which occur between family members, rather than about how people feel about the situation, or about how they interpret or understand it. For example the therapist might ask one of the children in a family questions such as the following:

> What does your father do when Billy loses his temper and swears at his mother? (Then, when the father's reaction has been described): And what does your mother do then? And if your big sister is around, what would she be doing?

(b) As well as asking about them directly, differences may be highlighted by asking people to rank the family members in terms of specific behaviours. For example, the members of a family in which one child is physically aggressive to a younger one, might be asked the following questions:

> When Pete hits Dorothy, who is most likely to step in and try and stop him? And who is the next most likely to do this? And then?... (And so on, until it is determined who is least likely to intervene.)

(c) It can be helpful to ask questions concerning changes in the patterns of relationships; these may concern differences before and after certain specific events. Thus members of a family which has recently moved from one place of abode to another might be asked about differences in the behaviours of members relative to one another before and after the move; similarly the situation before and after a marital separation, a remarriage, an illness or accident affecting a family member, or a child's entry into school or departure to university, might be explored.

(d) Questions can be asked about how the behaviour of family members varies in different circumstances, whether these are real or hypothetical. For example:

- Who would be most upset if Eric was seriously ill?
- Do Frances and Gillian fight more when Dad is at home than when he is not?
- What does Mummy do when Harry misbehaves? Does she react differently in any way when Dad is at home?

Neutrality is the last of the three attributes that the Milan group consider desirable, even essential, in the therapist. When asking questions in the way described above, the therapist may seem to be allied with the person being questioned, while that questioning is occurring, but the alliance shifts when the questioning moves to another family member. During the session the therapist will be allied in turn with all the family members, and 'the end result of the successive alliances is that the therapist is allied with everyone and no one at the same time.' The Milan authors also advise that the therapist declare no judgements, whether implicit or explicit, while interviewing the family; to do so would have the effect of allying the therapist with one or more of the individuals or groups within the family.

There are other approaches to interviewing families, and not everyone uses the methods advocated by the Milan associates. Karpel and Strauss (1983), for example, in their book *Family Evaluation*, describe a more direct style of questioning. They use questions and remarks like:

- Can you tell us a little bit about how you were feeling after your father died? *Or*
- So when he died you felt responsible? (Both from page 124)

These authors sometimes address intrapsychic processes quite directly. They are clearly concerned with intrapsychic processes (which the above questions address), as well as interpersonal ones. The Milan group therapists might have preferred to ask other members how they thought the person concerned felt when the father died. They might also have asked each member to rate the family in terms of who was most upset, down to who was least upset; similarly each member could have been asked who they thought felt most responsible for the father's death, who came next, and so on.

Karpel and Strauss (1983) also describe a series of 'probe questions', designed 'to probe the broad area of family structure in a routine, organized fashion that is both direct and non-threatening' (page 136). The probe questions cover such subjects as the layout of the home, a typical day in the life of the family, rules, regulations and limit setting within the family, and the alliances and coalitions within the family. Thus Karpel and Strauss might say:

I'd like to get a better idea of who spends a good deal of time with whom in the family, whom each of you is most likely to talk to when something is on your mind. (Page 142)

It seems that these authors use many more direct questions than the Milan group. For example, they describe asking a daughter how she reacted when her mother behaved in a particular way, whereas the

Milan associates would probably have asked this question of another family member.

Other areas which Karpel and Strauss suggest as subjects for probe questions are family disagreements, previous family crises, and the changes the family members desire to make. The latter issue, however, is one I deal with separately in Chapter 6.

Although the subjects of the 'probes' Karpel and Strauss (1983) suggest can often be usefully raised with families, I prefer less direct enquiry and tend to use a more circular type of interviewing. There are, however, many ways of obtaining information about families, and there is little scientific evidence to tell us which is best. Therapists need to develop their own personal styles, and use techniques with which they are comfortable and which fit their theoretical models of how families can be helped to change. Moreover some interview styles seem to suit certain families better than others. The important things for the family therapist to keep in mind are that it is the family system that is being assessed, not the individuals, and that the relationship patterns and habitual ways of interacting are what we seek to understand during this process.

Developing a diagnostic formulation

At this stage it is necessary for the therapist, or the therapy team, to review the information that has been obtained and develop from it a diagnostic formulation. This involves considering how the family functions, whether the presenting problems are related to its way of functioning and, if so, how they relate.

While the human systems to which a person belongs are always relevant, in some instances other factors appear more important. Physical conditions such as hyperthyroidism, porphyria, cerebral tumours and many other diseases of the nervous system have particular psychiatric manifestations, for which family therapy is not the treatment of choice. Some psychiatric disorders also appear to have causes which are physical, rather than being related primarily to family factors; for example in many cases of bipolar affective disorder, the swings between moods of depression, normality and mania occur in a regular cyclical pattern with no evident relationship to external circumstances. Family therapy may be needed in such cases, and in families containing members with physical disorders, since the presence of such conditions does not provide immunity from family dysfunction. Quite the reverse is true; such disorders make family dysfunction more likely, since they provide additional stress. Emotional factors – which are often closely tied in with the family situation– can also be important in the genesis and the exacerbation, of certain physical conditions. These issues were explored by Minuchin and his colleagues (1978) in the book *Psychosomatic Families*, where they also discuss the relationship between family factors and the physical disorders in cases of diabetes, asthma and anorexia nervosa.

An important issue to be decided when formulating a case, therefore, is the extent to which the presenting problems are a feature of family dysfunction on the one hand, and how far they are due to other – perhaps physical – causes on the other. In many instances it is not an 'either-or' question that must be answered. Indeed, even if there are no relevant physical *disorders* affecting any of the family members – and in most of the cases that come to the attention of family therapists this is the case – the temperamental characteristics of the family members are relevant, and often important, factors. Any individual's symptoms must be viewed in the light of that person's temperament and personality characteristics, and of the family and wider social context.

The idea of a formulation is to convey, or put on record, the therapist's understanding of the family. It is not just a listing of factors, but a description of their interplay and relative importance. It should include a description of the family system, using whatever theoretical model the therapist favours; there should also be mention of the family's developmental stage, and of whether the family is having any difficulty dealing with one of the 'transition points' discussed in Chapter 2. It is best to put it in writing. It should be concise and clearly written, and should constitute a logical explanation of the case, leading to a treatment plan or, perhaps, a plan for further assessment of the family. In most cases it will contain the following information:

1. A brief description of the problems which have led the family to seek help, and of the changes they hope will result from therapy.
2. Mention of the family's constitution, with the members' ages, relationships and occupations, and a summary of their developmental stage; much of this information can usually be provided by attaching the genogram to the formulation.
3. The therapist's understanding of the family, the nature of its current problems and how these are being maintained, using whatever theoretical model the therapist finds most helpful. The relative importance and interrelation of the various factors maintaining the current situation should be described.
4. The family's strengths, assets and motivation for change.
5. Information about the family's ecological context or suprasystem, and how this is affecting the family.

When treatment appears to be needed the formulation should lead logically to a treatment plan and, usually, a prognosis – that is, a statement of the expected outcome, with and without treatment.

Offering the family feedback and recommendations
I usually give the family a short break while I develop the formulation. When one or more observers have been watching the session, the formulation will be developed by the group; similarly, if the family has been interviewed by co-therapists, these will want to discuss their findings and develop a joint formulation.

The form the feedback takes will depend on the theoretical orientation of the therapist(s), as well as on the nature of the family's case. Most therapists would probably agree that it is not simply, or even mainly, a matter of explaining the formulation to the family. Generally, insight in itself is not particularly helpful. Knowing how the therapist understands their problems does not necessarily lead to change; in fact when a strategic approach to treatment is planned it may impede it.

The feedback should always include any recommendations the therapist has regarding further investigation or assessment of the family, and it should state whether treatment is recommended and, if so, what type. The feedback is often the start of therapy. Depending upon the therapist's theoretical orientation, it may take the form of agreeing a contract for the family to do certain things, as is the practice of those who use the McMaster Model of Family Therapy; or it may be quite indirect, and be intended to reframe the situation in a therapeutically helpful way.

I find it useful at this stage to 'positively connote' what the family members are doing, as suggested by Palazzoli and her colleagues (1978a). What is positively connoted is the *intent* behind the actions of family members, not necessarily the actions themselves. Thus parents may be using quite inappropriate methods in their attempts to discipline a child, and may even be physically abusing the child, but their intent – namely to rear their child to behave in a socially acceptable way – is nevertheless commendable. The concept of 'best choice', derived from the work of Milton Erickson and described by Lankton and Lankton (1983), is also helpful at this stage of the assessment. Erickson believed that people always make the best choice of behaviour available to them in their particular circumstances; it may prove most unfortunate, even highly destructive, but is the best available to those concerned, taking into account their state of mind and situation. Therapy, therefore, is a matter of giving the family members more choice, and alternative, more effective, options. Sometimes the therapy plan can helpfully be presented in this way.

Arranging the next step

It is important that the family leave the first interview knowing what is to happen next. The next step, in most instances, will be setting the date and time of the next appointment. Sometimes other recommendations may be made, such as referral to a colleague for further investigation or specialized treatment; when the family contains a child or children who are having social or academic problems at school, contact with the school, and perhaps a visit to the school, may be suggested. Indeed, Aponte (1976) recommended that when the main problems are at school, the first interview should be a family–school interview. The therapist may sometimes wish to obtain information from professionals who have previously treated the family, or members of it. In that case the necessary forms of consent, authorizing release of this information, should be signed by the appropriate family members.

The question of who should attend future sessions sometimes arises at this stage. If one or more important people were absent from the first interview, the therapist should either ask the family to bring the missing person(s) to the next session – which is quite appropriate if the person concerned is a child – or should discuss with the family how to approach the missing individual(s). If these are adults it may be better for the therapist to make the approach, with the permission of the family. I have outlined a metaphorical approach to this issue elsewhere (Barker, 1985, pages 25-27).

Sometimes it may be helpful to have extended family members who do not live in the household present at certain sessions. On the other hand, the therapist may wish to see fewer people, perhaps just the marital couple, next time or even for a series of sessions; in that case, also, the plan should be discussed with those concerned and agreement sought.

Feedback to referring professionals and others

When a family is referred by another professional person it is both courteous and good clinical practice to send that person a written report of the results of the assessment. This should make it clear how the therapist thinks the referror can assist in the ongoing treatment of the family; this may involve no more than the referror not getting involved in the issues the therapy is addressing, but referring questions the family may ask about those issues back to the therapist. It may be helpful to supplement the written report with a telephone call.

Sometimes more active participation, such as joint planning and action, with family physicians, paediatricians, child welfare social workers, school staff and others may be important. In that case the appropriate contacts should be made with the outside people and agencies concerned at this stage, and with the family's permission. Formal permission to send a report to a referring professional is not, however, normally needed.

Summary

This chapter has reviewed some research-based models of family functioning, namely the McMaster model, the Process model, Minuchin's structural model, Tseng and McDermott's triaxial model, the circumplex model of Olson et al, and the Beavers model. Each of these models can be of value as a guide, or map, for the therapist wishing to make sense out of the complex and sometimes confusing information presented by familes when they are assessed.

The assessment process itself should be systematic but flexible. The initial contact should lead to the establishment of rapport and the gaining of the family's trust. Therapist and family must then define the desired outcome – the subject of the next chapter. Whatever model of family functioning is employed, the focus must be on the family system – that is the pattern of the relationships between the members. In family therapy these, rather than the individuals in the family, are the primary focus. A 'triadic' approach to interviewing families, which involves thinking about groups of three individuals, or collections of individuals, and how they interact, is helpful. The family's developmental stage, and whether it is having difficulty making the transition from one stage to the next, should also be considered.

The assessment of the family unit and its ecological context should lead to a diagnostic formulation. Appropriate feedback is then provided to the family, which is also told what treatment is recommended, if therapy appears to be needed. It is important to keep referring sources informed, especially if they are still involved with the family. Other outside professionals may also need to be informed and, perhaps, become involved in some way as therapy proceeds.

Chapter 6

Establishing Treatment Goals

Most human endeavours are more successful if they are carefully planned and have well-defined objectives. Family therapy is no exception, though some schools of therapy place more emphasis on the setting of objectives than do others. It is, however, hard to know whether you have achieved a successful outcome unless therapy has started with clearly defined goals. It is important also that the goals are defined in such a way that therapist and family can tell whether they have been met.

The importance of having a clearly defined outcome is emphasized by the developers of neurolinguistic programming (NLP) (Dilts et al, 1980). NLP is concerned with the processes of communication, both verbal and non-verbal. One of its aphorisms is that 'the meaning of a communication is the response it elicits' – regardless of what the communicator intended (Bandler et al, 1976). It assumes that communications from one person to another are intended to elicit some sort of response. This is the 'outcome frame'. While in everyday conversation outcome frames are not usually consciously formulated, they nevertheless exist. Thus if you say 'Good morning' to a colleague you probably expect a similar reply; this is your outcome frame. How important it is to you to achieve your desired outcome will vary with the circumstances of the conversation or interaction.

Outcome frames, or treatment objectives, are important in psychotherapy generally, but in family therapy, where there are a number of parties involved in the process, they are especially so. All the verbal and non-verbal messages that pass from therapist to family should be designed to elicit responses which will assist the family to achieve their objectives. Family therapy is thus a meeting of therapist and family members for the purpose of exchanging communications with a view to making changes; these changes may be in the behaviour of family members, in their emotional states or relationships, or in the family's overall functioning. To achieve this purpose the establishment of agreed and clearly defined objectives is imperative – at least if much time is not to be wasted. Much family therapy nowadays is 'strategic' – that is to say it is based on a strategy or plan which, the therapist has reason to believe, will lead to the changes the family seek. The effective use of strategic methods is, however, difficult, perhaps even impossible, without well defined objectives.

Negotiating the objectives of treatment and reaching agreement may not be easy, especially when there is much pre-existing disagreement between family members. It may take a whole session, sometimes several, but the time usually proves to have been well spent, and in fact this process itself can have therapeutic value.

Steve and Terri had been married eight years; they had two daughters, one aged 7 years and the other 6 months. Steve was a busy professional man and Terri a homemaker who had occasionally worked as a receptionist. They presented as their problem the behaviour of their 7-year-old daughter, Vivienne.

Vivienne was an attractive, highly intelligent but rather sulky and sullen girl. She was having some relationship difficulties with other children at school, where she also exhibited some mild behaviour problems and was thought not to be performing to her academic potential. A much bigger problem, it soon emerged, existed in the marital relationship.

Steve and Terri had met hitch-hiking at a time when Steve was still a student and Terri had just left a home where she had not been happy. They married soon afterwards, both of them still in their teens. At first things went well for the couple; until Vivienne's birth Terri worked as a waitress, then as a receptionist, helping support Steve as he continued his studies at university. Terri realized that Steve had to study hard and for long hours, and at first accepted cheerfully the fact that she got little of his attention. Vivienne arrived sooner than the couple had planned to start a family, and with her birth Terri started to feel increasingly unhappy and lonely. Her parents disapproved of her marriage and also looked down on her, she felt, because she was the only child in their family who had not gone on to higher education.

Eventually Steve completed his university degree. He obtained a job working for a large company which demanded much of its trainee executives. He also started attending evening classes, playing squash with colleagues after work and staying out drinking with his friends after these activities. Terri was left, literally, holding the baby at home.

This family pattern had persisted, with little change occurring when the new baby was born six months previously. Terri felt trapped in the relationship, estranged from her family of origin and generally worthless.

The therapist's entire first session with this family was spent exploring their situation and what they wanted to achieve from therapy. When the seriousness of the marital situation became clear, the therapist asked each spouse, in turn, to describe exactly how he or she would like the marriage to be. In other words, each was asked to paint a word-picture of their desired 'outcome frame'. Both partners found this an interesting experience and each was surprised by the picture of the 'ideal marriage' which the other one presented. This exercise took up the remainder of the first session, so that no time was left for any other therapeutic work; the therapist therefore made an appointment to see the couple the following week.

When they came next week Steve and Terri reported a big change for the better in their relationship. While not all their problems were resolved, and Vivienne continued to cause them some concern, the process whereby each partner learned what the other wanted of the marital relationship seemed to have helped them considerably.

The setting of objectives and the description of an outcome frame do not always have as positive an effect as they did in the case of the above couple; indeed this family was a little unusual in that the marital partners were able to make significant changes simply in response to the discussion of the desired objectives. It does, however, illustrate the point that one reason at least why some relationships are unhappy is that the partners in the relationship are each unaware of what the other wants.

Even if agreement is never reached, so that treatment is not started, time spent discussing treatment objectives is not wasted; therapy embarked upon on the basis of misunderstood goals seldom produces results that are satisfactory to any of those concerned. The one possible exception to this is the long-running therapy into which some clients get to achieve 'emotional growth' or 'make gains' – the 'gains' never being defined in any precise way. Such therapy resembles a hiking trip upon which the hikers embark with no idea of where they want to go, nor of what they will do when they finally land up wherever their hike takes them. This kind of therapy – like this sort of hiking – can be enjoyable, of course, but it is probably not the best way to achieve particular results quickly, which is the aim of most therapists and their clients.

Defining the desired state

It is helpful to obtain a clear picture of the 'desired state' which families coming for therapy wish to reach. Therapist and family members should also define as precisely as possible how this differs from the present state of affairs.

Many family members – and individual clients – come to therapy with negative goals. Parents want their children to stop having tantrums, or fighting with each other; or a spouse wants his or her partner to stop arguing; or a couple want their teenage daughter to stop refusing to eat the food they offer her. These are all good reasons for seeking professional help – assuming that commonsense measures have proved ineffective – but they are not adequate as outcome frames. To put it another way, a description of your 'desired state' requires more than a statement of what you *don't* want to be happening. A comprehensive picture of how you *would* like things to be is as useful to both client and therapist as an architect's mental image is – to the architect – of the building for which plans must be developed.

So it is often useful to ask family members to reframe their objectives in positive terms. If the children are not to have tantrums, how should they react in situations in which they have been having tantrums? If they are not to fight, what should they be doing when they would otherwise be fighting? What should replace the arguments the couple have been engaging in? Presumably the arguments have served some purpose. So too, we may assume, has the teenage girl's refusal to eat; while it is certainly more positive to frame the objective as that of having the girl eat more, it may also be helpful to take matters a little further and ask what is to serve the purpose refusing food has served.

Surprisingly, perhaps, such questions have often scarcely been considered by families seeking therapy. And even when goals are stated in positive terms, they are frequently vague and ill-defined. Perhaps they want 'to be a happy family', or 'to get along well together'. These are reasonable enough things to want, and they may be useful starting points for the discussion of treatment goals, but they are not in themselves adequate outcome frames. What do the family members mean when they talk about being a 'happy family'? How, exactly, would they be relating to each other if they were getting along 'well'?

The aims of therapy are also sometimes described by families in comparative terms; they want to be 'happier' or 'to do more things together'. It can be helpful to ask the members to elaborate on such statements. If they are to be happier, the next question may be 'happier than what'? And in what circumstances? What would the family look like, and what would it be doing, if it were happier? And so on. Similarly it could be useful to ask a family that wants to do more things together, what sort of things it would like to be doing, where they would be done, how often and so forth. There may prove to be disagreement on some of these points, so that what looks like an agreed objective is not really one at all; indeed it may simply serve to conceal some fundamental differences in the family. If so, resolving these differences might become a goal of therapy.

I have found it a good plan to get families to describe, in as much detail as possible, how things will be when (and not if!) therapy is successfully concluded. This is the process referred to above when the case of Steve and Terri was described. (By talking about how things will be *when* therapy is complete, you embed in your statements the message that it will end successfully; on the other hand, if you discuss how things will be *if* therapy reaches a successful conclusion, you are implying doubts about this – which is hardly the way to inspire confidence in those who come to you for help!)

Once the desired state has thus been described there are still some questions to be considered:

1. Will there be any drawbacks to the desired state? Will anything that at present offers gratification to someone in the family, or serves some useful purpose, be lost, without its being replaced by a satisfactory alternative? For example, if the daughter who at present won't eat starts to eat the food her mother prepares, will this result in less closeness between mother and daughter, since there will no further need for battles or discussions about the daughter's diet? ... Or will it mean less closeness between the parents because they will not now need to spend long hours discussing their daughter's eating problem?
2. What other consequences will follow once the changes the family seek have occurred? Careful consideration of how things will be for all members of the family when the specified changes have been made may lead to second thoughts. This in turn might lead to further modification of the objectives.
3. What has so far stopped the family making the changes they say they would like to make? This question is closely related to the foregoing ones but asking it in this way places the issue of what is causing the symptoms to continue in a different perspective.
4. Under what circumstances are the changes desired? Context is important in the setting of objectives. Thus while it is generally a good thing to be happy, there are circumstances in which this may not be appropriate, for example following a bereavement or other loss. Disagreements and even arguments, especially if they are

constructive, can be useful in the right context; so can most other behaviours. Aggression may be needed to defend your loved ones, or even yourself, and there may be times when lying may be the best course of action. Would anyone say it was wrong for members of households being questioned by the Nazis to have lied and said there were no Jews in the house, knowing that any Jews taken by the Nazi troops would probably be killed? Most 'symptoms' therefore have value in some circumstances, and there are times when it is appropriate to refuse food, or to get angry, or to feel tired, or to be undecided about something.

5. How quickly does the family want to change? This is not only a useful thing to know, but it is also a good question to ask because of the statement embedded in it – namely that change *will* occur if therapy is undertaken. By asking such a question you dismiss, by implication, the issue of whether the changes are possible, and replace it by that of how quickly the changes should, and will, occur.

Intermediate and final goals

Sometimes it is helpful to distinguish short-term from long-term goals. Psychotherapy may be likened to travelling through a jungle, where it is impossible to see your final objective and where you cannot survey, from your starting point, the route which will get you there most quickly and easily. You need to know where you are aiming to end up – since otherwise you could wander aimlessly and die of starvation or be eaten by a wild animal. So it is often best to plan your journey in stages. A good way to proceed is to climb a tree, survey your route to the next landmark – it may be another large tree – and then repeat the exercise as often as necessary until you reach your objective.

Family therapy, similarly, is often best approached in stages. Intermediate goals, equivalent to the trees the traveller climbs to survey the next stage of the journey, may need to be set and achieved along the way. Each one of these is an opportunity to review progress and perhaps even to set a new course. The intermediate goals do not always have to be made explicit to the family, but the point that every journey starts with the first step can sometimes usefully be made; setting goals should also be done in such a way as to suggest that they are attainable. The metaphor of an avalanche, which starts with the movement down the mountain of a small quantity of snow or a few rocks, leading to a massive shift of material down the slope, may also be useful. In the same way what look like small therapeutic interventions may have disproportionately large results.

Motivating families to consider and set objectives

Many families readily understand the desirability of defining their objectives, but some question it and seem satisfied with vague ideas and ill-thought-out notions about what they want from treatment. In such cases the importance of well defined objectives can be explained metaphorically. The following story, reproduced from *Using Metaphors in Psychotherapy* (Barker, 1985), is an example of this process.

Norman, a man who was well skilled with his hands, wanted to build a garden shed. So he went to a store that sold materials and supplies for the do-it-yourself market and asked for advice. The salesman he spoke to asked him a lot of questions, many of which he was not immediately able to answer. He wanted to know what kinds of things Norman planned to keep in the shed, how big it should be, on what sort of ground it was to be built and with what materials, what kind of floor Norman wanted it to have, what tools and equipment Norman already had at home and how much he could afford to spend on the shed.

Norman realised that he needed to give a lot more thought to his project than he had done so far. So he first gathered together all the items he intended to keep in the shed, including his lawn-mower, electric hedge-clipper and wheelbarrow, a whole collection of garden tools, the fertiliser spreader and a couple of bags of fertiliser, his children's bicycles, some flower pots and seed boxes and sundry smaller items. He was now able to estimate the size of shed he would need.

Next Norman assembled all his woodworking and other tools; these had been scattered in various parts of the house, and some had not been used for years. Indeed he was surprised by some of his finds – tools he had long forgotten acquiring. The total was impressive and it seemed as if Norman might have just about all the equipment he needed.

Norman now examined carefully the site where he planned to erect the shed. It was a damp area and it seemed safer to plan to have a wooden floor raised, perhaps on concrete blocks, above ground level.

Finally Norman reviewed his financial situation; the salesman had given him a rough idea of what sheds made of different materials would cost and it seemed that he would be able to afford a cedarwood shed, which was what he had originally hoped to build.

Norman now had a pretty clear idea of what the shed he was going to build would look like, the work that would be involved in constructing it and what it would cost in time and money. He decided to go ahead with it, and was ready to return, properly prepared, to the store to buy the materials he needed, to receive instructions and a plan of how to build the shed, and to purchase those few additional tools he required.

Maintaining and developing a family's motivation is important at all times during therapy, but the period when goals are being set is one during which this process can often be actively promoted. Sometimes certain family members do not believe that the changes they desire can be achieved; sometimes the whole family thinks this. Some families even come to therapists with the expectation that there will be no change! Their aim seems to be simply to prove that nothing can be done. (They are presumably examples of the sort of people Watzlawick (1983) writes about in his book *The Situation is Hopeless but not Serious.*) The process of goal-setting and the discussion of the outcome frame can, if approached optimistically and in a business-like fashion, enormously reassure families that they have the potential for change, along with the rest of the human race.

Summary

Family therapy, like most human activities, is more likely to be successful the clearer the goals with which it is approached. Time and effort spent in defining goals are usually well repaid; well defined goals greatly assist the therapist in developing a treatment plan, and they offer encouragement to the family, especially if the result is an agreed set of objectives which appear realistic to all concerned.

The *outcome frame*, or desired state, is that which, when achieved, will constitute a completely satisfactory therapy result. It should be stated in positive rather than negative terms; that is, it should describe how things *will* be at the successful conclusion of treatment, rather than how they will *not* be.

Other important points about goal setting are:

1. Aim for specific, definable objectives.
2. Determine the context in which the new behaviours are desired; the old ones may still have their uses under certain circumstances.
3. Have the family consider whether there will be any drawbacks to the desired state. If there will be, are the changes worth making?
4. What other consequences will follow once the desired changes have been made?
5. What has stopped the family making the desired changes so far?

6. How quickly do the family want to change?

It is sometimes helpful for the therapist to have intermediate goals to be achieved during the course of therapy. These do not always have to be shared, or agreed, with the family.

Chapter 7

Indications and Contradictions for Family Therapy

The indications for family therapy are less discussed in the family therapy literature than the treatment methods themselves. Many textbooks of family therapy, for example those of Hoffman (1981), Anderson and Stewart (1983) and Bross (1983), fail to discuss the indications for family therapy as a specific issue. Perhaps the reason for this is to be found in the words of Nichols (1984, page 91):

> Family therapy is not a method but an orientation to clinical problems...from a family therapy point of view, all psychological treatment *is* treatment of families, whether one, two, or several people are present, and whether or not the therapist includes the whole family in his or her assessment.

Discussion of the indications for family therapy is more often found in textbooks of psychiatry, and in journals which are not devoted primarily to family therapy. For example Steinberg (1983), in his book *The Clinical Psychiatry of Adolescence*, pays much attention to the question of when family therapy should be used in the treatment of adolescents. He considers family therapy a distinct form of treatment and clearly does not subscribe to the views which Nichols, in the above quotation, ascribes to family therapists.

While Nichols is probably right in his description of how many family therapists view clinical problems, his statement begs a number of questions. One is that of deciding what approach to psychotherapy we are to take in any particular case. It is all very well to take the view that all psychotherapy is family therapy, since change in any one family member inevitably has its impact on the whole family group, but this does not tell us whether we should be working with the whole family, with a part of it, or with one individual member. In practice the various forms of family therapy *are* different from therapies which take the individual as their focus, even though the latter, when effective, have effects in the family as a whole. Moreover, therapists skilled in working with families are often less skilled in work with individuals than those who concentrate on individual psychotherapy, and vice versa.

A second issue is that of physical illness. Psychiatric symptoms can be due to endocrine disorders (for example hypothyroidism and hyperthyroidism), metabolic disorders (such as porphyria), infections (for example syphilis) and various forms of brain disease. Medical and surgical therapies are available for such conditions, and family therapy should not be the primary treatment for them – though families containing members with such conditions may need therapy.

A third point is that other psychiatric treatments, pharmacological as well as psychotherapeutic, are available. It is therefore necessary to consider when one of these may be the treatment of first choice. Schizophrenia is nowadays usually treated pharmacologically, and most psychiatrists caring for such patients do not see family factors as being the principal ones to be addressed in treatment. The role of family therapy in schizophrenia is, however, discussed further in Chapter 11. Similarly antidepressant drugs are sometimes the best treatment for depressed individuals, and the use of anxiolytic drugs for anxious patients may have to be considered, if only because some people ask for them when they come for help.

Basic criteria for employing family therapy

Two conditions should exist before family therapy is recommended. These are:

1. Evidence of a malfunctioning group; and
2. Evidence that the family dysfunction is related to the problems for which help is being sought.

The problem with these criteria is that, for them to mean anything, the terms 'malfunctioning' and 'dysfunction' have to be defined, but unfortunately there are no agreed norms for the functioning of families. Some families which seem to be functioning in quite unusual ways appear to be free of clinical problems, while others appear relatively 'normal', at least at first acquaintance, and yet contain members with severe clinical problems. In addressing issues of this sort the models of family functioning reviewed in Chapter 5 are useful; they direct our attention to specific aspects of family interaction which can be the focus of therapy. This is more important than deciding whether a family is 'normal' or not, although the attempt by Beavers (1982) to define 'healthy, midrange, and severely dysfunctional' families is a bold step on the way to the development of norms for the functioning of families. Another helpful concept is that of 'optimal family process', described by Kirschner and Kirschner (1986) in the book *Comprehensive Family Therapy*. This book also addresses in a helpful way the issue of when whole family groups should be treated, and when therapy should focus on individual members.

Whether or not you choose to compare the families you see with some theoretical norm, it is important to make the best judgement possible of whether the presenting problems can be understood on the basis of the way the family functions. In doing this, it can again be helpful to use as a guide one of the models suggested in Chapter 5, or one of the several other models that are available. Sometimes families present themselves as family units and define their problems in family terms, and with increasing public awareness of family therapy this seems to be happening more often; in such cases family therapy is usually the best approach. Nevertheless families more often present with symptoms in one, sometimes more, members. Indeed often only one, or perhaps two, family members present initially, and involvement of the family occurs on the initiative of the therapist.

Differing views on the place of family therapy

Some therapists pay more attention than others to the assessment of whether or not family therapy is indicated. Beal (1976) investigated the differences between therapists, using a modified version of a scale developed by the Group for the Advancement of Psychiatry (1970) when it rated the theoretical orientation of therapists. He found that therapists at the A end of the scale, that is those who are primarily concerned with the appropriate expression of emotion in the family, are more concerned about the indications and contraindications for therapy than are therapists at the Z end, those concerned chiefly with family structure and communication pathways. To this latter group problems are interactional – that is they do not reside in individuals but in the processes of interaction going on in a family or other social system; and behavioural – that is consisting of behaviour 'which is stimulated and shaped by the behaviour of others' (Weakland, 1977, page 23). Weakland (1979, page 57) also wrote of how the family approach to treatment has come to be applied to 'the whole spectrum of recognized psychiatric problems, except the manifestly organic'. He describes family therapy as an entirely new way of looking at problems and their resolution, making a new approach to practice necessary.

Haley (1976, pages 170-178) explains the difference between orientation A and orientation B in his usual lucid way. The A therapist, he says, is attempting to achieve understanding of the problems and emotional growth in individuals, whereas the Z therapist is working to produce specific changes in particular behaviours without being concerned about understanding or insight. The indications which each type of therapist considers appropriate are therefore bound to be different. In addition the A therapist is typically willing to use traditional group therapy techniques, whereas the Z therapist sticks to the family or other naturally occurring groups.

Weakland's exclusion of 'manifestly organic' problems presents difficulties. The system of an identified patient with an obviously organic problem, for example cerebral palsy, may or may not be badly functioning. Moreover in modern medical practice many problems are seen as having multiple and complex causes. Bronchial asthma is a good example. In severe cases there are often structural changes in the lungs, and in all cases the physiological control of respiratory function is abnormal. In addition, allergy and infection are important factors in precipitating attacks. A comprehensive treatment plan cannot overlook these factors. In a sense asthma is 'manifestly organic', certainly once there are structural changes in the lungs, but there is reason to believe that attacks of asthma can be precipitated by processes occurring in the family system (Minuchin et al, 1975).

Then there is the question of schizophrenia. Is *it* organic? Some psychiatrists believe it is. There are certainly strong genetic factors involved, as has been demonstrated by twin and adoption studies reviewed by Kinney and Matthysse (1978). There is also evidence pointing to various biochemical abnormalities in the brain. Yet there is also reason to believe that the likelihood of relapse in schizophrenic patients discharged from hospital is influenced by family factors (Leff and Vaughn, 1985). Family dysfunction may also be related to the onset of the schizophrenic symptoms, but these issues are discussed further in Chapter 11.

It may be relevant that few of the proponents of the extreme Z position, such as Haley and Weakland, are physicians. Such therapists have perceived certain important truths about families and how they function, but they may, in their enthusiasm, have given insufficient weight to biological, intrapersonal and intrapsychic factors. The extreme Z position cannot be taken as the basis for deciding upon indications for family therapy unless other treatments, for example individual therapy or medication, are seen as methods of conducting family therapy. A therapist might conceivably prescribe an antidepressant drug for a depressed family member as part of a strategy aimed at changing the way the family functions, but this is not what is normally meant by family therapy. It is possible also that some depressed individuals may need antidepressant medication regardless of the family situation.

Current views on indications

Although many family therapists regard all psychological problems as interactional, most probably do consciously consider when to use a family approach and when not to do so. They make this judgement, however, in the light of a family systems-oriented view of the situation.

The indications for family therapy, like the objectives of treatment, should be positive ones. Some authors have failed to take this position. Thus Glick and Kessler (1974) included such criteria as the failure of individual therapy (failure which might perhaps have been avoided if greater care had been taken over the selection of the treatment method in advance); the inability of an individual to use the 'intrapsychic, interpretive mode' which is employed in individual therapy (which suggests that individual therapy is the mode to be tried first); and the subject's presence in a hospital or somewhere other than his or her home.

Walrond-Skinner (1978) reviewed the indications and contraindications for family therapy, which she defined as 'the psychotherapeutic treatment of the family system, using as its most basic medium conjoint interpersonal interviews', in a more positive way. She identified four approaches to the subject. The first is the *exclusive approach* position. This is very much the Z therapist's position. Disturbance in an individual is to be dealt with by treating the system of which the individual is a part. Family therapy, perhaps better called systems therapy since systems other than family groups may be the subject of treatment, thus becomes a new orientation to both understanding and treating psychiatric disorders – and one suitable for almost universal application.

At the other extreme, Walrond-Skinner defines the *treatment of last resort* position, family therapy only being employed when all else has failed. If this view of the place of family therapy is taken, it is liable to mean that it is applied only to particularly severe and serious disorders, so that its chances of success are likely to be limited.

The *diagnostic aid* position is taken, Walrond-Skinner says, by those who see family therapy as an adjunct which may be used to assist in treatment selection and to promote the more effective use of individual, group or inpatient treatment. It may also be used intermittently, perhaps during 'a crisis phase of therapy', and can be useful in overcoming intrapsychic or interpersonal resistance to therapy.

Finally there is the *differential treatment* position taken by clinicians who consider family therapy along with other treatments which might be used. Whether it is selected depends in part on whether the therapist's theoretical model suggests that it will be effective. Such clinicians also take into account their clinical experience and their understanding of the literature on the subject in deciding what treatment to recommend.

Neither of the first two of the above positions seems tenable. While the 'systems approach' to families and their treatment is indeed a new way of tackling mental health problems, it does not mean that all other approaches must be abandoned or are of no value. It is clear also that family therapy can be more than a treatment of last resort; indeed there are probably few therapists who nowadays take that point of view. The 'diagnostic aid' position may be tenable if family therapy is not conceived as limited to it. It does, however, seem that family therapy can be a powerful treatment when properly used in the right cases, but it should only be embarked upon after a careful consideration of the relative merits of the full range of available treatments.

Walrond-Skinner (1978) went on to suggest the following indications:

(a) *Symptoms considered by the therapist to be embedded in a dysfunctional system of family relationships.* Thus if the symptoms appear to be expressing the 'pain or dysfunction' of the family system, family therapy will probably be the best treatment. There remains the difficulty of assessing whether this criterion is met. How to set about this has been discussed in Chapter 5.

> Tracie was a shy, timid and anxious eight-year-old, the third child and youngest daughter in a family of four. She was referred because of her inhibited behaviour and social isolation at school. Her mother also felt that she was slow learning to read, though the school disagreed with this opinion. This was a consequence of the mother's belief that Tracie was 'super-intelligent' – a view not substantiated by intelligence testing, which showed her cognitive functioning to be within the average range.
>
> There was much emotional distance between the parents. The father disagreed with the mother's attitudes towards the children, which he thought were over-controlling, but he let her do as she wished. Tracie had always been a difficult, frail and rather special child, in mother's view, and a close, anxiously enmeshed relationship between the girl and her mother had developed, apparently at the expense of the relationship between mother and father.

In this case it was quite easy to understand the presenting problems in the light of the family's way of functioning. In structural terms, mother and Tracie had an enmeshed relationship. Using the McMaster or

Process models she had a special role, that of frail, special child, regarded by mother as 'super-intelligent'. Father was relatively disengaged from the rest of the family, and there was a poorly functioning parental system. Tracie's inhibited behaviour and overdependence on her mother were integral parts of the pattern of family functioning. It was unlikely that her behaviour would change much, if at all, until the family system changed.

The situation could also be formulated in family developmental terms: Tracie had remained dependent on her mother to a degree more appropriate to the infant or toddler years. The normal emotional separation of mother and child which occurs as toddler becomes schoolchild had not taken place. The reasons why this situation had arisen are another question. Such situations often turn out to have multiple causes. Temperamental and/or physical factors in child and parents may interact with relationship difficulties in the nuclear family, extended family systems problems, and perhaps extra-familial factors also. The causes are, however, less important than the cure, and if there is a family systems problem related to the presenting symptoms, family therapy may be helpful.

(b) *Problems presented by those seeking help to produce some change in a relationship, rather than to deal with problems in an individual family member.* Examples are marital difficulties, including those involving sexual problems, child-parent relationship problems and problems between siblings.

(c) *Separation difficulties.* These are considered by many therapists to be best treated by family therapy. Indeed they are really no more than examples of the kind of relationship difficulties mentioned above. Thus a family containing an adolescent girl trying to separate from her family, or an overprotected younger child who is having difficulty growing up, may be helped very effectively by family therapy. Family therapy may be equally useful when members need to become closer to each other – that is when the separating process has gone too fast, or when marital partners have never become sufficiently close. During the latter parts of the family life cycle, however, many of the tasks with which families have difficulty concern the separating process as children leave the home and go their various ways.

(d) Family therapists with a psychoanalytical viewpoint believe family therapy to be of value with *families 'functioning at a basically paranoid–schizoid level, with part object relationships, lack of ego boundaries and extensive use of denial, splitting and projection'* (Skynner, 1969a). Such families bear similarities to those in which Bowen (1966) described an 'undifferentiated ego mass'. The idea is that basic psychological functions are scattered among the family members, who are not properly functioning individuals in their own right. It may be that such a description is only another way of referring to many of the families covered under sections (a), (b) and (c) above.

(e) Family therapy has been used for *severely disorganized families, functioning badly and in poor socioeconomic circumstances.* A project to help such families was described by Minuchin and his colleagues (1967) in the important book *Families of the Slums.*

The 'decision tree'

Clarkin, Frances and Moodie (1979) reviewed the limited research literature on the indications for family therapy and employed this to construct a 'decision tree' for use in determining whether family therapy or some other form of treatment should be used. These authors proposed four steps:

Step I: Is family or marital evaluation indicated?
The authors defined family evaluation as one or more family interviews designed to assess the structure and process of family interaction, in order to discover how this is related to the behaviour and symptoms of individual members. They concluded that situations in which family or marital evaluation are almost always essential include the following:

(a) When a child or adolescent is the presenting patient.
(b) When the presenting problem is sexual difficulty or dissatisfaction.
(c) When the presenting problem is a serious family or marital problem, especially when the future of the marital relationship, the adequate care of the children in the family or family members' vocational stability or health are at stake.
(d) When there has been a recent stress or emotional disruption in the family, caused by such family crises as serious illness, injury, loss of job, death or the departure from the home of one of the family members.
(e) When the family or the marital pair, or an individual within the group, defines the problem as a family issue and family evaluation is sought.

Clarkin and his colleagues also consider that family evaluation is usually indicated when admission of a family member to hospital for psychiatric treatment is being considered. In such circumstances family evaluation is of value for history-gathering, to clarify the relationship between family interaction patterns and the course of the identified patient's illness, and in order to negotiate a treatment plan with the whole family. Other 'less powerful' indications for family evaluation include:

(f) Situations in which more than one family member is simultaneously in psychiatric treatment.
(g) When improvement in a patient coincides with the development of symptoms in another or a deterioration in their relationship.
(h) When individual or group therapy is failing or has failed, and the patient is very involved with family problems, has difficulty dealing with family issues or shows evidence of too intense transference to the therapist; or when family co-operation appears necessary in order that the individual can change.
(i) When, during individual evaluation, it appears that the advantages to the family of the patient's symptoms can be understood in the light of the psychological functioning of the family.

Step II: Deciding whether either family or marital treatment is required
This next step involves deciding whether treatment using a family or marital therapy approach, as opposed to individual treatment, sex therapy or inpatient treatment in hospital, is required. Clarkin and his co-authors suggest that family or marital therapy may be indicated:

(a) When marital problems are a presenting problem.
(b) When a family presents with current problems in the relationships between family members.
(c) When there are chronic and severe problems in perception and communication. These include projective identification, in which members blame each other for the problems and disclaim their own parts in them; paranoid–schizoid functioning, as mentioned above; and various severely disturbed forms of communication such as are seen in schizophrenia.
(d) In the presence of adolescent antisocial behaviour, such as promiscuity, drug abuse, delinquency or violent behaviour.
(e) When there are adolescent separation problems.
(f) When there is found to be control or manipulation of the parent by the child.
(g) Following the failure of other treatment, for example when individual therapy sessions have been used mainly to discuss family problems.
(h) When the family group is motivated to accept treatment but an individual is not.
(i) When improvement in one family member leads to symptoms or deterioration in another.
(j) When more than one person needs treatment and resources are available for only one treatment.

The next choice is between family and marital therapy. In making this choice the therapist must consider whether the main problems are in the spouse subsystem or in the family as a whole, and the motivation of the different family members to become involved in one or other type of therapy.

If marital therapy is selected, the decision then has to be made whether or not to include sex therapy as a part or even the major part of this. The decision will depend upon whether sexual problems are present, how severe they are and whether the marital problem is clearly centred around the sexual difficulties. In addition the couple must be motivated to have sex therapy and be willing and able to carry out the appropriate tasks.

Finally the therapist must decide whether 'family crisis therapy' should be considered as an alternative to admission to hospital. Family crisis therapy is an approach described by Langsley et al, 1968; 1969). It consists of an intense but brief family intervention performed at the time of crisis. It is discussed further in Chapter 16.

Step III: Deciding on the duration and intensity of therapy
The choice here is between family crisis therapy, brief family therapy and long-term family therapy. The first-named is most likely to be indicated when the problems with which the family presents are associated with a developmental or other crisis, and particularly when the problems are acute and urgent.

Brief family therapy, which the authors define as lasting less than six months and consisting of sessions no more often than once a week, is indicated for less urgent problems. These include the following situations:

(a) When there is a focal symptom or conflict involving a child, adolescent or marital pair and the family is highly motivated to change.
(b) When family involvement is necessary to support another method of treatment, such as regular attendance at a day hospital.
(c) When a couple presents seeking help in deciding whether to separate.
(d) In family situations too complex to be understood in a brief evaluation. In this situation brief family therapy may enable the therapist to learn more about the situation and test the response to treatment.

Long-term therapy may be indicated for more complex and chronic problems, especially where a family's motivation to change is strong and in instances where the family has failed to respond to family crisis therapy or brief treatment.

Step IV

This step is not explored by Clarkin and his colleagues (1979) in their paper, but consists of determining which family therapy approach is likely to be most useful in a particular case. Currently there is little scientifically sound data on this subject. Few controlled trials have been reported comparing different methods of family therapy, using matched or randomly allocated families. This issue is discussed further in Chapter 16.

The practical value of the 'decision tree' is unclear. While it was derived from an extensive review of the literature, this in turn has many limitations; it consists largely of personal views arising out of therapists' own clinical experiences, rather than being based on scientifically sound studies. Nevertheless, the principle of using a decision tree along the lines suggested, first considering the circumstances in which family or marital evaluation is indicated, then considering a number of steps, leading up to the selection of a particular form of treatment – if any is required – seems a sensible one.

In addition to the above indications certain authors have advocated the use of specific approaches to family therapy in particular disorders, for example psychosomatic conditions (Minuchin et al, 1978) and 'families in schizophrenic transaction' (Palazzoli et al, 1978a).

Contraindications for family therapy

There is even less hard data on the contraindications for family therapy than there is on the indications. Walrond-Skinner (1976) commented that lists of contraindications may say more about therapists' own areas of defensiveness than about the likely effectiveness of the therapy. She also commented that what to one therapist is a contraindication may to another be a challenge. Nevertheless she did suggest the following contraindications:

(a) There may be practical limitations to family therapy. If key family members are unavailable for geographical or other reasons, or are completely unmotivated to become involved in treatment, family therapy may have to be ruled out. Another factor is the availability of a suitably trained and experienced therapist; family therapy is a complex and sometimes very difficult undertaking, and it is important that the skills of the therapist be matched to the needs of the family. If this is not so it may be better not to start until a suitably skilled therapist is available, either to carry out the treatment or to provide 'live' supervision.

(b) Family therapy may be contraindicated because the family presents too late in the course of the disorder. The outlook may be too poor to justify the necessary expenditure of time and money – though this is very much a value judgement and the question of whether a family wishes to spend its money on family therapy is perhaps its decision, rather than the therapist's. Ackerman (1966a) mentioned as a contraindication 'the presence of a malignant, irreversible trend towards breakup of the family which may mean that it is too late to reverse the process of fragmentation'. Yet the fact that a family is likely to break up, or is in the process of breaking up, does not necessarily mean that family therapy is inappropriate; sometimes people seek help in separating or divorcing amicably, and with as little damage as possible to all concerned, and the therapist may be able to help them achieve this aim.

(c) It may be dangerous to attempt family therapy when 'the emotional equilibrium is so precariously maintained that attempts to change the relationship system may precipitate a severe decompensation on the part of one or more family members'. It is certainly the case that many families maintain themselves in a precarious and stressful adjustment. In some cases an alteration in the family situation could increase the stress faced by one or more individuals; this in turn could lead to a worsening of their condition with perhaps depression and even suicide. These are issues requiring mature clinical judgement, including careful assessment of suicidal and other risks. Such risks should always be borne in mind when deciding whether or not to embark on family therapy – or any other treatment for that matter. Walrond-Skinner (1976) also mentions that it may be felt unwise to embark on family therapy when one or more members are organically ill, lest this raises hopes of a 'magical' cure of the organic illness. This risk can usually be avoided by the clear setting of objectives, as discussed in Chapter 6.

(d) Some therapists consider that family therapy may be contraindicated in the presence of depression or severe emotional deprivation in one or more members; Walrond-Skinner suggested that the combination of individual treatment for the members with these symptoms may in such cases be combined with sessions for the whole family. Recently Kirschner and Kirschner (1986), in their book *Comprehensive Family Therapy*, have described an approach which takes into account, and provides treatment for, both family systems problems and individual psychopathology in family members. CFT, as the authors abbreviate their approach, seems to offer the prospect of helping families in which there is severe psychopathology in one or more members. These are challenging families; with most forms of family therapy treatment failures, and even failure to engage such families in therapy, are common.

(e) Finally, Walrond-Skinner advocates caution when the family is referred by an agency such as a court or school. In such cases there may be a hidden agenda, for example the family's desire to avoid a more severe sentence, or to prevent a child from being expelled from a school, rather than any real wish to change. If the family is deeply involved with other agencies, the therapist's relationship with these agencies, and their role in the treatment and the disclosure of any information arising from it, should be clearly defined before therapy is begun. Sometimes it is found that it is the family/agency system that should be the focus of treatment.

Clarkin et al (1979), in describing their 'decision tree' for the selection of patients for family therapy, also list contraindications which have been mentioned in the research literature. Many of them are the same as those mentioned by Walrond-Skinner and they include various signs of lack of motivation for, or strong prejudice against, family therapy. The inclusion of members who are in the process of 'individuation', for example a young adult who has just left the family, may not be desirable, lest it compromise the individuation process (Glick and Kessler, 1974).

Deterioration in family and marital therapy

Gurman and Kniskern (1978a; 1978b) reviewed the research literature on the outcome of family therapy, looking for data about deterioration in the course of marital and family therapy. The literature they surveyed had various defects, including the lack of a category for 'deterioration' in many of the outcome studies. In many reports 'no change' and 'worse' were bracketed together. Nevertheless they found evidence that deterioration can occur, and that it may be greater than in appropriately matched control couples and families; that is to say the treatment seems sometimes to cause a worsening of the family situation.

Deterioration was more common, Gurman and Kniskern found, with individual or group marital therapy than when marital partners were seen together (conjoint marital therapy), or were seen concurrently by collaborating therapists (concurrent-collaborative therapy). Even more striking was the difference between treatments which involved both partners simultaneously (that is conjoint, group and concurrent-collaborative therapies) and that which involved only one partner (individual marital therapy). The rate of deterioration where both partners were being treated (5.6 per cent) was only half that reported to occur with individual marital therapy (11.6 per cent). Moreover the overall improvement rate reported for the latter treatment was only 48 per cent, a poor rate compared with that associated with other forms of therapy. It seems, therefore, that marital therapy that does not involve both partners should generally be avoided. Hurvitz (1967) and Kohl (1962) both described some of the serious problems and pathological reactions that can follow individual marital therapy.

Gurman and Kniskern's (1978a) study showed that deterioration can occur with 'whole family' treatment as well as with marital therapy, but apparently less often. They also found evidence that improvement in the identified patient was sometimes accompanied by deterioration in the condition of other family members or in the marital relationship. This suggests that careful thought should be given to this possibility when indications and contraindications are being considered.

Summary

Some family therapists regard family therapy as an effective treatment for virtually all non-organic psychological disorders. There is also a school of thought which sees anything that produces change in a family system as family therapy, even the treatment of an individual family member. In practice, however, it is necessary to decide whether or not to make the family system the main focus of therapy.

Family therapy should be considered when (a) there is a malfunctioning family group and (b) the problems which therapy is to address are related to the functioning of the family. It is likely to be of value when the presenting problems concern children or adolescents; when families present complaining that members have problems in relating to each other; and when a family appears to be having difficulty making the changes required to pass from one developmental stage to the next – for example when adolescents start to become more autonomous.

Family therapy should be regarded as neither a 'cure-all', nor a treatment of last resort, but rather as an effective way of dealing with problems which are embedded in a dysfunctional family system – as many personal problems are. The combination of family therapy with treatment for individual family members, while not always advocated by family therapists, may be helpful. It is a key feature of 'comprehensive family therapy' (Kirschner and Kirschner, 1986).

The 'decision tree' approach offers promise. It involves a number of steps. The first is to decide whether family or marital *assessment* is indicated; the next is to decide whether family or marital *treatment* is required, and if so whether the family or the marital couple should be the focus of the therapy; then the duration and intensity of treatment needed are considered; and finally it is necessary to decide upon the particular type of family therapy which is to be used.

Deterioration may occur during family therapy, and the treatment of marital problems without involving both partners simultaneously is relatively ineffective.

Chapter 8

Practical Points in the Treatment of Families

In this chapter we will consider some of the practical issues that arise from time to time in the course of family therapy.

What should the therapist do when one or more family members declines to attend?

In Chapter 5 we considered how best to make the initial contact with a family, and outlined some points which can be made to family members who do not understand why the whole family need be present at the initial assessment interview. Sometimes making these points is sufficient to persuade the family of the value of seeing them all; this applies especially when reluctance to have everyone come is due simply to a lack of knowledge of how family therapists view problem situations. Once the key family members realize how interdependent family members are, reluctance to have everyone attend often disappears. They may also need to understand that emotionally healthy and well-functioning family members usually contribute helpfully to the therapeutic process.

Karpel and Strauss (1983), in their book *Family Evaluation*, also discuss how a therapist may negotiate full attendance at a family assessment interview. They also make suggestions about when to compromise, and when not to compromise, on the matter of full attendance. They recommend that, at least in the initial phone contact, the reluctant family members should be told simply that the goal of the interview is to gather as much information as possible about the presenting problem. They warn that:

> Going beyond a variant of the 'information-gathering' rationale for the family evaluation...may lead the caller (usually a parent) to feel that he or she is being blamed for the family's troubles. Or it may

cause the caller to become angry and defensive over someone implying that there is something wrong with his or her family. (Karpel and Strauss, 1983, page 100)

Reluctance, or outright refusal to attend, may be met with at the very beginning, so that one or more members are unwilling to come to the first session; or people may drop out of treatment later. The therapist then has various choices. One is to decline to start, or continue, with therapy. While this may occasionally be the best course of action, you should bear in mind that the refusal of the reluctant family member(s) to attend is probably but one manifestation of the family's problems; there is a certain lack of logic in declining to offer help to a family because of the very problems for which they require help. It is therefore usually wise to consider alternative strategies.

There are four categories of family member who may decline to attend: parents or marital partners; dependent children; 'adult' children; and extended family members (grandparents, uncles, aunts, cousins and so forth).

A missing parent or marital partner

If the presenting problem concerns a child, or the marital relationship, and one parent (or marital partner) declines to attend while the other wishes to do so, this suggests that there may be serious marital problems, or major difficulties in the functioning of the pair as a parental couple. When one parent is reluctant to be involved from the start, direct communication with this person by the therapist may help. In making contact, taking a 'one-down' position may be helpful; this means that you say, in effect, to the person who is reluctant to attend that you need to have that person present in order to do a good job. Your message is, 'I need your help in order to be effective in helping your son (or your daughter, your family, your wife, or whoever is being presented as the problem)'. This is very different from saying that the person must come because the therapist, as an 'expert', decrees it; or because the person concerned is a part of the problem. It is also true.

If marital difficulties are the main presenting problem it is important to involve both partners. If one asks for help and the other is unwilling to come, even after a direct request from the therapist, I am usually willing to see the partner who is asking for help, at least once. The purposes of such a meeting are, first, to explore in a face-to-face interview possible means whereby the other partner may be induced to attend; secondly, to assess the mental state of the partner who is seeking help, since that person may have a disorder which can be treated other than by marital therapy; and thirdly, to explore whether there may be any possibility of starting treatment of the marital difficulties by seeing the one partner – although, as we saw in Chapter 7, this is a plan which carries considerable risk of failure or deterioration, and therefore should not be entered upon lightly.

If the identified patient is a child, and it is a two-parent family, it is important to involve both parents from the start. If only one agrees to come, or actually shows up for the first interview, my own practice is usually to see the children with the one parent, but during the first interview I focus on the issue of the missing parent and how that person might become involved in the treatment. Sometimes the reluctant parent becomes willing to attend when the family returns home and talks about the session, mentioning that the things the absent parent feared (perhaps that they would be told the family was a 'bad' one, or that the problem was the parents' fault), did not happen.

If after two or three sessions one parent is still failing to attend, a further direct approach by the therapist, perhaps by telephone, may be successful; again it is often helpful to use the 'one-down' approach. In other words the therapist is saying, 'After two (or three) sessions with your family, I find I need your help more than ever; I'm sure the information you can give me will make things a lot clearer to me'. Another approach is to plead confusion. You may say you feel defeated by the problem the family presents, and can only get further with the help of the person concerned. If this approach fails, and the presence of the missing parent seems vital if progress is to be made, this may be the time to suggest that there should be no further sessions until the missing parent is available. This may precipitate a crisis – which sometimes leads to the involvement of the missing parent – or the family situation may have to deteriorate further, or the child's symptoms worsen, before the family can be fully involved in therapy.

When the problems are marital and one partner fails to attend, a similar approach is indicated, except that it may be best to say you can proceed no further without the missing partner even sooner – perhaps after one, or no more than two, sessions.

When parents are divorced or separated, and the identified patient is a child, therapy normally starts with the family in which the identified patient lives. But parenthood is not ended by divorce, and involvement of the other parent is usually desirable at some stage, even if the children do not have regular contact with that parent. When there *is* regular contact, problems in the relationship between the two parents, or families, may continue to exist, despite the separation; when this is so they usually need to be the focus of therapeutic attention. Having both parents present at some sessions may be helpful. This emphasizes that they are still the children's parents, despite the separation or divorce. It can also be a means of dealing with unresolved issues between the separated parents. Such issues may persist for many years, and the children may be used as pawns in a game in which the parents continue to play out their feelings towards each other.

Achieving a joint meeting of two separated parents can be difficult, but is often worth working hard to achieve. It may be best to start by meeting separately with each parent, and any new marital partner either one may have. These meetings can be used to explain how important both parents are to their children, and why separated parents should still work together. The purpose of the sessions should be defined as that of dealing with children's issues, rather than aiming to repair the marital relationship. Once this has been made clear, parents often become more willing to come.

Missing dependent children

Children, including adolescents, who are living at home in the care of their parents sometimes object to coming to family therapy sessions; or their parents may be willing to bring only the identified patient, on the grounds that that child has the problem and therefore no one else need be involved.

We thus have two possible problems. The simpler problem is that of children or adolescents – and it is often adolescents – who object to coming. If the parents have decided that the family should have therapy, and that the children should attend, the children should be expected to come – just as they are expected to go to school, or to bed at night, or to do any of the other things which parents reasonably expect of their children. If a child refuses to come, this is an issue to be dealt with in therapy, and it may be necessary to see the parents, and any children who will come, and work out a means of enabling the parents or parent to gain control of their child(ren).

The situation is different when it is the parents who are reluctant to have a child or children attend. They may not want the other children involved because they see the problems as residing in the identified patient; involving anyone else in the treatment might threaten that assumption. Another question – which arises in many situations in which there are problems concerning who should attend – is that of who is to control the therapy process: is it to be the therapist or the family? It is a paradox that a family will seek the help of a therapist, but will then dictate how the treatment should proceed. Yet this often happens, probably because change, though desired, is also threatening. To allow such a situation to develop is a good recipe for therapeutic failure.

Many rationalizations are offered for parents' refusal to bring certain children; they do not want them to miss school, because they are already behind in their studies and may fail if they miss any more; or the other children are unaware of the identified patient's problems (something which in reality is only rarely the case) and should not be bothered about it, or might even be harmed in some way by knowing about it; or the other children would miss out on some sporting or other activity which is important to them.

The simplest way of dealing with parents' objections to bringing the other children is to explain, as set out above, why it is helpful to see everyone, at least at the first session. Who should attend future sessions can be discussed at that meeting, and this can be an ongoing process as treatment proceeds. The therapist's interests in meeting everyone in the family and obtaining as much information about the family as possible can be emphasized; so can the fact that no one will be compelled to reveal information or discuss topics which they do not wish to mention – a truism of course, since we have no means of forcing family members to reveal things they do not wish to reveal.

Sometimes it is possible to achieve a meeting of the whole family by starting where the family are, and progressing gradually from there, a procedure at which the late Milton Erickson was an expert.

Jason, aged 11, his father, Ken, and his stepmother, Lynn, presented themselves for the first interview; one full sister, two stepsiblings and a baby recently born to Ken and Lynn were left at home, although Ken and Lynn had been asked to bring the whole family. The parents complained that Jason was presenting a host of behaviour problems and that these were getting steadily worse. As a result, he had recently been placed in a foster home. Ken and Lynn were unshakable in their belief that the problem was solely Jason's, though there seemed to the therapist to be evidence of a number of family systems problems. Ken, supported by Lynn, insisted that Jason required hypnosis, which would solve all his behavioural problems.

The therapist decided to go along with this idea and saw Jason three times, each time doing some hypnotherapy. Jason proved to be an excellent hypnotic subject and the sessions were used to help him gain access to some good feelings about himself, related to various successful past experiences, and to improve his self-image generally. At the conclusion of these three sessions the therapist suggested a meeting of the whole family to discover what changes the other family members had observed in Jason, who had been spending his weekends at home.

Presented in this way the parents found the idea of a family meeting quite acceptable. They even asked if they could bring the baby – before the therapist had had a chance to tell them that he did want everyone, including the baby, to come. When at last the family meeting occurred, it proved possible to do a great deal more than ascertain the changes the other family members had observed in Jason, although the session started as an enquiry into Jason's recent behaviour. Moreover the family seemed to find the sort of family interview that was carried out neither alarming nor threatening to them, nor did they feel they were being criticized, as they had apparently thought they would be.

Missing adult children
'Adult' children may be divided into those who have physically left home, and those who are still living in the parents' home. It is not reasonable to expect the former group to come to sessions against their will, though many are glad to help resolve a problem in their family of origin. All the therapist should do in these cases is invite the independent children to come for sessions whenever it appears that this would be helpful; if the reasons for inviting them have been explained to them, and they refuse, this should be accepted.

The situation is different when adult children are still living at home, even if they are wage-earning and contributing their share of the household budget. Sometimes such children decline to come to therapy sessions. Whether the parents should expect them to do so, even unwillingly, depends in part on the 'contract', written or more probably unwritten, on the basis of which these children are still living at home. This contract may be unclear, and an aim of therapy might be to make it clear and achieve acceptance of it by all concerned. Such families may not have resolved the issue of whether these children should obey certain family rules, rather than doing exactly as they like in their parents' home. In practice there have always to be some rules family members must obey, but whether mandatory attendance at family therapy sessions should be one of them may be a matter for negotiation.

While the above issues may need to be dealt with in therapy, the decision as to whether children, young or adult, should attend rests ultimately with the parent(s). We must tell family members what we believe will lead to the best and quickest therapeutic outcome, and why. When our clients decline to accept our advice we have always to consider whether we can still hope to treat them effectively; if we believe we cannot, it is important to tell them so. What look like blocks to therapy, because our clients decline our advice, may however sometimes be overcome by careful development of rapport and the use of strategic therapy devices such as are discussed in Chapter 10.

Missing extended family members
Extended family members are usually best contacted through the family member to whom they are most closely related. Most often this is one of the marital pair. Extended family members often willingly attend, but if they are reluctant to do so direct contact by the therapist, to explain why seeing them would be helpful, may be required.

Maintaining control of the therapy

Some families arrive asking for help, yet have firm views on the form the treatment should take. These are usually based on their understanding of the family's problems – an understanding which, obviously, has not led to their resolution. The problem may be blamed on one particular family member – the family scapegoat. This may lead to demands that this family member be seen for individual therapy, or that the other children do not attend sessions. In other cases the family has preconceived ideas about how frequently the sessions should occur, or makes demands to be seen at times which are incompatible with the therapist's schedule.

These views and demands must be recognized for what they are – namely attempts to control the treatment process. If the therapist passively accepts them, the prospects of success are limited. On the other hand, to confront the family immediately with a denial of their point of view may lead them to withdraw from treatment. What then should the therapist do?

In the early stages of therapy it may be best to go along with the family's viewpoint, at least in some measure, but without losing sight of what is happening. As rapport and trust develop, the family members may become more willing to follow the therapist's suggestions. Taking a 'one-down' position, as described above, may also be helpful. Strategic approaches, such as the use of paradox or of metaphorical methods of communicating your point of view, may also help. Telling stories such as the following can sometimes assist the family to view the situation differently, and get involved constructively in therapy.

I remember a very caring family I worked with before I came to this city. The parents were deeply concerned about their 13-year-old daughter, Patricia, who had started running away and getting into trouble with the law. Her mother brought her to see me and told me they also suspected that she was on drugs, though she denied it and the parents had no proof. There were two other children in the family, both girls and both older than the daughter who was in trouble. Neither of them had been in trouble and the parents had no particular concerns about them.

As none of the other members of the family appeared to have any problems the reasons for the daughter's behaviour were a real puzzle to the family. Their family doctor suggested that they bring Patricia to see me, and she came to my office with her mother. I had long talks with both of them and at the end of it all I was as puzzled as the family. They seemed delightful people and both mother and daughter appeared quite open in the interview situation. From what the mother told me it seemed also that the parents had handled their daughter's problem behaviour quite sensibly; they hadn't over-reacted, they'd spent long hours discussing the problems with her, trying to figure out what had gone wrong and what they could do about it, and they had imposed reasonable sanctions in response to Patricia's misdeeds, though these had not been effective.

In those days I didn't ask the whole family to come when I first saw a child, as I do nowadays. But I now felt I needed more information. Naturally I first thought of the father. So I called him and said I needed his help. I asked him to bring the whole family, including the other two daughters, to see me. I said I thought probably he, and perhaps the other girls too, could help me understand the youngest daughter's problems. He wasn't too keen on the idea nor, he told me, would the other girls be. He was very busy at his work and therefore reluctant to take time off. He feared losing his job – a fear which I felt probably wasn't fully justified as he had a long and excellent work record with the same firm. The other girls were good students at school, they had exams coming up and didn't like missing school. I commented that this was interesting since Patricia was reported to have a negative attitude towards school and was not doing well there. Eventually, after a good deal of discussion, the father agreed to come and to bring the whole family.

I was quite new to family therapy in those days and was surprised by how much I learned from that first interview with the whole family. The father was a perceptive person. He told me a lot about the relationship between Pat and her mother that I hadn't even guessed when I just saw the two of them. The other daughters, too, gave me much new information. Seeing them together made me realize how close they were emotionally. The mother had said they were close, but it wasn't till I met them, and saw how they interacted, that I realized the true nature of their relationship.

It was also only when I saw the whole family that I appreciated how different the two older girls were in looks compared with Patricia. They were both strikingly attractive blondes with slim figures, whereas Pat was a little overweight, had mousy-coloured hair and an altogether less striking appearance.

Seeing the whole family helped me a lot. The problem for me was to understand how, in what seemed a basically healthy, normal family, there could be one member with problems as serious as Patricia's.

This story, reproduced from *Using Metaphors in Psychotherapy* (Barker, 1985), makes a number of points which might be useful in motivating reluctant family members to attend for an assessment interview; it also offers those to whom it is told a different way of looking at family situations, especially those in which there may appear to be only one person who has a problem. The various points it makes are discussed further in the book from which it is quoted, but one of the functions it could serve, in addition to motivating familes to attend as a group, is to put the therapist back in control of the situation.

Involving children in family sessions

Once the therapist has achieved the attendance of the whole family, it is important that all members are involved in the treatment process, even very young ones. Concern has sometimes been expressed, especially by professionals skilled in individual psychotherapy with children, that children's needs may be neglected when the family unit is considered. Dare and Lindsay (1979), Guttman (1975) and Ackerman (1970) are among the authors who have addressed the issue of how to involve children in family therapy.

Dare and Lindsay mention two other concerns. One is that family therapists may not learn the skills needed to communicate effectively with children and to provide them with settings in which they can express what is going on in their inner worlds, an issue also raised by McDermott and Char (1974). The other is that the changes in personality structure which individual therapy seeks to bring about in children will not occur in the course of family therapy. They believe, however, that none of these concerns is justified if suitable steps are taken to involve the children.

But why is it so important to involve children in the family therapy process? Dare and Lindsay (1979), like Satir (1967), Skynner (1976), Kirschner and Kirschner (1986), and many others, are concerned both with the family system and with the psychological development of its members. A system cannot exist without transactional content and they believe that systems theory and psychodynamic views are complementary rather than antagonistic. Along with Boszormenyi-Nagy and Spark (1973) and Bowen (1976) they are interested in the relationship between the current interactional pattern in the family and the interpersonal patterns of the past. The way family members have interacted in the past often seems to be reflected in the present intrapsychic structures of the family members. In other words, developing children take into themselves, and incorporate into their internal models of the world, patterns of behaviour, attitudes and beliefs – and family myths – learned from their parents, and to a lesser extent from other family members. These in turn have been learned from *their* parents, and so on.

Byng-Hall (1973) discussed the role that family myths may play in the functioning of some families and regards their use as a form of defence against the examination of the real issues facing the family. Children are often repositories of such myths, and through them a family's defences can sometimes be penetrated. Byng-Hall's paper is recommended to those interested in this aspect of family functioning.

Children are, and should be seen as, active participants in the current interactional system and as repositories of the history of the family. The content of their play and other communications is important, and many therapists believe that steps must always be taken to help child members of the family to express themselves.

Dare and Lindsay (1979) recommend the provision of a few good quality materials, chosen specially for each family. They keep the toys or play materials for each family in a separate locker. A small dolls' house has been found to be a useful adjunct for young children. A 'family' of people for the house provides a group upon which young children can project their family knowledge and fantasies. For older children, and those who are well defended against direct expression using family figures, domestic or zoo animals are useful. A toy telephone, bricks, a dolls' tea set, plasticine, modelling clay, pencils, crayons and paper are useful items. Dare and Lindsay (1979) make it clear that the children's drawings will be kept as records of their work, not taken home by the family.

From the start of the first session children should be actively involved, if they are present at all. They should be asked their names and greeted individually. Little ones can sometimes be held for a time by the therapist. Interest should be shown by the therapist in both the verbal and the non-verbal contributions of the children. By all these means the therapist shows that he or she is approachable at a childhood level, and that childlike feelings are acceptable.

Making free and accepting contact with the children need not undermine parental authority, though the latter must always be acknowledged and respected. Dare and Lindsay take care to refer to the parents either as 'mother' and 'father', or as 'Mr' and 'Mrs'. Interruption of their speech by the children is not permitted.

Throughout therapy Dare and Lindsay (1979) make every effort to attend to and understand the children's communications. Their play materials and drawings are given careful attention, and it is made clear that the therapist wants everything to be understood by the children, who should ask about things which they do not understand. Giving children and childhood things high status sometimes produces scepticism or disbelief in the parents, but this is usually soon shaken by the accuracy, perceptiveness and unexpectedness of the children's knowledge. Dare and Lindsay have found that the material produced by children can be 'extraordinarily forceful'. It can help overcome parental resistance, and historical and other data the parents thought were secret may be revealed.

Involving children in family therapy in this way not only facilitates the production of content, but it also helps reveal the transactional patterns of the family and current interpersonal processes. Children, like adults, reveal a great deal non-verbally. Thus those who sit stiffly on their chairs during a therapy session raise questions about the family's control structure. Fear, dependency, depression, the seeking of attention and the response of parents to their children's play or the overtures they make to them – all these provide indications of the family's way of functioning.

Dare and Lindsay (1979) usually construct a genogram, as described in Chapter 5, during the first or second session. The children are invited to participate in this and usually enjoy it. It is another way of involving them and helps establish the family as a unit in the context of the extended family system.

All these devices are designed to prevent 'family' therapy becoming marital therapy in the presence of the children. There are, of course, times when marital therapy is needed, but Dare and Lindsay believe that many therapists move towards it because they are more comfortable communicating verbally with adults than they are making contact with children, rather than because it is needed. Regardless of how frequently it is desirable to move from whole family to marital therapy, however, family therapists should certainly have the skills, and be familiar with the techniques, needed to contact and involve children in therapy as members of the family group. This is probably true whatever the orientation of the therapist, and whether or not intrapsychic processes are given prominent consideration by the therapist.

The therapist's use of self

Family therapy differs from many other forms of psychotherapy, and especially from psychoanalysis, in the active role played by most therapists. They generally avoid just sitting with a family, and reflecting back or interpreting what the family members are saying and doing. Instead they aim to devise active strategies which will in some way unbalance the systems of the families they work with or otherwise result in changed family functioning.

In producing change in families in these ways the therapist's personality is important. Many of the pioneers of family therapy have been powerful, charismatic figures and it may be more difficult for shy and diffident people to learn to be effective therapists. But whether or not this is so, every therapist must learn to use her or his personality to best advantage. Particular techniques may suit therapists with particular personalities and temperamental styles. Some therapists have difficulty using certain techniques effectively, but quickly become skilled with others. It is important, though, to learn a wide range of techniques, even those that do not at first come naturally. Practice, with skilled supervision, will enable you to gain confidence, and use effectively any of the techniques mentioned in this book. (I still remember the trepidation with which I offered a family my first paradoxical injunction; but nowadays I feel perfectly comfortable in using paradoxical methods where they are indicated.) Some therapists, probably a minority, do use a reflective approach, although not in a context of passivity. An example is the 'group analytic' approach of Skynner (1969b; 1976). This gives considerable attention to psychodynamic processes and their understanding. The relative merits of this approach and the more active approaches of many family therapists are at present unclear.

Transference issues

The term 'transference' is used here to mean the feelings projected on to a therapist by family members. This process is not stressed in the family therapy literature, but it merits consideration, as such feelings do develop.

Skynner (1976, pages 206–208) has discussed the development of transference phenomena during family therapy. Like most therapists he does not encourage transference. He also points out that it is less likely to develop the less the therapist is a 'blank screen'; since family therapists are generally more active and spontaneous, and reveal more of themselves than individual therapists, the projection of patients' own feelings on to them is less likely.

Transference can nevertheless develop. Family sessions can, for example, cause hostility previously kept under control by mental defence mechanisms to be projected into the transference. This may need to be interpreted and discussed.

> James, a 13-year-old boy, lived with his father, Tom, aged 35, and the 19-year-old young woman, Kate, with whom Tom had been living since he and James' mother separated three years before. Many tensions existed between Tom and Kate, and these seemed to be exacerbated by James' violent resentment of Kate whose arrival in the family he had never accepted. He was not, however, allowed by his father to express his anger directly, though he did so indirectly by means of various behavioural problems. The tensions between Tom and Kate were also kept under wraps and were not openly acknowledged. As the various unacknowledged feelings in the family came to light during family therapy sessions, the whole family, led by Tom, attacked the therapist with a variety of accusations. This process had to be worked through, and judiciously discussed, over the course of several sessions.

Transference can also develop as a result of the therapist's needs. Skynner (1976) believes that members of helping professions tend to have defensive systems which deal with inner conflict by taking 'parent' roles towards clients or patients. The latter then take the 'baby' role in response. The possibility that transference issues may be interfering with treatment should always be borne in mind during family therapy. They are more likely to surface the more the therapist takes a passive role; and the less intense and frequent the sessions the greater the chances of avoiding problems of this sort. It is better if previously repressed feelings are expressed between family members rather than towards the therapist; they can then be dealt with in the course of therapy.

Contracts

Many family therapists establish specific contracts with the families they treat. These often concern the number of sessions proposed and their frequency, who should attend, the goals of therapy, the fee and other issues. We have seen that some, like Epstein and Bishop (1981), have family and therapist sign a written contract at the end of the assessment process and before treatment begins.

Establishing a contract, which specifies the number of sessions and their frequency, has several advantages. First, it can define the length of time the therapist considers will be needed to produce the changes sought. It thus sets a programme for change. Secondly, it can define the part to be played in the process by the family members and the therapist. Thirdly, it can provide for 'homework' to be done between sessions, with the implication that the families will work on their problems between sessions, as well as during them.

A time-limited contract also has the advantage that an exit point is available for the family, which is therefore less likely to feel trapped into extended therapy. Knowing that there is a projected end-point may make it easier for them to enter treatment.

Perhaps the most important part of a contract is the specification of the changes which the family and therapist are meeting together in order to bring about. Without a clear understanding of this the chances of success are lessened, and indeed there is no way of knowing when therapy has been successfully completed – a point we have already made in Chapter 6.

The spacing of sessions

Therapists' views on the spacing of family sessions vary. In the early days of family therapy many therapists saw families weekly, or even more often, perhaps because in individual therapy this had been the usual practice. Nowadays, therapists tend to see families less often – as infrequently as once a month, sometimes even less often.

Palazzoli and her colleagues (1980) have set out a rationale for seeing families less often, and demonstrated that, in their practice, families seen less often did as well, or better than, those seen more frequently. It seems that when strategic and systemic methods are used, more widely spaced sessions are often best, whereas when more direct, and especially behavioural, methods are employed it may be preferable to see families more frequently. Spacing sessions at greater intervals has several advantages. One is that a therapist can handle a bigger caseload. Another is that, as we have seen, there is less likelihood of the family becoming overinvolved with the therapist, so that transference problems are diminished or avoided. Modern family therapy also often involves family members in carrying out tasks or performing rituals between sessions. These can often, with benefit, extend over the course of several weeks. Finally, systems change often takes time, and a week, or even two, may not be long enough for a well designed intervention to have its full impact on the family system.

Confidentiality

An important feature of family therapy is the openness which it promotes; when all members of the family are meeting together and talking about the issues with which treatment is dealing, the question of keeping certain information confidential, as between family members, does not arise. We can model free and frank communication, and can encourage it, for example by positively connoting the sharing of information between family members when it occurs. For example, a therapist might comment, when one person says something uncomplimentary to another, 'I'm impressed that you decided to clear the air and get those feelings out in the open.' It is thus the intent behind the action or statement, rather than the action or statement itself, that is positively connoted.

In family therapy, information emerging in therapy naturally becomes available to all members of the family. So if a member is absent from a session, the others normally feel free subsequently to share with that person what happened and what was said during the session. It may be helpful to make this clear at the start of treatment, especially when treating families that have had difficulty sharing information and communicating effectively with one another (i.e. disengaged families).

Family members sometimes try to obtain individual attention or communicate information to the therapist outside the therapy sessions. This may be done by phone calls to the therapist, or by taking the therapist aside at the end of a session and requesting a private talk; another, healthier approach is to ask openly for a private talk, while the other family members are present. The meaning of such behaviours should be carefully considered. Whether private interviews should be granted, and how telephone calls should be responded to, must be decided in the light of what is known about the family system. Such issues may be best brought to the family sessions for discussion. Positive connotation of them often proves possible, and at the same time any adverse effects they might have had are countered by bringing them out in the open.

Sometimes therapists see subgroups of families for certain sessions or parts of sessions, and ask those present not to share what is said with the other family members. If this is to be done it should, of course, be made clear to the other family members that this is a private talk the therapist and the family members concerned are having, and that its content may not be shared with the rest of the family; their agreement should be obtained to this. Some strategic therapy plans involve such confidential talks with certain family members.

A thirteen-year-old with a severe sleeping problem and school refusal had an enmeshed relationship with her mother, while father was largely uninvolved with the family. The father declined to come to therapy, but the mother and daughter were seen on one occasion, and during the latter part of the session they were interviewed separately. The daughter, when seen on her own, was told to see how long she could stay awake each night and telephone the therapist, without her mother's knowledge, at certain set times to tell him. She was not to discuss her sleeping habits with her mother at all. The mother was told, when she was seen alone, that she could talk to her daughter about any subject except sleeping, which must not be discussed. She could however discuss it, when the children were not present, with her husband.

The therapist's plan was to separate mother and daughter, having the daughter become involved with the therapist by reporting to him how long she was staying awake, while at the same time promoting sleep by a paradoxical injunction. Because the daughter's sleep problems were her mother's main preoccupation and something she could scarcely help talking anxiously about, she was given permission to discuss it with her uninvolved husband as a means of bringing him more into the family.

The strategy was successful and the sleep problem had resolved within two weeks; school attendance also became normal shortly afterwards, and the mother found that when she told her husband of her concerns regarding their daughter he showed a lot more interest than she had expected. In this case some secrets between family members were essential to the treatment strategy employed.

The content of therapy sessions is, of course, strictly confidential so far as people outside the family group are concerned. Information should not be released by the therapist without the family's permission.

Observers

Family therapists make extensive use of one-way observation screens, through which treatment is observed by one or more other therapists; these assist the therapist in understanding the family and devising intervention strategies. Dealing with families is a complex process; many things, both verbal and non-verbal, are going on at once and it can be helpful to have several people watching and listening. De Shazer (1982), in his book *Patterns of Brief Family Therapy*, regards the total team as being 'the therapist' and refers to the member who goes into the therapy room with the family as 'the conductor'.

Observation through one-way screens is also commonly used by supervisors in teaching family therapy; it enables them to watch their students in action and, using a telephone, to intervene in the treatment if necessary. Communication by telephone between therapist and/or family, and those observing, can also have other therapeutic uses (Coppersmith, 1980).

Closed circuit television can serve a similar purpose to observation through a one-way screen, especially when a large audience, or one situated at a distance from the treatment room, wishes to watch a therapy session. Videotape recording can also be useful, both for supervision and review of sessions, and to enable therapists to watch themselves in action. By this means you can learn more about your own functioning, as well as that of the families you are treating; videotape recordings are not, however, a substitute for live observation, since intervention during sessions by supervisors or other observers is not possible when a videotape is reviewed. Ideally sessions should be observed and taped for subsequent review. Videotape replay has itself been used as a therapeutic device (see Chapter 11).

Whatever form of observation or recording is proposed should be explained to the family in advance and their consent obtained; it is usual to get a signed consent to record sessions. Written consent is usually not considered necessary in order to have observers watch, but the family should always be told who is watching; if they wish they should be allowed to meet the observers. Only rarely do families object to being observed, once it is explained that they have not just one therapist, but a team, devoted to helping them. Families raising objections to being videotaped may be told that records are always kept of therapy sessions, usually in written form, and that the tape recording is only a better, more comprehensive form of clinical record; they should also, of course, be assured that the tape will not be released to anyone outside the clinical team without their permission.

What should the therapist do if family members do object to being observed and/or tape recorded? This depends in part on the philosophy of the institution in which the therapy is being conducted. If team therapy, as described for example by de Shazer (1982), is the basic approach of a centre, it might be better, unless the centre can offer other treatment approaches, to suggest that the family seek help elsewhere. On other occasions it may be quite appropriate for an experienced therapist to proceed without the help of observers or recordings, perhaps after warning the family that treatment might take longer, or be more difficult, without the additional help. The situation is different when the family is to be treated by a student; in this case proper supervision, which might need to be 'live' depending on the nature of the case and the experience of the therapist, is essential. To proceed without it, when it is needed, would be unethical. In such cases it is necessary to consider whether any other way of treating the family is available.

Serious objections to being observed or tape recorded come mostly from individuals with paranoid personalities or paranoid psychoses. When this is the case the management of the paranoid person, or family system, becomes part of the clinical problem – often a difficult one – with which the therapist or team has to deal.

Co-therapy

From the early days of the family therapy movement there have been those who have believed that a co-therapy team – that is two therapists working in the room with the family – is preferable to having a single therapist work with the family, at least in many instances. As with many other issues which arise in family therapy this is one on which there is a lack of good data. Gurman and Kniskern (1978b), however, found some evidence in their review of the literature that there is little difference between the results of co-therapy and those of single-therapist treatment. This global finding could nevertheless conceal the fact that co-therapy is advantageous in certain circumstances, and the use of but one therapist is better, or as good, in others.

The advantages claimed for co-therapy include:

(a) Better observation of what is going on in the family group. It is certainly true that a single therapist cannot take note of all the events, verbal and non-verbal, that take place in a family interview. If two therapists are present, less is likely to be missed.

(b) The therapists can supply each other with mutual support. Each can also watch for signs that the other is getting overinvolved with the family or is losing objectivity in dealing with the family system.

(c) The therapists can model healthier ways of relating and commun-icating than the family use. When the co-therapists are a man and a woman, they may help to model a better relationship for marital and parental couples.

(d) In that type of strategic therapy in which two incompatible alternative courses of action may be presented to the family, the therapists can say they disagree about which would be the better; one of them can present one alternative while the other presents the second.

(e) It can be a valuable learning experience for the therapists. Each may learn from the other, and a less experienced therapist may learn much from a more experienced one.

(f) Two, or even more, therapists may be required for very large families and, especially for multi-family therapy (see Chapter 11), simply to monitor events, keep the therapy process under control and maintain contact with all members of the family.

Most of these advantages have been questioned:

(a) It has been said that experienced therapists are able to observe enough of the family process to make appropriate interventions. There is no hard evidence that observing everything, or more than one therapist can observe, improves results.

(b) Experienced therapists in their day-to-day work do not require the support of co-therapists; when they require assistance with families they can seek consultation with colleagues. Students and other inexperienced therapists should receive support from their supervisors, either by means of live supervision or through review of videotapes of their work.

(c) Modelling can usually be done by therapists working on their own, using members of the family group as partners in the process. When family members do not have the appropriate skills these can be taught by the therapist; this can be a useful therapeutic strategy.

(d) It is not necessary to have two therapists in the room to present two different viewpoints to a family; one view can be put forward as the therapist's while the other can be that of the observing team, or the two views can be presented as those of two groups within the team. Even if you are working without a team, it is still possible to say that you can see two possible courses of action but are unsure which would be better.

(e) Other learning experiences are available without the use of co-therapy. One-way observation and review of videotapes enable students to watch skilled and experienced therapists at work without the necessity of being in the therapy room.

(f) While it seems to be generally agreed that more than one therapist is needed for multiple family therapy, it is less clear that this applies with big families. My own experience in trying to see on my own a family of two parents, fourteen children and the marital partners of two of these suggests, however, that it would have been helpful to have someone else present. It was hard even to remember everyone's names, let alone form a clear view of how the family system operated!

Two other problems with co-therapy are the additional cost of paying two therapists, and the greater complexity of the process. Careful planning is necessary, as well as subsequent review of each session by the co-therapists, who should also have similar theoretical orientations, comparable skills and a satisfactory working relationship.

It seems that co-therapy is used in some centres more than in others, perhaps more as a matter of policy than because of firm evidence that it yields better results than treatment by a single therapist. Most therapists probably work on their own. Of the eleven case studies in the book *Family Therapy: Full Length Case Studies* (Papp, 1977), only two were treated by co-therapy teams. In one of these Carl Whitaker started out as the sole therapist, but was joined by David Keith in the fourth interview. The decision to bring in a co-therapist was made because of the 'close lock-in' or 'profound intimacy' which Whitaker felt had developed between himself and the mother, herself a professional therapist. The other co-therapy case was a marital one treated by James Framo and his wife who had worked together as co-therapists for five years. There are other instances of marital couples working together as co-therapists, for example Robin Skynner and his wife (1976) and Stephen and Carol Lankton (1983).

While there are no clearly established benefits of co-therapy, it seems that it has its place in certain circumstances. For example co-therapy of a creative and fascinating kind is reported in the book *The Family Crucible* (Napier and Whitaker, 1978), which describes the co-therapy treatment of a family (actually a composite of a number of families) in a singularly clear and well written way.

Summary

This chapter has considered some practical points which may require attention during family therapy. Attendance of the whole family for assessment, which is usually desirable except when the problem is purely a marital one, may be resisted; it can usually be achieved by persistence, careful explanation and avoidance of confrontation in the therapist's early contacts with the family. It is important that family therapists maintain control of the therapy process as it occurs in and between sessions. They need also to learn to use their own personality characteristics to best advantage; all of us have characteristics which we can turn to good use in family therapy, and we need to identify and capitalize on these. Involving children in family sessions is important too; children are often repositories of their families' myths and histories, and much can be learnt from their contribution to family sessions.

Family therapists should be aware that family members may project their feelings and attitudes on to them, though this happens to a lesser extent than in individual therapy; at times, however, such transference issues require to be dealt with. Also discussed have been the spacing of sessions; issues of confidentiality; and the use of observers and of team members who are not in the room with the therapist. Finally we considered the place of co-therapy teams in family therapy; their use is characteristic of the philosophy of certain centres, and while their value generally is unclear, they can be used creatively in some circumstances.

Chapter 9

Common Family Problems and Their Treatment

Family problems come in many forms and degrees of severity. This chapter will look at some of the more common ones and will discuss direct approaches to their treatment. More complex problems and treatment approaches are discussed in later chapters.

Many of the concepts used in this chapter are derived from the McMaster Model of Family Functioning (Epstein et al, 1978) and the closely-related Process Model of Family Functioning (Steinhauer et al, 1984). These were discussed in Chapter 5, and provide convenient ways of conceptualizing family functioning. Concepts derived from the structural school of family therapy (Minuchin, 1974; Minuchin and Fishman, 1981) and from communication theory (see Chapter 3) are also employed.

Task accomplishment problems

Task accomplishment problems (as defined in the Process model), or problem solving difficulties (the McMaster model term) were discussed in Chapter 5. Failure to provide for the basic needs of family members can be severe and serious. An extreme example was reported by Oliver and Buchanan (1979). These authors presented a horrifying story of an extended family network, starting with a mentally retarded young woman, the six men with whom she successively lived and her children, and continuing with their descendants. Altogether forty members of the family, and their spouses or partners, were studied. Throughout all the family groups there was a gross failure of basic task accomplishment, with physical neglect, assaults on the children, incest, prostitution – sometimes taught to the children by the parents – and an utter failure to provide the basic elements of care.

Oliver and Buchanan's paper is replete with reports of assaults on children with hammers or knives, burns causing persisting poker marks, bites, beatings and hair pullings. Unfortunately cases as severe as this are not uncommon, as reports which appear in the media from time to time reveal.

Tonge and his colleagues (1975) also provided a tragic picture of the failure of basic task accomplishment in their study of problem families; and for every extreme example of the failure to accomplish basic tasks, there are many other serious, though milder, cases. Most families in which there is serious failure of basic task accomplishment do not, however, present themselves at family therapy clinics or therapists' offices. Instead they are more often encountered by the social workers employed by child welfare agencies.

Developmental tasks are those associated with the growth of individuals or changes in a family's composition or situation. Examples are the changes necessitated by the birth of children, their entry into school, the onset of adolescence or the departure of offspring from home as grown-up children. There may be problems in surmounting any of the 'transition points' described in Chapter 2.

Certain families cope well at some stages in their development but have difficulty at others; for example development may proceed smoothly until the children reach adolescence – a time when a lot of adjustments may be needed over a short time span.

Some families function well until faced with a crisis such as serious illness or death of a family member, job loss, migration from one culture to another, or the loss of the family home by fire or foreclosure; others seem able to deal well with a whole series of disasters.

Basic, developmental and crisis tasks comprise a sort of hierarchy, in that if basic tasks are not performed well it is unlikely that developmental or crisis ones will be; similarly crisis tasks will probably not be handled well if developmental ones are not. The reverse does not necessarily apply, however; that is to say it does not follow that if crisis tasks cause a family difficulty, developmental ones will also do so, nor that the failure to cope with developmental tasks is likely always to be associated with failure in basic task performance.

In the *treatment* of task accomplishment problems direct methods may be effective, although when there are severe problems affecting all three categories of task, therapy often presents great difficulties; indeed 'multi-problem' families present some of the greatest challenges family therapists meet. It is important, however, not to be overwhelmed by the immensity of the problems some of these families face.

The first step, as always, is to establish rapport and have the family come to trust you. Families with basic task accomplishment problems are often composed of people with poor self-images who readily feel criticized, and are easily threatened by authority figures; so the establishment of the right sort of relationship is vital if the family's motivation is to be maintained and developed.

'Positive connotation' of family members' motives, even though their actions may have had unfortunate results, or failed to achieve any of the results sought, can be enormously useful in achieving this. Very few parents, for example, deliberately harm their children. Their attempts to care for them, though, may fail for many reasons, some of these residing in their own life experiences and personality limitations. The actions of parents who yell at their children in a demeaning way, or beat them to the extent of causing serious injury, can be connoted as representing their attempts to train their children to behave well; they are unsuccessful, even harmful, attempts to be sure, but they are the best choices available to them at the time. Their histories, personalities, and emotional states, and the current circumstances, all place limitations on the choices they find they have. Such parents usually expect to be blamed or criticized, and may have a strong sense of guilt about what has happened. They do not expect to meet someone who positively connotes their intentions by saying that they obviously care a lot about their children - enough to go to perhaps quite extreme measures to bring the children's behaviour under control. Perhaps they will think, 'Here is someone who sees things differently from other people, someone who is on our side, and wants to understand what has happened and how we can get out of this mess we've got ourselves into'.

By attributing good intentions to whatever the family members have done, therefore, we can establish ourselves as being on the family's side. Once this has been achieved, we can proceed to explore alternative means of achieving the family's goals - means that are more likely to be successful and which will not have destructive consequences. In other words we give the family members more choice. Reaching this stage represents an important breakthrough; once it is achieved it is surprising what some families will do at the therapist's behest.

The next step is to break down the therapy task to manageable proportions. Milton Erickson many times advocated aiming first at small changes, just as every journey, however long, starts with the first step.

The processes involved in task accomplishment - identifying the task, exploring alternative approaches, taking action, evaluating and adjusting - were set out in Chapter 5. In treatment it is sometimes possible to go through these processes directly with the family members, concluding with an agreement, or even a written contract, that the family will take some action between now and the next session. Much depends on the family's motivation, but even more important is the therapist/family relationship.

When trust has been established, therapy can follow the stages described by Epstein and Bishop (1981). This will be described more fully in Chapter 12, but after dealing with the first two stages – that is identifying the problem and exploring alternative approaches – an agreement is made with the family for them to take a certain course of action, the third stage. This may address the problems in quite a direct way – though it need not do so and could approach the problems indirectly. At the next session the results are evaluated and any necessary adjustments are made – the fourth stage. Another problem is then examined and alternatives are explored in the same way as the first one was. This leads to another task being set the family, and so on.

This generally direct approach is not always successful, of course; indeed no one approach is uniformly successful in family therapy. Any of the 'strategic' or other special approaches described in later chapters may be required, but if direct methods have not been tried previously it is usually best to start by using them.

Communication problems

Communications theory and its relevance to family therapy have been discussed in Chapters 3 and 4. Communication problems exist in many families coming for therapy. In our assessment of families we must take note of both their verbal and their non-verbal communication; there are often discrepancies between the messages sent by each of these two means. We must also assess the clarity, directness and sufficiency of communications, both verbal and non-verbal, and the availability and openness of those to whom communications are addressed.

> Frances (10) and George (8) attended with their parents, Harry and Irene. Irene was a homemaker, while Harry had a job which took him away from home four to five months of the year, with individual trips lasting up to six weeks.
>
> The presenting problems were George's severe temper tantrums and Irene's reported inability to control him, to the extent that she was fearful that he would do her serious physical harm. George had been referred to the emergency department of a hospital because of a severe outbreak of violent behaviour at home a few day's previously, while his father was away.
>
> When the history of George's temper attacks was explored Harry, who had returned home early because of George's admission to hospital, said they were a new phenomenon, of which he had just become aware. Frances, however, chipped in, saying that George had been losing his temper for at least two years, 'but my Mum doesn't

tell my Dad because she's afraid he'll hit George, and he doesn't lose his temper when Dad's at home'. The therapist turned to Irene, who confirmed that Frances' statement was true. The therapist then asked Harry if he was aware of what had been going on when he was away; he said he was not. Irene then admitted that she had been afraid to tell Harry about George's behaviour at home, and also about behaviour problems the school had reported.

During the remainder of the interview several other pieces of information emerged of which Harry, and in one case Irene, had been unaware. For example the children agreed that when George was worried about something the only person he would confide in about his worries was Frances; neither parent realized that this was the case, nor did they seem to know how close the relationship between George and Frances was. Frances, it also emerged, confided freely in her mother, but neither child ever confided in Harry.

In this family the failure of communication, especially between the father and the other members, became obvious when it emerged that the father knew little of what went on in the family; it was also evident during the assessment interview itself. The information passing between Harry and the rest of the family was certainly not sufficient, although when the family members did speak to each other they did so with a good degree of clarity. There was, however, a tendency for communication to be indirect, with Frances acting as a sort of telephone exchange; she seemed to have freer communication with the remainder of the family than did anyone else, and she did not appear afraid to tell her father things which might upset him – or at least which the other two members of the family thought might.

This family was treated using direct methods; the members had never given much thought to the question of how information was communicated within the family, and when this was discussed they became interested. Initially work on the communication problem was carried out during the therapy sessions. At the very first session, when Irene's obvious failure to keep her husband informed about their son's behavioural problems emerged, there was progress towards resolving the difficulties. Harry did not react in the way Irene had feared he would; instead of becoming angry and threatening he expressed concern about the situation, and regretted that he had not been more involved in the family. The family 'myth' – that father would become angry, perhaps even violent, if he was told what was going on – was exploded.

With the therapist's encouragement, the other family members proved willing to share with the father the important facts about what had been going on. A 'same-sex parenting program' was also prescribed; Irene was put in charge of Frances, so that Frances was to come to her with any issues she wished to discuss, or requests she had to make, and similarly anything of significance that the parents wished to communicate to Frances was to be told to her by her mother. Harry's role was that of consultant to Irene, who was to consult him on matters concerning Frances on which she needed a second opinion. Harry could also offer input unasked, though the final decision on matters concerning Frances was to be Irene's.

When this had been explained to the parents and to Frances, and they had agreed to follow the prescribed plan, the therapist turned to George. Before the therapist could say anything, however, George pointed to his father and said, but with a smile, 'So that leaves me with him', 'Yes, it does', replied the therapist, who went on to explain that Harry's role in relation to George was to be exactly analogous to Irene's in relation to Frances. Harry accepted this readily, and George seemed quite delighted, though he could not bring himself actually to say so.

This quite direct intervention was designed to serve several purposes. It was aimed at altering family members' roles (an issue discussed later in this chapter), and it was intended to promote increased communication between Harry and his son, as well as between the parents, who would need to consult with each other on issues concerning their children. It was also a structural intervention, aiming to get Harry more involved in the family and to break down the boundary between him and the rest of the family. Finally the parents were instructed to set aside ten minutes before they went to bed each night to discuss how the same-sex parenting programme was going, and to ensure that they were keeping to the plan as prescribed. This would also be an opportunity for them to exchange any information about the children which they had not been able to share earlier in the day.

This was a lot of work to do in a single therapy session, but the therapist felt he had been able quickly to establish good rapport with the family. All members seemed well motivated, even desperate, for help. In some cases, however, the work done in this one session would have been spread over several sessions. In the event the interventions were successful and only four therapy sessions were needed.

In the above family, communication – though insufficient – was usually clear when it occurred. In many families with problems, however, this is not so, and communication is either ambiguous or vague, or conflicting messages are given simultaneously. Sometimes the verbal message says one thing and the non-verbal another; it is easy to disqualify a statement by one's tone of voice, body posture or actions.

The double-bind, already mentioned in Chapter 1, is a more extreme example of this kind of thing. Its main features, as described by Bateson et al. (1956), are:

- the presence of two persons
- an oft-repeated experience
- a 'primary negative injunction' to do, or not do, something with a threat of punishment if the order is not obeyed
- a 'secondary injunction' which conflicts with the first at a more abstract level, often communicated non-verbally, again with threats of punishment, and
- a situation from which the subject cannot escape

To put it another way, we have a person in an intense relationship, with a strongly felt need to understand the messages being communicated by another person who is giving two orders of messages, one of which denies the other. The subject is also unable to comment on or discuss the messages so as to come up with a suitable response; that is to say metacommunication – communication about the communication – is not possible. Once the individual has learned to perceive the universe in 'double-bind patterns', the complete set of conditions may not be needed and a part of it may be enough to provoke panic or rage.

Although the double-bind was originally described as occurring in the families of schizophrenic patients, it soon became clear that it is by no means confined to such families. It is perhaps best regarded as a special example of unclear communication, likely to occur more often in seriously dysfunctional families than in better functioning ones.

Direct treatment of families in which communication is unclear consists of raising questions about whether the communications family members offer each other are clear. Thus if family member A has said something to member B, the therapist might ask B, 'What was A trying to tell you?' or, 'Would you like to tell A what you thought she meant?' or, 'Perhaps you would like to check out with A what you thought she meant?'

As with everything else a therapist may do, this process is greatly facilitated if there is good rapport with the family members; this makes it easier to get the family to do what is asked than it otherwise would be. The introduction of humour may help, and the process of clarifying communication need not be a deadly serious one. The therapist should use his or her personality in a warm, empathic, kindly, but firm way, to insist that the family do as they are asked. The procedure must be repeated until a pattern of clear, direct communication has been achieved. Once A is communicating satisfactorily with B, the process can be reversed, and other family members can then be brought in, as necessary. When the process has got well under way during sessions, the family may be asked to practice it at home, usually for specific and quite short time periods.

Similar approaches may be used to deal with both insufficient communication and indirect communication. Family members are rehearsed until they learn to exchange information which is sufficient for the purpose in question, or until they have learned to address directly those people with whom they formerly communicated indirectly.

As well as teaching family members better communication skills, the above approach also draws their attention to the importance of communication; the value the therapist places on it can often heighten family members' awareness of the need to communicate clearly and in a straightforward way. Therapists can also help promote better communication by appropriate modelling. It is important that our own communications are sufficient, clear and direct. A model of frank, open communication, in a context of emotionally warm relationships, characterized by courtesy and respect, can be of real value to many families. It often happens that after a few sessions family members begin to adopt some aspects of their therapist's style of communicating.

The process of examining, clarifying and modifying the communication occurring between family members can be applied to non-verbal as well as verbal communication. Analogic communication – the voice tones, facial expressions, body postures and other non-verbal behaviours – may be examined, clarified and changed during therapy. Thus the therapist may ask family member B what it was like being spoken to by A in a particular tone of voice. By asking such a question the therapist is disqualifying, at least for the moment, the digital meaning of the message and concentrating on its analogic qualities. Examples of other questions which might be put to family members are, 'What does it make you want to do when A talks to you like that?' or, 'How do you feel when A talks to you in that way?' A series of questions such as the following might be helpful.

To B: 'What is it like for you when A talks to you with that voice?'
To A: 'Did you know that B feels like that when you use that voice? Would you like to ask her to tell you a bit more about what it's like?'
To B: 'Tell A what you feel like doing when he speaks to you in that way'.
To A: 'Did you know that? Would you like to say the same thing in a different way?'

The next step might be to get the two people to practise talking in different tones of voice.

Similar approaches can be used with other forms of analogic communication, for example facial expression, gestures and body posture, failure to look at a person being spoken to, or sitting apart from or too close to another person. Communication can also occur through silence; since it is impossible not to communicate, therapy may have to address problems of silence, avoidance and the like.

A good account of how improved communication can be taught to families was presented by Richard Bandler, John Grinder and Virginia Satir in their book *Changing with Families* (1976).

Role problems

A family is liable to develop problems if the various functions which have to be performed are not properly allocated to, or carried out by, appropriate family members. The importance of role allocation and performance was discussed in Chapter 5, in which we considered what are called by the authors of the McMaster Model of Family Functioning, 'idiosyncratic' roles, for example that of family scapegoat.

Families containing children require at least two subsytems, or groupings of people; the parental subsystem and the child subsystem. The simplest situation is that of a one-parent family with a single child. In such a family the parent should take responsibility for the care of the child, by providing the basic necessities of life, and by giving the child love, emotional security and the feeling of being a worthwhile person; the parent should also provide a sound role model for living in the society of which parent and child are members.

Children's roles depend on their ages. Normally developing children become progressively less dependent on their parents as they get older. Depending on cultural norms, they should take increasing responsibility for instrumental tasks within the household, and by adolescence should have a significant role in running it. Emotionally, too, children normally become more independent with increasing age; and when adolescence ends, with emancipation from the family of origin, they should be relating to their parents much more nearly as equals. Parents' roles change in a reciprocal way as their children mature.

In two-parent families, and families with more than one child, role allocation is more complex than when there is only one parent and one child. The same roles have to be performed, however. The parents also need to work together as a team, though their respective roles will differ. In larger families there may be more than two subsystems.

Role performance problems exist when appropriate roles are either not allocated or, if they are allocated, are not properly performed. In most families roles are mainly implicitly understood, though some may be deliberately discussed and consciously decided upon. They also evolve as the family passes through its various developmental stages. Symptoms often develop in family members who are cast, because of the nature of the family system, into idiosyncratic roles.

The family scapegoat. This is probably the idiosyncratic role about which most has been written, though the term seems to be used less nowadays that it was in the earlier days of family therapy. It was first described, in relation to family functioning, by Vogel and Bell (1960). It has biblical origins, however. The use of a scapegoat was one of the procedures laid down by Moses for use by the people of Israel. The priest was to lay his hands on the head of the goat and 'confess over it all the iniquities of the Israelites and all their acts of rebellion, that is all their sins'. Having laid the sins on the goat's head, the goat was to be sent into the wilderness, 'to carry all their iniquities upon itself into some barren waste' (New English Bible, 1970). The way the term is used in the family therapy literature is however not strictly accurate. While the 'scapegoated' family member – often a child with symptoms – appears to act as the person on to whom all the family's problems are projected, that person is usually maintained in the family system rather than being sent out into a 'barren waste'. Sometimes, though, the scapegoat is placed in an institution, which presumably plays the role of the 'barren waste'. Some families depend on having a 'bad' child for their, often precarious, stability. The scapegoat's difficult behaviour may be the only thing that keeps the family together; sometimes a symptomatic child appears to be all that parents can agree about.

The parental child. The role of 'parental child' is another special, or idiosyncratic, one. It is sometimes appropriate to give older children some 'parental' functions in the care of younger children in the family, but if too much responsibility is given to a child – and especially if the delegation of authority is not explicit – the child may be unable to function as required and may develop symptoms. The parental child may be involved in 'parenting' younger children or in performing a similar role in caring for one, or even both parents. In extreme cases there is reversal of roles, the child looking after the parent, though this process may be camouflaged (Skynner, 1976, page 417).

Other special roles. These include the roles of martyr, 'family angel', sick member, handicapped member and disturbed or 'crazy' member. The martyr perpetually sacrifices his or her interests for the good of the family. The 'family angel', described by Gross (1979), performs a role analogous to that of the scapegoat – that of someone others can be agreed about, and may co-exist in the same family with a scapegoat. Sometimes the adoption of special roles by one or more members enables the family to function quite smoothly, but this may be at considerable cost to those in the special roles. Not all special roles are undesirable, however, and we must take care to understand the function that each one has in any family we are treating. It is also necessary to know whether the pattern of role performance is related to the problems for which the family is seeking help.

Treatment of role performance problems

Direct measures are sometimes effective. Once the problems have been identified, it is necessary for the therapist and family to agree how family members' roles need to change in order to resolve the problems. In doing this it can be helpful to start with the historical development of the dysfunctional roles. These may have had useful purposes at one time, but have since outgrown their usefulness, or even have become inimical to healthy family functioning. The therapist then negotiates with the family members for them, or some of them, to play different roles. An example is the 'same-sex parenting' procedure mentioned above. It is a way of enhancing, and making more appropriate, the roles of parents. It may be a useful intervention when there are one or more parental children, when there is enmeshment between parent(s) and child(ren), or when there are deficient behaviour control mechanisms. Kirschner and Kirschner (1986), in their description of 'optimal family process', comment as follows:

> The same-sex parent (SSP) tends to function as the primary programmer and disciplinarian. The SSP promotes maximum ego development by setting limits as well as progressively higher level goals and standards intrinsically suited to the child's unfolding skills and talents. The SSP uses rewards and discipline, education, inspiration, and modelling to help the child to attain these goals. The opposite-sex parent (OSP) functions primarily as the facilitator or mediator within the triangle...
>
> If the SSP disciplines a misbehaving child in an inappropriate fashion, the OSP takes responsibility for correcting the interaction... In a manner that creates a satisfactory rapprochement, the OSP is stable and loving and points out that the SSP still loves the child. (Kirschner and Kirschner, 1986, page 35)

'Same-sex parenting' interventions are based on the above view – which is set out more comprehensively in the Kirschners' book – of 'optimal' family functioning. They involve putting the father in primary charge of the boys in the family, especially in the fields of discipline and 'programming' and the mother of the girls. 'Programming', as the Kirschners use the term, refers to the way children are helped to develop a particular view of themselves and the world.

Programming is much like the kind of informal hypnosis that occurs in all families. As Laing and Esterson (1970) have pointed out, children are raised in a trancelike state vis-a-vis their parents. In this state, they are programmed regarding themselves and the world...Programming can be targeted toward three areas: the definition of the self; the description of the world; and one's behaviours, attitudes, and values (Kirschner and Kirschner, 1986, page 69).

In making a 'same-sex parenting' intervention the family is told that, except when the SSP is absent and a major decision cannot wait until that parent returns, all decisions, advice, rewards, punishments and permissions concerning each child are to be made by the SSP. The OSP's role is that of consultant and adviser to the SSP. I usually explain the rationale for this procedure by pointing out that the parent concerned has had the experience of being a boy, or girl, as the case may be. That parent is therefore in the best position to advise, assist and make important decisions about the welfare of the boys, or girls, in the family. The OSP supports both the child and the SSP, and may mediate between them when necessary, but always emphasizing that the SSP loves the child. Embedded in such instructions, there is also the implication that parents are in charge of their children, and are responsible for making certain decisions concerning them. When parental roles have been unclear, interventions of this sort can bring greater clarity and definition to them, and lead to better parenting of the children.

Sometimes direct approaches to the treatment of role performance problems fail, and it is then necessary to use more indirect or strategic approaches. A useful one is the 'odd-days/even-days' type of intervention. This, along with other indirect approaches, will be considered in Chapters 10 and 11.

Behaviour control problems

The behaviour of one or more family members is the presenting problem in many families that seek therapy. It is usually one or more of the children in the family who are presented as the identified patient or patients, but parents and other adults may also present behaviour which causes concern to others or to themselves. 'Conduct disorders' and their milder variant, 'oppositional disorders' are much the commonest child psychiatric disorders, although these terms do little more than describe certain patterns of behaviour. Both, however, refer to various forms of disobedient, antisocial and aggressive behaviour. Children to whom they are applied have failed to learn the types of socially acceptable behaviour expected in their families and/or the wider social environment. Conduct disorders usually start as behaviour control problems in the children's families. They are discussed further in *Basic Child Psychiatry*. (Barker, 1983, Chapter 4)

Various types of behaviour control – rigid, flexible, laissez-faire and chaotic – were described in Chapter 5. Although in reality there is an infinite number of ways in which family systems may be organized, this is a useful framework for examining the control structure of families. Whether the parents work together can also be an important factor in determining how successful their control of their children is.

The various aspects of family functioning we considered in Chapter 5 are closely interrelated. Behaviour control depends to a considerable extent on, for example, role allocation and performance, and on the family members' affective involvement and their values and norms. We have seen, in the previous section, how parents can 'programme' their children to achieve a certain understanding of themselves and the world, something which depends much on parental roles and the nature of family relationships. If we take a structural view, there need to be clear subsystem boundaries, with a well defined parental system adequately in touch with, but also distinct from, the child system. When these conditions do not exist, direct work to create them may be successful. Using the McMaster model of therapy, this might involve contracting with particular family members to do certain things. For example, the parents might be asked to work out together agreed limits to their children's behaviour, and then to communicate these to the children. They would then take specific steps to enforce these limits and, perhaps, to reward the children for keeping within the limits.

Control problems are not, of course, limited to children's behaviour, but may involve the family system as a whole; task accomplishment depends in part on how well behavioural control operates, and role performance is closely related too. Sometimes direct discussion of the tasks that need to be performed, who is to perform them (role allocation and performance) and how the family system will be organized to see that roles are performed (behaviour control) may be undertaken as a single therapeutic process. By giving conscious thought to such issues the family may be able to make the necessary changes, with the therapist's help. This is 'first order' change, but it may suffice. Often, however, it is not sufficient and less direct therapy methods, designed to produce 'second order' change, may be needed.

Poorly functioning subsystems and boundary problems

Structural theory has been outlined in Chapters 4 and 5. Many family problems can be conceptualized as structural ones, but statements about the 'structure' of a family system have implications for its communication patterns, the affective involvement of the family members, the behaviour control system and other aspects of its functioning. We need not be concerned, therefore, to decide whether there are, for example, either communication or structural problems. In fact if there is one there is likely also to be the other. The structural therapist, however, tackles the therapeutic task using the structural model – which might, however, mean doing things very similar to what a therapist using another model (the McMaster one, for instance) – would do.

Generally speaking families require well-functioning spouse, parent and child subsystems (where there are children in the family). There should be clear, but not unduly rigid boundaries between the subsystems. In large families there may be more than one child subsystem, and there may also be a grandparental subsystem. The existence of a suitable hierarchy, as between generations, is important, and something that Haley (1976, Chapter 4) emphasizes. Yet there is no 'normal' or universally ideal family structure. The questions must always be, 'Does it work without anyone suffering or developing symptoms?' and, 'Does it provide for the healthy growth of the family and its members?' Thus giving a child parental power can, as we have seen, cause problems, but it can also be appropriate, at least in some measure, in large families.

In *structural therapy* the therapist works on the boundaries between systems and subsystems, promoting communication and emotional interchange where it is inadequate (as in disengaged relationships), and helping erect barriers and create a necessary sense of separation where there is undue enmeshment. The structural approach to therapy, a valuable and widely applicable one, is described further in Chapter 12.

Suprasystem problems

The suprasystem, or 'ecological context', contributes to the difficulties some families experience. It is well known that middle-class families are careful to live in areas in which there are good schools, and recreational facilities suited to their families' needs and tastes, together with an absence of serious problems of delinquency and social decay. Well functioning suburban areas are preferred to declining inner city areas.

Such choices reflect awareness of the effects different neighbourhoods can have on families.

Satisfactory family functioning can be harder to maintain in some areas than in others. While in some poor areas there are helpful neighbourhood and extended support networks, in others this is not so. Families living in decaying areas with high crime rates, widespread drug abuse, open and active prostitution and large numbers of alienated people and truants from school face great difficulties. In such situations the family needs to establish and maintain an adequate boundary between it and the surrounding environment. Therapy may need to focus on this particular aspect of family functioning.

Auerswald (1968) provided a description of the use of the 'ecological' approach to people's problems, illustrating it with a striking example. This was the case of a 12-year-old girl who had run away from home. The involvement and roles of the police, the mother, a sister, the girl's therapist at the local mental health clinic, the clinic psychiatrist, the school staff, the after-school group worker, the maternal grandparents, the Department of Welfare and the staff of the local adolescent ward are all described. The inadequacy of looking only at the girl, or her nuclear family, becomes very clear as one reads this account. The girl, and her family, were part of a complex suprasystem; only if this were understood could rational treatment be planned and carried out.

The *treatment of suprasystem problems* consists of either strengthening the boundary between the family and the suprasystem, where the latter is having an adverse effect on the family; or working with the relevant parts of the suprasystem, which may include extended family, school staff, social agencies, other therapists, even employers – though all this can only be done with the permission of the clients.

Delivering direct injunctions

'Direct injunctions' – or instructions given to clients to change their behaviour in direct ways – are an important part of the treatment approaches discussed in this chapter. How families respond to them depends largely on how they are delivered. Good rapport with the family is an essential prerequisite, but attention to the following points increases further the likelihood of their being effective.

1. Make the instructions as precise as possible. Thus rather than saying, 'Be kind to X', or 'Don't be rude to Y', say more precisely what the person concerned should do to be kind, or to avoid being rude.
2. Enlist other family members, when available, to remind the sub-

ject(s), in a calm, non-critical and non-judgmental way, of the injunction.

3. Use the force of your personality. Convey your enthusiasm for the plan of action you are putting forward, and your conviction that it will work. Another application of therapists' own personalities is the use of hypnosis, which seems sometimes to increase people's suggestibility, as well as helping convince themselves that they *can* do what they are being asked to do.

4. Consider setting up a system of rewards or punishments, preferably rewards. This can be very appropriate for children, but even parents and other adults can be told to reward themselves, perhaps by going out to dinner together, or perhaps just by exchanging a few words of approval or praise, for successful implementation of the treatment programme.

5 Whenever possible tell clients to do something different rather than to stop doing something. The 'different' thing must be incompatible with the behaviour which you wish to discourage. Thus it is better to tell people who are talking rudely to others what they *should* be saying, rather than what they should *not* say.

6. Tell clients to do things in a different sequence. This can be effective in disrupting established, dysfunctional patterns of behaviour, for example between spouses, or between parents and children.

Summary

In this chapter we have examined some of the more common family problems and how they may be treated by direct methods of intervention. Such methods may be successfully applied to task accomplishment problems; communication problems; problems of role assignment and performance; behaviour control problems; 'structural problems' – that is those involving poorly functioning subsystem patterns; and supra-system problems – those related to the nature and characteristics of the wider social environment of which the family is a part. Problems in several of these categories or even all of them, may co-exist.

The first step in the use of direct methods of treatment should be the establishment of rapport and a trusting relationship with the family. The problem or problems are then made explicit, and a plan of action designed to overcome the problems is then suggested, or worked out with the family.

There are also several ways in which the likelihood of direct injunctions being successful may be increased. Instructions should be precise, positive rather than negative, and delivered with conviction. Rewards for compliance may help, family members may offer reminders to each other and altering the sequences of behaviours may be useful too.

Direct interventions involve 'first order' change and this is not always sufficient, especially in the more seriously troubled families. In these cases other approaches are needed. These are often indirect and part of a strategic plan.

Chapter 10

Strategic and Systemic Therapies

In Chapter 9 we considered some of the simpler and more straight-forward ways of intervening in families. It *is* sometimes possible to identify specific problems in the functioning of a family – for example communication difficulties, or poor role assignment or performance – and then to discuss with the family members how they can change their interactions so as to resolve such problems. This is the promotion of 'first order change', or the modification of the existing order of things.

In many cases first order change is not enough: direct injunctions, even if their rationale has been fully discussed and a plan of action negotiated with the family, do not bring about the desired results. More fundamental changes are therefore required. These 'second order' changes involve alterations of perspective; the family's situation, or some aspects of it, come to be looked at differently and understood in a new way. This is the process of 'reframing' – the giving of a different meaning to behaviour, feelings or relationships. For example, in 'developmental reframing' (Coppersmith, 1981), the antisocial behaviour of an adolescent might be reframed as behaviour that is young for the individual's age; the young person is thus neither 'mad' nor 'bad', but instead is regarded as immature and needing to grow up.

Strategic and systemic therapy methods are designed to bring about second order change. They have both been discussed in Chapter 4, but the distinction between them is not always clear. MacKinnon (1983) reviewed some of the approaches to therapy which have been called 'strategic' – those developed at the Mental Research Institute (MRI) (Watzlawick et al, 1974), and those developed by Haley (1976; 1980) and Madanes (1981) – and contrasted them with those of the Milan associates (Palazzoli, 1978; Palazzoli et al, 1978a), which have been labelled 'systemic'. Her paper provides an incisive and valuable analysis of the main features of the therapy schools she discusses.

The three main approaches – MRI, Haley/Madanes and Milan – are different in several respects, and MacKinnon's paper is recommended as a source of information on the differences. The Milan therapists tend to be even more 'systemic' in their approach than the others considered, but this is probably more a matter of degree than anything else. But all look at families as systems, and so can reasonably be called 'systemic', and all use strategies to help families change, so could be called 'strategic'. But then, as I have pointed out in Chapter 4, in a sense all therapy that has any aims at all could be called strategic, since the therapist is presumably always using some strategy intended to help produce change. To some extent, therefore, we are dealing with a semantic issue.

This chapter will consider various approaches that have been called 'strategic', and which all involve looking at the family, perhaps to varying degrees, systemically.

Looking at families systemically

Although it is hard to distinguish a school of 'systemic family therapy' – that of the Milan associates is perhaps better just called the 'Milan school' – looking at families as systems is basic to most family therapy. Sometimes it is not just the immediate family system that must be considered, but the extended family; grandparents, for example, can exercise a powerful influence on a family, even though they may live at a great distance.

General systems theory and its application to family therapy have been discussed in Chapter 3. The essence of the systemic approach to therapy is the belief that the family system is more than the sum of its parts, and that the system as a whole can be the focus of therapy. The symptoms of individual members of the family thus become simply manifestations of the way the family system is functioning. Concentrating on them, rather than on wider systems issues, will not bring about their resolution; it may even make matters worse, since it can reinforce the idea that it is the behaviour of the 'identified patient' that is the problem, rather than the way the family system as whole is structured or is functioning.

Among the most systemic of all therapists are the Milan associates (Palazzoli et al, 1978a), and others who adhere to their model (Tomm, 1984a; 1984b). In order to help maintain a systemic perspective, therapists of this school tend to work as teams; one or more colleagues observe through a one-way screen, and offer input to the therapist. This may be done during sessions by telephone, or it may be achieved by having one or more 'intersession breaks' during which the whole team discusses the family system. There are usually also pre and post session discussions.

Perhaps the least systemic are behavioural family therapists, who tend to focus on the interactions between specific family members, working mainly with dyads or, at the most, triads. Between these two extremes therapists may be placed on a continuum, according to the extent to which they use a systemic approach to clinical problems.

Taking a systemic perspective is itself a form of reframing, at least in cases in which such a perspective has not been taken previously. Rather than seeing the problem as being the mother's depression, the father's alcoholism, the son's behaviour disorder or the daughter's anorexia – or whatever else may be the presenting symptom – it is conceptualized as lying in the family system. The symptoms of individual family members are necessary, given the nature of the system as a whole. The concept of 'coherence' – or understanding the family as an 'organized coherent system' (Dell, 1982, and see also Chapter 3) – is helpful. The family is regarded as a unit with certain properties. It will respond in certain ways to particular interventions – or 'perturbations' – and the therapist's job is to find the perturbations which bring about the desired changes.

Whether the therapist makes the systemic view of the family's problems explicit during a therapy session is a matter of technique. It is not always necessary, or helpful, to do so, though the systemic perspective is usually implicit in what the therapist does.

Powerful support for a systems view, at least of children's behaviour, was provided by the Isle of Wight study of 10- and 11-year-old children (Rutter et al, 1970). In this large-scale epidemiological research project it was found that there was little overlap between the group of children identified as disturbed at home, and those showing disturbance at school. Evidently children's behaviour depends, to a great extent, upon their social context, as opposed to their own characteristics. It is also common to find that children's behaviour differs according to which family members are present; sometimes they are better behaved with one parent than with the other, and in other instances they may behave much better – or worse – with grandparents.

A systemic approach and indirect methods of promoting change are often employed together. Direct methods can, however, be systemic if they are addressed to the family as a whole, and are designed to produce change in the way the family functions as a group. Conversely, indirect methods, such as paradoxical ones, can be applied to individuals. Indeed Victor Frankl, one of the pioneers of the use of paradox in psychotherapy, was not a family therapist and worked mainly with individual patients. (See, for example, his report of the treatment of a woman with an obsessive–compulsive disorder (Frankl, 1960)).

Strategic methods of therapy

The term *strategic* is generally used to describe therapy that uses a plan, which may be quite complex, to produce change, rather than a simple directive or mutually agreed task. As Cloe Madanes puts it in her book *Strategic Family Therapy*, 'The responsibility is on the therapist to plan a strategy for solving the client's problems' (Madanes, 1981, page 19). Madanes considers that strategic therapy stems from the work of Milton Erickson. Many examples of his work are to be found in *Uncommon Therapy* (Haley, 1973) and in his own publications (Erickson 1980a; 1980b; 1980c; 1980d; 1980e). Erickson was certainly a master at working strategically with patients in his psychiatric practice, although according to Hammond (1984) he used direct methods of therapy most of the time. Strategic methods of solving human problems are not, however, new. 'Paradoxical intention', described by Frankl (1960) and referred to above, is an example of the use of a strategic plan in psychotherapy; and the book *Change: Principles of Problem Formulation and Problem Resolution* starts with the following account of a strategic approach to solving a problem:

> When in 1334 the Duchess of Tyrol, Margareta Maultasch, encircled the castle of Hochosterwitz in the province of Carinthia, she knew only too well that the fortress, situated on an incredibly steep rock rising high above the valley floor, was impregnable to direct attack and would only yield to a long siege. In due course, the situation of the defenders became critical; they were down to their last ox and had only two bags of barley corn left. Margareta's situation was becoming equally pressing, albeit it for different reasons: her troops were beginning to be unruly, there seemed to be no end to the siege in sight, and she had similarly urgent business elsewhere. At this point the commandant of the castle decided on a desperate course of action which to his men must have seemed sheer folly: he had the last ox slaughtered, had its abdominal cavity filled with the remaining barley, and ordered the carcass to be thrown down the steep cliff on to the meadow in front of the enemy camp. Upon receiving this scornful message from above, the discouraged duchess abandoned the siege and moved on. (Watzlawick et al, 1974, page xi)

This commandant would probably have made a good strategic therapist, since he apparently had a creative way of finding solutions to problems – if this was typical of him.

To Madanes (1981), strategic therapy is not a specific method to be applied to all cases but rather an approach which depends on devising a strategy for each clinical problem. The therapist takes responsibility for the therapy, clear goals are set and a strategy is developed, involving intervention in the client's social context, to deal with each problem. In many instances the social context concerned is the family, and strategic methods are widely used as the means of intervening in families.

There is an infinite number of possible therapeutic strategies, and the range of interventions available to us extends as far as the limits of our imagination and creativity. The following list of strategic techniques is not exhaustive, nor are the strategies mutually exclusive. Some of them – especially those described by the Milan group – would be called 'systemic' rather than 'strategic' by certain therapists. For our purposes, however, it is convenient to consider them all together.

• Reframing, including positive connotation.
• The use of metaphorical communication, which may take various forms.
• Giving paradoxical directives, including instructions to change either slowly or not at all.
• Prescribing rituals and other tasks.
• Declaring therapeutic impotence.
• Prescribing interminable therapy.
• Using humour.
• Using a consultation group as a 'Greek chorus'.
• Staging a debate.

This list is not exhaustive. Other strategic techniques are to be found in the literature, some of them in *Paradox and Counterparadox* (Palazzoli et al, 1978a), but I believe the above comprise a good representative sample.

Reframing and positive connotation

Reframing has been mentioned several times already. Any of the other devices listed above may be used to reframe situations, but reframing may also be done without using any of them. For instance, a child's non-compliant behaviour may be reframed as the parents' problem in controlling the child. This can be done during the course of conversation: when the parents have described the child's difficult behaviour, the therapist might comment, 'So you're having a hard time finding effective ways of handling Billy and getting his behaviour under control'. This kind of statement is hard to deny, though some parents may respond by saying they, and perhaps others, have tried 'everything' and 'nothing works' – the implication being that the child is 'impossible' and that the laws of learning theory have been suspended. Families may try to disqualify attempts to reframe situations in this way, but whatever the response, statements such as that above do offer a new perspective on the situation.

Other situations may be reframed during conversation as more serious, or less serious, than they have been considered, or as funny (when they have been considered serious), or surprising – or indeed anything they have not previously been considered to be by the clients.

Positive connotation is the ascribing of 'positive' or noble motives to the symptomatic behaviour of family members. It is thus a form of reframing, since usually the symptoms have previously been considered by all concerned to have 'negative' value – that is to be 'bad', or undesirable, behaviours. The value of positive connotation has been stressed by Palazzoli and her colleagues (1978a), who devote a chapter of their book *Paradox and Counterparadox* to the subject. Positive connotation, these authors believe, can be important, even essential, in the treatment of many of the more difficult families.

> It ... became clear that access to the systemic model was possible only if we were to make a positive connotation of *both* the symptom of the identified patient and the symptomatic behaviours of the others, saying, for example, that all the observable behaviours of the group as a whole appeared to be inspired by the common goal of preserving the cohesion of the family group. In this way, the therapists were able to put *all* the members of the group on the same level, thus avoiding involvement in any alliances or divisions into subgroups, which are the daily bread of such systems' malfunction. Dysfunctional families are in fact regularly, especially in moments of crisis, prone to such divisions and factional battles, which are characterized by the distribution of such stereotyped labels as 'bad', 'sick', 'weak', 'inefficient', carrier of hereditary or social taints', etc. (Palazzoli et al, 1978a, page 56)

It is not the symptomatic behaviour itself which is positively connoted, but the intent behind it. Palazzoli and her colleagues (1978a), on the basis of their study of severely disturbed families, make the assumption that the intent is to maintain the homeostatic balance within the family, so that it does not 'fall apart'. Positive connotation is also an important preliminary to the prescription of a paradoxical injunction; it makes a lot more sense to prescribe a behaviour which has been connotated as 'good' rather than one which has been called 'bad'.

Metaphorical communication

Metaphor offers many possibilities for the indirect communication of ideas and for strategic intervention in families. Two books – *Therapeutic*

Metaphors (Gordon, 1978) and *Using Metaphors in Psychotherapy* (Barker, 1985) – deal specifically with this therapeutic device, but the use of metaphor is described by many other authors, for example Madanes (1981) and Erickson, who used this device extensively, both in therapy and in teaching his students. *My Voice Will Go With You* (Erickson, 1982) is a collection of his 'teaching tales' and makes fascinating and entertaining reading. In *A Teaching Seminar with Milton H. Erickson* (Erickson, 1980a, edited by Zeig) Erickson again makes extensive use of metaphor, seldom answering a question from a student other than by telling a story with a meaning that in some way addresses the issue raised.

Metaphorical devices that may be used in therapy can be classified as follows:

1. Major stories designed to deal comprehensively with complex clinical situations. The construction of such stories is the main subject of Gordon's book *Therapeutic Metaphors* (1978).
2. Anecdotes and short stories aimed at achieving specific, limited goals.
3. Analogies, similes, and brief metaphorical statements or phrases that illustrate or emphasize specific points.
4. Relationship metaphors. A relationship metaphor uses one relationship, for example that between the therapist and one or more members of the family, as a metaphor for another relationship. Thus the therapist might explore the reason why a family member is absent from a session by asking the family members who *are* present questions like, 'Did I say something tactless to your father last time?', 'Did he feel left out of the discussion?', 'Have I shown him insufficient concern?', 'Did he feel in some way blamed for the family problems?' and 'How could I have made him feel more a part of the therapy process?'

   Such questions may cause family members to think about their own relationships with the missing family member. The discussion of the relationship between therapist and the father thus serves as a metaphor for that between other family members and the father.
5. Tasks with metaphorical meanings. These may be carried out during therapy sessions, or they may be prescribed to be performed between sessions. An example of the former category is the 'couples choreography' described by Papp (1982); in this procedure couples are asked first to close their eyes and have a 'dream' or 'fantasy' about their spouse. They are then asked to visualize themselves in the same fantasy. The fantasy is then enacted, under the therapist's guidance. The marital relationship is thus defined in metaphorical terms, and 'penetrates the confusing morass of verbiage that often sidetracks both couple and therapist...and reveals the ulterior level of

the relationship' (Papp, 1982, page 455). Papp's paper contains several interesting examples of this process.

6. Metaphorical objects. These are objects used during therapy to represent something other than what they actually are. Angelo (1981), for example, described the use of an envelope containing a blank sheet of paper to represent a family 'secret', that is an issue the family members were having difficulty dealing with, namely the fact that the son was adopted. By this means the family was able to talk about what was 'in the envelope' without specifying its nature. This enabled that particular block in the therapy process to be overcome.

7. Artistic metaphors. These are artistic productions, such as drawings, paintings, clay models or structures built with 'Lego', which are used to represent a feeling state, experience, or something else which may be significant in the treatment process.

The therapeutic use of artistic metaphors has been pioneered by Joyce Mills and Richard Crowley, and the creative way they have employed them is described in their book *Therapeutic Metaphors for Children and the Child Within* (Mills and Crowley, 1986). The essence of this technique is that clients who say, for example, that they are angry, or sad, or in pain, are asked to draw their pain, or to draw what 'angry' looks like. They can then draw the same thing getting better. The drawing thus becomes a metaphor for feelings, which people often have difficulty expressing in words. Mills and Crowley suggest that artistic metaphors can be useful when the therapist wishes to reframe a subject's experience in another sensory modality. The technique can be used during family therapy, or in individual work with children or adults.

The above classification is taken from *Using Metaphors in Psychotherapy* (Barker, 1985), in which the uses of the various types of metaphor are more fully discussed, and many examples are quoted. Further information about artistic metaphors is provided by Mills and Crowley (1986).

The use of paradox

People sometimes fail to do what therapists suggest. In other words, they do not respond to direct injunctions, even if all the facilitating devices described in Chapter 9 are used. This may be because they have reached a stable state, one that is comfortable for them despite the fact that one or more family members have symptoms. When a particular way of functioning has continued for a long time change may not occur easily. This applies especially in some families containing a psychotic member or members – that is people who are functioning in a way that is based on a false view of reality. If the family, or one or more members of it, are operating on the basis of delusional ideas, rather than in a rational, reality-based fashion, then rational and logical treatment methods may prove unsuccessful.

There is extensive literature on paradoxical psychotherapy. Frankl (1960) developed the technique of replacing efforts to extinguish symptoms by intentional, even exaggerated, efforts by the subject to carry out the symptomatic behaviour. He called this 'paradoxical intention'. Paradoxical techniques are discussed in detail, with examples, in the books *Change* (Watzlawick et al, 1974) and *The Tactics of Change* (Fisch et al, 1982), and many examples of the use of directives, both direct and paradoxical, are to be found in *Uncommon Therapy*, Haley's (1973) fascinating description of the work of Milton Erickson. In 1982 Weeks and L'Abate published a bibliography of the literature on the use of paradoxical injunction, and an outline of paradoxical methods and their application was provided by Barker (1981). In *Paradox and Counterparadox* (Palazzoli et al, 1978a) the Milan associates described creative ways, many of them involving the use of paradox, of treating families in 'schizophrenic transaction'. In 1982 the important book *Paradoxical Psychotherapy* by Gerald Weeks and Luciano L'Abate appeared; it also is a valuable source of information on the use of paradoxical therapy in various clinical situations.

Paradoxical methods are usually employed when direct methods have failed. Weeks and L'Abate (1982) recommend their use 'when a family and/or any of its subsystems is in a developmental crisis' (page 58). They also describe some 'dysfunctional transactions where paradoxical intervention appears especially appropriate' (page 60). These are:

1. Expressive fighting and bickering, which describes the situation in which members of a system relate to one another overtly by fighting. Weeks and L'Abate suggest that therapists who attempt to deal with such families in a straightforward way will find themselves at odds with them.
2. Unwillingness to cooperate with each other and complete assignments, which is a more passive and subtle way of expressing hostility than that found in families in the previous category. Such families may express verbal compliance with one another, but defeat each other non-verbally. There is often one marital partner who is more verbal and articulate than the other and who defeats the other by continuous complaints and diatribes; on the other hand, the second partner is more skilled non-verbally and achieves defeat of the first by non-verbal means.

3. Continuation of the same patterns in spite of all types of intervention, as is seen in the 'rigidly resistant' family.
4. 'Divide and conquer', the term used by Weeks and L'Abate for the situation which is especially seen in some families with teenagers skilled at separating the parents, and exploiting any polarization there may be in the marriage.
5. Using disqualifying communications, such as self-contradictions, inconsistencies, subject switching, metaphor (which can be used by clients to avoid defining or facing issues directly), and making cryptic statements.

As with other strategic techniques, the use of paradox presupposes that a desired outcome has been agreed upon by therapist and family. The family should also be actively engaged in the therapy process before these techniques are employed.

Weeks and L'Abate (1982, Chapter 5) provide an excellent account of how to work paradoxically. They define five 'basic principles', which are applicable to individuals as well as to couples and families. These are:

Principle One: New symptoms are positively relabelled, reframed, or connoted.

The value of reframing and positive connotation, as means of using symptoms to positive effect has been discussed above.

Principle Two: The symptom is linked to the other members of the family.

Family therapy is based on understanding the relationship context of clients' symptoms, and positively connoting the intent behind symptoms is often an effective way of putting symptoms in such a context.

Principle Three: Reverse the symptom's vector.

This procedure aims to put those concerned in charge of the symptom. In the case of individuals it involves the intentional enactment of the symptom, and sometimes also its deliberate amplification. In working with families, reversing the vector may be achieved either by having other members help the symptom-bearer have the symptom, or by having the other members play a paradoxical role; to use an example of the latter process provided by Weeks and L'Abate (1982), consider the case of a single-parent family in which a daughter is acting out and taking charge. To reverse the vector, the mother might be told to assume the role of child, giving up her position of authority and pretending to be a helpless child. Such measures place the people concerned in charge of the symptom or symptoms, which is the first step towards bringing about change.

Principle Four: Prescribe and sequence paradoxical interventions over time in order to bind off the reappearance of the symptom.

By this principle Weeks and L'Abate mean that a series of interventions over a period of time is usually needed, rather than a single one. A sequence of interventions which these authors recommend as often effective is:

1. Positive relabelling, reframing, or connotation.
2. Symptom prescription.
3. Predicting a relapse.
4. Prescribing a relapse.

Prescribing a relapse in families which respond 'negatively' to injunctions is, of course, a way of preventing relapse.

Principle Five: The paradoxical prescription must force the client(s) to act on the task in some way.

Good rapport is a basic requirement in ensuring that therapeutic prescriptions are carried out, but in addition they may be ritualized, for example by prescribing them in a fixed sequence, or by laying down that whenever event X occurs the client is to have the symptom. Paradoxical prescriptions can also be put in writing.

Haley (1976, pages 72-75) suggested eight steps in giving paradoxical directives:

(a) A relationship must be established with the client(s). This should be defined as one directed to producing change.
(b) The problem must be clearly defined.
(c) Clear goals must be set. The therapist must understand precisely the changes the directive is designed to bring about.
(d) A plan must be offered. It is helpful to offer some rationale for the paradoxical directive. This may be that it is necessary to continue with the symptom, or even increase its intensity, because to abandon it would be 'too risky' or 'too difficult for the rest of the family'. For example a thirteen-year-old boy and his stepmother were told that it was essential that they express their hostile feelings towards each other, since 'bottling them up' would create too much tension in them both. At the same time a specific fifteen minute time each day was agreed for the expression of these feelings.
(e) Anyone who is an authority on the problems must be disqualified. One way is to suggest that the person would be upset if the symptom disappeared. Another is to praise that person's self-sacrifice but suggest another area of the subject's life where self-sacrifice would be more important. In the case above the stepmother initially raised objections to the plan, saying that she did not believe in children and their parents insulting each other. It was, she

said, against the principles she lived by. Her views were commended as praiseworthy, and the therapist said that he too did not believe in this sort of thing. He realized that it seemed crazy to encourage undesired behaviour, but it was important for him to know how the experiment would work out, in order to plan further treatment. He complimented the stepmother on her willingness to consider compromising her principles for this purpose, whereupon she agreed to take part in the suggested plan of action.

(f) The paradoxical directive is given. In the case of the boy and the stepmother, they were to meet at a set time every day when each would say what he or she disliked in the other, and how the other person had irritated or annoyed him or her during the previous twenty-four hours. They could be as frank and insulting as they chose. Such matters were only to be discussed at that time, however; if the son and stepmother were tempted to discuss them at other times they were to postpone doing so until the set time.

(g) The response is observed and the therapist continues to encourage the undesired behaviour, especially if the behaviour shows signs of improving. The therapist's pleasure at this turn of events should be hidden, and doubt expressed that the improvement will continue. In the case mentioned above there was a rapid improvement, but the therapist warned that it might not continue.

(h) The therapist should not accept credit for change as it occurs. Puzzlement is often better, combined with some scepticism about whether the changes that have occurred are real and will continue.

There is often an element of challenge in paradoxical directives.

A family came for therapy with complaints about the antisocial behaviour of the thirteen-year-old son, but actually talked about little except their nineteen-year-old unmarried daughter and her son, aged one-and-a-half. Father, mother, son, and seventeen-year-old daughter all complained about the behaviour of the nineteen-year-old who – characteristically – had refused to come to the family interview. They said that she took no part in caring for her son, consistently failed to contribute from her wages the sum she had agreed to pay for her keep and that of her son, was dirty, lazy, self-centred, a liar and prone to take things without asking. She often 'borrowed', and damaged, her sister's clothes and other property. It seemed she had total control over the household. As an infant she had had a kidney removed for cancer. Her parents had expected that she would die and had apparently indulged her greatly when she was younger.

The situation was discussed fully with the family. The parents were aware of the need to achieve control of their wayward daughter, but had tried 'everything' without any success. It seemed that the daughter used the family's apartment as a sort of free hotel. It was pointed out that she would undoubtedly continue to do this if allowed, and that the only alternative would be to make staying in the household conditional upon certain specific behaviours, such as paying her 'rent', doing her share of caring for her son and of the household chores, and generally acting as a constructive adult member of the family. If these conditions were not met she would have to be asked to leave and live elsewhere; changing the locks or seeking the help of the police to remove her might even be necessary.

Having spelt this out, the therapist said he believed this course of action would be impossible for the parents. Their concern and love for their daughter was too great. It would be better, and less distressing, for them to accept continuation of the present situation. So he advised against this plan – though not until after he had spelt it out in detail. The parents, led by the father, immediately said no, they *would* take control of their daughter; she was quite capable of taking care of herself and had done so when she first left home two-and-a-half years previously. She was earning enough to rent her own apartment. The present situation had gone on long enough, they said. The therapist expressed doubts about whether the parents could ever bring themselves to offer this choice to their daughter – at least if they were sincere in their intention to tell her to leave the home if she didn't shape up.

The parents left expressing their intention to carry through with the plan, and they did so. The daughter decided to leave and found her own accommodation; she continued in her job, became financially self-supporting, and signed over guardianship of her son to her parents – a situation with which all concerned seemed well satisfied.

A simple, and often effective, example of the use of paradox is 'prescribing the symptom'. The case of the mother and stepson who were told to meet together for fifteen minutes daily, mentioned above, is an example of this process. Another was described by Hare-Mustin (1975). This was the case of a four-year-old with temper tantrums which occurred frequently and unpredictably. The therapist negotiated with the child and his family where the tantrums should occur, picking a safe place at home. If the boy started to have a trantrum he was to be taken to that place – the 'tantrum place'. By the next session a week later Tommy had had only one tantrum, so the therapist then said it was necessary to decide what time the tantrums should take place. The period 5.00 to 7.00 pm was agreed upon. As expected it proved hard for the child to have tantrums to order and the symptom was soon extinguished.

It is also possible to prescribe that a symptom occur during a therapy session. In most cases the symptoms are not produced under these circumstances. This was so, for example, in the case of William, aged eight, and described at greater length elsewhere (Barker, 1985, pages 30-32).

William also had severe tantrums, and these had failed to improve despite several attempts at therapy. In the course of a family interview he was asked to have a tantrum, so that the therapist could see exactly what his tantrums were like. He declined to do so, despite some pressure from the therapist. The parents were therefore asked to have a cassette recorder ready in the home at all times, so that the tantrums could be recorded and played back to the therapist at the next session. This proved a remarkably effective way of eliminating the problem. The cassette recorder functioned as a metaphorical object and represented the therapist. William was now supposed to have tantrums, so that the therapist could be given recordings of them. His tendency to respond negatively to what he was told to do, however, led him to abandon having them.

How and why do paradoxical directives work? It seems that an important factor is the taking over of the symptom by the therapist who, instead of attempting to stop it, is perceived by the client(s) as encouraging it, at least in certain circumstances. This is a new situation for the individual or family, and it evokes a new response. When it is a family that is being treated it disturbs the family's homeostatic processes, so that some change in their way of functioning becomes necessary. A metaphor for this situation might be the situation of a man who is trying to open a door that is stuck closed; he is encouraged to push harder and harder, until suddenly it gives, and then a quick change in the direction of his energies is required or he will fall to the floor.

It is worth noting, too, that in the case of the rebellious nineteen-year-old recounted above, the therapist implicitly reframed the family situation. He was presented, after the son had been used as an 'admission ticket', with a rebellious teenage girl as the problem and was, it seemed, expected to do 'something' about it – despite the fact that the parents had already tried 'everything'. To enter into treating the family on this basis is a recipe for failure. So he reframed things so that the issue became the parents' problem. This was realistic. The daughter was quite happy living in her free hotel, and from her point of view there was no need to make any changes. She did not even deign to come with the family to see the therapist. If there was to be change the rest of the family had to make a move and it was through a paradoxical intervention that they were enabled to do so. Note, too, that the problem was that of overcoming a developmental hurdle – that of letting the daughter leave the nest and become an independent person in society – a situation in which paradoxical methods seem to have particular application.

Rituals and tasks

The setting of tasks and the performance of rituals are used by many family therapists as devices to promote change. Wolin and Bennett (1984) have pointed out that rituals are 'a powerful component of family life', and one that is 'central to the identity of the family'. Providing new rituals, or altering pre-existing ones, can therefore be powerful change-promoting devices. The ritualizing of tasks set as part of a strategic (or other) therapy plan can also help ensure that the tasks are performed.

Wolin and Bennett (1984) divide family rituals into family celebrations (weddings, baptisms, bar mitzvahs, religious celebrations and so forth); family traditions (ritualized activities specific to the family, such as summer vacations, visits to extended family members, family reunions, birthday and other parties and so on); and patterned family interactions, often not consciously planned (such as regular dinner-times, bedtime routines for children, customary treatment of guests and weekend leisure activities). The modification, or prescribing, of rituals in any of these categories may be used to promote change in families. Otto van der Hart, in his book *Rituals in Psychotherapy* (1983), provides another valuable account of the use of rituals, both in psychotherapy and in other situations.

Discussing the therapeutic use of rituals in family therapy, Sutcliffe et al (1985) list the following purposes they can serve: supporting competence; increasing skills; differentiating roles; establishing hierarchies; influencing expectations; altering communication patterns; developing support systems; challenging stereotypes; introducing rewards; and promoting proximity or challenging enmeshment. Tasks, whether ritualized or not, may be used as a form of direct therapy as, for example, when parents are told to get together to decide on rules for their children's behaviour, or on the rewards to be given to the children when they conform to the rules. In strategic therapy, however, tasks usually have a hidden meaning, as well as a more obvious one.

Rituals are often employed as components of strategic plans, which may also involve one or more other strategic devices or concepts. For example, the case of the boy with temper tantrums reported by Hare-

Mustin (1975), and mentioned in the preceding section, involved the ritualization of the symptom as well as the use of paradox. Not only was the child told to have tantrums, but these were to occur at a particular time and place.

Rituals have long been used to assist people in moving from one developmental stage to another. Van der Hart (1983) discusses the 'rituals of transition', which are features of the lives of many primitive tribal communities. They include initiation rites for women, marriage rituals and birth rituals. In western society, as Wolin and Bennett (1984) point out, we too have marriage ceremonies, funerals, house-warming parties, retirement parties, birthdays and so forth. The Jewish bar mitzvah is, however, one of the few currently practised rites marking the assumption of a more adult role in society; it seems our adolescents therefore often stage their own rites of transition, which tend to take the form of wild parties and the rather conspicuous rejection of the 'child' role which they have previously played. In some other societies, however, formal puberty rites are given great importance.

According to Wallace (1966, page 203), 'rites of passage are a type of ritual which educates participants for, announces publicly, and initiates a new relationship'. Similarly therapeutic rituals can educate people for, announce and initiate new relationships, which therapy often aims to promote.

Therapeutic rituals are discussed at length by van der Hart (1983). His book contains examples of rituals dealing with detoxification, healing in various forms – including exorcising illness – saying goodbye, bereavement, transitions, spoiled children, and separation, among other things. Most rituals have a symbolic or metaphorical meaning. The following, for example, is one such, reproduced from *Using Metaphors in Psychotherapy* (Barker, 1985).

Fay had lived in a common-law relationship with George for 18 months. The relationship was a stormy one and Fay was highly ambivalent about it. When she eventually decided to leave George she and her two sons nevertheless mourned his loss a great deal. Fay complained that she couldn't sleep at night, thought constantly about George, was unable to concentrate and felt lonely. At interview she also appeared moderately depressed. It seemed important that she discard the unhappy associations and memories, as she came to terms with the separation. Had she not resolved her feelings she might have been tempted to seek a reconciliation with George, as she had done with men she had previously lived with.

Fay still had a number of items in the house which reminded her of

George. Some were things which had belonged to him but he had left behind, while others were things he had given her.

After exploring Fay's feelings and situation carefully with her, the therapist gave her the following task. She was to go through everything in the house that had belonged to George and decide whether it was worth keeping or whether it was something that would be better got rid of. The two classes of things were to be placed in different boxes. Fay was then to take the box of things that were not worth keeping, make a fire in the backyard and burn the box and its contents. As she did so she was to feel free to weep as much as she felt like doing.

The other box now contained all those things of George's that Fay valued. These were to be packed carefully and Fay was to dig a hole in her backyard and bury them. This was a symbolic act of preserving the good things about George and the happy times they had spent together.

Fay carried out the task as directed. When she returned to the therapist, however, she reported that she had been unable to weep at the burial because 'so much trash was not worth wasting tears over'. She also reported that she was now feeling a lot better and was once again getting a good night's sleep. She no longer appeared depressed and seemed to be making good progress in the business of mourning and coming to terms with the loss of George.

Fay was faced with the problem of making a transition in her life – and quite an abrupt one too. The ritual actions prescribed were designed to have appropriate metaphorical meanings and to assist her in making the transition. They did indeed appear to be helpful to her.

Rituals can be used at any stage in the therapy process, including termination. When finishing treatment it can be helpful to give clients something to take away with them, as a continuing resource. Imber-Black (in press) describes the creative use of rituals in terminating therapy. In one case, that of a family containing a 12-year-old girl with an eating problem, two metaphorical objects were offered the family, to be used in a ritualistic way. Among the very few foods the girl would eat were french fried potatoes. She had also been seeing a dietician who urged her to eat kiwi fruit, something she hated.

At the final therapy session the therapist handed the family a potato and a kiwi fruit, and told them to put them in a plastic bowl, fill the bowl with water, and place it in the back of the freezer. Then if at any time in the future they found themselves unsure what to do about a family problem, they were to remove the bowl from the freezer, allow the contents to thaw, and have a family discussion about the seriousness of the problem and the course of action they should take. The two objects symbolized the process the family had been going through, and the ritual was designed to help them recall and again make use of the problem-solving skills they had learned during therapy. The ritual may also have been helpful because it gave the family time to reflect on the situation while the contents of the bowl thawed, rather than reacting precipitately.

The prescribing of rituals is also described by the Milan associates (Palazzoli et al, 1978a), and Palazzoli et al, (1978b) coined the term 'ritualized prescription' and applied it to 'odd days and even days' tasks. They use this strategy with certain families in which children are the identified patients. Its essence is that one parent – let us say the father – makes all the decisions about the 'problem' child on even days, that is Tuesdays, Thursdays and Saturdays; while the mother does the same thing on odd days, that is Mondays, Wednesdays and Fridays. On Sundays everyone is to behave spontaneously. Each parent, when it is his or her turn to be in charge, has absolute discretion to make decisions about the identified patient. The other parent acts as if not there, as far as such decisions are concerned, and the parent who is in charge must note in writing any infringement of this rule by the other one.

There is more to most strategic therapy devices than simply the carrying out of the task; indeed they can be effective even though the tasks or rituals are not carried out at all. Thus the 'odd days–even days' prescription carries a number of important messages, which are implicit in the task. One is that *someone* has to be in charge of the children and make the key decisions concerning them – a point that is not directly stated and might be disputed by some families if it were. ('They're old enough to look after themselves', might be the response.) Another is that both parents need to share the responsibility of caring for, and making decisions relating to, the children. The setting of the task makes these points even if the ritual is never carried out. The ritual may also suggest that the parents need to have different roles, or that one may be a more effective, or more appropriate, disciplinarian in certain circumstances. Finally, there is an implied contrast between 'spontaneous' and controlled behaviour, and the opportunity is provided to observe, on Sundays, how far family members have progressed in internalizing the lessons they have learned in therapy, and thus behaving 'spontaneously' in an acceptable fashion.

Declaring therapeutic impotence

Chapter 16 of the book *Paradox and Counterparadox* (Palazzoli et al, 1978a) is entitled 'The therapists declare their impotence without blaming anyone'. This strategic manoeuvre, which is really another example of the use of paradox, can be effective when the family and the therapist have become locked in a symmetrical relationship. In such a situation every intervention the therapist attempts to make is in some way blocked or disqualified, so that the strength of the symmetrical conflict steadily increases. The Milan associates described the delivery of this intervention as follows:

> We say that in spite of the willing collaboration of the family, which has done everything possible to facilitate our understanding, we find ourselves confused and incapable of forming clear ideas, of helping them, and that the team has in no way clarified our ideas. The attitude of the therapists should be neither indifferent nor overdramatic but simply that of those who dislike acknowledging their incapacity in doing what has been asked of them.
>
> In saying this, we attentively observe the feedbacks of the various members of the family. We leave a pause of 'suspense', fix the date for the family's next session, and collect our fee. (Palazzoli et al, 1978a, page 148)

The timing of this intervention is important. Palazzoli and her colleagues emphasize that it should not be done too soon. They suggest that the right time is when the 'angry obstinacy of the therapists' (the Milan group usually work as a team, so we will use the plural), together with the family's reinforcing of its disqualifications of the therapists, indicate escalation of the symmetrical battle. The intervention is, of course, designed to put an end to the battle, and is another example of the use of the 'one-down' position in therapy. It also avoids the therapists appearing as the initiators of change; if they did seem to be playing that role, in a family such as we are discussing, the family would regard them as hostile, and would continue to defend its position.

This device has the effect of creating a complementary relationship between therapists and family; it might seem to be one in which the therapists are giving over control to the family, but in reality they are taking control. There is also a paradox in the contrast between the declaration of impotence on the one hand, and the collection of a fee and the making of a further appointment on the other. At a certain level the intervention involves an invitation to the family to come up with something new, and challenges them to prove that the implication in the intervention – namely that their case is hopeless – is wrong.

Prescribing interminable therapy

Yet another strategic device is the prescription of interminable therapy. Its purpose is similar to that of declaring therapeutic impotence. The symptoms, or the family problem, are labelled as chronic and unlikely to change quickly; such a prescription might be indicated when efforts to get the family to change quickly – or perhaps to change at all – have failed. In effect, the family is told it will have to attend indefinitely at prescribed intervals. This intervention, too, incorporates a paradoxical element.

Humour

It can often help to see the funny side of things – in family therapy as much as in many other of life's activities. Pauline Sutcliffe, Jane Lovell and Marianne Walters (1985), in an article entitled, 'New directions for family therapy: rubbish removal as a task of choice', point out that 'family therapists, if they take families seriously, need to be able to laugh and joke with them'. The article reframes the disposal of rubbish – in North America it's known as garbage – as a worthwhile, indeed valuable activity, and one which we should not feel guilty about asking our children to perform. Nor need we be reluctant to perform it ourselves, for it may be just what we, as therapists, need to do.

Frankl (1960) encouraged his patients to laugh at their symptoms, and Erickson also advocated the use of humour. For example he said:

> In teaching, in therapy, you are very careful to use humour, because your patients bring in enough grief, and they don't need all that grief and sorrow. You better get them into a more pleasant frame of mind right away. (Quoted in Erickson, 1980e, edited by Zeig, page 71)

The use of humour is a very personal thing and depends, perhaps more than any other therapy device, on the therapist's personality, and on non-verbal communications as well as verbal ones. The aim, usually, is to laugh *with*, not *at*, the family. Doing this can both help establish and maintain rapport, and assist in reframing things. For example, children's behaviour, which may have been arousing their parents' severe disapproval, can sometimes be shown to have a funny side – another example of reframing.

Humour is a double-edged therapeutic weapon. Its use presupposes some understanding of the family's sense of humour. Without this our jokes may fall flat or – more serious – remarks which are intended as jokes may be taken seriously. Yet despite these possible disadvantages, humour is a valuable therapeutic tool and skill in its use is well worth developing.

The 'Greek chorus'

The use of the 'Greek chorus' in family therapy was described by Papp (1980). This technique was devised by the staff of the Ackerman Brief Therapy Project, who regularly used a 'consultation group' to aid the therapist working with the family. This group, watching the session through a one-way observation screen, sent a series of messages into the therapy room, rather like a Greek chorus. Papp (1980) lists some of the types of message sent:

- Support messages. These simply praise or support certain aspects of the family.
- Public opinion polls. These take, and report to the family, the odds on the family changing. They can thus present families with challenges.
- Messages designed to surprise and confuse. Surprise and confusion can be important elements in promoting change, and these messages are intended to arouse the family's curiosity, stir their imagination, or provoke them into revealing hidden information.
- Messages disagreeing with the therapist's expressed opinion. Therapeutic 'splits' can help promote change; usually the therapist in the room advocates change, while the 'Greek chorus' advises against it at the present time, or against the proposed speed of change. This is a process similar to that described in the case history included in the section on the use of paradox (page 181), though in that case the therapist offered both alternatives himself.
- Messages offering advice from outside the circle of therapist and family. These can reframe situations, and bring psychological pressures to bear on families in various ways.

While a consultation group can always be helpful, it is especially so when complex paradoxical and other strategic devices are used. It is costly in terms of staff time, but this may be considered worthwhile for severely disturbed families, resistant to other interventions, and as a method of speeding up therapy. Moreover the Greek chorus may consist mainly, even entirely, of students, and thus be a valuable learning experience for them.

The debate

The debate as a strategic therapy device is described by Sheinberg (1985), another member of the staff of the Ackerman Institute. It is a development of the use of the Greek chorus. The consultation group, or 'strategic team', come out from behind the one-way screen and stage a debate in the presence of the family. The debate concerns 'a dilemma that is a strategically constructed isomorph of the family situation. From this position, therapists have the option of changing levels between themselves and the family, asking the family to help solve the therapists' dilemma so that they can be free to help the family (Sheinberg, 1985, page 259).

The family members are able to observe the therapists' struggles to resolve their difficulties from a 'meta' – or outside – position. From this different perspective they may be able to find new solutions to their own dilemma.

Summary

Most family therapists prefer to consider families systemically, rather than paying attention primarily to the psychopathology of the individual members. Taking such a view is a form of 'reframing' – that is, causing something to be looked at from a different perspective. Systemic approaches to therapy use methods which address the family system as a whole. The 'direct' methods discussed in the previous chapter are sometimes effective, but often fail to bring about the desired changes. When this is so indirect, or strategic, methods are required.

The strategic therapist devises a strategy, or plan, which is intended to bring about the changes the family seek - changes which must first have been defined. If the strategy is not effective, the therapist will nevertheless have acquired some useful new information about the family. This will assist in the planning of another strategic intervention. This process may need to be repeated several times before the changes sought have been achieved.

Reframing, and positive connotation – the ascribing of 'positive' intent to symptomatic behaviours – are basic strategic manoeuvres and are aimed at giving new meaning to the actions and attitudes of family members. Other strategic devices include metaphorical communication, the use of paradox, giving families ritualized tasks to perform, declaring therapeutic impotence, prescribing interminable therapy, using humour to give situations different meanings or values, employing a 'Greek chorus' to comment from behind the one-way screen, and staging a debate by members of the therapy team in the presence of the family. The devices in this list are not mutually exclusive, nor are they the only ones which may be used. The range of possible therapeutic strategies is restricted only by the limits of the imagination and creativity of the therapist. Most, however, involve the reframing of situations or behaviour to give them new meaning.

Chapter 11

Other Therapeutic Techniques

In addition to the direct therapy methods mentioned in Chapter 9, and the strategic approaches discussed in Chapter 10, many other therapeutic techniques have been described. In this chapter we will examine some of the more important of these.

Family sculpting

'Sculpture' as a family therapy technique was developed by Frederick Duhl and his colleagues (1973). It has also been used extensively by Peggy Papp, who has made a commercial videotape to illustrate it (Papp, see references). The essential feature of family sculpting is the placing of family members in positions and postures that represent aspects of their relationships and interactions with each other. Any aspect of family functioning may be sculpted, for example closeness or power.

Family sculpting requires a *sculptor*, whose view of the family it is that is revealed in the sculpture; a *monitor*, namely the therapist, who guides and supports the sculptor and the others involved in the process; and the *actors*, usually the family members, who portray the sculptor's system. There may also be an *audience*, but usually the family members and the therapist both play the other roles mentioned and comprise the audience.

An excellent account of family sculpting was given by Walrond-Skinner (1976), who included in her description of the process drawings of the sculptures created by the different family members in a particular case. Walrond-Skinner (1976) believes that the technique is useful for involving young children in therapy; for them non-verbal methods of expression are more natural. It can also be a useful diagnostic procedure and a substitute for asking a family to describe their problems. Families can be asked to describe the changes they want to see by sculpting their idealized family. Walrond-Skinner also considered sculpting as a useful way of helping family members get in touch with their feelings; another use is in overcoming families' resistance to therapy, and it can be something to do 'when the therapist just feels stuck'.

The therapist introduces the idea of sculpting to the family, perhaps by suggesting that they try something different. The idea should be put forward enthusiastically and a family member should be selected to be the first sculptor. It is best to start with someone likely to respond willingly to the suggestion. This may be an adult or a child. If there is in the family a child who has been having difficulty putting things into words, this may be a good person to choose; or someone who has been relatively uninvolved in the therapy may be chosen.

Once the sculptor has been chosen the other members of the family are asked to stand up and then move to whatever position and posture the sculptor directs. The therapist must make it clear what everyone is to do, and initially some encouragement may be needed. The rules of the procedure have to be clearly defined, especially the one that the actors must do whatever the sculptor says. Once this has been accepted, so that the sculptor is not overcome by the family's power struggles, the therapist can begin to observe what happens and comment upon or interpret it. It is usually helpful to emphasize from time to time that this is just one view of the family, and that the other members will be able to express their points of view in the same way later.

Once the tableau is completed, which may not be until after a lot of discussion and comment, the therapist may ask the sculptor also to enter it, in an appropriate position and posture.

The therapist should have, at the outset, an idea of what the family sculpting is designed to achieve, that is of how it is intended to help the family achieve the objectives of therapy. Both the process of sculpting and the finished tableau are therefore used to assist in restructuring the family, or for some other purpose, such as clarifying or changing communication, feelings or roles. Sculpting can thus be an adjunct to other treatment approaches.

Role playing

Role playing is another 'action technique' which can be useful when verbal approaches prove ineffective. It can be especially valuable in families which intellectualize, that is discuss things on a cognitive level and produce intellectual ideas and explanations, rather than real change. Facilitating real change in such families presents a considerable challenge, and it can help to have them act out scenes or events from their life. For example, a family might be asked to act out what happens when father returns home from work or when it is time for the children to go to bed, if these appear to be times when the family dysfunction is evident. If the family members are hesitant or reluctant about role playing, the therapist may start with a simple, non-threatening scene; but if rapport has been well established, obtaining agreement to what is suggested usually does not present difficulty.

Like sculpting, role playing brings the reality of family life into the therapy session, and gives the therapist material with which to work. This is especially valuable when the family is inhibited in the therapy room and so does not behave 'naturally' – that is, in the way it does in other situations. Role playing can also serve to bring a family's mode of functioning to life in an assessment interview, when this is needed.

Videotape replay

Alger (1969, 1973) has written extensively on videotape replay – the playing back to families of tapes of their therapy sessions. Whole therapy sessions may be played back, or arbitrarily selected portions may be used. Another alternative is 'focused replay' (Stoller, 1968), in which brief sections considered by the therapist to be of particular significance are played back.

Videotape replay enables family members to see what is going on in the family 'from the outside', as it were. They can observe not only what they are saying, but also their tone of voice, facial expression, body posture, and other non-verbal behaviour. For families with a strong conscious desire to change, videotape replay can be an effective way of defining and getting members to understand how they may be able to change. In other families it can promote understanding of the need to change.

The effects of seeing and hearing oneself and one's family on tape can be salutory.

A family in which the children were anxious to know how the videotaping process worked was taken, following a therapy session, into the viewing room in which the recording equipment was installed. Part of the tape was played back for them to see. This was not intended as a therapeutic move, except insofar as it provided a model of openness about the process. Having watched a few minutes of tape, however, the four-year-old son commented, apparently in all innocence, 'Why do you talk all the time, Daddy?' The segment of tape had indeed included a lot of talking by the father, who tended to be a bombastic, controlling and very talkative person.

This remark, said openly in front of the family, therapist and technician, seemed to have a marked effect upon the father. He returned to the next session much more aware of his over-dominant role in the family, and open to making changes.

Alger (1973) points out that the availability of relatively inexpensive closed circuit television equipment makes the use of videotape replay in therapists' offices a practical and economic proposition; and equipment has come down in price even further, as well as improving in quality, since 1973. The basic requirements are a camera, a videotape recorder, and a monitor. Such equipment can readily be operated by the therapist, though Alger suggests that it can be helpful to have family members operate the camera at times; what they choose to focus on can be revealing, and family members can sharpen their observational skills by this means.

Alger (1973) also mentions the use of such special effects as shutting off the sound and viewing the picture only; making serial recordings, that is recordings consisting of short segments from a succession of interviews; and videotaping role play. All these things can be done with simple equipment. Also possible, though needing more expensive equipment and facilities, are the use of split-screen techniques, slow motion, fast motion, and still framing. Split-screen techniques can be used to show people side-by-side when they are really sitting apart; this can draw attention to how they react to each other.

The uses of videotape we have discussed serve to draw family members' attention to how the family functions generally, and particularly to the interactions between its various members. They are perhaps primarily a means of promoting insight into the processes occurring in the family, and the relationships between the members. Videotape applications are therefore likely to fit most easily into a direct therapeutic plan, though indirect and strategic uses of videotape replay are certainly possible.

Network therapy

Network therapy was described by Speck (1969; 1971). In its classical form it is probably used rather rarely. It consists of getting the family's complete 'network' together; the network consists of the kinship system, the family's friends, and other significant people. This may mean that as many as thirty or forty people are assembled to work on the problem. It is claimed that by having all significant people present, progress in therapy may be possible where it otherwise would not be. One advantage of the procedure is that blame cannot be placed on absent family members, because they are all there; another is to add the voices and opinions of healthier, better functioning people to the therapy process.

Various examples of the application of network therapy are to be found in the literature. A useful one is reported by Rueveni (1975), who describes the use of four network sessions in the treatment of a couple who presented with conflicts in their relationship. There was major disagreement about their sixteen-year-old son. Network therapy was started when the crisis continued despite more conventional therapy. In addition to the family members, six of the son's friends came to the first session. Rueveni's paper describes the considerable improvements in the family situation that were achieved in four sessions. Network meetings, without the therapist present, continued for three months after the last of the four sessions. The author believed that the breakthrough that occurred as a result of network sessions was possible 'because of the intensity of the involvement and caring on the part of those network activists who maintained a continuous support'. Each of the three 'nuclear' family members was henceforth able to rely on other family members for advice, suggestions and support when needed. The process is thus, in part, a way of mobilizing the extended family supports which so many contemporary families lack.

Gatti and Coleman (1976) described what they called *community network therapy*. Their approach arose out of school consultation work in a small New England town. Using structural family therapy techniques as their basic approach, they also established and maintained continuing contact with all the 'important extra-familial people and institutions', to which they could gain access. They report contacts with extended family, neighbours and friends; responsible people from schools, public welfare, the housing authority, employment agencies and courts; interested members of private groups such as charitable, church and children's organizations; and such professional groups as doctors, lawyers and ministers of religion. Gatti and Coleman considered themselves also to be a part of the wider community network, and their paper contains a number of interesting ideas about how to involve, work with and help families get into contact with those people in the community who may be of help to them.

Network therapy is a means of tackling the problems in the suprasystems of families. There is a limit to the effectiveness of therapy which stops short at the boundary of the nuclear family. Many therapists recognize this, and Minuchin (1974, page 130), in his classical account of the structural approach, makes it clear that the therapist should review 'the family life context, analyzing the sources of support and stress in the family's ecology'. Family boundaries are not impermeable, and what happens outside them can help or hinder family functioning.

An important part of a school-age child's ecological context is the school, and the school/family relationship often requires the therapist's attention. A child's behaviour and adjustment in school can be regarded as a function of the family situation; if the parents want the child to behave well in school, then it is reasonable to consider it as a family problem when the child is not so behaving. But while children's failure to behave or perform satisfactorily in school sometimes seems to be related to the situation at home, this is not invariably so. There can be systems problems in school classes or even in entire schools (Rutter et al, 1979).

When a schoolchild is the identified patient, the school is part of the family's suprasystem, or network, to which attention most often needs to be given during therapy. There are various ways of involving schools in the therapy process. One or more meetings of family – or at least the parents and the child concerned – and the relevant school staff, may be useful. It is important that all the key members of the school staff are present. These normally include the child's own teacher or teachers; the person who has the authority in the school, usually the principal but perhaps a vice-principal; and the guidance teacher, school counsellor or school psychologist – if these people are involved. Aponte (1976) provided an excellent account of the purposes of family-school interviews, and how to conduct them, together with an illustrative case. The procedure he recommends is a good one, and his paper is worthwhile reading for therapists dealing with school/family problems.

Aponte recommends that, when referral comes from the school because of problems there, the first interview should be at the school, and should include family and school staff.

Multiple family therapy

Multiple family therapy, or multi-family therapy, apparently had its origin in 1951 when, as Peter Laqueur (1973) explained much later, he started bringing family members together to explain to them the insulin therapy that was being carried out in a psychiatric hospital unit. According to Laqueur the term *multiple family therapy* was coined by Carl Wells in 1963; Wells was co-author of a paper on the subject published later (Laqueur et al, 1969).

As described by Laqueur (1976), multiple family therapy consists of a meeting of four or five identified patients, who may be inpatients or outpatients, together with their families – parents, siblings, spouses, children. The sessions are usually weekly and last one-and-a-half hours.

Videotape and playback facilities are considered useful and the groups are open-ended, that is members may join and leave during the life of the group. The theoretical basis of the work is general systems theory, and multiple family therapy is designed to effect changes in the family systems. Opening exercises include asking the mothers in the group to say what they think of themselves and how they rate themselves as mothers and wives. The fathers are then asked to describe themselves and rate how they perform their roles. Next the children may be asked to divide themselves into a 'good' and a 'bad' group, and then to state briefly their problems with their families.

As therapy proceeds various action techniques, including family sculpting procedures modified from those of Peggy Papp (discussed earlier in this chapter), and videotape playback, may be used. Laqueur believes that the presence of several families can assist in various ways. One of these is by breaking the 'family code' – its own secret means of verbal and non-verbal communication. The presence of several families may also stimulate competition between the families to produce change; it may help the families learn through trial and error, and by observing the different responses of the other families; and it may promote change through learning by analogy and identification. The therapist can also use one family as a model for another; or one can be used as a challenge to motivate another. In addition the adoption by a member family of a healthier or more realistic way of behaving can be a 'focus of excitation' for the whole group. Raasoch and Laqueur (1979) discussed the teaching of multiple family therapy. They recommend the use of workshops with simulated families as the best and quickest method.

A helpful review of 'multiple family therapy systems' is that of Anna Benningfield (1980), who includes a summary of the main pioneering articles on the subject.

Vector therapy

We owe the concept of vector therapy to the work of John Howells, Director of the Institute of Family Psychiatry, in Ipswich. This form of treatment is designed to effect 'a change in the emotional forces within the life space to bring improvement to the individual or family within the life space' (Howells, 1968, page 102). Vector therapy aims to alter either the magnitude or the direction of the relevant emotional forces. These may be within the individual, outside the individual and within the family, outside the family and within the community, or outside individual, family and community, but within the culture.

Vector therapy involves such procedures as advising family members to seek work outside the home, sending a child to boarding school, and the use of various individuals, agencies and institutions in the family's suprasystem. When it deals with forces outside the family, vector therapy seems to be another way of conceptualizing therapy with a family's suprasystem. In other words it is then a form of network therapy.

Although Howells has long been a proponent of the concept of vector therapy, the term has not gained wide acceptance among, nor been much used by, family therapists generally. As Howells himself has suggested by his frequent reference to 'family psychiatry', rather than 'family therapy', it is perhaps more a 'family psychiatry' concept than a 'family therapy' one. Yet the therapist struggling to promote change in a family that seems stuck in its way of functioning does well to bear in mind the possibility of altering the emotional forces bearing upon the family from outside.

Multiple impact therapy

Multiple impact therapy was developed by Robert MacGregor (1962) at the University of Texas Medical Branch Hospitals at Galveston. The Youth Development Project, a research project treating adolescents referred from correctional services, found itself dealing with families in crisis who often lived long distances from the clinic. The team therefore developed a plan which involved treating entire families for intensive therapy for two or two-and-a-half days, while they slept overnight in a neighbouring motel. A team of therapists of various disciplines would meet with the family on their arrival at the unit. This initial team–family conference was the beginning of a therapy process which would continue intensively for two days.

What happened after the initial conference varied from family to family, but typically each family member was seen individually by a team member, and subsequently in overlapping sessions in which, for example, the therapist who had been seeing the teenage identified patient might join another therapist during the course of that therapist's interview with the teenager's parents. The parents' therapist would then summarize the session so far, with perhaps some interpretation of what had happened, and then the session would continue.

At midday the team would confer, and further and varied interviews would be held in the afternoon, the day ending with another team–family conference. The procedure, though with more variability, would continue the next day and end with a final conference with the family. If satisfactory progress had not been made the team might arrange a further half-day of treatment the next day. A follow-up visit was a requirement and in one quarter of the cases that MacGregor (1962) reported, a further day's treatment was arranged after about two months. Community resources such as local treatment agencies, teachers and minister, were used extensively in the follow-up period.

The treatment and its results were documented in the book *Multiple Impact Therapy with Families* (MacGregor et al, 1964). Although multiple impact therapy is an interesting concept it has not been widely practised, perhaps because of the practical difficulties associated with admitting whole families, or accommodating them nearby, and assembling a team to work intensively with them. It may be particularly valuable when families live at great distance from clinics, a situation which is likely to exist for progressively fewer families as family therapists and clinics become more numerous. Nevertheless some centres, for example the Philadelphia Child Guidance Clinic and Thistletown Regional Center for Children and Adolescents in Toronto, do admit whole families for varying periods of time. At Thistletown the procedure has also been found to be useful for looking at the instrumental skills of families, and for making an in-depth assessment of family functioning.

The admission of whole families for treatment has been reported by some other therapists. Thus Portner (1977) described the admission of families, one at a time, to a seventeen-bed mental health unit in a general hospital. The treatment of eleven cases is described in Portner's paper. Length of stay varied from three days to three weeks. The admission of the whole family, rather than only the patient or the patient and one other family member, seemed to be valuable, but the numbers were too small for definite conclusions to be drawn.

Abroms, Fellner and Whitaker (1971) described the admission of additional family members, along with the primary patients, to the inpatient psychiatry service of the University of Wisconsin Hospitals. They believed the procedure to be valuable and reported a number of individual case histories in which this certainly seemed to be the case; but this study, like the aforementioned one, was uncontrolled.

Catanzaro and his colleagues (1973) coined the term (which happily has not been widely adopted) *familization therapy*, for an inpatient programme involving the treatment of artificial 'family' groups of about thirty people. These consisted of patients aged from 14 to 82. The aim was to help each patient become a 'responsible and caring member of a family'. Towards the end of this inpatient treatment members of the natural family were admitted as 'co-patients' for several weeks. The authors considered the treatment to be valuable, but this is another isolated report of a treatment approach which has been neither properly evaluated nor widely adopted.

Behavioural approaches

The main principles of learning theory, upon which behavioural approaches to psychotherapy are based, were outlined in Chapter 3, and Chapter 4 included a summary of behavioural family therapy methods. The essence of behaviour therapy is the modification of events either preceding or following particular behaviours, so as to produce changes in the behaviours. The two procedures are called, respectively, respondent and operant conditioning.

As we saw earlier, behavioural methods are best suited to the modification of interactions involving two, or at the most three people; they are less readily applicable to whole family systems. Nevertheless the rules of learning theory apply to the transactions occurring between family members, and between therapist and family, as much as they do to any other human interactions. Therapists are therefore wise to bear these rules in mind whenever they are working with families. Thus paying attention to a symptom often tends to reinforce or strengthen it – at least when it has been serving the function of obtaining attention for the individual concerned, as it so often does. Ignoring a symptom, for example tantrum behaviour, often leads to its disappearance, perhaps after some initial increase. Turning attention to another behaviour, or to a different topic – for example talking about the extended family – may also reduce the attention given to the presenting problem. This may lead, in time, to the partial or complete extinction of the problem behaviour.

Not only does the therapist's behaviour inevitably affect the responses of family members, but the behaviours of family members affect each other. Changes in family systems can therefore be brought about if the family respond to instructions as to how they should interact. This is 'first order' change, and in many of the more seriously disturbed families that present for treatment this is insufficient; sometimes, however, it can be effective.

> Sylvia was a 21-year-old single parent. Her 3-year-old son, Tom, had twice been removed from her care for short periods by the child welfare authorities, because of her alcoholism and the effects it had on the care she gave him. She had then entered a detoxification centre and started attending Alcoholics Anonymous meetings. When she presented for therapy she was no longer drinking and her son had been returned to her. He was, however, presenting a severe behaviour management problem; he had long been in the habit of disregarding, or defying, his mother's inconsistent shouted injunctions and threats – threats which were rarely followed by any action.

Sylvia herself had had an unstable childhood. Her mother also had a drinking problem and had been married six times. As a child Sylvia had been cared for by a variety of relatives, and she had spent several short periods in foster homes which, she told her therapist, she hated. She ran away from home at the age of 15 and lived an unstable life for several years, drinking excessively, using street drugs and living with a series of physically abusive young men, who themselves abused drugs and alcohol.

Sylvia had never experienced stable, consistent, loving care and discipline as a child; consequently she had no suitable internal model of parenthood. Yet she had made good progress in many areas of her life; she had ceased using alcohol and drugs, and no longer seemed to need to associate with abusive men – Tom's father had been one – as she had done previously.

Therapy with Sylvia and Tom used a behavioural model. It was designed first to help Sylvia realise that shouting at children, especially if this includes threatening consequences which do not occur, is unhelpful. Instead Sylvia was given specific instructions about what to do in response to behaviours in Tom which she wished to alter or have cease. One behaviour was dealt with at a time, starting with the behaviour Sylvia considered most important – which was Tom's habit of running recklessly out into the road in front of the house.

A detailed plan for dealing with this problem was developed. This was done in discussion with Sylvia, since it is important that whatever behavioural management is prescribed be tailored to the specific situation, resources and personalities involved. Tom was only to be allowed out of the house to play at times when Sylvia could observe his activities and had nothing else to distract her. As soon as he stepped on to the roadway, Sylvia was to bring him into the house and sit him on a chair for five minutes. If he yelled or protested actively in any other way the five minutes did not start until he had settled down. When Tom was playing safely in the area his mother permitted him to use, she was to give him intermittent approving attention.

The above programme was strikingly successful, and within a week of its implementation, in good summer weather when Tom could play outside every day, he had ceased running on to the roadway.

As well as dealing with one specific behavioural problem, treatment plans such as the above offer families a model of healthier functioning, and a way of dealing with other problems. It often happens that once they have developed behavioural plans for one or two problems with the help of the therapist, they can devise ways of dealing with other problems without the help of the therapist.

Behavioural interventions such as the one used with Sylvia and Tom can also play a part in restructuring families. Implicit in the plan worked out was the assumption that parents should be in charge of their children and have a right, indeed a duty, to set limits on the children's behaviours and to enforce these – both by encouraging desired behaviour and by placing defined limits on undesired behaviour. A more functional hierarchical system thus tends to be created.

The classical studies of Alexander and Parsons (1973) also deserve mention here. These authors carried out, early in the history of family therapy, a controlled study of behavioural intervention in the families of delinquent teenagers. A carefully planned procedure was used in order to:

(a) Assess the family behaviours maintaining the delinquent behaviour.
(b) Modify family communication patterns to bring about greater clarity and precision, increased reciprocity and the presentation of alternative solutions.
(c) Institute a pattern of contingency contracting in the family to modify the maladaptive patterns and institute more adaptive behaviours.

In addition to studying the delinquent youths, these authors also studied two comparison groups, one receiving other forms of family intervention and one receiving no treatment. Certain changes in the families undergoing the 'short-term behavioural family programme', as the treatment was called, were hypothesized. These were less silence, more equality of speech and greater frequency of positive interruption, that is asking for clarification of unclear messages and providing feedback on messages received. Another hypothesis was that there would be less recidivism in the experimental group than in the comparison groups.

A treatment programme designed to extinguish in a systematic way maladaptive interaction patterns and substitute reciprocity was devised. Families were randomly assigned to this treatment or to one of the comparison groups. The latter received either client-centred family group treatment, a psychodynamic family programme or no treatment.

Statistically significant differences were found between the 'short-term behavioural family programme' and the families in the other groups. The differences were in the directions hypothesized. Significantly better recidivism rates at six and eighteen month follow-up were also demonstrated. The rates were:

- 'Short-term behavioural family programme' – 26 per cent.
- 'Client-centred' treatment group – 47 per cent.
- 'Psychodynamic' group – 73 per cent.
- No treatment group – 50 per cent.

This was an important study. Precise therapeutic goals were set, and the treatment procedures were carefully defined. Recurrent delinquency was reduced in youths from families which showed the changes in interaction which the therapists aimed to achieve. On the other hand, it was not reduced in the families in which interaction patterns did not change.

Behavioural methods have also been widely used in marital therapy. Their application in this work is discussed in Chapter 13.

Family therapy and schizophrenia

The early work of such pioneers of family therapy as Bateson, Jackson, Haley, Weakland, Wynne, Lidz, Bowen and Laing was reviewed in Chapter 1. They started out by studying, and attempting to treat, the families of schizophrenic patients. Since those early days, however, the attention of most family therapists has shifted to the clinical problems of a much wider range of troubled families. McFarlane, in his introduction to the book, *Family Therapy in Schizophrenia*, says:

> During the 25 years that family therapy has been developing, there has been, until very recently, a nearly linear decline in interest in the family treatment of schizophrenia. Reports of treatment techniques and even research studies have dwindled in the family literature, while most family therapists have become increasingly reluctant to treat the families of schizophrenic patients...Drug therapy is still the mainstay in dealing with schizophrenic psychoses, while research on this baffling condition has become almost completely oriented toward its biological aspects. (McFarlane, 1983b, page 1)

McFarlane goes on to suggest that 'conventional' family therapy has not provided enough in the way of results to warrant its continued use, and that the evidence for a family 'cause' for schizophrenia is lacking. On the other hand, the evidence for a biological component seems to McFarlane to be 'overwhelming', and the efficacy of drug therapy is apparently greater than that of conventional family therapy.

It is also clear that genetic factors are involved (Kinney and Matthysse, 1978). The many pieces of evidence supporting this have been listed by Gottesman (1978). Of particular interest to family therapists is the evidence that children of schizophrenics placed early for adoption in non-schizophrenic families still develop schizophrenia at rates higher than the population rate, sometimes as high as those reared by their schizophrenic parents; adoptive relatives of schizophrenics do not have elevated rates of schizophrenia, but the biologic relatives of the adoptees do have higher rates; and children of normal parents fostered into homes in which a parental figure became schizophrenic do not show an increased rate of schizophrenia. Some of the above statements are based on the study of small samples, and not all have been replicated, but there have also been twin studies which are of good quality and show that the concordance rate for schizophrenia is 3 times greater in monozygous (MZ) twins than in dizygous twins, and 30 times the general population rate. Nevertheless, more than half the MZ pairs are discordant for schizophrenia, despite the fact that they have identical genes. Genetics is therefore not the whole cause, and there is room also for social factors.

What, then, are these social factors and what can the family therapist do about them? Two reviews (Jacob, 1975; Goldstein and Rodnick, 1975) concluded that there was no good evidence, in the research on family interaction, for the concept of a 'schizophrenic family', although there did seem to be some evidence that 'communication deviance' (CD) and 'expressed emotion' (EE) were relevant concepts in these families. Since then evidence has been accumulating that social, and particularly family, factors *are* important – at least in determining whether schizophrenics relapse after discharge from hospital, but perhaps also in contributing to the onset of the condition. These developments have led to new approaches to the treatment of these families. According to McFarlane, 1983b, page 2) they differ from the approaches used in the past in two ways:

1. They seem to have major therapeutic effects on the schizophrenic process, beyond those achievable with drug therapy.
2. They all – except for the systemic variety – start from a major expansion of family systems theory that also takes extra-family factors into account.

Expressed emotion and its relevance have been the subject of a series of studies of the families of schizophrenics carried out in Britain by staff of the Medical Research Council's Social Psychiatry Unit (Brown and Birley, 1968; Birley and Brown, 1970; Brown et al, 1972; Leff et al, 1973; Vaughn and Leff, 1976; Leff and Vaughn, 1981; Sturgeon et al, 1981). The findings of these studies are summarized, reviewed and discussed in the book *Expressed Emotions in Families* (Leff and Vaughn, 1985). They are of particular interest, both because of the scientifically sound research methods used, and because the findings have been confirmed in replications of the work done. The research has also been approached more from a sociological perspective than from a 'family therapy' one; this has meant the investigators have not set out with a commitment to family therapy as a treatment for the disorders concerned.

These studies have shown that certain characteristics of the families to which schizophrenics discharged from hospital return, have significant effects on the patients' relapse rates. Expressed emotion was measured using scales developed over a period of years (Leff and Vaughn, 1985). Five scales were developed: two involve 'a recognition of particular comments ("critical" and "positive") and consist of a count of all such comments occurring at any point in the interview' (Leff and Vaughn, 1985, page 37). The other three – emotional overinvolvement, hostility, and warmth – involve the recognition of particular kinds of comments; the interviewer then makes a judgement of the degree to which the emotion concerned was shown. In all cases the information was obtained in the course of interviews with relatives, usually spouses or parents.

In brief, these studies showed that high scores on the EE scales were associated with high rates of relapse in schizophrenic patients discharged from hospital; the best results occurred when there was both the regular use of antipsychotic drugs and low expressed emotion in the relatives. The British workers also investigated a group of 'depressed neurotic' patients, with a view to discovering how specific their findings were for schizophrenia. They found that the depressed neurotic patients were even more vulnerable to critical comments by relatives, but that face-to-face contact between patients and relatives did not relate to relapse, as it did in the schizophrenic group. Low face-to-face contact appeared to protect schizophrenic patients in 'high-EE' homes, but it had no such function for depressives. The researchers concluded:

> We interpret this as an indication of a poor relationship between a patient and a relative that predates the illness. We consider it likely that low contact and high criticism are both indicators of a poor marriage (virtually all these relatives were spouses) and that the poor quality of the marriage predicts relapse of depression. (Leff and Vaughn, 1985, page 93)

It seems that high EE may predispose to relapse in schizophrenia, but there is no clear evidence that it is a significant causal factor.

Communication deviance (CD), on the other hand, may play at least a small role in the aetiology of the condition. Margaret Singer and her colleagues (1978) and Wynne (1981) developed instruments for measuring CD, and found it to be present in the parents' communication with each other, as well as in communication involving the patient. CD consists of various forms of vague, ambiguous, wandering, illogical and idiosyncratic language, similar in some respects to schizophrenic thought disorder – though the researchers found the abnormalities of language to be much less severe than in schizophrenics. These abnormal speech patterns may be present in the parents some years before the onset of the schizophrenic disorder in their offspring, and they are similar in type to those that develop in the offspring; they may therefore play a part in the aetiology of the disorder, along with genetic and biological factors.

If 'conventional' family therapy is not effective, what are we to do to help these families? This question is the main one that is addressed in the book *Family Therapy in Schizophrenia* (McFarlane, 1983a), in which various possible ways of intervening are discussed. Hatfield (1983), for example, suggests that what families want of their therapists is often different from what therapists wish to provide. 'Families', Hatfield (1983, page 63) says, 'are turning to mental health professionals for assistance in becoming more effective care givers for their disturbed relatives and in coping with the many problems that develop'. Yet professionals seem, at least to Hatfield, to be reluctant to give this kind of help. Other chapters in the book discuss crisis intervention, psychoeducational programmes for families, behavioural interventions, multiple family therapy, supportive group counselling for relatives, and the coordination of family therapy with other therapies.

Leff, Kuipers and Berkowitz (1983), from the MRC Social Psychiatry Unit, describe a trial of an intervention programme designed to reduce EE in the families of patients in which there was a high risk of relapse. All the patients received medication, but in addition the experimental group also received a programme of social treatment. This had two components. One was an educational programme, designed to help relatives understand the nature of schizophrenia and its symptoms; the other was a relatives' group. The idea behind setting up this group was that those relatives falling into the 'low-EE' group and living with schizophrenics admitted to hospital (who comprised almost half of the total), would help teach the necessary coping skills to the 'high-EE' relatives. In addition to these generally-applied measures, specific measures were applied in particular cases, for example conjoint marital therapy or attempts (usually unsuccessful) to move the patient out of the family to another living setting.

The results of this small-scale treatment trial – there were 12 families in the experimental group and 12 in the control group – have been encouraging. The researchers found that it was possible to reduce the critical comments in the experimental group, while there was virtually no change in the control group. In many of the experimental families there was also a significant reduction in the social contact between patients and relatives, a change which seldom occurred in the control families. In their 1983 paper, Leff et al also report a significantly lower relapse rate in the experimental group, compared with the control group, but the trial was not complete and the number of cases was small, though they were high-risk ones.

While 'conventional' family therapy techniques are apparently generally ineffective when applied to the families of schizophrenic patients, it seems that certain systemic approaches may help these families. The Milan group reported work with what they called 'families in schizophrenic transaction', in the book *Paradox and Counterparadox* (Palazzoli et al, 1978a). These authors, however, used the term 'schizophrenic transaction' to describe a particular family communication pattern. But as McFarlane (1983c) has pointed out, this pattern is neither specific, nor unique to schizophrenia.

Although Palazzoli and her colleagues (1978a) state that 5 of the 15 families they describe contained children with 'serious psychotic behaviour' and the other 10 were 'acute schizophrenics' between the ages of 10 and 22, McFarlane points out that they focus on family characteristics and processes, rather than diagnostic entities. In any event it is doubtful whether they were treating schizophrenics similar to those referred to in the other research reports we have considered. Nevertheless, their methods are creative and seem often to be effective in the severely disturbed families they describe. What effect they would have applied to the general run of schizophrenic patients seen in adult psychiatric clinics and hospitals is unclear, however, but there is no reason to presume that they would in themselves constitute an adequate treatment.

In conclusion, evidence is lacking that family factors, in themselves, cause schizophrenia. They may, however, contribute to its development in genetically-prone individuals. They may also play a part in precipitating relapse in schizophrenics who have improved during treatment in hospital. It seems clear that there is a connection between the degree of 'expressed emotion' in the family and relapse. In addition 'communication deviance' (CD) may play some part in causing a predisposed person to develop schizophrenia, so the possibility of lessening the chances of this happening by reducing the CD in the family exists; whether this is effective remains to be demonstrated, however. Other systemic interventions may also be helpful to these families, but family therapy should not normally be the sole therapy; it seems to be most effective when combined with the use of antipsychotic drugs such as the various phenothiazine compounds, or haloperidol.

nmary

ious special therapeutic techniques can be useful in treating families. ong these are 'action techniques' such as family sculpting and role ing; when bringing the reality of a family's functioning into the apy room proves difficult, such techniques can help do so. otape replay of sessions, or parts of sessions, can perform a similar tion and can assist families in understanding and then modifying actions.

twork therapy – (treatment which includes the wider family and l network); and multiple family therapy (the treatment of several ies together) can also be valuable. Other approaches which may useful include vector therapy, which aims to alter the emotional bearing upon the family; and multiple impact therapy, which ts of an intensive two or two-and-a-half day process during which ety of therapeutic inputs are offered the family and its various stems by a team of therapists.

nis chapter we also considered the application of concepts derived behaviour therapy in the treatment of families. Being aware of, ing, the principles of learning theory can increase the effective- many other forms of family therapy.

ie treatment of the families of schizophrenic patients, conven- family therapy techniques have proved largely ineffective. hrenia appears to have multiple causes, and while social, arly family, factors are among these, treatment of them alone t seem to be adequate. However, there is good evidence that pressed emotion' in patients' families predisposes to relapse, and nication deviance' may contribute to the development of irenia in genetically predisposed individuals; both may there- appropriate targets for therapeutic intervention.

Chapter 12

A Method of Therapy

Every family therapist must develop a method of therapy, using concepts derived from one or more schools of family therapy – unless she or he aims to invent a totally original method. We need therefore to consider how existing knowledge may be used in developing such a model. It is not necessary to adopt, in complete form, any of the therapy models we have discussed so far, nor any other specific model. It is important, though, to have a coherent model, and to subscribe to a theory of how change may be brought about in families.

Most therapists use ideas, concepts and techniques derived from a variety of schools. This chapter will describe a model of therapy derived from various sources. I have found it useful, but it is not put forward as necessarily the best way of practising therapy, but rather as an example of a method derived from several sources. I believe also that it is a good starting model for novice therapists, though I am sure many other starting points could also be used with good results.

How therapists work, and the methods they use, depend partly upon their personalities, partly upon who has taught them, and usually largely upon what they find works for them. The personalities of some therapists are better suited to the use of certain types of therapy than others; for example some feel comfortable with the use of humour while for others this is difficult. The therapist's type of practice is also important. What is effective for many middle and upper income families functioning well in instrumental ways, may not be helpful to some families in different socio-economic circumstances, and vice versa.

Most therapists – and surely all who have not reached a state of professional stagnation – are constantly developing their skills and refining the therapy techniques they use. Once you have established your philosophy, adopted a theory of change and developed a way of working with families, you will want to continue incorporating new

d approaches as you learn of them. The techniques you add later
:lude some of those mentioned in this book – for instance
g or videotape replay; others may be techniques you learn
re, or acquire in the course of your clinical experience with
and in working with colleagues. The method which follows,
, like any other derived from existing knowledge, is offered as
ng – a foundation for you to build on.

ionship between assessment and treatment

rapy should normally follow a proper assessment of the family
eful formulation of its problems, way of functioning and
the complete separation of assessment and treatment is
. Virtually anything the therapist says or does during
t may be either therapeutic or anti-therapeutic, and many
: interventions also result in the therapist acquiring new
about the family; at the very least they tell you whether or
ticular intervention brings about the desired changes.
es a family's problems – or some of them – quickly emerge,
the first few minutes of their first session. The family
ay also quickly make clear the changes they seek. For
re may be a concern that communication, or the control of
ehaviour, is not the way they would like it to be. If
on were a problem, the therapist might choose, even in the
to try to promote communication between the family
is would be both a diagnostic and a therapeutic procedure.
the hypothesis that verbal communication between the
rs concerned was poor; and it would reveal whether the
oach employed to improve communication was effective.
above considerations, it is good practice both to carry out
as set out in Chapter 5, and to establish clear therapeutic
sed in Chapter 6. By the time these processes have been
e may already have been changes in the family. These
e members review their situation in conversation with
d think about family issues, perhaps from new points of

ages

lished rapport and reached agreement with the family
of therapy, my usual plan is to employ direct methods
g the use of more complex, indirect and strategic
e main exceptions are some families that have had

much previous unsuccessful therapy, and those that take an oppc
tional attitude towards therapy from the start. Most families nev
presenting for therapy are, however, keen to receive input that n
help them resolve their problems. If a family fails to respond satisfact
ily to direct interventions, I proceed to use one or more of the ot!
approaches discussed in Chapters 10 and 11.

The importance of *the establishment of rapport* cannot be exaggeratec
enables the process of 'joining' the family (Minuchin, 1974) – referree
as 'bonding' by Kirschner and Kirschner (1986) – to occur. How to b
rapport has been discussed in Chapter 5. If adequate rapport has
been established it is hard even to assess families properly, let alone t
them.

Interesting examples of apparent failure to establish rapport are t
found in a book by Peck (1985). This author reports two serio
disturbed families, each containing a depressed teenage boy. Neither
family of Bobby (described in Chapter 2 of Peck's book), nor tha
Roger (Chapter 3), became engaged in therapy following brief cor
tations with the author. Peck chose to regard both sets of paren!
'evil', because they did not accept the treatment he consid
necessary. Their unwillingness may, however, have been due to a
of rapport between therapist and family – itself a result of the
nature of the consultations, which may not have allowed time
rapport to develop.

Once rapport is established, therapy can proceed. A syste
scheme is described by Epstein and Bishop (1981) in their pape
'problem centred systems therapy of the family'. These au
distinguish 'macro stages' of therapy from 'micro moves'. The 'n
stages' Epstein and Bishop list are:

(a) Assessment.
(b) Contracting.
(c) Treatment.
(d) Closure.

Each macro stage is composed of four steps. The assessment
comprises:

1. Orientation. The therapist explains to the family members w
   or she proposes to do, and seeks their agreement to it.
2. Data gathering. This is the process of learning about the fa
   history, structure and organization, as discussed in Chapter .
3. Problem description. This comprises more data gathering, b
   focus now is on the problems with which the family present

si-
ly
ay
·r-
.er

and agreement of a problem list. Epstein and Bishop
e that therapy should not start without a full knowledge
's problems and strengths, and they like to commit this

It
to
.ild
not
eat

essentially just a way of ordering the process we
pter 5. I find it a useful approach, but I usually put more
ired changes than on *problems*. While these are closely
to speak of changes sought rather than problems
se this helps define therapy as a change-producing
to use written problem and strength lists, rather than
verbally, is a matter of the therapist's style and

be
.sly
the
. of
sul-
· as
·red
.ack
·rief
for

nd Bishop (1981) describe as their *contracting* macro
roughly to the process described in Chapter 6, on the
reatment objectives. They list the following steps:

.atic
r on
.ors
acro

in the orientation in the previous stage, the therapist
what is to happen.
ns. The therapist tells the family about the treatment
·red; the family members must then decide whether
, work on their own or not pursue treatment.
pectations. These are the expectations family
f each other and of the therapist, and the therapist's
hem.
. Epstein and Bishop require all concerned to sign a
listing the problems, what would be a satisfactory
· negotiated treatment conditions, including the
proximate number of sessions.

make a written contract, but find them to be
sorganized families, and some that fail to honour
h contracts are a means both of clarifying what
·en sessions, and of emphasizing the importance
·s to this and to the therapy process generally.

stage

:ro stages identified by Epstein and Bishop (1981),
.ps:

.at he

nily's

.t the

This is a good model for use when direct, as opposed to strate
therapy methods, as described in Chapter 9, are to be employed – tho
it need not be confined to direct methods. The setting of tasks is a m
feature of Epstein and Bishop's 'problem centred' approach, but m
other therapists also set their clients tasks to perform between or du
sessions. The final macro stage described by Epstein and Bishop (198
that of *closure*. It is dealt with in Chapter 14.

Epstein and Bishop's scheme is a good example of a planned appr
to therapy, based on the use of a particular model of family functio
– the McMaster model. This, and the related Process model,
summarized in Chapter 5. They are quite closely related to
structural model which, however, complements them in some resp
Together, they provide the material needed for effective therap
many family problems.

Direct treatment approaches

Direct injunctions, or directives, are a central feature of direct the
methods. They are sometimes called *behavioural prescriptions*, for exa
by Watzlawick and his colleagues (1974) – though these authors us
term to describe mainly paradoxical directives. In many cases, how
it is not necessary to use paradoxical methods; families whic
strongly motivated to change are often willing to follow the instru
or directives of the therapist.

It appears that even Milton Erickson, who was a past mas
indirect and strategic methods, used direct methods 80 per cent
time (Hammond, 1984). It is in more severely disturbed fa
including some containing psychotic members, that direct injun
tend to be resisted, ignored or even defied. The novice family the
should first practise the giving of direct injunctions, becoming cc
table in doing this before starting to use paradoxical ones.
behavioural prescriptions of any sort is foreign to many the
trained in more reflective, passive or interpretive methods. Le
this more active approach can be hard, but it is necessary for most
of family therapy.

Direct interventions for some common family problems
discussed in Chapter 9. Whether they are successful depends n
on the existence of adequate rapport, but also on how the directi
delivered. Haley (1976, Chapter 2) has provided an excellent acc
how to do this. He acknowledges his debt to Erickson, about
work he wrote in an earlier book (Haley, 1973). He points out t
difficult or impossible not to give directives. These are not nec
framed as orders. Thus if a person says two things and a com
responds to one but not to the other, this is effectively a directiv

gic,
igh
ijor
any
ing
1) is

ach
iing
vere
the
icts.
for

though at first sight it may not look like one. The
ressing interest in the one thing rather than the other,
to hear more about that subject than about the other

rectives in non-verbal ways. These include showing
om in our faces; turning our back on, or facing, a
rticular tones of voice; and taking care or showing
lack, in responding to a request. Indeed Haley (1976,
t that it is difficult not to give directives, even when
give them. Thus a therapist may not wish to give a
ther to quit his job or divorce his wife. Yet simply not
erbally does not prevent the therapist's opinion being
y that the therapist's views will be communicated, at
sure, through such channels as voice tone, facial
re.

rapy
nple
e the
ever,
are
tions

ectives is not a one-way process. Just as therapists
many subtle ways, so also do clients influence
onding differentially to the therapist's statements
l for therapists to be fully aware of these processes
basic assumption on which therapy is based is that
e understanding of these processes than their
use of the self in the giving of directives, both
l, is moreover an important part of most, perhaps

er at
f the
ilies,
tions
rapist
nfor-
Using
apists
rning
forms

(1976, page 49), there are three purposes which
The first is the straightforward one of causing
eir behaviour by telling them to do things
nd purpose is to increase the involvement of
ing treated. When directives concern tasks to be
ssions, they help maintain the relationship with
he period until the next session. This applies
isks are performed, since the family is either
ing the therapist's wishes.

were
t only
es are
unt of
whose
at it is
ssarily
panion
by the

ostic purpose to the use of directives. Whether,
rmed provides useful information, particularly
ess and ability to change. Thus a task may be
not done at all, half done, attempted and failed,
about a proposed task often reveals useful
e about the family's mealtime behaviour, if the
erformed at mealtimes.

nctions be given? We have three alternatives:

doing something.

2. Telling people to do something different.
3. Telling people to do things in a different sequence.

1. *Telling people to stop doing something* may not be effective. In many cases our clients already want to stop doing whatever it is, and simply having the therapist tell them to stop does not help. There are, however, ways of increasing the effectiveness of direct injunctions. These were mentioned in the final section of Chapter 9 and, in brief, are:

(a) Making the instructions as precise as possible. This may involve repetition and having the family members repeat, in detail, what they are to do.
(b) Enlisting other family members to remind those concerned of what has to be done.
(c) Using the force of the therapist's personality. How effective this is will depend on the quality of rapport that has been established.
(d) Setting up a system of rewards or punishments.

2. *Telling people to do something different* is often more effective than telling them to stop doing something. Thus, rather than telling parents to stop arguing about how to handle their child's behaviour, the therapist might tell them to list the possible ways of dealing with certain troublesome behaviours. These could then be discussed and a joint plan of action agreed. If it seems unlikely that the parents will be able to reach agreement on a joint plan, they could be asked to return with their list of possible courses of action for discussion and agreement at the next therapy session. With some families it may be necessary for the whole process to be carried out during therapy sessions with the therapist's active help, at least for the first few problems tackled.

Procedures such as the above can have more value than that of simply resolving particular problems. They can help couples learn to communicate and discuss issues, and then to resolve them by the use of compromise and the rational consideration of alternatives.

3. *Telling people to do things in different sequence* can lead to changes in set, problematic patterns of behaviour. A good example is an instruction given by Milton Erickson, and reported by Haley (1973, page 225). A husband and wife had run a restaurant business for many years, but were constantly quarrelling about how it should be managed. Although the wife said the husband should manage it, he protested that she would not allow him to do so. She insisted on nagging him about the buying, the book-keeping, and even when the floor needed scrubbing. Erickson discovered that they opened the restaurant at 7.00 am. Both partners carried keys and the wife would open the restaurant door while her husband parked the car. Erickson's behavioural prescription to the wife

was to see that her husband arrived at least half an hour before she did. He thus carried the keys, opened the door, unlocked everything and started setting up the restaurant for the day. By the time the wife arrived, the husband had got things going and was managing satisfactorily. She stayed at home, washed the breakfast dishes and did some housework before she left. Gradually she found she could be later and later, and that her husband could still run the restaurant. By this simple intervention, Erickson unbalanced the game the couple had been playing by changing the rules, and set in train a sequence of events which led to the resolution of their problems.

Motivating people to follow directives can be a challenge to the therapist. In addition to choosing from the above three ways of giving direct injunctions, there are some other important points to be considered. It is necessary to persuade the family that carrying out a directive will lead to a result they want. In other words, there must be something in it for them. This is easier when the family are agreed on the changes they want; when they disagree, the therapist's efforts are usually best directed to devising tasks which will help the family members reach agreement. Such tasks must offer the prospect of leading to some advantage for everyone concerned. Another possibility is to start with small non-threatening tasks and work up to more complex ones.

Another way of motivating families is to rehearse with them the various ways in which they have attempted to solve their problems. The family members can be asked to list everything they have tried, and to explain what resulted in each case. As it becomes clear that everything tried so far has failed, this may help them become more responsive to the therapist's suggestions. On the other hand, if they state that things have been improving recently, the therapist may present directives as building on this, and as ways of adding to the improvement the family has achieved by its own efforts.

As well as promoting motivation by the above means, the therapist should be sensitive to what is acceptable to the family. Some families respond better to the challenge of what is presented as a big task, while others prefer the less-threatening idea of a small one. Some respond better than others to the weight of the therapist's professional authority as an expert. You will often find it best to use directives during sessions, before you offer them for use between sessions. Remember that almost everything you do or say during any session with a family has directive properties. Selective attention given to different things can itself be a powerful factor in bringing about change.

Assigning tasks

We have seen that assigning families tasks is a major part of the direct treatment of family problems, and of the 'problem centred' approach of Epstein and Bishop (1981). Once the objectives of treatment have been agreed, the therapist can embark on this phase of treatment. Tasks may be assigned to be carried out during therapy sessions or between them, or both. Ultimately, however, the family has to practise new ways of functioning outside the therapy sessions.

Provided that the family's problems have been carefully explored and defined during the assessment, the tasks set by the therapist should be more successful than the family's own past attempts to overcome their problems. It is often hard for families to come to an objective view of their problems, but the therapist can help them do this. This can lead to a better understanding of what may lie behind the presenting problems, and thus to better 'solutions'. In many families the problems turn out to be rather different from what they were initially thought to be. In other words some reframing takes place. The following case illustrates this.

Mr and Mrs C complained of the behaviour of their eight-year-old son, David. They said he lied, stole money and other items from family members, generally defied his parents' authority, and had tantrums when confronted about his behaviour. They had tried many ways of dealing with these problems, but had difficulty agreeing on what approach to take. Mr C preferred to be the 'heavy', imposing severe prolonged sanctions, like early bedtimes, or no television, for a month; while Mrs C thought he was too harsh in his punishments. She sometimes managed to persuade her husband to modify the sanctions he had imposed on David, and tended to make concessions when he wasn't present; for instance she might let David watch a few cartoons on television when he arrived home from school, even though his father had said he should not be watching any TV.

Further exploration of the family situation revealed longstanding marital tensions. The parents came from very different families of origin, and their marriage had been precipitated by Mrs C's pregnancy with David; before that she had been far from sure she wanted to marry Mr C. The therapist hypothesized that David's difficult behaviour was a secondary problem, related to the tensions between the parents. It was these tensions that seemed to be behind the parents' failure to agree on how to deal with David. By behaving badly David also gave his parents something other than their own marital problems on which to focus their attention.

When the time came for therapist and family to agree on a problem list, and the changes desired by the family, the therapist proposed that the parents' disagreements regarding David should come high on the list. During the discussion of this 'problem' – namely the parents' disagreements – the original 'presenting problem' became reframed. Now the top priority was to enable the parents to find means of agreeing on how to handle David and his problem behaviours. His behaviour per se became a secondary issue.

The initial tasks set the family addressed parenting issues; they were designed to help Mr and Mrs C communicate better, and learn to problem-solve in a cooperative way. The difficulties they had in functioning as an effective parental couple were also closely related to their marital problems. These too were included in the problem list, and in due course became a focus of therapy.

The C family did well in therapy. David's behaviour ceased to be a problem, and indeed it was not long before the presenting symptoms were forgotten, as the underlying issues were tackled and resolved. Left to themselves, however, the parents would probably have continued their futile (because they were disunited) attempts to control their son.

The 'C' family had a number of problems. The most obvious concerned behaviour control; not only were the parents' efforts to control their son ineffective, but neither one could control what the other did in dealing with David. But there were other, perhaps more fundamental, problems. Communication between the parents was poor; many important issues were not discussed, and sometimes communication was through David, rather than direct. The affective involvement of the parents was also less than optimal. Indeed it appeared that Mrs C was emotionally closer to her son than than she was to her husband.

There are other ways in which the 'C' family's problems can be conceptualized. The structural therapist would see the essence of their problem as being the lack of a clear boundary between parents and son. The parents appeared relatively disengaged emotionally, while there was an unhealthy degree of enmeshment between mother and son. The structural therapist would endeavour to establish a clearer boundary between parents and child, while opening up that between the parents. Represented graphically as recommended by Minuchin (1974, Chapters 3 and 5), the structure:

```
        .                          FM
 M  .  Son      needed to change to:      - - - -
        .                          Son
  ‿‿‿‿‿
       F
```

The diagram on the left represents a subsystem pattern in which there is a diffuse boundary (shown by vertical dotted lines) between mother and son, and a coalition (shown by the horizontal bracket) between mother and son on the one hand, and father on the other. The diagram on the right shows a parental subsystem consisting of mother and father working together, separated from the son by a clear boundary.

The above change in the family structure would probably represent quite well the objectives of a therapist using the 'problem centred systems therapy' of Epstein and Bishop (1981); such a therapist would not, however, conceptualize the process in the same way. But the tasks set the family would probably be aimed at getting the parents to work together in a united way in dealing with their son, and at improving the communication of both information and feelings between them.

Structural therapists generally use the power of their personalities to help alter the structure of the family system. In this case the structural therapist might for part of a session join with father, supporting him in the view that the sanctions he imposes should not be undermined or ignored by mother; this procedure would have to be balanced by supporting mother in her desire that the sanctions imposed on her son should not be too severe or prolonged. The opening up of the boundary between the parents could be promoted by addressing the parents collectively as a couple during sessions, having them sit together apart from their son, or even seeing them on their own without the son present at all. These actions would help create an appropriate boundary between the parents and their son. Tasks set the family between sessions would have the same aims. Implicit in all the therapist's words and actions should be the assumption that parents are in charge of their children, and have a duty as well as a right, to teach them society's ways and the limits to behaviour that are acceptable.

Haley (1976), employing his 'problem-solving' approach, would probably concentrate on the confused hierarchy in the 'C' family. It was not clear who was in charge, and there was a lack of a properly functioning parental subsystem. The therapist takes charge of the family for a while, and puts the parents in charge of the children.

Direct treatment approaches to common family problems were discussed when these problems were described in Chapter 9. These are the basis for the setting of tasks in this phase of treatment.

Other therapeutic options

The 'problem centred systems' approach, structural therapy and Haley's 'problem-solving' therapy are all relatively direct – though not necessarily easy – methods of resolving family problems. Each requires the therapist to assess the family situation, and conceptualize it according to the relevant model of family functioning. This may involve redefining the problem, or even reframing it – although the distinction between redefining and reframing is hard to make. In the case of the 'C' family the problem was redefined as being the parents' inability, in the past, to agree on a common approach to David's problems, and generally to work together as a parental pair. This, in turn, was related to longstanding marital conflict.

Some therapists might prefer to say that the problem was reframed, rather than redefined, but this is really a matter of semantics. Reframing is not an all-or-none process. A more drastic reframing would have been to tell the family, for example, that it appeared to the therapist that David was doing an excellent job in drawing attention to the problems between the parents, and that he should be congratulated because his behaviour had had the effect of bringing the family to therapy. This reframe would have changed the meaning attributed to the presenting symptoms to a greater extent than what the therapist actually did. In this case the therapist's actions were designed to redirect the family's attention to the marital problem, rather than have it remain on the presenting symptoms.

Reframing and strategic therapy

Therapy methods which have come to be labelled 'strategic' usually involve a greater degree of reframing than was used with the 'C' family, but the borderline is a vague one. Reframing is, however, 'fundamental to strategic therapy' (Coyne, 1985).

We must now consider what the therapist should do when direct injunctions prove ineffective. Such injunctions fail either because they are not obeyed, or because the changes the family seek do not occur even though they are obeyed. Sometimes there is improvement in one area of family functioning, but this is accompanied by deterioration in another area. It is important to remember, however, that giving direct injunctions can be successful even though the instructions are not carried out. This is usually because the content of the injunction, or the nature of the task, serves to reframe the situation. Thus, setting a task that is concerned with communication in the family may draw attention to the family's communications problems and cause the family members to think differently about them. This can lead to change; indeed it can sometimes be difficult to persist in the same pattern of behaviour once your attention has been drawn to it.

The failure of direct approaches is a signal to consider indirect, or strategic, ones. A less straightforward, or more sophisticated, strategy may be required to achieve the changes the family seek. (In a sense all therapy is 'strategic' in that every therapist must have some sort of plan, or strategy, to help the family, even if this has not been clearly thought out or consciously articulated. In practice, however, the term 'strategic therapy' is usually reserved for therapy of the type described under that heading in Chapter 10 – that is, therapy aimed to reach specific goals, by indirect means.)

The therapeutic use of reframing

If therapy addressed to the unreframed problem has failed, it is usually best to consider next how the problem, or the family's situation generally, may be reframed. To quote Coyne again:

> The reframing of problem behaviour is a basic tool of strategic therapists. This class of therapeutic interventions involves shifting the perspective within which a client experiences a situation in a way that fits the 'facts' of the situation at least as well, but that changes its entire meaning. (Coyne, 1985, page 337)

Developmental reframing (Coppersmith, 1981) is a relatively simple form of reframing. It usually involves labelling behaviour which has been regarded as in some way disturbed as 'young' or 'immature'. Coppersmith's (1981) three clinical examples were entitled, respectively, 'He's not bad, he's just young'; 'She's not mad, she's just young'; and 'They do not need to divorce, they're just young'. Talking of behaviour as immature can give it a meaning quite different from what it had before. The teenage terror, who seems out of control and perhaps has temper tantrums like a toddler's, is spoken of as being just a young child who has yet to grow up. It can be difficult for teenagers to continue to behave in the same way once their behaviours have been reframed in this way. At the same time the parents may be encouraged to treat the young person as a child several years younger. This will probably mean less responsibility and fewer privileges than hitherto. The latter become dependent on age-appropriate behaviour, and temper tantrums are not age-appropriate in the teenage years.

Other therapeutic strategies

Strategic therapy has been discussed in Chapter 10, and the various techniques described there should be considered when direct methods fail. Several may be used simultaneously or in succession.

In planning and delivering strategic interventions the use of a consultation team is helpful. In addition to assisting the therapist in devising interventions, the team can act as a 'Greek chorus', as described by Papp (1980) and discussed in Chapter 10. The novice therapist in particular is wise to seek help from colleagues, preferably having them watch sessions 'live'. Even one observing colleague can help greatly. In family therapy training centres live supervision is usually the routine, but it is valuable whatever the circumstances and however great the experience of the therapist.

Having several therapists involved simultaneously in a single case may sound like an expensive proposition, but it is not necessarily so; it may greatly speed treatment, or even lead to the successful treatment of families which otherwise might fail to respond, even to prolonged therapy.

Summary

Every family therapist needs a coherent theory of change, and a systematic way of tackling families' treatment needs. We must each of us pick out, from the vast range of accumulated information, that which is most helpful to us in assisting families to make the changes they seek.

As an example of how available knowledge may be used, this chapter has described an approach to family therapy which employs techniques from different schools of family therapy. While this is certainly not the only possible approach, it is presented as a useful model for therapists as they begin to work with families, and then further sharpen their clinical skills.

The establishment of rapport is the first step in helping any family. Only once this is accomplished can assessment and treatment proceed. Treatment commences following assessment and the establishment of agreed objectives; assessment is, however, an ongoing process, and strict separation of assessment and treatment is impossible. Direct methods of therapy are used first, unless they have already been given a fair trial and have failed, or unless the family is assessed as having oppositional attitudes such as would make them unresponsive to direct injunctions.

When direct methods prove unsuccessful, indirect ones are indicated. These involve reframing the problems and/or the family situation; in doing this the family is usually offered a more radically different way of looking at things than the redefining of problems which is often necessary with direct methods. Any of the strategic therapy techniques described in Chapter 10, or the other special techniques discussed in Chapter 11, may be needed at this stage.

In dealing with the more complex family problems the use of a consultation team is recommended. For students just beginning to use strategic methods this is particularly important.

Chapter 13

Marital Therapy and Sex Therapies

The treatment of marital problems is an aspect of family therapy. As Kirschner and Kirschner (1986, page 25) put it, 'a healthy marital interaction is the key to optimal family process'. According to 'comprehensive family therapy' (CFT), the model to which these authors subscribe, there is a natural drive towards a healing marital relationship; this 'not only replicates, but also transcends the transactional gestalts that the spouses experienced in their families of origin'.

The marital relationship is also the basis of the parental one; it is hard for a couple to work effectively together as a parental couple if they are not happy as a marital pair. Many problems which manifest themselves in the behaviours of individual family members – whether parents or children – can be related to marital tensions. In families in which there are no children, marital therapy and family therapy are the same thing.

A couple's sexual relationship is an important part of their total relationship. Sometimes sexual problems are but one aspect of a wider set of problems. When this is so, the sexual difficulties may disappear as the marital relationship improves in the course of marital or family therapy. In other cases the sexual difficulties may be the primary problem, or even a separate one, and therapy directed specifically to them may be required. The treatment of sexual disorders has, however, become a specialized field, and will not be discussed in detail in this book.

The development of marital therapy

The development of marital therapy has paralleled that of therapies for larger family groups. When psychodynamic theories held near-exclusive sway, marital problems were seen as being consequences of the intrapsychic difficulties of the partners. Treatment therefore tended to concentrate on individual therapy with one or both partners. This is, theoretically at least, a valid approach. When there is marital conflict, the individuals concerned usually do have unresolved intrapsychic conflicts which are interfering with their marital relationships; and if these intrapsychic problems can be resolved, improvement in the marital relationship may be expected.

Unfortunately individual therapy often proves difficult, and needs to extend over a long period. Quicker, and often better, results can usually be achieved when the marital partners are seen together. Much the same could be said about family therapy; in theory at least, family problems could be dealt with by providing treatment for individual family members. It seems, however, that when the presenting problems are interactional, work with the whole family usually yields better and quicker results.

An important development was the publication of the book *Marital Tensions* by Henry Dicks (1967). Although Dicks viewed marital problems primarily from a psychodynamic viewpoint, he looked also at the interactional processes occurring between marital partners. He recommended conjoint treatment of marital couples, but emphasized intrapsychic processes and mental mechanisms, as well as the use of the transference relationship, in helping the partners gain an understanding of themselves and their problems in relating to each other. Other approaches, such as those of Nathan Ackerman and Jay Haley, were also reviewed by Dicks in his book.

Why does individual treatment for marital problems often yield poor results? The reason is probably to be found in the factors which lead people to marry. Couples usually marry, or enter into some other form of intimate relationship, because each of them sees something attractive in the other, and at some level feels the other partner would meet her or his needs. Individual therapy, however, aims to change the partners and may remove some of those characteristics each found attractive in the other. Someone who has undergone effective therapy is no longer the same person the partner married. If there have not been reciprocal, or in some way compatible, changes in the other partner when one changes, much of the basis of the relationship may have been removed. This is probably why, when an alcoholic partner in a marriage stops drinking, the marriage sometimes breaks up. The non-alcoholic partner may feel a sense of superiority over the one who drinks; the latter plays the role of marital or family scapegoat. Crafoord (1980, page 72) puts the situation well, describing the situation when the husband is the alcoholic:

There is an extreme polarization of the role distribution between man and wife in the family, an inequality which makes it impossible for the man to get rid of the role as the 'family bastard' if the wife would not lose her role as the 'angel'. If she is very dependent on being an angel, she has an interest in keeping the husband as a 'bastard'.

It is easy to see how, in a situation such as the above, treatment of the apparent problem – the husband and his excessive drinking – could upset the balance in the family. The wife might have married her husband in order to feel, at an unconscious level, the 'angel', that is the superior partner in the relationship. This, in turn, might have been a reaction to her own deep-seated feelings of insecurity. In conjoint marital therapy, however, it is the relationship that is the primary focus of therapy; changes in the individual partners occur as the relationship changes and vice versa. Individual and relationship changes are part of one and the same process.

As family therapy developed, and therapists increasingly found that looking at family problems interactionally, and from a 'systems' perspective, generally yielded better results than the more traditional methods, similar approaches were adopted for marital therapy. The marital *system* became the focus of therapy, rather than the marital *partners*.

We have seen that behaviour therapy techniques can readily be applied in the treatment of dyads, though they are less easily adapted to larger groups. This has led to their extensive use in marital therapy. It is usually easy, once a behavioural analysis has been carried out, to discover how each marital partner, by responding differentially, is reinforcing or extinguishing particular behaviours in the other. From this information, behaviour modification programmes can be developed.

Current approaches to marital therapy

Marital therapy – sometimes called 'couples therapy', since similar methods can be used for unmarried couples living in an intimate relationship – has much in common with other forms of family therapy. Most of the treatment methods for families discussed in previous chapters can be used as well for marital problems as for problems in larger family groups. The McMaster Model of Family Functioning, for example, is equally applicable. Thus couples may have problem-solving difficulties, communication problems, role definition problems, difficulties with affective responsiveness and affective involvement, and behaviour control problems. Such problems can be tackled using the various treatment approaches discussed in Chapter 9.

Any of the therapeutic approaches mentioned in Chapters 10 and 11 may also be used with marital couples. As with larger family groups, it is usually best to use direct methods first – unless they have already had a fair trial. Then, if the desired results have not been achieved, indirect strategies may be employed. Whether, and when, to use behavioural methods in preference to the others that are available is not always clear, but an interesting comparison of behavioural and 'interpretative' methods was reported by Crowe (1978). Forty-two couples with marital problems were randomly allocated, so that each received one of three types of treatment. These were:

- A 'directive' approach.
- An 'interpretative' approach.
- A 'supportive-control' approach.

The 'directive' approach was based on the work of Stuart (1969) and Liberman (1970), who described behavioural methods using operant conditioning. The basis of this treatment is the belief that when there is marital strife, the partners each fail to produce enough rewarding behaviours to encourage 'positive', that is gratifying, behaviours in the other partner. Therapy is designed to increase such positive behaviours; the approach is discussed further in the description below of behavioural marital therapy. In addition to these techniques, where there were sexual problems some of the techniques of Masters and Johnson (1970) were also used.

The 'interpretative' approach was based on the work of Skynner (1969b; 1976). In this, the therapist analysed and interpreted the feelings of the couple, as in group therapy with small groups. The therapist's reactions were openly shared with the couple and no advice was given. The therapist may, however, take sides or give challenges which help the couple face 'real' issues. This approach involved making interpretations dealing with the couples intrapsychic conflicts, defences, manipulation and avoidance of responsibility, and such underlying traits as depression or anger. Ventilation of feelings was encouraged. The therapist often intentionally took sides, but few interpretations of the transference relationship were used.

The 'supportive-control' approach aimed to avoid both giving advice and offering interpretations. The therapist endeavoured to remain passive and impartial, encouraging the clients to talk to each other and intervening only to make peace during prolonged quarrels or to prevent long silences.

A variety of outcome measures was used. Although the study had some methodological weaknesses, mostly acknowledged by the authors, it was an important attempt to assess the effects of different types of marital therapy. Results were assessed at the end of treatment and at follow-up three, nine and eighteen months later. While the relative improvement rates varied according to which outcome measures were considered, and with the time at which the comparisons were made, the directive approach was generally the most effective of the three treatments. This applied particularly when specific problems and target behaviours were considered. This also seems to be the consensus of other literature on the topic.

Behavioural marital therapy

The objective of the behavioural analysis which must precede therapy is to look at the interactions occurring between the couple entering treatment. Behavioural therapists believe that marital conflict is related to the rate of reinforcement of various behaviours directed by the partners towards one another, and by the proportions of reinforcement and of punishment that are delivered.

Reinforcement is defined as any response which is followed by an increase in a behaviour. *Punishment* is any response which is followed by a decrease in a behaviour. These processes can each be applied to desired or to undesired behaviours. The behavioural approach does not concern itself primarily with the origins of the present behaviours; these can vary from biological and temperamental factors, through childhood rearing patterns and other childhood experiences, to deficiencies in problem-solving or other skills. The therapist is concerned with what is *maintaining* the undesired behaviours, regardless of their origins which are, in any event, often hard to determine – especially when the problems have been present for a long time.

In this form of treatment, as in any other, the therapist must first establish rapport. The rapport building techniques discussed in Chapter 5 are as important in behavioural therapy as in any other. The therapist's interest in helping, concern for the couple, and belief that change for the better is possible, should be made clear from the start. The marital partners are usually assessed and treated as a couple, though many therapists see the partners individually in the course of the assessment; if one partner is seen, however, it is important that the other is afforded the same attention.

It is important to assess also the couple's objectives and motivation for change. Not all couples coming for help want to repair their marital relationship. Some want to end it. They may come in order to demonstrate that the situation is hopeless, or for help in ending the relationship in as constructive a way and with as little harm to all concerned as possible.

An excellent account of behavioural methods of marital therapy is to be found in the book *Marital Therapy* (Jacobson and Margolin, 1979). A basic principle, as illustrated in the brief summary above of Crowe's (1978) research, is to increase the 'positive' exchanges between the couple. Highly specific agreements are usually worked out with the clients. Each partner agrees to do certain things in relation to the other. These agreements may be committed to writing so that they can be regularly reviewed by all concerned. This helps reduce uncertainty about what actually has been agreed. While different interpretations of written agreements are possible, they are less likely than with verbal ones.

The more flexible the couple, and the less well-established and chronic their problems, the more likely it is that a straightforward approach which identifies the behaviours to be changed, and then deals directly with them by prescribing changes in the partners' behaviours, will be effective. Various examples of this approach are to be found in the book by Jacobson and Margolin (1979, Chapter 6).

Needless to say, the above approach is not successful in every case. Some couples have other problems which must be tackled first, especially communication difficulties and poor strategies for problem-solving. In treating problem-solving difficulties, it is helpful to keep in mind certain general principles of learning theory. These include the pin-pointing of target behaviours, the use of specific behaviour management strategies, for example 'shaping', and the use of positive rather than aversive principles of control. Shaping is the gradual changing of behaviour by rewarding each step, even if it is only small, towards the behavioural goal.

Behavioural communication training comprises three processes. The first is the provision by the therapist of *feedback*, that is information about clients' current communication patterns, and how these fail to serve their intended purposes. The second step is the provision of *instructions*: the therapist suggests alternative communication patterns which appear likely to be more effective. Then, during *behavioural rehearsal*, the clients practise the new communication patterns. The therapist continues to give feedback, and further instructions may be needed as treatment progresses. The three processes may thus continue together.

This form of communication training is similar to that used by therapists of other schools, and discussed in Chapter 9, but behavioural therapists tend to make the process more precise and specific. Role playing, and role reversal – in which the partners swap their usual roles – can be helpful when using these techniques.

Communication training may address various aspects of the interactions between marital partners. It may aim to make the partners respond more empathically to each other; to improve their listening skills; to increase their validation of each other; or to develop their skills in expressing feelings in appropriate ways – both angry feelings and positive, loving ones. *Validation* is the process whereby people affirm the legitimacy and reasonableness of others' opinions, suggestions or actions, even though they may disagree with them. It is discussed more fully in the self-help manual *A Couple's Guide to Communication* (Gottman et al, 1976).

A widely used technique, which can be used also in other forms of family therapy, is that of *contingency contracting*. A contingency contract is an agreement in writing between the people concerned, specifying a change in the relationship (usually a well defined behavioural change), and containing specific contingencies for compliance with the contract. ('Contingency' is a technical term for the consequences that follow an event or action.)

Contingency contracting, as Jacobson and Margolin (1979) point out, is the last stage in problem-solving. It presupposes that a solution to a problem between the couple has been found, and is a means by which the marital partners contract to put the solution into effect. If a couple already have adequate problem-solving skills but cannot make suitable agreements to apply them to their relationship, contracting skills may be taught without teaching problem-solving.

Contingency contracts are of two types, the 'quid pro quo' contract, so named by Weiss et al (1974), and the 'parallel' contract, which the same authors recommend as an alternative. In the first type there is a direct, simultaneous exchange of behaviours by the couple. In parallel contracts two independent change agreements are made. Although there is no specific exchange of behaviours, these are nevertheless accurately described as contingency contracts because specific rewards are agreed for compliance.

Other approaches to marital therapy

Behavioural marital therapy based on the theory that the relationships between spouses are controlled by reinforcement contingencies, as set out in the previous section, may not be the best way of dealing with all marital conflicts. Approaches which place more emphasis on psychodynamic factors seem also to have their place. For example, Knudson et al (1979) and Leadbetter and Farber (1983) believe that for many couples the promotion of mutual understanding and empathy are more important than the making of contracts concerned with instrumental behaviours. Knudson et al (1979, page 556) state that:

In healthy intimate relationships, people should behave in ways that are not controlled, whether positively or negatively, by the desires and expectations of others.

Leadbetter and Farber (1983, page 236) go on to suggest that, 'training in instrumental contracting may be helpful to couples who physically or verbally punish each other with negative or coercive stimuli'. In other situations it may not be the treatment of choice. Perhaps therapy should start with a 'behaviour exchange' approach when there is open strife between the partners. Then once there is no longer open conflict between the partners, it can proceed, as these authors put it, to promote 'mutual understanding, empathy, and reciprocal role-taking'. In cases where there is no open strife, therapy should from the start aim to help the partners understand each other, and the meaning behind each other's behaviour. The basis of the marital problems may be that the partners have different value systems, and differing ideas about the sort of marriage they want.

Kirschner and Kirschner (1986) provide two excellent chapters on marital therapy, one discussing the principles on which they work, the other describing the treatment of three cases. They recommend using conjoint sessions with both spouses, along with concurrent sessions with each spouse alone. By this means, 'the therapist gains access to the intrapsychic functioning of each spouse, the behavioural transactions, and the interface between psyche and system' (Kirschner and Kirschner, 1986, pages 152–53.

The Kirschners use a wide variety of techniques in their work with marital couples, some of them remarkably direct. They see marital therapy as involving the formation of a family triangle. Sometimes the partners compete for the therapist's attention and approval, and this can be used constructively. But 'the triangle of potent relationships formed in the course of CFT treatment can result ... in splitting and the potential formation of illicit coalitions'. The Kirschners discuss ways of dealing with such problems, and with such other issues as engaging resistant spouses, controlling abusive behaviour, equalizing overt power between the couple, enhancing the couple's sex life and 'fostering constructive fighting'. The latter term refers to the orchestration of 'constructive conflict and freer expressions of anger'. Once anger is accepted, it can become dissipated, and warm and loving feelings can emerge. The ventilation of hurt and anger must be done, 'in an assertive manner, with "I" statements rather than blaming "you" statements' (Kirschner and Kirschner, 1986, page 162).

The Kirschners' CFT model of marital therapy combines systems concepts, behavioural methods and individual therapy in a creative way.

It appears to offer a worthwhile and promising approach to many of the difficult but common problems that afflict marriages.

Self-help methods

Many self-help approaches to the alleviation of marital conflict are available. We have already mentioned *A Couple's Guide to Communication* (Gottman et al, 1976). Another self-help device is the *Marriage Contract Game* (Blechman and Rabin, 1982). This is 'designed to help couples negotiate problems in an explicit, rational manner'. The authors even suggest that the game may be, in some respects, 'superior to approaches which rely on a therapist to promote effective communication'.

Marital Choices, a book by William J. Lederer (1981), is described on its dust jacket as comprising:

A five-week program for improving relationships – a holistic system, to be conducted at home, which includes behaviour change, the development of full partner equality, and instructions for identifying unrecognized physical conditions which provoke trouble in many marriages.

This book presents its readers with a formidable series of tasks, which must test the motivation of many. Unfortunately there is little objective evidence about the relative effectiveness of this and other self-help devices, both compared with each other or when they are compared with 'live' treatment with a therapist.

Divorce therapy and mediation

Family therapists are increasingly being consulted by couples who are in the process of separating or becoming divorced. While some therapists specialize in this work, this is a field with which all who work with troubled families should be familiar. Sometimes marital partners decide to separate after entering therapy; it may only become clear that their marital goals are incompatible once they start exploring their difficulties, and the sort of marriage each wants.

Beal (1980) discusses divorce as an increasingly common feature of the family life cycle. How it occurs, and its consequences, vary greatly. Much depends on the length of the marriage, whether there are children and, if so, how old they are. Relationships between spouses rarely end with divorce, particularly when there are children of the marriage. The therapist may have much to offer couples during and after the divorce process, using any of the techniques mentioned in previous chapters, especially when there are problems with the children of the marriage.

Children of divorced parents are at risk in various ways. They may feel responsible for the divorce, and therefore be burdened with feelings of guilt; their lifestyle may have been greatly changed, perhaps because of the poorer economic situation of the parent caring for them; they may have had to move house, neighbourhood or school; and they may be used as pawns in a continuing game between the parents. It is important that the parents do not put each other down in conversation with the children; nor should one seek the children's support in criticizing and finding fault with the other. Divorced couples often continue, sometimes for many years, to feel anger, bitterness and resentment towards each other. Therapy can sometimes help in resolving these continuing problems.

Kressel and his colleagues (1980) have proposed a 'typology of divorcing couples', although their data is derived from a study of only fourteen couples. They identified four distinct patterns in the process by which the couples reached the divorce decision. This classification was based on 'three complex and highly intercorrelated dimensions':

- Degree of ambivalence.
- Frequency and openness of communication.
- Level and overtness of conflict.

The four patterns were labelled enmeshed, autistic, direct and disengaged. The *enmeshed* pattern was characterized by high levels of conflict, communication and ambivalence about the divorce decision. In the *autistic* type of divorce decision-making, communication and overt conflict about the possibility of divorce were almost absent, though there was a high degree of ambivalence. The *'direct-conflict'* pattern was characterized by high levels of overt conflict (but less intense than in the enmeshed pattern), and frequent and open communication between the parties about the possibility of divorce. Ambivalence was initially high, but moderated during a period of a year or more of 'working through'. The *'disengaged-conflict'* pattern was distinguished by low ambivalence, and communication and conflict which were nearly as low as in the autistic pattern.

Although this was a small study, confined to a particular socioeconomic group – all the husbands were in professional or managerial positions – it appeared that task-oriented mediation worked best for the couples in the 'direct' and 'disengaged' groups. In the 'enmeshed' and 'autistic' types it was less successful; in addition the post-divorce adjustment in these groups was poor – worse than in the other two groups.

'Divorce conciliation' or 'divorce mediation', sometimes known as 'family mediation', is increasingly being sought by divorcing couples, as an alternative to adversarial legal processes. In the USA there are both a Family Mediation Association and an Academy of Family Mediators. In 1982 the president of the latter organization reviewed the status of family mediation, and the training needed to practise it (Haynes, 1982). There have also been many other publications on the subject (for example, Coogler, 1978; Haynes, 1981; Irving, 1980, 1981; Kaslow, 1984; Lowery, 1984; Marlow, 1985a, 1985b). Although agreements reached in the course of mediation usually have to be confirmed by the court, Marlow (1985b) contends that, 'divorce mediation represents a rejection of a legal model of divorce and a substitution of a mental health model'. He also identifies 12 steps in the process of mediation:

1. Referral.
2. Intake/orientation.
3. Budget development.
4. Reconciliation of budgetary needs.
5. Identification of assets.
6. Identification of parenting goals.
7. Clarification of issues.
8. Rank ordering of issues.
9. Identification of options.
10. Bargaining.
11. Drafting the memorandum of understanding.
12. Consultation with the lawyer(s) or attorney(s).

It will be clear from the above list of steps that this process requires more than an understanding of family dynamics, and of communications and other theories of human behaviour. Haynes (1982) points out that knowledge of bargaining and negotiation – in which lawyers are usually expert – is also necessary. Family therapists should therefore undergo some additional training if they are to undertake this work effectively.

Sex therapy

Sexual difficulties between the marital couple sometimes exist as part of a wider marital or family problem. It is then necessary to assess the role of the sexual problems in the total marital or family problem. Sexual problems may be the cause or the effect of other family problems, or they may be but one feature of a larger set of systems problems. Sometimes they are an associated feature with little evident aetiological connection – though it is always helpful to enhance a couple's sexual satisfaction if this is less than optimal.

Sex therapy, like much other psychotherapy, used to be based principally on psychodynamic theories. These looked at sexual problems in terms of the psychopathology of the individuals concerned, rather than examining the processes going on between the partners with the troubled relationship. But in much the same way as family therapists have concerned themselves with interpersonal, rather than intrapersonal, processes, sex therapists too have taken to considering interactional phenomena. It has also become clear that many sexual problems can be successfully treated using direct approaches.

An important event in the development of sex therapy was the publication in 1966 of *Human Sexual Response*, by Masters and Johnson. In this book the authors reported the results of a careful study of human sexual behaviour. This led to the development of therapy methods based on the understanding of sexual behaviour the authors had achieved. Masters' and Johnson's approach was primarily a behavioural one, rather than one based on the uncovering and resolution of intrapsychic conflict. It was described in *Human Sexual Inadequacy* (Masters and Johnson, 1970). These two books became standard works of reference, and are the basis for much modern sex therapy.

In 1974 Helen Singer Kaplan's book *The New Sex Therapy* appeared. Building on the work of Masters and Johnson, it examined the anatomy and physiology of the sexual response and then looked at the various factors which may affect sexual performance. These include physical illness, age, drugs, intrapsychic causes, relationship difficulties and faulty learning experiences. Kaplan recommended an assessment along these lines of both members of the couple, leading to the development of a plan directed to the specific cause or causes of the problem.

Kaplan (1979) took her understanding of sexual disorders further in *Disorders of Sexual Desire*. In this book she is careful to distinguish the many different types of sexual problems, and she also points out the error of the old ways of looking at them:

> The psychoanalytic establishment, consistent with the prevailing monistic concept, regarded all sexually troubled patients – the fetishists, asexuals, those with disturbances of romantic attachments, the sexually phobic, patients with gender disturbances, impotence, anorgasmia, vaginismus, etc. – as variants of the same psychopathological population. The second error involved the belief that the cause of sexual difficulties was specific and profound. It was thought that all sexual problems were produced by specific and serious unconscious conflicts about sex which were acquired during specific developmen-

tal phases in early childhood. Thus, all sexually inadequate patients were believed to be in need of psychoanalytically oriented treatment which has the capability of resolving such unconscious conflicts (Kaplan, 1979, page 4).

Kaplan asserts that therapy was formerly impeded by a failure on the part of therapists to realize that sexual response is not an entity, but consists of a series of phases.

Masters and Johnson (1966) divided the sexual response into four stages: excitement, plateau, orgasm and resolution. Kaplan (1979), however, suggested that a 'triphasic' model best fits the facts. The three phases she recognizes are:

• The desire phase.
• The excitement phase.
• Orgasm.

Masters and Johnson's 'excitement' and 'plateau' stages correspond to Kaplan's 'excitement' phase, and their 'orgasm' phase to Kaplan's phase of the same name. Resolution is simply the termination of sexual arousal. Masters and Johnson did not describe a 'desire' stage.

Kaplan (1979) describes separate treatment approaches for sexual problems, according to which of the three phases is involved. Problems of the orgasm phase include premature, retarded or absent ejaculation in the male and inhibition of orgasm in the female. Inhibition of the excitement phase produces impotence in the male and a failure to become excited and to produce adequate vaginal lubrication in the female. Desire phase problems are characterized by low libido; this is manifest, in both sexes, in reduced or absent desire for intercourse. It is possible for problems to exist in two or in all three phases simultaneously. Generally speaking treatment of orgasm phase difficulties has the highest success rate, and that of desire phase problems the lowest.

Kaplan's approach is generally directive and behavioural, but when this proves ineffective she looks at psychodynamic factors which may be responsible for resistance to treatment. This, she believes, is the main importance of a psychodynamic understanding of the case. She pays less attention to the symbolic meaning of the symptoms and their historical origins.

Further information on sex therapy is available in the books that have been mentioned. *Principles and Practice of Sex Therapy* (Leiblum and Pervin, 1980) also provides a wide-ranging look at the field, and sex therapy has spawned its own journals – for example the *Archives of Sexual Behaviour*, *The Journal of Sex and Marital Therapy* and *The Journal of Sex Research*. Advances in this fast-growing field are reported in these journals, often in preference to family therapy journals or other publications in the mental health field.

Summary

Marital therapy is an aspect of family therapy. Sometimes a marital problem is at the heart of a problem which presents as dysfunction in the wider family system. Marital therapy has increasingly concentrated on the interactional processes occurring between the marital pair, rather than on the partners' intrapsychic processes.

Any of the therapy methods which have been described for use in larger family groups may be applied to marital couples, but behavioural methods are particularly well suited for use with dyads, such as marital pairs. They seem to be especially valuable when there is open strife, and much 'negative' interchange between the partners. They can promote the substitution of 'positive' exchanges for the negative ones. There are often also psychodynamic aspects of the relationship which need to be addressed in therapy. Individual treatment of one partner, independent of help with the other, tends to lead to poor results. Various self-help programmes for couples with marital problems are also available.

With the rising frequency of divorce, therapists are increasingly being consulted by couples who want help during this process – both in preventing any more psychological harm than necessary befalling family members, and in mediating disputes about the custody of children and about financial and other issues. This has led to the development of specialist 'family mediators'.

Problems of sexual dysfunction are often present when there are other marital and family problems, though they may also occur in the absence of other serious problems. Sex therapy, too, has become a largely separate field of study and clinical practice, but all therapists need to be aware of what it has to offer. They should always consider whether sexual problems are contributing to the other marital and family problems which they are investigating and treating.

Chapter 14

Terminating Treatment and Dealing With Treatment Interruptions

The family therapy literature has less to say about how to terminate treatment than about how to start and how to continue it. The way treatment is ended is nevertheless important. Lankton and Lankton (1983, page 345) point out that:

> The termination of a therapy session, as well as the termination of the entire therapy relationship, has special meaning to clients...the therapist orients clients away from dependence on therapy to the interdependence of their social network. But individual coping styles and mechanisms for frustration tolerance will determine just how clients consciously anticipate their adjustment.

Treatment contracts

Some of the purposes of making formal contracts with families were discussed in Chapter 8. When a specific time-limited or session-limited contract exists, the family can prepare for termination from the start. Having a time limit can also motivate families by providing a sense of urgency. 'If we don't get these issues sorted out by the fifth (or tenth, or whatever) session', they may say to themselves, 'we shan't be able to achieve a solution to our problems'.

A time-limited contract also helps families see therapy as a discrete process extending over a certain period of time, following which they will be able to continue their lives without needing the help of a therapist.

There can be some flexibility about contracts; the frequency of sessions may be decreased as changes in the family occur and the intensity of the problems lessens. Some therapists foreshadow, at the outset, the possibility of negotiating a further contract at the end of the initial one. While there are advantages in a flexible approach, and in keeping options open, early talk about renewing time-limited contracts tends to remove much of the point of setting them up. I prefer not to mention the possibility of renewing any contracts I negotiate when they are first made. Some families, however, raise the issue, and in that case I tell them I am sometimes willing to do this.

When is a time-limited contract indicated? There seems to be no available data on which to base a firm answer to this question. Some therapists use such contracts and others do not, but no controlled trial, in which comparable groups were treated with and without time-limited contracts and results compared, has been reported. Moreover, the number of sessions recommended does not seem necessarily to be related to the severity of the family problem. For example the Milan group (Palazzoli et al, 1978a), reported that they used ten-session contracts for the very severely disturbed families they treated. Occasionally they renewed the contracts for a further ten sessions, but in most cases they did not. The Brief Therapy Centre of the Mental Research Institute in Palo Alto also worked on the basis of limited-session contracts. The 97 cases reported by Watzlawick and his colleagues (1974, page 115), comprising identified patients with a wider range of problems than those treated by the Milan group, were seen for an average of seven hours each.

If there is a previously agreed contract which specifies when therapy is to end, the therapist should have a contingency plan ready for use if the family ask for an extension. The choice lies between negotiating another contract, perhaps for a small number of further sessions, assuring the family they do not need any more treatment, or suggesting some other treatment; the latter could be something quite different – for example individual therapy for a family member, involvement in a therapeutic group or self-help organization, non-time-limited family therapy (such as the 'interminable' treatment mentioned in Chapter 10), or referral to another therapist or agency.

Sometimes a family's request for further treatment once their initial contract has come to an end can be the occasion to get therapy on to a new footing. If treatment has failed to achieve the hoped for results because of a lack of commitment on the part of the family, new conditions may be built into the contract at this stage.

Open contracts

The alternative to a time-limited contract is an open one – one which does not specify the length of the treatment, nor the number of times the family will be seen. This seems to be a more commonly used procedure. In the book *Family Therapy: Full Length Case Studies* (Papp, 1977), there are accounts of the treatment of eleven families by eminent family therapists. In none of them is there mention of the setting up by the therapist of a contract for a fixed number of sessions. This is despite the presence among the authors of two therapists (Weakland and Fisch) associated with the Brief Therapy Centre in Palo Alto, and of Papp herself, describing a family seen in the brief therapy project of the Ackerman Institute. This book, and the family therapy literature generally, suggest that open contracts are more commonly used than closed ones.

When the therapy contract is an open one the management of the termination process is even more important. With closed contracts families know from the start when treatment will end, and can prepare themselves for this. With open contracts this is not so, and at some point the subject of termination must be raised and related issues discussed.

Indications for ending treatment

The termination of family therapy may be initiated either by the therapist or by the family.

Termination on the initiative of the therapist may be indicated under any of the following circumstances:

(a) When the objectives set at the start of treatment have been met. Assessing whether or not this has happened is greatly helped if clear goals and objectives were agreed at the outset. Ideally therapist and family should, throughout treatment, bear in mind the 'outcome frame', as we have described this concept in Chapter 6.

When it appears that the desired state has been achieved, or is being approached, it is a good plan to review with the family the changes that have taken place during treatment. If the family members feel things have changed, it can be helpful to have them examine the changes that have occurred. What exactly has changed? What specific things are different compared with the situation at the start of therapy? Do these changes amount to the achievement of the goals set when therapy began, or at later stages?

Termination is often better accomplished when the family is able to see the extent of the changes that have occurred, and when family members realize that their problem-solving skills have improved. Tomm and Wright (1979) suggest that a paradoxical question, such as, 'What would each of you have to do to bring the problem back?' helps the family understand better what has happened during treatment.

(b) When, although the objectives originally specified have not been fully met, there has been a change in the family's functioning such that further treatment is not necessary. That is, the family now has the resources it needs to deal with any remaining problems. Outside help is no longer required.

There may have been structural changes in the family, or improvement in the family's problem-solving skills. These may now enable it to cope with problems which previously defeated it. For example there might have been an improvement in the effectiveness of the parental couple's ability to work together in caring for their children. So although their children's behaviour might still present problems, the parents would now be able to handle them appropriately. If treatment is to be terminated in these circumstances, it is important that the changes that have occurred are labelled, explained and agreed by the family members – even though the means whereby they have been achieved may not be made explicit.

(c) If therapy has proved ineffective, despite having had a fair trial. This may be an indication for stopping therapy, at least of the type that has been used so far. A possible source of failure, as Watzlawick et al (1974, page 105) point out, is the setting of unrealistic or inappropriate goals. It is unrealistic to suppose that every family can achieve all the changes its members might desire, and sometimes there is a lack of agreement among the members about what they really want – though this may initially be camouflaged.

Coleman and Gurman (1985), in the final chapter of the fascinating book *Failures In Family Therapy* (Coleman, 1985), list as some of the causes of failure:

- Inadequate understanding and analysis of the circumstances surrounding the referral, particularly with regard to the assessment of the problem.
- Insufficient goal setting, particularly with regard to who sets the goals.
- Conflictual goals that affect therapy outcome.
- Overlooking the role of the presenting problem.

Coleman and Gurman's analysis of therapeutic failures confirms the importance of the initial assessment of family problems, and of defining and agreeing therapeutic objectives, as set out in earlier chapters of this book.

(d) Loss or lack of family motivation. This is really an aspect of therapeutic failure, but issues of motivation merit separate consideration. If therapy appears to be failing to achieve its objectives it is wise for the therapist to consider whether the family wants to change, or whether perhaps some members do while others do not. This is a delicate issue, for it is always possible for the therapist to blame a family's lack of motivation for the failure of therapy, yet a more important factor may be the therapist's limitations, or lack of the skills or experience needed to treat the family successfully. Sometimes a family's apparently weak motivation, or fear of change, may be part and parcel of the problem that brought it to therapy in the first place. We should therefore be cautious about blaming failure on the family's motivation; part of our job is to motivate the families we see to do what they need to do to achieve their objectives. Therapists who are in doubt about the relative roles of families' poor motivation and their own limitations should seek consultation from experienced colleagues.

There are various ways of motivating families. An optimistic attitude on the therapist's part, combined with mention of how things will be when (not if!) therapy is successfully concluded, and the embedding in conversation of statements that look forward to that situation, are useful. In more difficult families a strategic approach may be needed. Metaphorical methods may succeed where direct ones do not; a number of examples are to be found in *Using Metaphors in Psychotherapy* (Barker, 1985, particularly pages 94–101). Stories about people who have come to a crossroads, or a fork in the highway, may be useful. The excitement, challenge or happy outcome of taking a new direction may be stressed, and may serve as a metaphor for the adventure of entering therapy. For those who believe that discontinuous change is not possible, Milton Erickson's story of Joe, the chronic and apparently incorrigible criminal whose life became suddenly and dramatically transformed, can be used. (It is to be found in Erickson, 1980e, pages 211–216, and is summarized in Barker, 1985, pages 55–56.)

Another possibility is to use a paradoxical approach, for example telling the family that while changes such as they say they want are possible, it would nevertheless be unwise to start treatment since the family is really unsure whether it wants to make the changes in question. Therefore they are advised to leave things as they are for the present. A challenge of this sort may cause the family to react by insisting upon therapy. This approach may be used when termination is being considered because of an apparent lack of interest, on the family's part, in making changes. When termination is being discussed, the family is told that, though change is certainly still possible, this appears to be the wrong time to undertake the work involved; to do so would be more difficult – or stressful – than the status quo. If the family really wishes to make changes this may stimulate them to action. If it does not, its response to such a statement may confirm this. Either way, nothing is lost, and in ending treatment the therapist may motivate the family to seek help later.

(e) Tomm and Wright (1979) point out that when continuing treatment does not appear to be cost-effective, it may be wise to consider termination. Sometimes progress is very slow, despite all the therapist's efforts. It that case it may be best for the therapist to clarify his or her limitations and initiate termination.

Termination on the initiative of the family may occur in various ways. The desire of the family to stop therapy may be manifest in failure to attend sessions, but there are often warning signs that this may be about to happen. These include failed appointments, last minute cancellations, late arrival for sessions, and the absence from sessions of family members who are supposed to be present. The content of sessions may also provide hints about what is happening, as when family members express dissatisfaction with the course of therapy, or begin complaining about the practical difficulties of attending, the loss of time at work, or the children's lost schooling.

Tomm and Wright (1979) recommend that whenever initiatives such as those above become apparent, the therapist should take certain steps. These include considering what problems remain and what goals have not been achieved, assessing why the family is inclining towards termination, and looking especially for any evidence that there is serious danger of deterioration if treatment stops at the current stage. Depending upon these considerations, the therapist may take any of the following steps:

(a) Exploring with the family their motives for wishing to end treatment. This is almost always necessary. The aim is to establish whether the motives are reasonable. Families sometimes lose their motivation because the crisis that precipitated their request for treatment has passed. This may or may not be a good reason for stopping therapy.

(b) Reviewing with the family the present state of their problems and, if appropriate, renegotiating the therapy contract. It may be helpful for the therapist to point out the benefits which therapy may still offer.

(c) Actively encouraging the family to remain in treatment, should there be reason to believe that deterioration is likely if treatment ceases at its current stage. It can be helpful to seek the support of any people, inside or outside the family, who are likely to benefit if therapy continues. It may be necessary for the therapist to bring to the notice of such people the benefits that are likely to accrue.

(d) Accepting the family's wish to end treatment, and indicating respect for their right to make that decision. This is appropriate when there is evidence that termination is inevitable, and the therapist's wish to continue is stronger than the family's. In such circumstances the chances of further change occurring as a result of therapy are slight.

How to terminate treatment

Epstein and Bishop (1981) identify four steps in the closure process in their therapy model. These are:

- Orientation.
- Summarizing what has happened during treatment.
- Discussing long-term goals.
- Follow-up (which is optional).

The following steps are modified from the above scheme. During the *orientation* stage the therapist explains why the question of termination is being raised. This may be because the expectations with which therapy started have been met, because the contracted number of sessions has been or is about to be completed, or because there has been little or no progress.

The summary of what has happened during therapy provides an opportunity for all concerned to review the progress that has been made, and the present situation in the family.

The discussion of long-term goals should include also discussion of how family members will know whether or not they are meeting them. It is usually appropriate to present treatment as part of a continuing process of family growth and development, and this in turn as something that is accompanied by the growth and development of the individual family members. I usually identify challenges the family may face in the future, and discuss how the family may use its strengths and psychological resources to meet such challenges. It can be helpful also to identify the outside resources that are available – extended family, friends, social and other agencies, the family doctor, professional workers in the mental health field, school counsellors and so on.

Follow-up, the final stage, is considered below.

During the closure process I like to take an optimistic view of the situation and the family's prospects, even if closure is due to the family's unwillingness to continue to attend rather than because the goals of therapy have been attained. I emphasize the family's strengths, the changes they have made and the effort they have put into achieving these changes. Even if the changes have been small, it is worthwhile pointing them out. It may also be helpful to mention that family therapy is not the only means by which families make changes; indeed most families, most of the time, are making changes, meeting challenges, and overcoming developmental hurdles, without the help of therapists.

As at other stages of therapy, families should be affirmed as treatment is terminated. I like to express confidence in their ability to continue to make necessary changes. The message to be given should be, 'You've done well during treatment, and I believe you know what you have to do in the future, and how to set about making any further changes you want'. It is not usually a good idea for us as therapists to take credit for the changes families make, however clever we may think we are. As professional therapists we are only doing the job we are paid for, like bus drivers, plumbers, architects or the people who work in our factories.

Termination tasks and rituals

It can be helpful, when therapy sessions end, to leave the family with resources they can continue to use. These can consist of straightforward tasks, like arranging family meetings at regular intervals, or when major decisions have to be made. Another possibility is to prescribe symbolic or metaphorical tasks, perhaps of a ritualistic nature.

These tasks or rituals will often build on processes started during therapy. They can be a means whereby the therapist can remain psychologically with the family, even though the sessions have ended. They are similar to post-hypnotic suggestions. Indeed Ritterman (1983, page 316), in her book *Using Hypnosis in Family Therapy*, describes the deliberate use of post-hypnotic suggestion in work with a client who was having difficulty dealing with issues concerned with the death of her husband. Erickson, too, made frequent use of post-hypnotic suggestion, as implied in the title of the book *My Voice Will Go With You* (edited by Rosen, 1982; the phrase is taken from one of Erickson's 'teaching tales', which appears in the book).

Termination metaphors (Barker, 1985, pages 184-185) can keep alive, at the unconscious level, something of what has happened during treatment. Imber-Black (in press) describes the use of a ritual and a metaphorical object in the termination of treatment. The ritual was designed to help normalize the relationship between a mother and her young adult daughter. The daughter had previously been diagnosed as a 'paranoid schizophrenic'. Prior to treatment the relationship had been more that of custodian and patient than mother and adult daughter.

They were instructed to go shopping together, which they heartily enjoyed, and to find the most elegant, most expensive pair of kid gloves possible. When they returned home the mother, with the daughter watching, was to soak the gloves in a bowl of water and put the bowl, gloves and all, in the freezer. She was then instructed to continue to treat her daughter with kid gloves when she needed to, but only *after* she had removed the gloves from the freezer and let them thaw out. Mother and daughter did the ritual with great care and lots of laughter. The daughter continued to grow in responsible action and the mother stopped being afraid of her or of making appropriate demands on her. The kid gloves stayed in the freezer and became part of the family's 'inner language'. (Imber-Black, in press)

This is an example of a creative device for enabling a family to remain symbolically in touch with the therapist after the actual sessions with her had ended. The pair of gloves served as a metaphorical object (see Angelo, 1981; Barker, 1985), and could continue to serve the family's therapeutic needs even though they reposed, frozen, in the freezer.

Emotional and psychological aspects of termination

The ending of therapy may be a time of great emotional significance to family members. It may, consciously or unconsciously, remind them of previous separations or losses. Inexpertly managed, it can appear to clients as a rejection but, just as the death of a loved one can be the occasion to celebrate that person's life and achievements, so can the ending of treatment be an occasion to celebrate what has been achieved. Nevertheless the therapist should always be on the look-out for signs that termination is proving difficult for the family, or for some of its members. The Lanktons put it well:

The business of other unfinished 'goodbyes' may be revived. These may have nothing to do with the expressed purpose of the therapy but nevertheless be stimulated by the parallel situation. For example the death of a friend from college may have had nothing to do with the marital therapy sought by the client. Yet, at termination, the client or therapist may find the need for adequate adjustment to this past situation stimulated by the end of the session or the therapy. This is often typified by negative emotions, tensions, 'dead' spots, internal dialogues with deceased loved ones, unexplainable preoccupations, or unexpected delayed stress reactions from involvement in, for instance, the Vietnam War. (Lankton and Lankton, 1983, pages 345-346)

Similar reactions, I have found, may occur in response to my being late for or cancelling an appointment with a family. Punctuality and reliability on the part of the therapist are very important (not only in family therapy either). When lateness or cancellations are unavoidable, the family should be told the reasons at the earliest opportunity, and the therapist should be prepared to deal with any emotional reactions that may occur. (Being late, or even failing to appear at all, may occasionally be used deliberately as a strategic device, but this is a different matter.)

Follow-up

Deciding whether or not to offer follow-up contacts, designed simply to obtain information about a family's progress, can be difficult. It may be tempting to offer an appointment or a telephone contact a few weeks or months ahead, when a family's case is closed, in order to check on whether progress is being maintained. While it may help families to feel that the therapist is still available to them, there is a danger of giving the message that further problems are likely. The family should not leave feeling they are likely to fall apart again! After you have expressed a positive view of the family's competence, the message should not be weakened by any implication of doubt about the longer-term outcome. There is a good case for making it clear that therapy is finished: no further treatment will be needed. It may be permissible to add, 'I (or we) will always be here if you need me (or us), of course, but I (or the team) really don't believe you will'.

The problem with the above approach is that it deprives the therapist of any follow-up information. Yet it is important for our professional development that we know whether changes that occur in families during treatment are maintained. Fortunately there is a way of resolving this dilemma, at least partially. This is for the therapist to make it a policy to follow up every family at certain predetermined intervals, perhaps at four or six months, or at both six and twelve months. If we do this we can truthfully say to families, at closure, 'You don't need any more treatment, but it is my policy (or perhaps the policy of the agency), with all the families I see, to contact them after six months (or whatever interval or intervals are chosen), because I am interested in knowing how they are getting along, and what further progress they have made'. An alternative is to say that the information is needed 'for research purposes', but this would only be appropriate if the data were indeed being used for research purposes.

Follow-up contacts may be made by telephone, letter or an appointment at the clinic or office. A face-to-face meeting with the family generally gives the most information; it may need to be no longer than half an hour. Some families are willing to respond to a telephone call, but not to pay a visit to the therapist. Some also respond to letters or questionnaires requesting information, but this seems to be the method which yields the least return.

Treatment interruptions

Sometimes the course of treatment is interrupted by such things as physical illness in the family, illness affecting the therapist, vacations, or a move out of the area by family or therapist. Occasionally these circumstances may lead to the termination of therapy, but more often there are other appropriate ways of dealing with them.

As far as possible these issues should be discussed well in advance. If you are expecting to be away from your work for a time during the family's projected course of treatment, the family should be warned of this, and the dates mentioned, before treatment starts. In the same way we should ask the families we see whether, and when, they expect to be away. In either case there should be agreement in advance about how absences will be managed; sometimes sessions can be specially scheduled to avoid vacations and other known forthcoming events, and sometimes longer breaks than usual can be used by the family to practise skills they have learned. If you are going to be absent for a long period, however, it may be best to arrange for a colleague to see the family in your absence, and in any case someone should be available to deal with any issues which cannot wait until you return.

We have already considered, in Chapter 8, what we can do when some family members fail to attend. If the entire family fails to attend regularly, this is an issue which usually needs to be addressed when the family does come. When this, or other breaches of the contract by the family, become serious problems, a session may be devoted to discussing them, and it may be necessary to renegotiate the contract. If the renegotiated contract is then broken this may be an indication for ending treatment.

Dealing with illnesses in families can present problems. While physical illness can afflict both therapist and family members, it can also be used as an excuse for non-attendance. If you have doubts about whether illnesses reported in family members are genuine, it is usually best to discuss these openly with the family. If therapy seems unlikely to be effective without the 'sick' member – whether the sickness is a 'genuine' physical illness or not – this may be a good reason to suggest suspending therapy until the person concerned has recovered, or even for ending it altogether. A new course of treatment, perhaps based on a new contract, may be offered when all necessary people can attend. The absence or sickness of family members may, however, be manifestations of the problems which have brought the family to therapy. It may not make sense, therefore, to suspend or terminate therapy because of these problems. Discontinuing treatment, or threatening to, is not always the best way of dealing with these difficulties. Through working with those family members who do attend it is sometimes possible to get the absentee members to come also.

Finally, it is important always to remember that we have an ethical responsibility to see families through, once we have accepted them for treatment, so long as they wish us to continue treating them. If we become incapacitated, or move away, we must ensure that they are properly handed over to the care of colleagues. Similarly, if families have to move away from us, we should do everything we can to put them in touch with help in their new locality, if that is their wish.

Summary

Bringing the treatment of a family to an end requires careful preparation. If a time- or session-limited contract has been made the family should be better prepared for termination than when an 'open' contract has existed.

Therapy may end on the initiative of either the therapist or the family. Termination may be indicated because the agreed goals have been achieved; because the family has acquired the skills to resolve the remaining problems on its own; because treatment has proved ineffective; or because the family does not wish to continue.

When therapy ends, the changes that have occurred should be identified, and any further long-range goals discussed. The family's progress, strengths and resources should be the focus of closing interviews, and an affirming, optimistic attitude is usually the best one for the therapist to take. Tasks and rituals, which may have metaphorical significance, can keep memories of the therapy, and reframed attitudes, in the minds of the family.

The therapist must be alert for evidence of the emotional significance of closure, which may bring out feelings related to past losses. Caution should be exercised in arranging follow-up, lest families interpret the plans to mean that relapse is expected.

How to deal with necessary disruptions of a regular schedule of therapy sessions should, whenever possible, be planned well in advance. When other disruptions occur, both the stated reasons and any underlying factors should be explored. When interruptions are therapist-related it is the therapist's duty to make suitable arrangements to meet the clients' needs, including referral to colleagues if need be.

Chapter 15

Teaching and Learning Family Therapy

Family therapy is taught to students of various disciplines both as part of their training in, for example, social work, clinical psychology or psychiatry; and as a postgraduate subject in which members of such professions choose to specialize. There is also emerging a new profession of family therapists – those who have not previously trained in another field. This is a recent development, however. The pioneers of family therapy all came from other disciplines. Many were physicians – usually psychiatrists – for example, Midelfort, Ackerman, Bowen, Wynne, Lidz, Whitaker, John E. Bell, Laing, Boszormenyi-Nagy and Minuchin, but there were notable exceptions, such as Haley, Weakland, Satir, Watzlawick and Bateson.

In the mid-eighties, most family therapy training is still designed for members already trained in other professions. Various aspects of our subject are, however, increasingly being taught as a part of social work, psychiatry (Sugarman, 1981), clinical psychology (Cooper et al, 1981), child care work, nursing (as evidenced by the appearance of *Nurses and Families*, by Wright and Leahey, 1984), and other courses. This does not make graduates of these courses fully trained family therapists, but exactly how much you need to know to set yourself up in practice as a family therapist is not generally agreed; in most jurisdictions anyone can legally do this, although this situation is beginning to change, especially in the USA.

Moves to establish professional standards and qualifications for family therapists have been underway for the last decade or so. Foremost among the organizations doing this has been the American Association for Marriage and Family Therapy (AAMFT), (1717 K Street, NW, Suite 407, Washington, DC 20006, USA). Founded in 1942, this association sets rigorous membership standards covering specialized academic training and supervised professional experience. It also examines and accredits centres which provide training in marital and family therapy. In the UK the Institute of Family Therapy and the Association for Family Therapy are similarly examining and seeking to formalize standards of training.

Whether family therapy should become a separate discipline, like dentistry or veterinary medicine, or whether it should remain primarily a field of practice in which professionals from other disciplines can choose to specialize, like hypnotherapy, is not currently agreed. There is much to be said for it remaining as one of the treatment skills possessed by therapists who are also adept in other approaches. Such therapists can choose which approach to use, according to the needs of their clients. On the other hand, there is also a need for expert, specialist family therapists, who make this their main or even their only field of practice. Many such experts exist already, and they act as consultants to other therapists, treat some of the more complex cases themselves, and play major roles in teaching family therapy and advancing the subject through research.

There is also a need for some means whereby the general public can discover who is properly trained and qualified to practice family therapy. The existence of university degrees in family therapy, such as we are now beginning to see, should help in this respect. In Britain a one-year full-time course of training in family therapy, leading to the award of a Diploma in Family Therapy, has recently been announced by the Institute of Psychiatry of the University of London.

Who learns family therapy?

As we have seen, family therapy is currently taught to three main categories of students:

- Those training in some other discipline, such as psychiatry, social work, psychology or nursing.
- Established practitioners of one of the above disciplines, or a related one.
- Students who have not previously trained in another discipline and are not currently doing so.

To become a properly competent family therapist, able to practice independently, a period of full-time instruction is desirable. Those with some professional experience in the mental health field often prove better equipped to undertake this training than those who lack such experience, and a range of varied life experiences, as well as emotional maturity and a secure family life, are helpful too. Part-time training courses are also offered in many centres; they can provide excellent training, and many family therapists have trained part-time.

An introduction to the main principles of family therapy is useful for all who are training in any of the mental health disciplines; it provides an understanding of what family therapy is, and when it may be useful. It is no substitute, however, for a comprehensive training in the field.

The AAMFT requires members to have a graduate degree in marital and family therapy, or its equivalent. Courses in the following subjects are required for such a degree: human development, marital and family studies, marital and family therapy, professional studies, and research methodology, together with supervised clinical work. Members must also have had 200 hours of supervision in the practice of marital and family therapy, of which no more than 100 hours may be in group supervision; 1500 hours of clinical experience of marital and family therapy; and two years' work experience after the graduate degree and while receiving supervision from an AAMFT approved supervisor.

The different possible learning experiences

It is helpful to distinguish training, teaching, supervision and consultation. Wendorf (1984) points out that supervision or training are often confused with therapy and consultation. He uses 'training' as a 'general term meaning the transfer of knowledge and skills', while 'supervision' is the 'hierarchical arrangement of training in which a superior "oversees", evaluates, suggests, gives feedback to, pushes or advises a trainee'. 'Consultation' means 'the giving of feedback and suggestions but with no hierarchical training relationship necessarily involved'. 'Teaching' is not differentiated from training by Wendhorf (1984), but is perhaps best used in this context to describe the more formal conveying of knowledge, as in lectures and seminars – though of course the term can be used also in a broader sense.

Methods of learning family therapy

The means whereby students learn family therapy probably vary as much as the various schools of therapy differ in their approach to treating families. For example, an issue on which there appear to be diametrically opposed views, is that of whether or not training should include an examination and review of the trainee's own family background and experiences. In some centres these are explored in depth, with role playing exercises and an examination of the trainee's current feelings towards, and relationships with, his or her own family, but in others nothing of this sort is done.

At the 1980 meeting of the American Orthopsychiatric Association there were several presentations on family therapy training. Views expressed on this issue varied from those of Epstein and Bishop (whose work I have referred to previously), who said that going into trainees' own family experiences was quite unnecessary and an unwarranted intrusion into their private lives, to those of Philip Guerin, of the Centre for Family Learning, New Rochelle, NY, who maintained that it was important to do this, and stressed it strongly in his description of the training programme at New Rochelle.

The wide divergence of views on this matter was also clear from the review of the literature on family therapy and supervision by Liddle and Halpin (1978). Liddle himself, however, believes that work with the trainee's family is not relevant to the learning of a therapeutic model oriented toward solving presenting problems within a family contract (Liddle, 1980). In this latter paper Liddle contrasts his approach with that of Murray Bowen, who requires each of his trainees to complete a 'family voyage' with his or her family of origin.

Keller and Protinsky (1984) describe what they call a 'self-management model for supervision' in marriage and family therapy, and adopt a point of view similar to Bowen's. They use 'a model of supervision that places emphasis on increasing self-awareness and the therapeutic management-of-self in the clinical setting'. They find Bowen's 'three-generational emphasis' useful in understanding how family interactional patterns are transmitted, and particularly the patterns of triangulation in which people, including therapists, get involved.

Keller and Protinsky (1984) also relate their concept of 'management of self' to Bowen's concept of 'differentiation', that is, 'ability to manage the tendency to emotionalize intellectual issues, to avoid emotional fusion with others, to maintain manageable emotional objectivity in the presence of a stressed emotional system'. They require each 'supervisee' to present a personal three-generational genogram; the supervisee's family of origin is then carefully examined and probed. That person's videotape therapy material is then presented, and the supervisor and the other 'supervisees' scrutinize it for 'evidences of his/her management-of-self processes'.

Like Bowen, Keller and Protinsky (1984) pay much attention to the process of *triangulation* – the tendency of two people to draw a third one into their relationship, especially when the relationship is in some difficulty. Triangles, as Bowen (1978) has repeatedly emphasized in his writings, are commonly found in troubled families. When spouses are in conflict they may involve a child and either, or both, of them may try to use that child as an ally, or in some other way, in their dispute. A parent/

child pair, or two children in a family, may similarly triangulate a third family member; or someone in the extended family, or outside it altogether, may be triangulated in by family members. Patterns of triangulation in therapists' families of origin may, Keller and Protinsky (1984) believe, be repeated in their interactions with their clients, supervisors and peers. Their paper describes how they assist therapists to be aware of such tendencies, and thus avoid reacting in ways which may not be therapeutically useful.

Coppersmith (1985) has reviewed the concept of 'triads', as it is used in family therapy. She points out that the ability to 'think in threes', and to analyze complex triads, is a skill required by family therapists. Indeed she considers teaching triadic theory 'a crucial aspect of family therapy training'. As an aid to teaching this she has developed an exercise, involving a series of role played simulations, to be enacted and discussed by trainees. These range from 'a simple non-problematic triadic organization to a complex, potentially problematic triadic system' (Coppersmith, 1985, page 62). This has been found to be a useful way of teaching both beginners and experienced therapists seeking further training.

It is not difficult to see how self-knowledge, and an understanding of one's family of origin and one's current family, might be of help in dealing with an emotionally challenging family situation. Yet whether such understanding *does* make for better therapy has not been established. Many effective therapists have not undergone an examination of their families of origin. Much may also depend on the style of therapy the therapist will be using. Examining one's own family background may be more important for those who use a 'Bowenian', or extended family systems approach, and perhaps also for those who use experiential methods, than for therapists of other schools.

Family therapy training usually consists of a combination of theoretical instruction and supervised practical experience, whether or not trainees are required or encouraged to examine their own family backgrounds. Theoretical knowledge may be obtained from formal teaching experiences, such as lectures, seminars and tutorial classes; it should always be supplemented by reading relevant books and journal articles. There has been an explosion of literature in our field over the course of the last twenty years, so that students – especially when they are first embarking on the study of family therapy – require guidance on what to read. (One of the purposes of this book is to provide such guidance, and in addition to the references an annotated list of relevant journals is provided in Appendix A.)

Audiovisual aids

The practical aspects of family therapy are learned by assessing and treating families under supervision. Audiovisual aids are used extensively in this process. I have referred in Chapter 1 to Minuchin's emphasis, in the early days of family therapy, on the importance of the 'live' observation of therapy, as opposed to the acceptance of trainees' reports of what they believed happened during their therapy sessions. It is probably better to supervise all therapy 'live', but it is especially important in family therapy, when there are several people to observe and a great deal is going on, both between family members and between therapist and family.

The simplest audiovisual aid is the one-way observation screen. This enables observers to watch therapy without themselves being in the therapy room. It is sometimes called a 'one-way mirror', but the 'therapy room' side is not necessarily, nor invariably, constructed so that it functions as a mirror. A sound amplification system enables those viewing the therapy to hear what is happening in the therapy room. This arrangement is the easiest way of conducting live supervision of therapy.

It is fortunate that as family therapy has developed, relatively inexpensive closed circuit television and videotape equipment has become available. Such equipment is now to be found in most family therapy training centres. Closed circuit television can serve the same purpose as observation through a one-way screen, especially when a large audience, or one at a distance from the therapy room, wants to view the therapy. The therapeutic uses of videotape replay have been outlined in Chapter 11, but videotape equipment is also invaluable as a training device. It can serve a number of purposes:

- Review by therapists of their own work.
- Review by supervisors of the work of their trainees.
- Demonstration of therapy techniques, as when the work of experienced therapists is reviewed by learners. Edited videotapes, some with commentary, are available from centres such as the Ackerman Institute and the Philadelphia Child Guidance Clinic.
- Review of the progress of therapist and family, when serial videotapes are made and kept for later use.
- Reviewing and learning from role playing exercises undertaken as part of a training programme.

Kramer and Reitz (1980) described a design for the training of family therapists which used the videotape playback of role playing exercises to groups of eight to ten students. Trainees were able to see themselves and other members of the group in a series of therapeutic situations, the complexity of which could gradually be increased. This led to sessions in which students learned to increase their 'personal awareness'. By such means students seen as aloof in therapy, or having recurrent difficulties in dealing with certain types of family, can be helped to overcome such problems. Personal relationship problems which may be affecting a therapist's work – as when a therapist has to deal with someone who reminds him of his dominant father, or the sister with whom he feels rivalry – can be rehearsed and explored, for example by setting up a role played session with a critical supervisor. Students can explore their own appearance on the screen, watching a 'video portrait' of themselves, while being coached in expressing, through their appearance and behaviour, what they want to convey to the group and, ultimately, to the families they treat.

Objectives

A teaching programme should have clearly defined objectives. If it does not, there is no way of discovering whether it is effective. Setting learning objectives was advocated by Cleghorn and Levin (1973), and Tomm and Wright (1979) also stressed the importance of objectives.

The setting of learning objectives for the teaching of family therapy implies that a clearly defined model of family functioning and therapy is to be taught. This should include an explicit theory of how families change (Liddle, 1980). As therapists acquire clinical skills, they can start investigating other models and techniques, and incorporate what they consider will be helpful into their own practice.

Learning family therapy skills

Cleghorn and Levin (1973) defined three types of family therapy skills which must be learned. These are perceptual, conceptual and executive skills. This remains a useful model.

It is probably best to start with *conceptual skills*. The trainee must understand the concepts and terms used in the model of therapy which is being taught. Conceptual skills can be taught by various means. The McMaster group used a combination of a 'semi-programmed text', reading materials in which theoretical concepts were explained, and tutorials in which the concepts the trainees had learned were integrated and problems and issues which remained unclear were resolved. The concepts taught were naturally those upon which the McMaster model of therapy was based, but this approach could equally well be used to teach any other conceptual scheme.

Before moving on to the next stage of training it is a good plan to test students' knowledge of what has been taught so far. Conceptual knowledge is probably the easiest category to assess, and can be tested using multiple choice methods. If the trainee has not come to a satisfactory understanding of the relevant basic concepts, learning perceptual and executive skills is likely to prove difficult.

The next stage is the learning of *perceptual skills*. Like conceptual skills, these can be learned without seeing families in therapy. Instead, videotapes of real or simulated families and role playing can be used. Teaching is best done in small groups. If, for example, it were the McMaster model which was being taught, trainees would be asked to rate families on problem-solving, communication, roles, affective responsiveness and involvement, and behaviour control, taking into account the sub-categories of each. Their responses would be discussed in the group and with the teacher. With practice, and appropriate feedback, trainees' skills in perceiving the processes occurring in family groups improve. Another way of learning perceptual skills is to use 'scenarios', that is short, one or two paragraph summaries of families. After reading each of these, the trainees rate them according to the various categories being used; there must also be categories for no data or insufficient data, since it is important to know when additional information is needed.

Perceptual skills can be assessed by having students rate videotapes, and by the use of 'scenarios'. The acquisition of satisfactory perceptual skills is necessary before students pass on to learning executive skills.

Training in *executive skills* should be carried out principally while students work treating families, although these skills can be practised initially using simulated families, made up of groups of trainees. The supervisor watches through a one-way screen, or on closed circuit television, and gives feedback. This may be done in breaks during therapy sessions, by using an intercommunicating phone, or after sessions have ended. Alternatively videotapes or – less satisfactorily – audiotapes of sessions may subsequently be reviewed. Live supervision has the advantage that the supervisor can, when necessary, intervene during the session. When sessions are being recorded for later review, novice students may get into difficulties if feedback is not available when things start to go wrong. For students with more experience, however, review of recordings can be quite adequate.

Evaluation of executive skills may be achieved by observing video-tapes of students' work, and rating this according to specific criteria.

Liddle and Saba (1982) also described a model for teaching family therapy at the introductory level. They drew a parallel between the process of therapy – using Minuchin's (1974) structural model and

Haley's (1976) more strategic one – and that of training family therapists. Just as therapy may be viewed in stages (Haley, 1976), so may training. According to Liddle and Saba (1982), three stages characterize both therapy and training – joining, restructuring, and consolidation.

Phase I, *joining*, requires the student 'to suspend ... his existing view of reality', and to adopt, 'at least in experimental spirit, ideas about the etiology and treatment of human problems which are often quite alien to the student's previous training and experience' (Liddle and Saba, 1982, page 65). Joining the training programme is thus seen as analogous to joining a family; this is the first stage of structural therapy, in which the therapist tentatively, but without being engulfed by the family's way of behaving and looking at things, becomes a member of the family group. The content of this phase has much in common with Cleghorn and Levin's (1973) stage of learning conceptual skills.

Phase II is that of *restructuring*. In structural therapy, this is the main change-producing phase of treatment. Similarly, the family therapy student, at this stage, is challenged 'to learn and experiment with new concepts from differing schools'. This has much in common with the learning of executive skills.

In phase III, *consolidation*, 'students are required to take personal and theoretical risks in integrating the various approaches into their professional identities'.

Liddle and Saba (1982) reported that the course, which introduced students to a variety of schools of therapy, had three main areas of impact:

1. It sparked student interest in clinical training in family therapy.
2. It affected the lives of some of the students, in that it made them more aware of their current families and their families of origin. Especially after studying the work of Bowen, Boszormenyi-Nagy and Framo, students asked to be allowed to write family autobiographies.
3. It affected the students' views of human problems. One student is quoted as saying:

   My eyes have been opened to a whole new way of viewing pathology. Clients are no longer isolates to me. I see them in relation to their environment which includes the family as well as myself, the therapist.

The content of training

Precisely what is taught in any course of training will depend on the orientation of those teaching it. As we have seen, there are many schools of family therapy, and it is possible to teach students the theoretical bases of a variety of them. But when actually teaching trainees to work with families it is necessary to use a specific, even if flexible, model. This need not be derived from any one particular school of therapy, but may be an eclectic one derived from various sources. An example of such an approach was set out in Chapter 12. The content of that chapter is one possible basis for teaching students how to work with families, and is the one I personally use.

Because approaches to therapy can vary so much, it is not appropriate here to say much more about the content of training, but it may be useful to summarize an approach to training described by Tomm and Wright (1979), and developed at the University of Calgary. These authors distinguished therapeutic *functions, competencies* and *skills*. Their four 'functions' are really four stages of therapy, namely *engagement, problem identification, change facilitation* and *termination*. For each function, or stage, certain competencies are required. These are:

(a) *Engagement* Four competencies are required for satisfactory engagement of families:
   (i) Developing a rationale for the use of a family approach. By this the authors mean the process of explaining why a family approach is being used and demonstrating what it involves by the way the interview is conducted.
   (ii) Establishing positive relationships with the family.
   (iii) Conveying to the family a feeling that the therapist is professionally competent.
   (iv) Maintaining the therapist–family alliance.
(b) *Problem identification* Five competencies are distinguished here:
   (i) Obtaining all the necessary information about the presenting problem or problems.
   (ii) Observing and becoming aware of the process currently at work in the family.
   (iii) Identifying and exploring interpersonal problems within the family.
   (iv) Identifying and clarifying problems affecting individual members of the family.
   (v) Integrating the assessment of the family.
(c) *Change facilitation* Six competencies are identified in this area:
   (i) Breaking maladaptive patterns.
   (ii) Clarifying how actions may lead to consequences which constitute problems for the family.
   (iii) Altering emotional factors that may block the family's attempts to achieve better functioning.

(iv) Initiating cognitive restructuring, that is helping family members think about their problems and their situation differently.

(v) Helping the family implement new, adaptive patterns of interaction.

(vi) Mobilizing resources outside the family as necessary.

(d) *Termination* Three competencies are recognized here:

(i) Assessing the situation when a family initiates the termination process.

(ii) Initiating termination when this is necessary.

(iii) Concluding treatment constructively.

In addition to the above, Tomm and Wright (1979) list various perceptual/conceptual skills, and their corresponding executive skills, which are considered to be required for each competency. It is an illustration of how complex family therapy really is that these authors identified twenty sets of skills required for the engagement function, forty-three for problem identification, fifty-seven for change facilitation and fifteen for termination.

Supervision

We have already seen that expert supervision, especially live supervision, has to be a central feature of any satisfactory training programme for family therapists. Indeed, the would-be student of family therapy might be well advised to avoid any centre that purported to provide training if good supervision were not freely available. This implies also that audiovisual aids, such as we have discussed above, are freely available, with adequate supporting technical staff. In fact the audiovisual technician should nowadays probably be regarded as an essential member of the team of any programme which takes the teaching of family therapy seriously.

It seems that the term 'live supervision' was coined by Braulio Montalvo (1973). In addition to making some of the points about supervision which we have already discussed, he suggested that the supervisor and the trainee should define in advance the limits within which they will operate, including the situations when it is obligatory for the trainee to do as the supervisor says, and when the supervisor's suggestions may be modified; that the supervisor should not unduly restrict the trainee's freedom to explore and operate within the family, and that if this does happen the trainee should tell the supervisor so; and that the supervisor should try to find procedures that fit the trainee's style and preferred way of thinking. Montalvo also advocates that the direction of therapy be worked out before each session, and reviewed after it. The better the advance planning the less likely it is that the therapist and supervisor will have to consult during the session. The intensity of supervision, and the frequency of interventions by the supervisor, may be expected to lessen as the trainee gains experience.

As stated above, live supervision is best provided by having the supervisor watch through a one-way observation screen, or on closed circuit television. Many supervisors like to be able to communicate with their trainees by telephone, but an alternative is the 'bug-in-the-ear', a device which enables the supervisor to talk to the therapist while the latter is interviewing the family, but without the need for the ringing of a telephone. Its drawbacks are that the therapist cannot reply to what the supervisor says, and may also have to listen while not appearing discourteous to the family by disregarding them. If either of these methods is used, it is suggested by both Haley (1976) and Liddle (1980) that only one or two ideas should be communicated to the trainee in the course of one call.

Another arrangement that can work well is for the trainee to leave the room during the session for one or more discussions with the supervisor; it is also possible for the supervisor to tell the therapist when to take a break to discuss progress by a pre-arranged signal, such as a knock on the door (if there is no telephone intercom system). Whatever the plan, the family should be told about it in advance. Families seldom raise objections to having supervisors watch, and intervene if necessary, especially if they are told that in this type of therapy the input of another therapist, or a team, often enables them to be helped more effectively and quickly. When the situation is properly explained, most families are pleased to learn that more than one person is involved in helping them.

The process of supervision differs from that of therapy in that the supervisor must consider both the family system, and how the family may be helped to resolve its problems, as well as the therapist/family system. It is this latter aspect that is the essence of family therapy supervision. A real danger which all family therapists face is that of getting involved emotionally with the families they treat. This can seriously impede therapy. Expert supervision is a good way of avoiding this danger.

Quinn et al (1985) offer an interesting model for the group supervision of advanced trainees. They call it the 'stuck-case' model. These authors established a special 'stuck-case clinic' for advanced trainees to bring families to when little or no progress was being made. They found it a useful way of bringing new thinking to difficult or 'stuck' families, so that progress in therapy can be resumed.

Learning to supervise

The importance of the supervision of family therapy is such that considerable attention has been paid to the process in the literature. Liddle and his colleagues (1984, page 139), however, comment that:

> Although the literature on supervision is impressive, it lacks the vital component specifying how supervisors best acquire this knowledge. Considerable clinical experience does not automatically qualify one to be a supervisor, but rather, just as the skills of family therapy can be taught, so also a separate and definable set of supervisory skills can and should be taught systematically to therapists who wish to be competent supervisors.

Liddle et al (1984), in the paper from which the above is quoted, describe the 'supervisor extern program' (SEP) at the Family Systems Program of the Institute for Juvenile Research in Chicago. The SEP comprises the following components:

- Live observation of supervision.
- A theory seminar.
- Opportunity for supervisors to receive feedback on their supervisory skills and styles (through videotape supervision, and case discussions with trainees).
- Learning and support from peers.
- The practise of the supervisory role and skills at their primary place of work.

Liddle and his co-authors point out that the above list resembles what might comprise any therapist training programme. There are, moreover, many principles common to therapy and supervision. For example the need to set goals, think in stages, be sensitive to contextual cues, establish rapport (called 'joining' by these authors) and challenge realities all apply to both. Yet there are specific supervisory skills also, and the training system itself, and its components, require that the supervisor has available an adequate conceptual map of the system.

Heath and Storm (1985) have described a four-stage course in marriage and family therapy supervision. This is adapted from the scheme described by Liddle and his colleagues (1984). It has four objectives:

(1) To encourage student supervisors to adapt and use their therapy theories as supervision theories.
(2) To facilitate the development of live supervision skills.
(3) To have student supervisors become expert in supervising student therapists with a variety of theoretical orientations.

(4) To provide student supervisors and student therapists with close and consistent supervision.

The course has two components; a seminar and a practicum. The seminar took up two hours per week, and aimed to develop the supervisors' conceptual skills. The practicum comprised four stages:

Stage One: During this stage the trainee supervisors, as a group, watched the live supervision of a student therapist by one of the authors of the article. The other instructor was with the trainee supervisors, and helped them begin to think as supervisors, rather than as therapists.

Stage Two: This was the stage of 'individual participation'. The students watched the authors while they supervised family therapy, asking questions and discussing the rationale of what was done. Each was also assigned three therapists to supervise in the next stage.

Stage Three: During this stage the trainee supervisors received live supervision of their supervision.

Stage Four: This was the stage of independent supervision.

These two related schemes for training supervisors, though expensive in the time of the instructors, seem to offer the prospect of improving what has in the past been something of a hit-or-miss process.

Consultation

Consultation is another means whereby therapists may both improve their skills and receive help in treating families that are presenting difficulties. It differs from supervision in two main respects. The first is that there is no hierarchical distinction between therapist and consultant; the second is that consultation is usually an occasional, rather than a regular event – though in theory there is no reason why a therapist should not seek consultation, or a consultant offer it, on a regular basis.

Bullock and Kobayashi (1978) described a number of situations in which 'live consultation' may be helpful. These are:

(a) Conflict between therapist and patient. The therapist may not be aware of this and the consultant may be able to intervene before the conflict escalates in a therapeutically unhelpful way.

(b) When the therapist becomes 'regulated' by the family, and starts to behave in ways similar to the dysfunctional behaviour of the family.

(c) When the therapist is drifting from the task. Therapists sometimes inadvertently stray from the course necessary to meet the goals and strategies which have been set out.

(d) The 'eureka' effect. This term is used to describe a situation in which the consultant becomes aware of a therapeutic move which would better help the family towards its goals, than the strategy currently being used by the therapist.

(e) When it appears that it may be helpful to create a therapeutic coalition. Thus the consultant may intervene to bring about an alignment of two parties against a third, when this seems likely to increase family members' motivation.

(f) When there is a misreading by the therapist of the family situation or the significance of members' statements.

The above circumstances might also be good reasons for intervention by a supervisor if one were involved. In most cases the therapist would, however, probably be unaware of precisely what had gone wrong with the therapy. Consultation is usually sought when unduly slow progress is being made with a family or a marital pair. It is the consultant's task to help the therapist discover what has gone wrong or, preferably, find a better approach than that used hitherto. The responsibility to seek consultation in such situations is one of our ethical responsibilities. It is not an admission of failure or inadequacy, for no therapist can expect to succeed, unaided, with every family; on the contrary, it is a sign of a mature and well-trained professional who realizes that he or she has limitations, and that good practice involves having consultants available and using them when necessary. The 'stuck-case clinic' (Quinn et al, 1985) is an example of how these situations may be tackled.

Max van Trommel (1984) also discusses the process of consultation and suggests three levels at which it can occur:

1. Expanding the field of the therapist but focusing on the family. Consultation initially places emphasis on the family with whom the therapist has reached a deadlock. This may be sufficient to free the therapeutic process.

2. Expanding the field of the family. The progress of therapy may be impeded because of the relationship of the family with other systems. These may be the family of origin, a friend, a couple with whom the family is very friendly, a school, a neighbourhood, an employer, a welfare system or the referring person or agency.

3. Expanding the field into a 'metadomain' to focus on the therapist/ family system. The system with which the family has become 'inextricably entangled' need not, van Trommel points out, be another person or organization but may be none other than the family therapist who is working with the family. The therapist/ family system therefore often has to be addressed in consultation. If

steps 1 and 2 do not lead to satisfactory progress, this area should be explored.

As therapists we have the difficult task of both observing and participating in the systems of which we become part. Van Trommel (1984) quotes Keeney (1982) who pointed out that 'there is no such thing as an observer-free description of a situation'. A system can only be analyzed as a mutual interactional process between the system and some other 'functioning unity...for instance, the therapist himself' (van Trommel, 1984, page 471).

Van Trommel goes on to describe a way of providing consultation to the 'family-plus-therapist'. This comprises the following stages:

- *A pre-session discussion.* The therapist provides basic information about the family, such as names, ages, who lives in the household, the aims of therapy and the strategies the therapist has used. Data about the content of the problem is not provided, since the consultation team (and this type of consultation is usually provided by a team) is concerned with a higher level of abstraction than that of the family processes themselves. For the second part of the presession discussion the therapist is absent, and the team draws up hypotheses about what has gone wrong with the therapist/family system.
- *A consultation session.* The interviewer, a member of the team, interviews the therapist-plus-family, using circular questions (Palazzoli et al, 1980; Penn, 1982). The questions are designed primarily to elicit information about the functioning of the system under investigation. Questions are asked equally of therapist and family. The team may telephone in advice or comments, and the interviewer may ask the team for advice.
- *An intersession break.* The therapist stays with the family; this emphasizes that it is the therapist-family system that is being investigated. Meanwhile the interviewer and the rest of the team discuss the information obtained. An intervention is then formulated.
- *An intervention.* During this short session, the family and therapist are informed of the intervention.
- *A post-session discussion, with team and therapist present.* The content of the intervention is not discussed, and this stage consists simply of a brief, general summing-up to conclude the procedure.

Van Trommel (1984) includes two examples of the above process, and a discussion of it. Those considering using the approach he recommends would do well to study his paper first.

Research into methods of teaching family therapy

Kniskern and Gurman (1979), in a special issue of *The Journal of Marital and Family Therapy* devoted to education and training, reviewed the literature on family therapy training and identified a number of issues which, they believed, needed to be addressed by means of research. They also commented on our 'collective empirical ignorance about this topic'.

The literature on the teaching of family therapy was also reviewed by Tomm and Leahey (1980), who went on to report a trial of three methods of teaching family assessment. These authors randomly divided a class of 72 medical students into three groups, each of which was trained in family assessment using a different method. The methods were:

1. Traditional classroom lectures, together with demonstration videotapes.
2. Small group discussions with the same videotapes.
3. Giving the students the task of conducting a family interview and presenting their own videotapes for small group discussion.

Tests to measure the students' knowledge and skills in family assessment were administered before and after the teaching pro-gramme, and it was found that students in all three groups gained in knowledge and perceptual–conceptual skills. There were, however, no significant differences between the gains made by the different groups.

The authors of this paper point out that the research had some methodological weaknesses, one of which was that there were only eight hours of instruction time for each group, which might not have been long enough to reveal differences between the methods. Never-theless, the paper is an important one in that it points the way to the more scientific assessment of the results of different teaching methods.

There remains a pressing need for the critical evaluation of teaching methods, though it is nowadays quite common to find that papers reporting teaching or supervision methods (like several of those mentioned in this chapter), do include some form of evaluation of their results.

Summary

Family therapy is taught to a wide variety of students, not all of whom aim to become specialists in this field. Increasing attention is being paid to defining what should be taught to students at different levels, and to the setting of professional standards for marital and family therapists. Formal teaching, supervised clinical work, role playing, and watching other therapists – live or on videotape – are all valuable components of training programmes. Modern training makes much use of the 'live' viewing of therapy, and for this adequate audiovisual aids are essential. How valuable it is for therapists to explore their families of origin and their current families is unclear; it may depend on the model of therapy to be used.

Well defined objectives are necessary in training therapists, as they are in therapy. Means of assessing students' progress in meeting the objectives should be built into programmes. The content of training depends on the theoretical model to be taught, but it should cover all phases of therapy, from joining and assessment to termination and follow-up.

It is important for teachers to learn the specific skills of supervision. These are not the same as therapy skills. Therapists should also be trained to use consultation when it is needed. Marital and family therapies are complex procedures and for the more difficult cases, when progress is unsatisfactory, the use of consultation is invaluable and one of our ethical responsibilities.

Chapter 16

Research in Family Therapy

Early work in the field of family therapy was mainly descriptive. Pioneers examined families from various points of view and described what they perceived to be going on in them. At the same time they formulated ideas about how family functioning might precipitate and maintain symptoms in individual family members. This led them to devise ways of intervening in families; these sometimes seemed to lead to happier family situations. Their initial studies were, however, inevitably tentative and exploratory.

In the 1950s, as Wynne (1983) points out, family research and family therapy were carried out by the same people; indeed research came first and therapy was initially a secondary activity. During the 1960s therapists and researchers apparently became two distinct groups. Haley (1978) also commented on this change, pointing out that originally therapist and researcher were 'of the same species (although the therapist had a more second-class status)'. By the time Haley was writing this, however, it seemed to him that, 'the research stance and the posture of the therapist [were] quite opposite'.

We have seen that many of the first family researchers and therapists were concerned to investigate the families of schizophrenic patients; various processes occurring in such families were identified, including the double-bind, schism and skew, pseudomutuality, pseudohostility and mystification. These discoveries led to further questions. Did these processes in the families *cause* the schizophrenic symptoms in the afflicted family members? Or could they be the *result* of the schizophrenic disorder in the individual (a less often asked question)? Does the resolution or modification of the supposedly pathological family processes lead to resolution or modification of the schizophrenic symptons? Are similar processes found in families in which no one is schizophrenic?

It proved harder to answer questions like the foregoing ones than it was to describe what was happening in the families, except for the last question, to which it soon became clear that the answer was yes. Most of the earlier authors who wrote about 'schizophrenic' families, however, acknowledged that the processes they described could be observed in other families. The double-bind, for example, seemed to be widespread, but it was suggested by some that its use was more frequent and intense in 'schizophrenic' than in other families.

Much of this early research into the families of schizophrenics was unproductive, insofar as finding a cure for schizophrenia was concerned; indeed psychopharmacological approaches to treatment gained more acceptance than family therapy ones during the ensuing years. This early work did, however, draw the attention of many therapists to families and family systems. It also raised questions about the relationship between the disorders of individuals and the families to which they belonged. Increasing numbers of therapists started trying new techniques which aimed to produce changes in family systems, rather than working with individuals. Many found they could produce changes more quickly than they had been able to do using traditional psychotherapy techniques – sometimes dramatically so. It did not take long for these therapists to conclude that the progress of many of those they had treated as individuals had been held back as a result of the characteristics of the family systems of which they had been part.

Unfortunately this newfound enthusiasm often became uncritical. A period was entered upon when a belief in a 'systems approach' to human problems became an article of faith among many, rather than the result of the consideration of scientific data. Research assumed a lower profile than it had done, and was increasingly left to 'family researchers', while the therapists got on with the 'real' work. Fortunately this situation now seems to be changing, as Wynne (1983) points out.

The need for family therapy research

The need for research in family therapy has been well set out by Alan Gurman (1983), and its methodological problems were discussed by Frude (1980). Gurman advocates adherence to traditional research approaches, despite the adoption of new attitudes to human problems by many 'avant garde' therapists – or, as Gurman describes them, those employing new epistemologies. He points out that research findings are needed by five categories of 'consumer'. These are:

1. Practising clinicians and students of family therapy who need, and

want, to know about the factors that affect clinical outcomes, as a guide to their clinical practice.

2. 'Theoretician/clinicians' who want to understand the mechanisms of change common to different treatment methods, as well as learning of findings of immediate application.

3. Practising clinicians, and students and teachers of psychotherapy, 'who are presently outside the family therapy circle'. Gurman hopes that this group may be open to 'the paradigmatic shift that is family therapy'.

4. The families, that is our potential patients or clients, who want to know how best they may be helped with their problems.

5. Public policy makers and third party providers of therapists' fees.

How far the employment of the 'new epistemologies' necessitates the use of radically different research approaches is unclear. To date, however, a good case for this proposition does not seem to have been made. Much of what those advocating a new approach write on the subject is hard to understand, and sometimes the writing seems as circular as the therapy. The following quotation is an example:

> Evolutionary feedback is the idea suggested by [Prigogine et al]: that random oscillations in self-regulating systems can go beyond the limits of self-correction and suddenly and unpredictably become part of the deviation-amplifying process, radically restructuring the system and creating increased (less probable) complexity in the system. It could be argued that this is still a cybernetic model, utilizing the basic assumptions of a cybernetic epistemology, e.g. information-guided, circular, mutual causal loops as a basic aspect of psychosocial reality. An evolutionary epistemology makes explicit the levels of organiza-tion that are already implicit in a cybernetic one. (Schwartzman, 1984, pages 231-232)

Approaches to family therapy research

As Wynne (1983) admits, the early research in the family field was 'primitive'. It mostly lacked controls. The disturbed families were not usually matched with comparable undisturbed families studied in the same way. Tests, self-report measures and rating-scales for use along with therapy had not been developed. 'Even worse,' Wynne (1983, page 114) says, 'we had very small samples of families'. Reports of the treatment of single families, or small series, were indeed common – as they are to this day, but such reports are not necessarily invalid or worthless.

Wynne (1983) may be unduly hard on himself and his colleagues from the early days, because the study of small groups and individual cases is probably an essential part of the development of new concepts and treatment methods; if a treatment method does not show signs of being effective in a small, uncontrolled study, there is little point in comparing it with other treatments, or with no treatment. But if it does appear effective when first tried, this may be an indication for investigating its value in a more rigorous way. Two questions then need to be asked. The first is whether the treatment is better than doing nothing – which is similar to asking whether the problem may be expected to clear up if untreated. The second is, how does it compare with other available treatments for the same condition? The comparison should consider effectiveness, the speed with which improvement occurs, cost, acceptability to those being treated, unwanted side effects, and whether any improvement achieved is maintained in the long term.

While questions such as the above were asked by workers in the family therapy field from early days, reliable answers have on the whole been scarce. Clinicians have often proceeded more on faith, or conviction, or even hunches, than on the basis of scientific evidence of the effectiveness of what they do. Yet they have *seen* dramatic changes in families they have treated. They *know* they can help some people through family treatment, and so they go ahead with therapy regardless of whether there is scientific support for what they are doing. In this respect family therapists probably differ little from practitioners of other forms of psychotherapy. Nor is such an approach necessarily wrong. In situations of uncertainty we must do something for those who come to us for help, even though we have no scientifically proven remedy available.

Nevertheless the desire of many workers to get family therapy on to a more scientific basis has led to the gradual adoption of more rigorous methods of studying families and their treatment. In research into the social and family aspects of schizophrenia, for example, the work of the Medical Research Council's Social Psychiatry Unit (described in *Expressed Emotion in Families* by Leff and Vaughn, 1985, and discussed in Chapter 11) has set a high standard.

Another development has been a great proliferation of books and journals devoted to family therapy, and to the holding of scientific conferences on various aspects of the subject. An important early conference was held at the Eastern Pennsylvania Psychiatric Institute, Philadelphia in March 1967. The proceedings were later published as a book entitled *Family Interaction: A Dialogue between Family Researchers and Family Therapists* (Framo, 1972). Wynne (1983) commented that the title of the conference showed that the split between family research and family therapy had already occurred by this time.

Many of the problems that family therapy research presents were explored, though not solved, at this conference. Jay Haley (1972, page 17), in his usual lucid way, got to the heart of the issues and defined many of the pertinent questions. He focused on four:

(a) Is there a difference between families containing a psychiatrically 'abnormal' member and other 'normal' families?
(b) Do families differ according to the type of abnormality present in the 'disturbed' member?
(c) Is one part of the family different from another part? For example, does the relationship between parents and the 'identified patient' differ from that between the same parents and their 'normal' children?
(d) Has the family system changed after successful individual or family therapy?

These are all basic and important questions, but none can be answered easily, even today. Haley went on to review previous studies addressing the above issues. He pointed out that studies in which the observer is also a participant have little value, especially if the observer is acting as the therapist. Non-participant observation is better and can readily be carried out using one-way observation screens or closed circuit television. Even under these circumstances standard conditions are necessary, control groups must be used, reliable measuring instruments are needed, and sufficiently large groups of families must be studied, in order to reveal real differences. We still have a long way to go before these conditions are met in most published research reports.

Areas for research

It became clear early in the history of family therapy that certain particular issues required investigation and clarification. Three broad areas present themselves:

(a) The assessment, description and classification of families. Certain families have features in common, much as certain individuals have common personality characteristics or present with similar psychiatric problems. The assessment and categorization of families, whether 'disturbed' or not, is, however, a more complex undertaking than the assessment of individuals.

(b) Describing and measuring the process of therapy. This book will have made it clear that 'family therapy' can mean a lot of different things. For

research into family therapy to mean anything it must be possible to characterize, in some replicable way, the nature of the treatment administered. If this is not done, measuring associated changes is of limited value.

(c) Measuring outcome. We must be able to measure, in valid and reliable ways, changes that occur during treatment. Both the functioning of the family as a whole, and the symptoms of the identified patient and any other members of the family, need to be considered and assessed. Since it is possible for improvement in one family member to be accompanied by the appearance, or worsening, of symptoms in another, all members must be considered. Outcome studies should also be planned to measure any deterioration that may have occurred, as well as the hoped-for improvement.

This is not an exhaustive list of areas which could be, and have been, addressed in family therapy related research, but it covers the main ones. We will now consider each in turn.

Assessing and classifying families

Assessment and classification are closely related. When assessing a family, with a view to placing it in some predetermined classification, it is necessary to examine those aspects of family functioning used in the classification system being considered.

Because of the necessity of ordering assessment data systematically, certain research-based methods of classifying families were described in Chapter 5, rather than being left to this chapter. This section should therefore be read in conjunction with the descriptions of those methods in that chapter.

Fisher (1977), on the basis of a review of the literature, suggested that schemes for the classification of families fell into five groups, according to the parameters used. These schemes were based on, respectively:

- Style of adaptation.
- Developmental family stage.
- The initial problem or diagnosis of the identified patient.
- Family theme or dimension.
- Type of marital relationship.

This list, derived from a review of various methods of classifying families, could in theory be the basis for the construction of a 'multi-axial' classification, in that it lists a number of separate, and presumably to some extent independent, features of families – as does the triaxial scheme outlined in Chapter 5.

Although there are clearly a number of ways of looking at families, including those in the above list, we will here confine ourselves to two:

(a) Considering the family's developmental stage.
(b) Considering the family's way of functioning, the essence of which is how the members relate to and interact with each other.

Ideally families should be classified, for clinical purposes, according to whether or not they are disturbed and, if they are, on the basis of the type of disorder present. Attempts have indeed been made to do this, for example by Richter (1974). He distinguished 'family symptom neuroses', and 'family character neuroses', the latter group being divided into 'anxiety-neurotic families', 'paranoid families' and 'hysterical families'. This method of classifying family disorders has not been adopted by family therapists, probably because it really consists only of the application to families of labels devised for use with individuals. Moreover it is not based on research data. Examples of other attempts to categorize family disorders are the concept of Minuchin and his colleagues (1978) of 'psychosomatic families'; and the Milan group's 'families in schizophrenic transaction' (Palazzoli et al, 1978a). These also have not been generally adopted, and we still lack a comprehensive classification of family disorders.

Categorizing families by developmental stage is a relatively straightforward undertaking. It is based on the developmental considerations discussed in Chapter 2, and the research literature referred to in that chapter. There are always two points to be considered: the stage the family *should have* reached (based on the ages of the children, whether they have left home, and so on), and the stage it *has* reached. When these differ, it probably means the family is having difficulty negotiating one of the family developmental hurdles we have considered earlier.

Categorizing families on the basis of the nature of family interaction is more difficult. An early review of family interaction research appeared in the book *Research in Family Interaction: Readings and Commentary* (Winter and Ferriera, 1969). Another review, by Jules Riskin and Elaine Faunce, appeared in 1972. Riskin and Faunce were concerned with studies which examined the interaction of family members directly, rather than by means of questionnaires, individual interviews or clinical material. Their excellent paper makes it clear that the subject is highly complex, and the methodological problems involved are considerable. These authors also found that investigators and groups of investigators worked in relative isolation from other workers, interdisciplinary cooperation was generally poor and replication studies – in which a worker or group attempt to confirm findings reported by others – unsatisfactorily few. They discovered many contradictory findings.

Nevertheless they found some encouraging signs of progress over the twenty years' history of research in family interaction. They also found some agreement in major areas, notably about the importance of certain variables in family interaction. These were 'humour', 'agreement-disagreement', 'support', 'positive affect', 'acknowledgment-commitment' and 'clarity of communication'. All these seemed, from the research reviewed, to be important factors in the study of family functioning; clearly it is essential to identify the particular things about families which should be examined in order to define different modes of interaction.

Since 1972 research has proceeded apace, although at times family therapists have tended to substitute polemic in the discussion of theoretical ideas, for the reporting of data. In *Family Process* especially, there have been many articles (for example those by Dell, 1982; Keeney and Sprenkle, 1982; and Allman, 1982 – all mentioned in Chapter 3) which have been followed by responses and rejoinders in which various protagonists put forward their points of view, claim that their ideas are better, castigate others for woolly thinking, and the like. There is, of course, a place for the formulation and discussion of theoretical ideas, but these should lead to research to test the ideas proposed. The presentation of data bearing on the issues, rather than the forceful expression of opinions, might better serve to advance the subject.

Despite some research, and much discussion, we still have no valid, reliable and generally accepted way of categorizing families according to their ways of interacting. Hodgson and Lewis (1979) did, however, point out that the 1970s saw the increasing use of systems theory in family research. They considered that systems theory is a 'logical extension of interactional theory'. Systems concepts certainly are dependent on, among other considerations, how family members interact, but they also consider boundaries, subsystem patterns, and the influence of suprasystems. They may therefore provide a good base for a model of family functioning which will be of practical value both to family therapists and to those wishing to carry out research on the categorization and classification of families.

There is more to family functioning than the issue of how family members interact. We have seen that many other aspects are addressed in the McMaster Model of Family Functioning (Epstein et al, 1978). This model is, however, only one of many that have been proposed, and an illustration of the complexity of the subject was provided by Fisher (1976) who reviewed research into family assessment. The studies reviewed concentrated on clinical assessment rather than on theories of family functioning. Twenty-nine schemes for assessing family functioning were reviewed, and there were substantial differences in the concepts used in them. Fisher managed to bring some sort of order into the data by dividing the assessment strategies used into four groups:

1. Single concept notions.
2. Theoretical notions.
3. Broadly-based clinical lists.
4. Empirically-based approaches.

Single concept notions emphasize either a limited range of assessment parameters, or redefine a range of dimensions as variants of a single concept. The single concepts Fisher identified were power, conflict, and conflict resolution. These seemed to make sense insofar as these issues, especially conflict and its resolution, often bring families to therapy.

Theoretical orientation is used as the basis for assessment procedures by such groups as that at the Philadelphia Child Guidance Clinic (Minuchin, 1974), which focuses on the 'structural' aspects of the family; and the behaviourists (Hammerlynck et al, 1973) who concentrate on specific interactional behaviours, and assess families according to the behaviours observed; treatment is then based on the assessment.

By *clinical lists* Fisher (1976) means lists of dimensions which have been found useful in clinical practice, although no great effort is made by those using them to tie the dimensions to an underlying theory. The Family Categories Schema, the predecessor of the McMaster Model of Family Functioning, is an example of this approach; it was considered by Fisher to be the one in which 'perhaps the best balance' had been achieved. The Process Model of Family Functioning (Steinhauer et al, 1984) is another example.

Empirically devised methods are usually based on the administration of scales, either to the family itself, or to observers who either watch the family perform certain tasks or observe them during therapy. The results may then be subject to factor analysis or other statistical procedures. One study (Otto, 1962) focused on family strengths, an unusual approach. Some marital couples were asked to list their strengths, and then met together as a group to discuss these strengths with a view to using them more effectively. The sessions were tape recorded and their content was used, together with material from a questionnaire previously administered, to identify twelve areas of family strengths.

Fisher (1976) went on to group the criteria used by the authors whose work he reviewed into five areas:

(a) Structural descriptors. These included the concepts of roles; splits; alliances and scapegoating; boundaries, both internal and external;

patterns of interaction and communication; conflicts and patterns of resolution; and 'family views of life, people and the external world'.

(b) Controls and sanctions. These comprised power and leadership; flexibility; exercise of control; dependency–independency; and differentiation–fusion.

(c) Emotions and needs. The criteria included under this heading were methods and rules for affective expression; need satisfaction; the relative importance of needs as opposed to instrumental tasks; and the dominant affective themes of the family.

(d) Cultural aspects. These included social position; environmental stresses; the family's cultural heritage; and social and cultural views.

(e) Developmental aspects. This category was concerned particularly with the appropriateness of structural, affective, and cultural aspects of family functioning to the family's developmental stage. It has thus concerned largely with the other approach we have mentioned – that of classifying families according to developmental concepts.

Fisher (1976) went on to divide these 'assessment dimensions' into a hierarchy as follows:

Level A		Cultural aspects	
		Developmental aspects	
Level B	Structural descriptors	Controls and sanctions	Emotions and needs

The idea of this hierarchy is that the level A factors provide the context for the understanding of those in level B. Thus every family must be considered against its cultural background and in the light of its cultural standards. Once these are determined, it is then necessary to consider its developmental stage. The level B factors have to be considered within the context of the situation defined by the level A variables.

Arising out of his review of the literature on the classification of families Fisher (1977) proposed six 'clusters of family types'. These were:

1. Constricted family types.
2. Internalized family types.
3. Object-focused family types.
4. Impulsive family types.
5. Childlike family types.
6. Chaotic family types.

The value of this grouping of family types is not clear, and it has not been widely adopted. It is nevertheless an interesting attempt to bring some order into a confused and confusing field.

Research on the process of family therapy

Defining the treatment given is probably the least difficult of the three research areas we are considering. Much of the family therapy literature consists of descriptions of therapy methods, often with less emphasis on the clinical problems treated and on outcome and longer term follow-up. Ideally a detailed description of a method of therapy should be accompanied by an equally detailed description of the families to which it has been applied, or is to be applied, and their problems.

It is important in psychotherapy research to ensure that the therapy methods that are supposed to have been employed actually have been. Unfortunately this has not been done in much of the family therapy research that has been reported in the literature. A study in which this was done is that of Crowe (1978). This compared three approaches to marital therapy and was referred to also in Chapter 13. Forty-two couples were randomly allocated to one of three treatment groups. They were given 'directive' or 'interpretative' or 'supportive' therapy. All sessions were tape recorded. A sample of forty statements by the therapist from each of four tapes randomly selected from each couple's therapy was analyzed by 'blind' raters, that is raters who did not know which therapy method was supposed to be represented on each tape. The raters correctly assigned 91.4 per cent of the 'directive' tapes, 74.4 per cent of the 'interpretative' tapes, and 72 per cent of the supportive' tapes; the overall accuracy was 78.2 per cent. While this result is better than chance and represents a highly significant degree of accuracy, it is nevertheless, as the author points out, less than ideal. It showed an overlapping of technique among the three approaches. It provides, however, an example of the kind of checks which are necessary in well-designed research.

Not only do few research reports indicate that checks were made to discover whether the treatments being investigated were properly applied, but many reports do not even provide adequate descriptions of the intended treatment. To quote but one example, Slipp and Kressel (1978), reporting an attempt to compare 'insight' and 'problem-solving' approaches, give little information about the latter. They state only that it 'consisted of concrete problem-solving advice and emotional support', and that no interpretations were made and no material outside the subjects' conscious awareness was brought to their attention. 'Emotional support' was not defined, and the above description seems a generally inadequate one – especially when it is compared with the several pages spent discussing the results. There was also no attempt to rate what actually did happen during the therapy sessions, as opposed to what was intended. (These authors were, however, aware that there were methodological problems in their study, and commented upon some of them.)

It is not surprising that, with new therapy methods based on innovative ways of looking at human behaviour coming into use, some workers in our field have questioned the appropriateness of applying traditional methods of research to them. Gurman (1983), however, advocates strongly the employment of 'standard research methods'. He points out also that such methods 'have already provided data of practical relevance to clinicians, patients and public policy makers', and considers they should not be abandoned in haste. In fact they should probably not be abandoned at all, despite assertions by those whom Gurman terms 'the new epistemologists' (for example Colapinto (1979) and Sheehan et al (1982)). These seem to feel that traditional research concepts are unsuited to the investigation of the newer therapy approaches they favour. These 'ecosystemic epistemologists' do, however, seem at times to let their enthusiasm for new ideas get the better of their scientific objectivity. Thus Keeney and Sprenkle (1982, page 16) state:

> From the level of aesthetics, the therapist's participation in therapy has more to do with being alive than with creating specific outcomes. The immediate implication for therapy is that efforts to make therapeutic problem-solving conscious (e.g. creating packaged cookbook cures) may result in manipulative techniques that are not adequately coupled to the ecology of which they are part.

Therapy, of course, *must* be concerned with specific outcomes. People come to us with particular problems, and ask that we assist them in making changes, whether it be in their family relationships, their ways of communicating with others, their instrumental functioning in various situations, their emotional states, their control over their children, or any one of a myriad of other issues. Certainly it is not necessary for our clients' problem-solving to occur at the conscious level, and it may not always be necessary for the therapist to have consciously formulated a precise change-promoting plan before intervening; yet if there is no describable and replicable therapeutic method, it is hard to see how any teachable body of knowledge can be accumulated. Nor would outcome research make any sense; for it to do so we must be able to define the process of which we are studying the outcome. Ambiguous and unclear statements (like the second sentence in the quotation above), clang associations, alliterations, even poetic language, may have their place in therapy – perhaps because they are meaningful to the right cerebral hemisphere (see Watzlawick, 1978; Barker 1985, pages 21–22) – but they should not be used in the scientific reporting of our work.

Despite the above problems, family therapy has perhaps been at its strongest in the descriptions it has provided of therapy methods, many of which have been outlined in this book. In measuring outcome it has been less strong.

Outcome research

There is much literature on the outcome of family therapy, but a great deal of it is of poor quality. In 1972, Wells, Dilkes and Burckhard published a review of outcome studies which had appeared in the literature from 1950 until 1970. In order to be included, studies had to cover three or more families and state explicitly the outcome measures used. The authors found eighteen studies that met these criteria, but of these only two were considered adequate. One was 'borderline', while the other fifteen had serious weaknesses, such as the absence of a control group.

A control group is important in psychotherapy research because many emotional and relationship problems improve without treatment, or simply following a process of assessment during which they are spelt out and discussed. Worthwhile preliminary information may, however, be obtained from studies which lack controls, as we have seen above, but this usually needs to be confirmed by controlled studies carried out subsequently.

Control groups should consist of comparable but untreated groups of patients or families, or of groups treated by a different method. There are obvious ethical difficulties in leaving those who are seeking help untreated for experimental reasons, though these are lessened when treatment services are insufficient to meet the demand. In such situations some would have to go without treatment anyway, at least while they remained on a waiting list, so it is sometimes possible to arrange that those on the waiting list are selected according to a sound research design.

When it is impossible for ethical or other reasons to have an untreated control group, an alternative is to use a standard treatment, the efficacy of which is known – though this is a difficult thing to find in the mental health field – or to use another commonly employed treatment which may be effective. An example is the study of Slipp and Kressel (1978), mentioned earlier. In that study the 'insight' group, which was seen on average twelve times over a three-month period, was compared with a randomly allocated group given 'concrete problem-solving advice' and seen on average only three times in three months. In this study, interestingly, the 'advice' group did better than the 'insight' group on most of the outcome measures, though there were several methodological problems with the study.

Of the studies reviewed by Wells and his colleagues (1972) the only 'adequate' studies were two, both of which reported results from a project carried out at the Colorado Psychiatric Hospital, Denver. In this study 150 families requesting admission to hospital for treatment of severe emotional disturbance in one of their members were treated by short-term crisis-oriented family therapy. These families were compared with a matched group of 150 families in which a member was admitted to hospital for conventional treatment (Langsley et al, 1968; 1969). The second paper describes the methods by which the results were assessed. 'Family crisis therapy', as the authors called their method, proved just as effective as inpatient treatment. Six months later the patients treated by family therapy were functioning just as well as those who had been admitted, and were less likely to have spent some part of the six months in hospital. The cost of family treatment was about one-sixth that of inpatient care. Although the methods used in this study were criticized by Wells and his colleagues, and later by Gurman and Kniskern (1978b), this remains a powerful piece of evidence of the value of family therapy.

Wells et al (1972) suggested that adequate studies of outcome should have the following characteristics:

(a) They should be controlled, ideally with subjects randomly allocated to experimental and control groups. An alternative is the 'A-B-A' Own Control design of Goldstein and Dean (1966), in which relevant variables are measured before, during and after treatment. This latter approach has not been favoured by family therapy researchers, however, and is inherently less satisfactory than the random allocation of families to their respective groups.

(b) The control and treatment procedures should be clearly described. Since the term 'family therapy' covers many different approaches, it must be clear what methods have been used.

(c) There should be adequate pre-treatment measures; that is to say, the state of the families before treatment should be sufficiently described.

(d) The assessment of the outcome should be done by an assessor who does not know which treatment has been given to which family (that is, it is done 'blind').

(e) There must be clearly stated and properly described outcome measures.

(f) There should be adequate follow-up.

Gurman (1973) published a review of research into the effectiveness of marital therapy. He found an overall improvement rate of 66 per cent, covering a very mixed bag of patients, therapists and treatment methods. He considered this significantly better than 'spontaneous' improvement rates. No support was found for the view that co-therapy was more effective than treatment by a single therapist.

Later, Gurman and Kniskern (1978b) examined and reviewed over 200 research studies. They found evidence of improvement in in the quality of the research, compared with that reviewed previously. They also devised a 'points system' for rating the quality of research designs. Fourteen criteria were used. Some, such as controlled assignment to treatment conditions and the use of pre- and post-treatment measurement of change, rated five points, while others, for example three months or more of follow-up, and outcome assessment allowing for positive or negative change, rated only one each. A score of 26 was possible. Zero to 10 was considered a poor rating, 10 ½ to 15 fair, 15 ½ to 20 good, and over 20 very good.

Overall improvement rates for non-behavioural family therapy were found to be in the range from 65 to 75 per cent, except when the identified patient was a daypatient, when it was 57 per cent. All the day hospital studies were of families in which the identified patient was an adult, and day hospitals tend to contain mainly chronic and intractable patients, which probably accounts for the lower improvement rates in this group.

Non-behavioural marital therapy was associated with improvement in about 66 per cent of cases when treatment was either conjoint (both partners treated by one therapist), conjoint group (in which groups of marital couples are treated) or collaborative-concurrent (in which spouses are treated by different therapists who communicate with each other); but when individual treatment was used for marital problems, there was improvement in only 48 per cent of cases.

The overall improvement rates, derived as they are from a very mixed group of studies, can at best give only a very general idea of the results obtained. Gurman and Kniskern (1978b) found the results from the Philadelphia Child Guidance Clinic to be the most impressive, especially their studies of anorexics, asthmatics and diabetics (Minuchin et al, 1975; Rosman et al, 1977; Minuchin et al, 1978).

Gurman and Kniskern (1978b) also reviewed both comparative and controlled studies of marital-family therapy. Conjoint marital therapy and conjoint group marital therapy were found to be superior to alternative treatments in 70 per cent of the comparisons, and inferior in only 5 per cent. In all six studies which compared these two types of therapy with each other, no differences were found. There were few comparative studies which included concurrent and collaborative marital therapy. In these studies also the results of individual marital therapy were found to be strikingly inferior to those of conjoint or conjoint group therapy. In only 10 per cent of the comparisons was individual therapy found to be superior to other therapies, and in only 5 per cent was it superior to conjoint or conjoint group therapy.

Every study that compared family therapy with any other type of treatment showed it to be either equal or superior to the other. The other therapies comprised individual therapy, 'service as usual' (such as inpatient treatment), standard probation programmes for delinquents, traditional parent counselling, and standard methadone or inpatient programmes for drug addicts.

Gurman and Kniskern (1978b) also reviewed 22 controlled studies of non-behavioural marital-family therapy, omitting some that were marred by serious defects. The marital therapies were reported as superior to control groups in two-thirds of the comparisons, with conjoint therapy and communications programmes (which are also conjoint) doing best. The controlled studies of non-behavioural family therapy showed that treatment was superior to no treatment in 8 of 16 comparisons. Altogether, non-behavioural marital and family therapies were found to be superior to no treatment in 18 out of 31 comparisons, with 11 showing no difference and 2 studies, though both of them non-representative, showing treatment to be worse than no treatment.

The data reviewed by Gurman and Kniskern seem to indicate that non-behavioural family and marital therapy is of some real value, but a substantial number of studies revealed no difference between treated and untreated groups. This might have been a function of the types of family therapy used, or the ways they were applied; or it may be that particular types of family therapy are suited to particular types of disorder and there was poor matching of treatments with families. This is an area which requires further research.

Another section of Gurman and Kniskern's (1978b) review dealt with non-behavioural marital-family therapy. They defined this as consisting of 'social learning theory approaches to the treatment of family systems', the essence of these being 'the exchange theory model of social psychological interaction'. According to this model, which was described in Chapter 4, the social behaviour of people engaged in any relationship depends upon the ratio of 'rewards' to 'costs'. The results were not clear-cut, especially in the treatment of marital problems.

There was a lack of studies of couples with severely disturbed relationships, and there were a number of controlled studies which failed to show the results of behavioural therapy to be superior to those found in untreated control groups. Nevertheless, couples receiving behavioural marital interventions did better than untreated control couples in 7 out of 11 studies, and behavioural interventions yielded better results than alternative treatments in 8 out of 16.

Behavioural family treatment strategies are different from the strategies used by behavioural marital therapists. They attempt to change parents' behaviour in ways which will lead to alteration in the problem behaviours of their children. Although children's behaviour is known to affect their parents' behaviour, therapy is essentially one-way, and there is not the same degree of 'exchange' or 'reciprocity' that there is in behavioural marital therapy. Most workers in this area acknowledge that many families require more extensive treatment than training the parents in more appropriate methods of managing their children's behaviour.

Gurman and Kniskern (1978b) suggest that there is evidence of the effectiveness of behavioural family interventions. In 5 out of 6 controlled trials this treatment proved better than no treatment, and in 5 out of 6 comparisons with other treatments it proved superior. Some of the best studies, however – notably those of the Utah group (Alexander and Parsons, 1973; Malouf and Alexander, 1974) – used methods which were not purely behavioural. There is also evidence that many patients either refuse behavioural treatment or drop out of it. It also seems that behavioural treatments can, like other forms of therapy, cause deterioration – as discussed in Chapter 7.

Gurman and Kniskern's review not only summarized the state of family therapy research in 1978, but also drew attention to the need for more information on a number of questions. These included the training, skill and experience needed by therapists to enable them to use particular treatment approaches successfully; the relative merits of co-therapy as opposed to treatment by a single therapist, in different conditions; the significance of the sex of the therapist; the significance of the diagnosis, severity and chronicity of the marital or family disorder in determining which treatment will be most effective, and what results may be expected; the optimal frequency with which families and marital couples should be seen; the length of treatment needed in order to ensure lasting results; the types of treatment appropriate to families of different socioeconomic and cultural backgrounds; and the question of which family members should be involved in treatment, and how far and in what circumstances the extended family and neighbourhood network should be involved. There is also need for research into the preventive aspects of family therapy.

Since the above review appeared, much further research has been reported, but many questions remain unanswered. Jacobson (1985) discerns 'encouraging signs that outcome research is becoming a growing concern among participants in the family therapy movement', but he also points out that, until recently, 'claims for the efficacy of family therapy have been based largely on speculation and anecdote'. Despite the work reviewed by Gurman and Kniskern (1978b), this is essentially true. Jacobson (1985) goes on to make a number of important points regarding family therapy outcome research. His paper perhaps charts, as well as anything that has been published, the course such research should take during the latter part of this decade. The issues he discusses are:

1. *The clinical relevance of research findings.* Differences may be statistically significant but clinically unimportant, for example because of fairly small changes in a large number of families. Statistically significant results are also more likely when large numbers of families are included in research studies, but the magnitude of the changes occurring may be small. Also important is the proportion of families in which changes occur. These points, Jacobson says, are often unclear from research reports.

2. *Comparative studies.* These are studies comparing different treatments, and they have limitations. One is that 'significant differences are rarely found between two bona fide treatments, and when they are, they are seldom replicable' (Jacobson, 1985, page 152). But just because no differences are found, we cannot conclude that no differences exist. Possible alternative explanations are that the experimental design was insufficiently powerful, the outcome measures were invalid or insensitive, or the treatments were inadequately applied. Statistically significant results can sometimes be obtained by increasing sample sizes, but this does not increase the magnitude of the effect nor its *clinical* significance. The fact that 10 per cent of people do better, on the basis of some outcome measure, with one treatment rather than another, may be statistically significant, but it may not represent a worthwhile clinical difference.

Comparative outcome studies also suffer from two other drawbacks. One is that many of the differences between the responses of families to treatment are due to the characteristics of the families; the other is that in clinical practice there is much technical overlap between models of therapy.

3. *Internal validity.* This is a function of the research design, which should ensure that what the experiment aims to measure is actually

measured. A good degree of internal validity can be hard to achieve in family therapy research. The two essentials are the appropriate use of random assignment of families to the treatment conditions being investigated, and the use of control groups. Random assignment is not used as often as it should be, yet it should present little difficulty when treatments of unknown efficacy are being compared. The use of *untreated* control groups obviously can present problems, but possible alternatives are the use of standard, established treatments, or comparison with a well-established 'spontaneous remission' rate for the category of family which is the subject of the research. Unfortunately there are, as Jacobson (1985) points out, 'in the family therapy literature few treatments which have received enough empirical support to be considered standard'. We similarly lack data on spontaneous remission rates in well defined clinical populations.

4. *Whether standardized or flexible treatments should be used in research projects.* 'Conventional wisdom,' Jacobson (1985) says, 'has experimenters writing standardized treatment manuals to guide the therapist in executing the treatment in question'. But this may detract from the efficacy of the treatment by placing constraints on the therapist which do not exist in normal clinical practice. Outcome research conducted on this basis may provide a conservative test of the efficacy of therapy, as suggested by Kazdin and Wilson (1978). On the other hand, these constraints may be balanced by such factors as the extra time and attention given to cases treated as part of a research project; the observation and taping of sessions which is more often carried out in research studies; and the support and help available when a team is involved, as is usually the case in a research project. There is therefore a case for studies comparing what Jacobson (1985) calls 'research-structured' and 'clinical flexible' conditions.

5. *Therapist variables.* Jacobson (1985) points out that, in family therapy, 'the abundance of charismatic school leaders increases the risk of confounding therapist with therapy'. He also cautions us against assuming that experienced therapists are necessarily more effective than inexperienced ones, and says that the 'scant evidence' on the subject does not support that view. There seems to be a need for studies of the relative effectiveness of experienced and inexperienced therapists. It is also unclear whether, when different therapies are compared, they should be administered by the same therapists or by different ones. Theoretically treatments should be assigned randomly to patients and therapists, but separate therapists are often used; the rationale for this is that by using experts who specialize in particular forms of therapy, such therapies are applied in 'purer' form. Jacobson, however, considers this notion 'naive'.

6. *The presenting problem.* Jacobson (1985) finally draws our attention to Haley's (1972) reminder that the primary criterion for successful therapy is whether the family 'got what they came for'. New problems, or problems which were not mentioned when the family first attended, may of course emerge during treatment, but we should never forget that our job, as therapists, is to provide a service to those who come to us for treatment, not to mould the functioning of their families to fit our own ideas of how they should be. He observes:

> But ultimately a successful outcome means that the presenting (or emergent) problem has been eliminated. Changes in family interaction are often the hypothesized means whereby a family therapist proposes to solve the problems that brought the family in. But this is only a hypothesis. The vindication of a model bent on changing family interaction is whether or not such change leads to elimination of the presenting problem. Except in those instances where dysfunctional family interaction *is* the presenting problem, measures of family interaction are at best indirect measures of treatment outcome (Jacobson, 1985, page 157).

Specialized areas of research

In addition to more general studies and reviews, there is substantial literature dealing with research in specialized areas, for example drug abuse and alcoholism (Steinglass, 1976; Janzen, 1977; Stanton, 1979; Kaufman and Kaufman, 1979; Steinglass et al, 1985), adolescent substance abuse (Levine 1985), psychosomatic disorders (Minuchin et al, 1978), cultural issues – for instance in the 'alcoholic family' (Ablon, 1980), and enrichment programmes designed to enhance the functioning of marriages and families.

The latter are interesting as they represent attempts to undertake preventive work in the family field, whereas the great bulk of family therapy research has dealt with established disorders. However, programmes such as Marriage Encounter and the Minnesota Couples Communication Program are widely used, and have been thought to help promote better communication and improved relationships. Giblin, Sprenkle and Sheehan (1985) reviewed and analyzed 85 studies of premarital, marital and family enrichment projects, involving 3886 couples or families. An examination of the results, using meta-analysis, a statistical device recently introduced into psychotherapy research, indicated that the average participant was better off than 67 per cent of those who did not participate. Yet many studies do not find evidence of significant benefit from these programmes. Giblin and his colleagues found that the studies that did produce significant findings tended to be those that were better designed, used behavioural measures, examined relationship skill areas, and used longer programmes, with less well educated subjects. Studies in which there were more 'distressed subjects' also seemed to be those in which greater effects were seen, perhaps because there was more scope for improvement. This is an interesting review, both on account of the information it provides about enrichment programmes, and because of the method used to review and evaluate the many research reports the investigators included.

There is also a need for research into the specific techniques used in family therapy. An example of such research is work that has been done on the use of paradoxical directives. Turner and Ascher (1979) reported a controlled comparison of progressive relaxation, stimulus control and paradoxical intention in the treatment of insomnia. All three treatments were found to be effective, but no significant differences in their effectiveness were discovered.

Subsequently the same authors (Ascher and Turner, 1979) reported a controlled study in which 25 subjects with insomnia were randomly assigned to three groups. One group was treated by paradoxical intention: the subjects were told to remain awake as long as possible, rather than continuing their efforts to fall asleep. They were not to engage in any activity which was incompatible with sleep, such as reading or watching television, but were to lie in a darkened room keeping their eyes open as long as possible.

The subjects in the second, 'placebo control' group were given a task previously described by Steinmark and Borkovec (1974); this involved imagining a number of bedtime activities and pairing them with neutral scenes. The 'no treatment' control subjects were provided with no treatment during the four weeks of the study, but contact was made with them every one-and-a-half weeks.

Four outcome measures were used. These were the latency period to sleep onset, the number of awakenings during the night with difficulty returning to sleep, a seven-point scale of 'restedness', and a seven-point scale of difficulty experienced falling asleep. The results were examined using appropriate statistical procedures, and it was found that paradoxical intention was significantly more effective than the two control measures on three of the four outcome measures. The rating of 'restedness' did not reveal any differences, however. The 'placebo' and 'no treatment' control groups did not differ from each other.

While this study suffered from some methodological weaknesses, including reliance on reports and ratings of sleep behaviour at home rather than observation by the experimenters, it is an interesting example of how specific treatment techniques can be evaluated.

Training family therapy researchers

Various training courses for those wishing to learn about family therapy research have been developed in recent years. Some of these are part of the general training programmes in family therapy. Sprenkle and Piercy (1984) described a graduate-level course which has been taught at Purdue University, West Lafayette, Indiana, since 1978. It consists of five units:

1. A review of the fundamentals of research methodology, which also aims to ground the student in the history of psychotherapy research.
2. An overview of family research through detailed analysis of major review articles.
3. Coverage of instrumentation tools and techniques.
4. Critical evaluation of 'key investigations' in the field.
5. Examination of the challenges of the 'new epistemologies' for family therapy research.

This course seems to cover the main areas necessary, apart from the practical experience of carrying out, or participating in, a research project.

Sources of further information

The family therapy journals regularly publish reports and reviews of research in the field. In addition, useful information is to be found in special sections of *The American Journal of Family Therapy*. This publishes periodically special reports on family measurement techniques, edited by Dennis A. Bagarozzi. These review new measuring devices as they become available. Developments in continuing education and training are reported in a section edited by Ian Alger, and a section entitled 'Research and Clinical Exchange' is edited by Alan S. Gurman. There is also a 'journal file' in which abstracts of important articles from other journals appear.

Summary

Although family therapy arose out of family research, especially research into the families of schizophrenics, there was subsequently both a separation of researchers and therapists, and a change of focus from 'schizophrenic' families to a wider range of family problems. A variety of groups, including potential clients, have need of research findings. In addition the desire of family therapists to demonstrate the efficacy of their approach has stimulated a recent resurgence in research activity.

Important areas for family therapy research are the assessment and classification of families; the description and measurement of the process of therapy; and the assessment of outcome. Major progress has been made in all these, but much remains to be done, and there is a need for improvement in both the design and the reporting of research projects. It also remains to be established whether or not radically new approaches to research are needed when the newer forms of family therapy are investigated. For the moment it seems important that family therapy, like other forms of treatment, is subjected to scientific scrutiny using established methods.

In addition to the above, there is a need for the investigation of specialized areas, such as the application of family therapy in alcoholism, drug abuse, and psychosomatic disorders. The field of prevention of family pathology is also one requiring evaluation, and already studies have been carried out to assess the value of 'enrichment' programmes designed to enhance the functioning of marriages and families. Specific therapeutic techniques, such as the use of paradoxical methods, also require evaluation.

Glossary

This glossary provides brief explanations of certain technical terms which appear in the text, for the benefit of readers who may not have training in the relevant disciplines. Terms which are explained where they occur in the text are not included here. Where a fuller explanation is provided in the companion volume, *Basic Child Psychiatry*, 4th edition, by Philip Barker (published by Collins, London 1983), the appropriate page reference is provided.

Affect. Mood.

Anorexia nervosa. A condition usually occurring in teenage girls but occasionally affecting boys. Characterized by failure to eat, loss of weight and cessation of menstruation. There may also be excessive activity, regurgitation of food and mood change. (See *Basic Child Psychiatry*, 4th edition, page 181)

Asthma. Bronchial asthma, the commonest type, is a condition in which there are attacks of difficulty in breathing with wheezing. There is contraction of the muscles in the walls of the respiratory passages, with swelling of their walls and the accumulation of liquid secretions. (See *Basic Child Psychiatry*, 4th edition, page 175.)

Aversive behaviour. Behaviour by an individual (or more than one) which tends to reduce the frequency or intensity of a particular behaviour in another individual. Thus if A shouts at, or hits B when B does a certain thing, A's behaviour might well turn out to be aversive – unless B likes being shouted at or hit, or for some other reason does not react by reducing the behaviour in question.

Client-centred treatment. A type of psychotherapy associated with Carl Rogers in which the client is encouraged to express feelings freely in the therapeutic relationship, based on the belief that clients have within them the potential for healthy growth.

Cybernetics. The study of living and non-living systems (the latter including machines and chemical and physical processes), with particular reference to control mechanisms and messages, including feedback processes.

Diabetes. In the commonest form, diabetes mellitus, the blood glucose level is elevated due to a lack of the hormone, insulin, normally formed in the pancreas. Prominent symptoms include excessive thirst, loss of weight and the production of large amounts of urine. The condition can proceed to coma.

Discriminating stimulus. A stimulus which differentially produces one of a number of possible responses.

Ego. A psychoanalytic term devised by Sigmund Freud, and denoting that part of the psychic apparatus which deals with the real-life situation. It is influenced by the *id* and the *superego*.

Factor analysis. A statistical technique which identifies the extent to which different variables fluctuate together and determines the relative contribution made by each variable to the combined result.

Hierachy/hierarchical structure. This refers to the existence in a family of clear generational boundaries, whereby the parents maintain control of the children, and exercise appropriate parental authority.

Id. A term used originally by Sigmund Freud to denote that part of the unconscious mind which contains the primitive impulses which influence, but are also regulated by, the *ego*. The primitive impulses were conceived by Freud as being primarily sexual and aggressive in nature.

Manic depressive disease. A disorder in which there are alternating episodes of mania (that is elated mood, overactivity and delusions of grandeur) and depression, often with periods of normality in between. The periods may be days, weeks or months. Also known as Bipolar Affective Disorder. (See also *Basic Child Psychiatry*, 4th edition, page 114)

Metacommunication. Communication about a communication, as when people discuss the meaning or structure of a statement made by someone.

Metalanguage. The rules and structure relating to a language. The concepts of syntax, semantics and pragmatics are metalanguage concepts.

Methadone programmes. Methadone is a drug with actions similar to morphine, but without some of the disadvantages of morphine. Methadone programmes use the prescription of methadone as a substitute for heroin in the treatment of addicts.

Modelling. Learning by observation of others.

Mucous membranes. The lining of the mouth, tongue and remainder of the alimentary tract, also of the respiratory passages and the urinary and genital passages. So called because all these membranes produce a liquid substance, mucus.

Obsessive/compulsive symptoms. Obsessions are intrusive and unwelcome thoughts and ideas which the subject wishes to resist but cannot. Compulsions are actions resulting from such thoughts, such as repetitive hand-washing which the subject feels compelled to carry out, although recognizing it as unnecessary. (See *Basic Child Psychiatry*, 4th edition, page 80)

Paranoid-schizoid functioning. A concept derived from the work of Melanie Klein, who described the paranoid-schizoid position as one of the stages of the emotional development of infants. Aggressive feelings are projected on to an external object or objects (i.e. persons), and at the same time there is a splitting of the internal representations of these objects into good and bad ones.

Projection/projected feelings. Projection is a mental mechanism in which a person's own disclaimed characteristics are attributed to another person. The process is one of which the subject is not consciously aware. Projected feelings are those attributed by the subject to others, usually because at the conscious level they are too anxiety- or guilt-promoting to be dealt with consciously. (See also *Basic Child Psychiatry*, page 7)

Reinforcing stimulus. In learning theory and behaviour therapy a reinforcing stimulus is one which results in an increase in the frequency or intensity (or both) of a particular response.

Schizophrenia. A major mental illness in which there are serious disorders of thinking, emotional responsiveness and motor functioning. Primary delusions (the attribution by the subject of special meanings to advertisements, newspaper headlines, items on TV etc.) and auditory hallucinations are also common. (See *Basic Child Psychiatry*, 4th edition, page 111)

Splitting. The division of objects by an individual into good and bad. The concept of this mental mechanism derives from the work of Melanie Klein, in whose theoretical scheme the good objects resulting from the splitting are incorporated into the self while the bad ones are projected on to another person or, in some case, several people.

Superego. That part of the unconscious mind which, in Freudian theory, is concerned with moral standards and self-criticism. It is derived from the ideals and standards of parents and others, and serves as a counter-force to the *id* in influencing the *ego*.

Trend analysis. A method of analyzing a series of measures. It takes into account all the measures in the series and statistically evaluates the contribution of each one to the total change occurring.

Triangulation. This term is used when conflict between two people is dealt with by the involvement of a third. This tends to stabilize the relationship between the two people concerned.

References

Ablon, J. (1980). 'The significance of cultural patterning for the "alcoholic family"'. *Family Process*, **19**, 127–144.

Abroms, G.M., Fellner, C.H. and Whitaker, C.A. (1971). 'The family enters the hospital'. *American Journal of Psychiatry*, **127**, 1363–1369.

Ackerman, N.W. (1956). 'Interlocking pathology in family relationships'. In *Changing Conceptions of Psychoanalytic Medicine*, ed. Redo, S. and Daniels, G. New York: Grune & Stratton.

Ackerman, N.W. (1958). *The Psychodynamics of Family Life*. New York: Norton.

Ackerman, N.W. (1961). 'A dynamic frame for the clinical approach to family conflict'. In *Exploring the Base for Family Therapy*, ed. Ackerman, N.W., Beatman, F.L. and Sherman, S.N. New York: Family Services Association of America.

Ackerman, N.W. (1966a). *Treating the Troubled Family*. New York: Basic Books.

Ackerman, N.W. (1966b). 'Family psychotherapy – theory and practice'. *American Journal of Psychotherapy*, **20**, 744–753.

Ackerman, N.W. (1970a). 'Family interviewing: the study process'. In *Family Therapy in Transition*, ed. Ackerman, N.W. Boston: Little Brown.

Ackerman, N.W. (1970b). 'Child participation in family therapy'. *Family Process*, **9**, 403–410.

Ackerman, N.W. (1970c). 'Family psychotherapy today'. *Family Process*, **9**, 123–126.

Alexander, J. and Parsons, B. (1973). 'Short-term behavioral intervention with delinquent families'. *Journal of Abnormal Psychology*, **81**, 210–225.

Alger, I. (1969). 'Therapeutic use of videotape playback'. *Journal of Nervous and Mental Disease*. **148**, 430–436.

Alger, I. (1973). 'Audio-visual techniques in family therapy'. In *Techniques of Family Therapy*, ed. Bloch, D.A. New York: Grune & Stratton.

Allman, L.R. (1982). 'The aesthetic preference: overcoming the pragmatic error'. *Family Process*, **21**, 43–56.

American Psychiatric Association (1980). *Diagnostic and Statistical Manual of Mental Disorders*. 3rd Edn. Washington, DC.

Anderson, C.M. and Stewart, S. (1983). *Mastering Resistance: A Practical Guide to Family Therapy*. New York: Guilford.

Andolfi, M. (1979). *Family Therapy: An Interactional Approach*. New York: Plenum.

Angelo, C. (1981). 'The use of the metaphoric object in family therapy'. *American Journal of Family Therapy*, **9** (1), 69–78.

Anonymous (1972). 'On the differentiation of self'. In *Family Interaction: A Dialogue between Family Therapists and Family Researchers*, ed. Framo, J. New York: Springer. (Reprinted in *Family Therapy in Clinical Practice*, ed. Bowen, M. New York: Jason Aronson, 1978.)

Aponte, H. (1976). 'The family–school interview: an eco-structural approach'. *Family Process*, **15**, 303–311.

Ascher, L.M. and Turner, R.M. (1979). 'Paradoxical intention and insomnia: an experimental investigation'. *Behaviour Research and Therapy*, **17**, 408–411.

Auerswald, E.H. (1968). 'Interdisciplinary versus ecological approach'. *Family Process*, **7**, 202–215. (Reprinted in *Progress in Group and Family Therapy*, ed. Sager, C.J. and Singer, H.S. New York: Brunner/Mazel, 1972.)

Bandler, R. and Grinder, J. (1979). *Frogs into Princes*. Moab, Utah: Real People Press.

Bandler, R. and Grinder, J. (1982). *Reframing*. Moab, Utah: Real People Press.

Bandler, R., Grinder, J. and Satir, V. (1976). *Changing with Families*. Palo Alto, California: Science and Behavior Books.

Barker, P. (1981). 'Paradoxical techniques in psychotherapy'. In *Treating Families with Special Needs*, ed. Freeman, D.S. and Trute, B. Ottawa: Alberta and Canadian Associations of Social Workers.

Barker, P. (1983). *Basic Child Psychiatry*, 4th Edn. London: Granada; Baltimore: University Park Press.

Barker, P. (1985). *Using Metaphors in Psychotherapy*. New York: Brunner/Mazel.

Barnhill, L. (1979). 'Healthy family systems'. *Family Coordinator*, **28**, 94–100.

Barnhill, L.H. and Longo, D. (1978). 'Fixation and regression in the family life cycle'. *Family Process*, **17**, 469–478.

Bateson, G. (1978). 'The birth of a matrix or double bind and epistemology'. In *Beyond the Double Bind*, ed. Berger, M. New York: Brunner/Mazel.

Bateson, G., Jackson, D.D., Haley, J. and Weakland, J. (1956). 'Toward a theory of schizophrenia'. *Behavioral Science*, **1**, 251–264. (Reprinted in *Theory and Practice of Family Psychiatry*, ed. Howells, J.G. Edinburgh: Oliver & Boyd, 1968; and in *Beyond the Double Bind*, ed. Berger, M.M. New York: Brunner/Mazel, 1978.)

Beal, E.W. (1976). 'Current trends in the training of family therapists'. *American Journal of Psychiatry*, **133**, 137–141.

Beal, E.W. (1980). 'Separation, divorce, and single-parent families'. In *The Family Life Cycle*, ed. Carter, E.A. and McGoldrick, M. New York: Gardner Press.

Beavers, W.R. (1981). 'A systems model of family for family therapists'. *Journal of Marriage and Family Therapy*, **7**, 299–307.

Beavers, W.R. (1982). 'Healthy, midrange, and severely dysfunctional families'. In *Normal Family Processes*, ed. Walsh, F. New York: Guilford.

Beavers, W.R. and Voeller, M.N. (1983). 'Family models: comparing and contrasting the Olson circumplex model with the Beavers systems model'. *Family Process*, **22**, 85–98.

Beckett, J.A. (1973). 'General systems theory, psychiatry and psychotherapy'. *International Journal of Group Psychotherapy*, **23**, 292–305.

Beels, C.C. and Ferber, A. (1969). 'Family therapy: a view'. *Family Process*, **8**, 280–318.

Bell, J.E. (1961). *Family Group Therapy*. Public Health Monograph, No. 64. Washington, DC: US Government Printing Office.

Bell, J.E. (1962). 'Recent advances in family group therapy'. *Journal of Child Psychology and Psychiatry*, **3**, 1–15.

Bell, J.E. (1975). *Family Therapy*. New York: Jason Aronson.

Benningfield, A.B. (1980). 'Multiple family therapy systems'. *Journal of Marriage and Family Counselling*, **4**, 25–34. (Reprinted in *Advances in Family Psychiatry*, vol II, ed. Howells, J.G. New York: International Universities Press.)

Bennis, W.G. and Shepard, H.A. (1956). 'A theory of group development'. *Human Relations*, **9**, 415–437.

Bentovim, A., Barnes, G.G. and Cooklin, A., eds., (1982). *Family Therapy: Complementary Frameworks of Theory and Practice*. London: Academic Press.

Bianchi S.M. and Spain, D. (1983). *American Women: Three Decades of Change*. Washington, DC: US Bureau of the Census & Government Printing Office.

Bion, W.R. (1961). *Experiences in Groups*. London: Tavistock.

Birley, J.L.T. and Brown, G.W. (1970). 'Crisis and life changes preceding the onset or relapse of acute schizophrenia: clinical aspects'. *British Journal of Psychiatry*, **116**, 327–333.

Blechman, E.A. and Rabin, C. (1982). 'Concepts and methods of explicit marital negotation training with the marriage contract game'. *American Journal of Family Therapy*, **10**, (4), 47–55.

Boszormenyi-Nagy, I. and Framo, J. (Eds.) (1965). *Intensive Family Therapy: Theoretical and Practical Aspects*. New York: Harper & Row.

Boszormenyi-Nagy, I. and Spark, G. (1973). *Invisible Loyalties: Reciprocity in Intergenerational Family Therapy*. Hagerston: Harper & Row.

Bowen, M. (1960). 'A family concept of schizophrenia'. In *The Etiology of Schizophrenia*, ed. Jackson, D.D. New York: Basic Books.

Bowen, M. (1961). 'Family psychotherapy', *American Journal of Orthopsychiatry*, **31**, 40–60.

Bowen, M. (1966). 'The use of family theory in clinical practice'. *Comprehensive Psychiatry*, **7**, 345–374. (Reprinted in *Changing Families*, ed. Haley, J. New York: Grune & Stratton, 1971; and in *Family Therapy in Clinical Practice*, ed. Bowen, M. New York: Jason Aronson, 1978.)

Bowen, M. (1976). 'Theory in the practice of psychotherapy.' In *Family Therapy*, ed. Guerin, P. New York: Gardner Press. (Reprinted in *Family Therapy in Clinical Practice*, by Bowen, M. New York: Jason Aronson, 1978.)

Bowen, M. (Ed.) (1978). *Family Therapy in Clinical Practice*. New York: Jason Aronson.

Bross, A. (1983). *Family Therapy: Principles of Strategic Practice*. New York: Guilford.

Brown, G.W. and Birley, J.L.T. (1968). 'Crisis and life changes and the onset of schizophrenia'. *Journal of Health and Social Behavior*, **9**, 203–214.

Brown, G.W., Birley, J.L.T. and Wing, J.K. (1972). 'Influence of family life on the course of schizophrenic disorders: a replication'. *British Journal of Psychiatry*, **121**, 241–258.

Bullock, D. and Kobayashi, K. (1978). 'The use of live consultation in family therapy'. *Family Therapy*, **5**, 245–250.

Byng-Hall, J. (1973). 'Family myths used as defence in conjoint family therapy'. *British Journal of Medical Psychology*, **46**, 239–250.

Cade, B. (1979). 'The use of paradox in psychotherapy'. In *Family and Marital Psychotherapy*, ed. Walrond-Skinner, S. London: Routledge & Kegan Paul.

Carter, E.A. and McGoldrick, M. (Eds.) (1980). *The Family Life Cycle: A Framework for Family Therapy*. New York: Gardner Press.

Catanzaro, R.J. Pisani, V.D., Fox, R. and Kennedy, E.R. (1973). 'Familization therapy'. *Diseases of the Nervous System*, **34**, 212–218.

Church of England (1662). *Book of Common Prayer*.

Clarke, R.V.G. (1985). 'Delinquency, environment and intervention'.

Journal of Child Psychology and Psychiatry, **26**, 505–523.

Clarkin, J.F., Frances, A.J. and Moodie, J.L. (1979). 'Selection criteria for family therapy'. *Family Process*, **18**, 391–403.

Cleghorn, J.M. and Levin, S. (1973). 'Training family therapists by setting learning objectives'. *American Journal of Orthopsychiatry*, **43**, 439–446.

Colapinto, J. (1979). 'The relative value of empirical evidence'. *Family Process*, **18**, 427–441.

Coleman, S.B. (Ed.) (1985). *Failures in Family Therapy*. New York: Guilford.

Coleman, S.B. and Gurman, A.S. (1985). 'An analysis of failures in family therapy'. In *Failures in Family Therapy*, ed. Coleman, S.B. New York: Guilford.

Coogler, O.J. (1978). *Structured Mediation in Divorce Settlements*. Lexington, Massachusetts: Lexington Books.

Cooper, A., Rampage, C. and Soucy, G. (1981). 'Family therapy training in clinical psychology programs'. *Family Process*, **20**, 155–160.

Coppersmith, E.I. (1980). 'Expanding use of the telephone in family therapy'. *Family Process*, **19**, 411–417.

Coppersmith, E.I. (1981). 'Developmental reframing'. *Journal of Strategic and Systemic Therapies*, **1**, 1–8.

Coppersmith, E.I. (1985). 'Teaching trainees to think in triads'. *Journal of Marital and Family Therapy*, **11**, 61–66.

Coyne, J.C. (1985). 'Toward a theory of frames and reframing: the social nature of frames'. *Journal of Marital and Family Therapy*, **11**, 337–344.

Coyne, J.C., Denner, B. and Ransom, D.C. (1982). 'Undressing the fashionable mind'. *Family Process*, **21**, 391–396.

Crafoord, C. (1980). 'Put the booze on the table: some thoughts about family therapy and alcoholism'. *Journal of Family Therapy*, **2**, 71–81.

Crowe, M. (1978). 'Conjoint marital therapy: a controlled outcome study'. *Psychological Medicine*, **8**, 623–636.

Dare, C. and Lindsay, C. (1979). 'Children in family therapy'. *Journal of Family Therapy*, **1**, 253–269.

Dell, P.F. (1982). 'Beyond homeostasis: toward a concept of coherence'. *Family Process*, **21**, 21–41.

De Shazer, S. (1982). *Patterns of Brief Family Therapy: An Ecosystemic Approach*. New York: Guilford.

Dicks, H. (1963). 'Object relations theory and marital studies'. *British Journal of Medical Psychology*, **36**, 125–129.

Dicks, H. (1967). *Marital Tensions*. London: Routledge & Kegan Paul.

Dilts, R. and Green, J. (1982). 'Applications of neuro-linguistic programming in family therapy'. In *Family Counselling and Therapy*, ed. Horne, A. and Ohlson, M. Itasca, Illinois: Peacock Publications.

Dilts, R., Grinder, J., Bandler, R., Bandler, L.C. and DeLozier, J. (1980). *Neuro-linguistic Programming: Volume I.* Cupertino, California: Meta Publications.

Dreikers, R. (1951). 'Family group therapy in the Chicago community child-guidance centers'. *Mental Hygiene,* **35**, 291–301.

Duhl, F.J., Kantor, D. and Duhl, B.S. (1973). 'Learning, space and action in family therapy; a primer of sculpture'. In *Techniques of Family Psychotherapy,* ed. Bloch, D.A. New York: Grune & Stratton.

Duvall, E.M. and Miller, B.C. (1985). *Marriage and Family Development,* 6th Edn. New York: Harper & Row.

Epstein, N.B. and Bishop, D.S. (1981). 'Problem centered systems therapy of the family'. *Journal of Marital and Family Therapy,* **7**, 23–31.

Epstein, N.B., Bishop, D.S. and Levin, S. (1978). 'The McMaster model of family functioning'. *Journal of Marriage and Family Counselling,* **4**, 19–31.

Epstein, N.B., Rakoff, V. and Sigal, J.J. (1968). *Family Categories Schema.* Monograph prepared in the Family Research Group of the Department of Psychiatry, Jewish General Hospital, Montreal, in collaboration with McGill University Human Development Study.

Erickson, M.H. (1980a) *The Nature of Hypnosis and Suggestion.* (Collected papers, vol. I, ed. Rossi, E.L.) New York: Irvington.

Erickson, M.H. (1980b). *Hypnotic Alteration of Sensory, Perceptual and Psychological Processes.* (Collected papers, vol. II, ed. Rossi, E.L.) New York: Irvington.

Erickson, M.H. (1980c). *Hypnotic Investigation of Psychodynamic Processes.* (Collected papers, vol. III, ed. Rossi, E. L.) New York: Irvington.

Erickson, M.H. (1980d). *Innovative Psychotherapy.* (Collected papers, vol. IV, ed. Rossi, E.L.) New York: Irvington.

Erickson, M.H. (1980e). *A Teaching Seminar with Milton H. Erickson, MD,* ed. Zeig, J.K. New York: Brunner/Mazel.

Erickson, M.H. (1982). *My Voice Will Go With You: The Teaching Tales Of Milton H. Erickson, MD.,* ed. Rosen, S. New York: Norton.

Erickson, M.H., Hershman, S. and Sector, I.I. (1961). *The Practical Application of Medical and Dental Hypnosis.* Chicago: Seminars on Hypnosis Publishing Co.

Fisch, R., Weakland, J. and Segal, S. (1982). *The Tactics of Change: Doing Therapy Briefly.* San Francisco: Jossey-Bass.

Fisher, L. (1976). 'Dimensions of family assessment: a critical review'. *Journal of Marriage and Family Counselling,* **2**, 367–382.

Fisher, L. (1977). 'On the classification of families'. *Archives of General Psychiatry,* **34**, 424–433.

Fisher, L., Anderson, A. and Jones, J. (1981). 'Types of paradoxical intervention and indication/contraindication for use in clinical practice'. *Family Process*, **20**, 25–35.

Fleck, S. (1980). 'Family functioning and family pathology'. *Psychiatric Annals*, **10**, 46–54.

Foley, V. (1974). *An Introduction to Family Therapy*. New York: Grune & Stratton.

Foulkes S.H. (1975). *Group Analytic Psychotherapy: Method and Principles*. London: Gordon & Breach.

Framo, J. (1970). 'Symptoms from a family transactional viewpoint'. In *Family Therapy in Transition*, ed. Ackerman, N.W., Lieb, J. and Pierce, J. New York: Little Brown.

Framo, J. (Ed.) (1972). *Family Interaction: A Dialogue between Family Researchers and Family Therapists*. New York: Springer.

Framo, J. (1976). 'Family of origin as a therapeutic resource in marital and family therapy: you can and should go home again'. *Family Process*, **15**, 193–210.

Framo, J. (1981). 'The integration of marital therapy with sessions with family of origin'. In *Handbook of Family Therapy*, ed. Gurman, A.S. and Kniskern, D.P. New York: Brunner/Mazel.

Frankl, V. (1939). 'Sur medikamentosen unterstutzung der psychotherapie bei neurosen'. *Schweizer Arshio fur Neurologie und Psychiatrie*, **43**, 26–31.

Frankl, V. (1960). 'Paradoxical intention: a logotherapeutic technique'. *American Journal of Psychotherapy*, **40**, 520–535.

Frankl, V. (1965). *The Doctor and the Soul: From Psychotherapy to Logotherapy*. New York: Simon & Schuster.

Friedman, E.H. (1980). 'Systems and ceremonies: a family view of rites of passage'. In *The Family Life Cycle*, ed. Carter, E.A. and McGoldrick, M. New York: Gardner Press.

Frude, N. (1980). 'Methodological problems in the evaluation of family therapy', *Journal of Family Therapy*, **2**, 29–44.

Gatti, F. and Coleman, C. (1976). 'Community network therapy: an approach to aiding families with troubled children'. *American Journal of Orthopsychiatry*, **46**, 608–617.

Giblin, P., Sprenkle, D.H. and Sheehan, R. (1985). 'Enrichment outcome research: a meta-analysis of pre-marital, marital and family interventions'. *Journal of Marital and Family Therapy*, **11**, 257–271.

Glenn, M.L. (1984). *On Diagnosis: A Systemic Approach*. New York: Brunner/Mazel.

Glick, L.D. and Kessler, D.R. (1974). *Marital and Family Therapy*. New York: Grune & Stratton.

Goldenberg, I. and Goldenburg, H. (1980). *Family Therapy: An Overview*. Monterey, California: Brooks/Cole.

Goldstein, A.P. and Dean, S.J. (1966). *The Investigation of Psychotherapy*. New York: Wiley.

Goldstein, M.J. and Rodnick, E.J. (1975). 'The family's contribution to the etiology of schizophrenia: current status'. *Schizophrenia Bulletin*, **14**, 48–73.

Gordon, D. (1978). *Therapeutic Metaphors*. Cupertino, California: Meta Publications.

Gottesman, I.I. (1978). 'Schizophrenia and genetics: Where are we? Are you sure?' In *The Nature of Schizophrenia*, ed. Wynne, L.C., Cromwell, R.L. and Matthysse, S. New York: Wiley.

Gottman, J., Notarius, C., Gonso, J. and Markman, H. (1976). *A Couple's Guide to Communications*. Champaign, Illinois: Research Press.

Gross, G. (1979). 'The family angel – the scapegoat's counterpart'. *Family Therapy*, **6**, 133–136.

Group for the Advancement of Psychiatry (1970). *The Field of Family Therapy*. Report No. 78. New York: GAP.

Guerin, P.J. (Ed.) (1976). *Family Therapy: Theory and Practice*. New York: Gardner Press.

Guerin, P.J. and Pendagast, E.G. (1976). 'Evaluation of family system and genogram'. In *Family Therapy*, ed. Guerin, P.J. New York: Gardner Press.

Gurman, A.S. (1973). 'The effects and effectiveness of marital therapy: a review of outcome research'. *Family Process*, **12**, 145–170.

Gurman, A.S. (1983). 'Family therapy research and the "new epistemology"'. *Journal of Marital and Family Therapy*, **9**, 227–234.

Gurman, A.S. and Kniskern, D.P. (1978a) 'Deterioration in marital and family therapy: empirical, clinical and conceptual issues'. *Family Process*, **17**, 3–20.

Gurman, A.S. and Kniskern, D.P. (1978b). 'Research on marital and family therapy: progress, perspective and prospect'. In *Handbook of Psychotherapy and Behavior Change*, ed. Garfield, S.L. and Bergin, A.E. New York: Wiley.

Guttman, H.A. (1975). 'The child's participation in conjoint family therapy'. *Journal of the American Academy of Child Psychiatry*, **14**, 490–499.

Haley, J. (1963). *Strategies of Psychotherapy*. New York: Grune & Stratton.

Haley, J. (1967). 'Speech sequences of normal and abnormal families with two children present'. *Family Process*, **1**, 81–97.

Haley, J. (1972). 'Critical overview of present status of family interaction research'. In *Family Interaction: A Dialogue between Family Researchers and Family Therapists*, ed. Framo, J. New York: Springer.

Haley, J. (1973). *Uncommon Therapy: The Psychiatric Techniques of Milton H. Erickson*. New York: Norton.

Haley, J. (1976). *Problem-Solving Therapy*. San Francisco: Jossey-Bass.

Haley, J. (1978). 'Ideas which handicap therapists'. In *Beyond the Double Bind*, ed. Berger, M.M. New York: Brunner/Mazel.

Haley, J. (1980). *Leaving Home*. New York: McGraw-Hill.

Haley, J. (1984). *Ordeal Therapy*. San Francisco: Jossey-Bass.

Haley, J. (1985a). *Conversations with Milton H. Erickson, MD Volume 2, Changing Couples*. New York: Triangle Press.

Haley, J. (1985b). *Conversations with Milton H. Erickson, MD Volume 3, Changing Children and Families*. New York: Triangle Press.

Hall, A.D. and Fagan, R.E. (1956). 'Definition of system'. In *General Systems: Yearbook for the Advancement of General Systems Theory*, ed. von Bertalanffy, L. and Rapopart, A.

Hammerlynck, L.A., Handy, L. and Mash, E.S. (1973). *Behavioral Change: Methodology, Concepts and Practice*. Champaign, Illinois: Research Press.

Hammond, C.D. (1984). 'Myths about Erickson and Ericksonian hypnosis'. *American Journal of Clinical Hypnosis*, **26**, 236–245.

Hare-Mustin, R. (1975). 'Treatment of temper tantrums by a paradoxical intervention'. *Family Process*, **14**, 481–485.

Hatfield, A.G. (1983). 'What families want of family therapists'. In *Family Therapy in Schizophrenia*, ed. McFarlane, W.R. New York: Guilford.

Haynes, J.M. (1981). *Divorce Mediation: A Practical Guide for Therapists and Counselors*. New York: Springer.

Haynes, J.M. (1982). 'A conceptual model of the process of family mediation: implications for training'. *American Journal of Family Therapy*, **10**, 5–16.

Heath, A.W. and Storm, C.L. (1985). 'From the institute to the ivory tower: the live supervision stage approach for teaching supervision in academic settings'. *American Journal of Family Therapy*, **13** (3), 27–36.

Heinl, P. (1985). 'The image and visual analysis of the genogram'. *Journal of Family Therapy*, **7**, 213–229.

Hodgson, J.W. and Lewis, R.S. (1979). 'Pilgrim's progress III: a trend analysis of family theory and methodology'. *Family Process*, **18**, 163–173.

Hoffman, L. (1981). *Foundations of Family Therapy: A Conceptual Framework for Systems Change*. New York: Basic Books.

Holman, A.M. (1983). *Family Assessment: Tools for Understanding and Intervention*. Beverly Hill: Sage Publications.

Howells, J.G. (1968). *Theory and Practice of Family Psychiatry*. Edinburgh: Oliver & Boyd.

Hurvitz, N. (1967). 'Marital problems following psychotherapy with one spouse'. *Journal of Consulting and Clinical Psychology*, **31**, 38–47.

Imber-Black, E. (In press). 'Towards a resource model in systemic family therapy'. In *Family Resources*, ed. Karpel, M. New York: Guilford.

Irving, H.H. (1980). *Divorce Mediation: The Rational Alternative*. New York: Universe Books.

Irving, H.H. (1981). 'Family mediation: a method for helping families resolve legal disputes'. In *Treating Families with Special Needs*, ed. Freeman, D.S. and Trute, B. Ottawa: Alberta and Canadian Associations of Social Workers.

Jackson, D.D. (1961). 'Interactional psychotherapy'. In *Contemporary Psychotherapies*, ed. Stein, M.T. New York: Free Press of Glencoe.

Jackson, D.D. (1965). 'Family rules: the marital quid pro quo'. *Archives of General Psychiatry*, **12**, 589–594.

Jackson, D.D. and Weakland, J.H. (1959). 'Schizophrenic symptoms and family interaction'. *Archives of General Psychiatry*, **1**, 589–594.

Jackson, D.D. and Weakland, J.H. (1961). 'Conjoint family therapy: some considerations on theory, technique and results'. *Psychiatry*, **24**, supplement to No. 2, 30–45.

Jacob, T. (1975). 'Family interaction in disturbed and normal families: a methodological and substantive review'. *Psychological Bulletin*, **82**, 33–65.

Jacobson, N.S. (1985). 'Family therapy outcome research: potential pitfalls and prospects'. *Journal of Marital and Family Therapy*, **11**, 149–158.

Jacobson, N.S. and Margolin, G. (1979). *Marital Therapy: Strategies Based on Social Learning and Behavior Exchange Principles*. New York: Brunner/Mazel.

Janzen, C. (1977). 'Families in the treatment of alcoholism'. *Journal of Studies in Alcoholism*, **38**, 114–130.

Kaplan, H.S. (1974). *The New Sex Therapy*. New York: Brunner/Mazel.

Kaplan, H.S. (1979). *Disorders of Sexual Desire*. New York: Brunner/Mazel.

Karpel, M.A. and Strauss, E.S. (1983). *Family Evaluation*. New York: Gardner Press.

Kaslow, F.W. (1984). 'Divorce mediation and its emotional impact on the couple and their children'. *American Journal of Family Therapy*, **12** (3), 58–66.

Kaufman, E. and Kaufman, P. (Eds.) (1979). *The Family Therapy of Drug and Alcohol Abuse*. New York: Gardner.

Kazdin, A.E. and Wilson, G.T. (1978). *Evaluation of Behavior Therapy: Issues, Evidence and Research Strategies*. Cambridge, Massachusetts: Ballinger.

Keeney, B.P. (1982). 'What is an epistemology of family therapy?' *Family Process*, **21**, 153–162.

Keeney, B.P. and Sprenkle, D.H. (1982). 'Ecosystemic epistemology: critical implications for the aesthetics and pragmatics of family therapy'. *Family Process*, **21**, 1–19.

Keller, J.F. and Protinsky, H. (1984). 'A self-management model for supervision'. *Journal of Marital and Family Therapy*, **10**, 281–288.

Keller, S. (1974). 'Does the family have a future?' In *The Family: Its Structure and Functions*, 2nd Ed., ed. Closer, R.L. New York: St. Martin's Press.

Kempler, W. (1981). *Experiential Psychotherapy Within Families*. New York: Brunner/Mazel.

Kinney, D.K. and Matthysse, S. (1978). 'Genetic transmission of schizophrenia'. *Annual Review of Medicine*, **29**, 459–473.

Kirschner, D.A. and Kirschner, S. (1986). *Comprehensive Family Therapy: An Integration of Systemic and Psychodynamic Models*. New York: Brunner/Mazel.

Kniskern, D.P. and Gurman, A.S. (1979). 'Research on training in marriage and family therapy'. *Journal of Marital and Family Therapy*, **5**, 83–94.

Knudson, R.M., Gurman, A.S. and Kniskern, D.P. (1979). 'Behavioral marital therapy: a treatment in transition'. In *Annual Review of Behavior Therapy and Practice*, ed. Franks, C. and Wilson, G. New York: Brunner/Mazel.

Kohl, R.N. (1962). 'Pathologic reactions of marital partners to improvement of patients'. *American Journal of Psychiatry*, **118**, 1036–1041.

Kramer, J.R. and Reitz, M. (1980). 'Using videotape playback to train family therapists'. *Family Process*, **19**, 145–150.

Kressel, K., Jaffee, N., Tuchman, B., Watson, C. and Deutsch, M. (1980). 'A typology of divorcing couples: implications for mediation and the divorce process'. *Family Process*, **19**, 101–116.

Laing, R.D. (1965). 'Mystification, confusion and conflict'. In *Intensive Family Therapy*, ed. I. Boszormenyi-Nagy and J. Framo. New York: Harper & Row.

Laing, R.D. and Esterson, A. (1970). *Sanity, Madness and the Family*. London: Tavistock; Baltimore: Penguin. (Republished by Basic Books, New York, 1971.)

Langsley, D.G., Flomenhaft, K. and Machotka, P. (1969). 'Follow-up evaluation of family crisis therapy'. *American Journal of Orthopsychiatry*, **39**, 753–759.

Langsley, D.G., Pittman, F.S., Machotka, P. and Flomenhaft, K. (1968). 'Family crisis therapy: results and implications'. *Family Process*, **7**, 145–158.

Lankton, S. and Lankton, C. (1983). *The Answer Within*. New York: Brunner/Mazel.

Laqueur, H.P. (1973). 'Multiple family therapy: questions and answers'. In *Techniques of Family Therapy*, ed. Bloch, D.S. New York: Grune &

Stratton.

Laqueur, H.P. (1976). 'Multiple family therapy'. In *Family Therapy: Theory and Practice*, ed. Guerin, P. New York: Gardner Press.

Laqueur, H.P., Wells, C.F. and Agresti, M. (1969). 'Multiple family therapy in a state hospital'. *Hospital and Community Psychiatry*, **20**, 13–22.

Leadbetter, B. and Farber, B.A. (1983). 'The limits of reciprocity in behavioral marriage therapy'. *Family Process*, **22**, 229–237.

Lederer, W.J. (1981). *Marital Choices: Forecasting, Assessing and Improving a Relationship*. New York: Norton.

Leff, J.P., Hirsch, S.R., Gaind, R., Rohde, P.D. and Stevens, B.C. (1973). 'Life events and maintenance therapy in schizophrenic relapse'. *British Journal of Psychiatry*, **123**, 659–660.

Leff, J.P., Kuipers, L. and Berkowitz, R. (1983). 'Intervention in families of schizophrenics and its effect on relapse rate'. In *Family Therapy in Schizophrenia*, ed. McFarlane, W.R. New York: Guilford.

Leff, J.P. and Vaughn, C. (1981). 'The role of maintenance therapy and relatives' expressed emotion in relapse of schizophrenia'. *British Journal of Psychiatry*, **139**, 121–134.

Leff, J.P. and Vaughn, C. (1985). *Expressed Emotion in Families*. New York: Guilford.

Leiblum, S.R. and Pervin, L.A. (1980). *Principles and Practice of Sex Therapy*. New York: Guilford.

Levine, B.L. (1985). 'Adolescent substance abuse: toward an integration of family systems and individual adaptation theories'. *American Journal of Family Therapy*, **13** (2), 3–16.

Liberman, R.P. (1970). 'Behavioural approaches in family and couple therapy'. *American Journal of Orthopsychiatry*, **40**, 106–118.

Liddle, H.A. (1980). 'On teaching a contractual or systemic therapy: training content, goals and methods'. *American Journal of Family Therapy*, **8** (1), 59–69.

Liddle, H.A., Breunlin, D.C., Schwartz, R.C. and Constantine, J.A. (1984). 'Training family therapy supervisors: issues of content, form and context'. *Journal of Marital and Family Therapy*, **10**, 139–150.

Liddle, H.A. and Halpin, R.J. (1978). 'Family therapy training and supervision literature: a comparative review'. *Journal of Marriage and Family Counselling*, **4**, 77–98.

Liddle, H.A. and Saba, G.W. (1982). 'Teaching family therapy at the introductory level: a conceptual model emphasizing a pattern which connects training and therapy'. *Journal of Marital and Family Therapy*, **8**, 63–72.

Lidz, R.W. and Lidz, T. (1949). 'The family environment of schizophrenic patients'. *American Journal of Psychiatry*, **106**, 332–345.

Lidz, T., Cornelison, A.R., Terry, D. and Fleck, S. (1958). 'Intrafamilial environment of the schizophrenic patient: VI – the transmission of irrationality'. *AMA Archives of Neurology and Psychiatry*, **79**, 305–316.

Lowery, C.R. (1984). 'Parents and divorce: identifying the support network for decisions about custody'. *American Journal of Family Therapy*, **12** (3), 26–32.

MacGregor, R. (1962). 'Multiple impact psychotherapy with families'. *Family Process*, **1**, 15–29.

MacGregor, R., Ritchie, A.M., Serrano, A.C. and Schuster, F.P. (1964). *Multiple Impact Therapy with Families*. New York: McGraw-Hill.

MacKinnon, L. (1983). 'Contrasting strategic and Milan therapies'. *Family Process*, **22**, 425–438.

Madanes, C. (1981). *Strategic Family Therapy*. San Francisco: Jossey-Bass.

Malouf, R. and Alexander, J. (1974). 'Family crisis intervention: a model and technique of training'. In *Therapeutic Needs of the Family*, ed. Hardy, R.E. and Cull, J.G. Springfield Illinois: Charles C. Thomas.

Marlow, L. (1985a). 'Divorce mediation: therapists in the legal world'. *American Journal of Family Therapy*, **13** (1), 3–21.

Marlow, L. (1985b). 'Divorce mediation: therapists in their own world'. *American Journal of Family Therapy*, **13** (3), 3–10.

Masters, W. and Johnson, V. (1966). *Human Sexual Response*. Boston: Little Brown.

Masters, W. and Johnson, V. (1970). *Human Sexual Inadequacy*. Boston: Little Brown; London: Churchill.

Maturana, H.R. (1978). 'Biology of language: the epistemology of reality'. In *Psychology and Biology of Language and Thought*, ed. Miller, G.A. and Lenneberg, E. New York: Academic Press.

McDermott, J.F. and Char, W.F. (1974). 'The undeclared war between child and family therapy'. *Journal of the American Academy of Child Psychiatry*, **13**, 422–436.

McFarland, D.J. (1971). *Feedback Mechanisms in Animal Behaviour*. London: Academic Press.

McFarlane, W.R. (1983a). *Family Therapy in Schizophrenia*. New York: Guilford.

McFarlane, W.R. (1983b). 'Introduction'. In *Family Therapy in Schizophrenia*, ed. McFarlane, W.R. New York: Guilford.

McFarlane, W.R. (1983c). 'Systemic family therapy in schizophrenia'. In *Family Therapy in Schizophrenia*, ed. McFarlane, W.R. New York: Guilford.

McGoldrick, M. (1982). 'Ethnicity and family therapy: an overview', in *Ethnicity and Family Therapy*, ed. McGoldrick, M., Pearce, J.K. and Giordano, J. New York: Guilford.

McGoldrick, M. and Carter, E.A. (1982). 'The family life cycle'. In *Normal*

Family Processes, ed. Walsh, F. New York: Guilford.

McGoldrick, M. and Gerson, R. (1985). *Genograms in Family Assessment.* New York: Norton.

McGoldrick, M., Pearce, J.K. and Giordano, J. (1982). *Ethnicity and Family Therapy.* New York: Guilford.

Midlefort, C. (1957). *The Family in Psychotherapy.* New York: McGraw-Hill.

Mills, J. and Crowley, R. (1986). *Therapeutic Metaphors for Children and the Child Within.* New York: Brunner/Mazel.

Minuchin, S. (1974). *Families and Family Therapy.* Cambridge, Massachusetts: Harvard University Press.

Minuchin, S., Baker, L., Rosman, B.L., Liebman, R., Millman, M. and Todd, T.G. (1975). 'A conceptual model of psychosomatic illness in children'. *Archives of General Psychiatry*, **32**, 1031–1038.

Minuchin, S. and Fishman, H.C. (1981). *Family Therapy Techniques.* Cambridge, Massachusetts: Harvard University Press.

Minuchin, S., Montalvo, B., Guerney, B.G., Rosman, B.L. and Schumer, B.G. (1967). *Families of the Slums.* New York: Basic Books.

Minuchin, S., Rosman, B.L. and Baker, L. (1978). *Psychosomatic Families: Anorexia Nervosa in Context.* Cambridge, Massachusetts: Harvard University Press.

Montalvo, B. (1973). 'Aspects of live supervision'. *Family Process*, **12**, 343–359.

Napier, A.Y. and Whitaker, C.A. (1978). *The Family Crucible.* New York: Harper & Row.

New English Bible (1970). Quotation from Leviticus, chapter 16, verses 20–22.

Nichols, M.P. (1984). *Family Therapy: Concepts and Methods.* New York: Gardner Press.

Oliver, J.E. and Buchanan, A.H. (1979). 'Generations of maltreated children and multiagency care in one kindred'. *British Journal of Psychiatry*, **135**, 289–303.

Olson, D.H., Russell, C. and Sprenkle, D.H. (1983). 'Circumplex model of marital and family systems: VI. Theoretical update'. *Family Process*, **22**, 69–83.

Olson, D.H., Sprenkle, D.H. and Russell, C. (1979). 'Circumplex model of marital and family systems: I. Cohesion and adaptability dimensions, family types and clinical applications'. *Family Process*, **18**, 3–28.

Otto, H. (1962). 'The personal and family resource development programmes: a preliminary report'. *International Journal of Social Psychiatry*, **2**, 329–338.

Palazzoli, M.S. (1978). *Self-Starvation.* New York: Jason Aronson.

Palazzoli, M.S. (1980). 'Why a long interval between sessions? The therapeutic control of the family-therapist system'. In *Dimensions of Family Therapy*, ed. Andolphi, M. and Zwerling, I. New York: Guilford.

Palazzoli, M.S., Boscolo, L., Cecchin, G. and Prata, G. (1978a). *Paradox and Counterparadox*. New York: Jason Aronson.

Palazzoli, M.S., Boscolo, L., Cecchin, G. and Prata, G. (1978b). 'A ritualized prescription in family therapy: odd days and even days'. *Journal of Marriage and Family Counselling*, **4**, 3–9.

Palazzoli, M.S., Boscolo, L., Cecchin, G. and Prata, G. (1980). 'Hypothesizing – circularity – neutrality: three guidelines for the conductor of the session'. *Family Process*, **19**, 3–12.

Papp, P. (1977). *Family Therapy: Full Length Case Studies*. New York: Gardner Press.

Papp, P. (1980). 'The Greek chorus and other techniques of paradoxical therapy'. *Family Process*, **19**, 45–57.

Papp, P. (1982). 'Staging reciprocal metaphors in a couples group'. *Family Process*, **21**, 453–467.

Papp, P. *Making the Invisible Visible*. Videotape available for rental from the Ackerman Institute for Family Therapy, 149 East 78th Street, New York, NY 10021, USA.

Patterson, G.R. (1971). *Families: Application of Social Learning to Family Life*. Champaign, Illinois: Research Press.

Patterson, G.R. (1976). 'The aggressive child: victim or architect of a coercive system'. In *Behavior Modification and Families*, ed. Mash, E.J., Hammerlynck, L.A. and Handy, L.C., New York: Brunner/Mazel.

Patterson, G.R. and Gullion, M.E. (1968). *Living with Families: New Methods for Parents and Teachers*. Champaign, Illinois: Research Press.

Patterson, G.R., Weiss, R.L. and Hops, H. (1976). 'Training in marital skills: some problems and concepts'. In *Handbook of Behavior Modification and Behavior Therapy*, ed. Leitenberg, H. Englewood Cliffs, New Jersey: Prentice-Hall.

Peck, M.S. (1985). *People of the Lie*. New York: Simon & Schuster.

Penn, P. (1982). 'Circular questioning'. *Family Process*, **21**, 267–280.

Portner, D.L. (1977). 'Hospitalization of the family in the treatment of mental patients'. *Health and Social Work*, **2**, 111–122.

Prigogine, I., Allen, P. and Herman, R. (1977). 'The evolution of complexity and the laws of nature'. In *Goals for Mankind: A Report to the Club of Rome*, ed. Laszlo, E. and Bierman J. New York: Pergamon.

Quinn, W.H., Atkinson, B.J. and Hood, C.J. (1985). 'The stuck-case clinic as a group supervision model'. *Journal of Marital and Family Therapy*, **11**, 67–73.

Raasoch, J. and Laqueur, H.P. (1979). 'Learning multiple family therapy through simulated workshops'. *Family Therapy*, **18**, 95–98.

Richter, H.E. (1974). *The Family as Patient*. London: Souvenir Press.

Riskin, J. and Faunce, E. (1972). 'An evaluative review of family interaction research'. *Family Process*, **11**, 365–455.

Ritterman, M. (1983). *Using Hypnosis in Family Therapy*. San Francisco: Jossey-Bass.

Rosen, S. (1982). *See* Erickson, M.H. (1982).

Rosman, B., Minuchin, S., Liebman, R. and Baker, L. (1977). 'Input and outcome of family therapy in anorexia nervosa'. In *Adolescent Psychiatry*, vol. 5. ed. Feinstein, S.C. and Giovacchini, P.L. New York: Jason Aronson.

Ruesch, J. and Bateson, G. (1968). *Communication: The Social Matrix of Psychiatry*. New York: Norton.

Rueveni, U. (1975). 'Network intervention with a family in crisis'. *Family Process*, **14**, 193–203.

Russell, C. (1979). 'Circumplex model of family systems. III: empirical evaluation with families'. *Family Process*, **18**, 29–45.

Rutter, M., Maughan, N., Mortimore, P. and Ouston, J. (1979). *Fifteen Thousand Hours*. London: Open Books.

Rutter, M., Shaffer, D. and Shepherd, M. (1975). *A Multi-Axial Classification of Child Psychiatric Disorders*. Geneva: WHO.

Rutter, M., Tizard, J. and Whitmore, K. (1970). *Education, Health and Behavior*. London: Longman.

Satir, V. (1967). *Conjoint Family Therapy*. Palo Alto, California: Science and Behaviour Books.

Satir, V. (1972). *Peoplemaking*. Palo Alto, California. Science and Behaviour Books.

Satir, V. (1981). Family Therapy Workshop. Denver, Colorado.

Schlesinger, B. (1979). *Families: Canada*. Montreal: McGraw-Hill Ryerson.

Schwartzman, J. (1984). 'Family theory and the scientific method'. *Family Process*, **23**, 223–236.

Searles, H.P. (1959). 'The effort to drive the other person crazy'. *British Journal of Medical Psychology*, **32**, 1–18.

Sheehan, R., Storm, C.L. and Sprenkle, D.H. (1982). *Therapy Based on a Cybernetic Epistemology: Problems and Solutions for the Researcher*. Panel presented at the Annual Meeting of the American Association for Marriage and Family Therapy, Dallas, October, 1982.

Sheinberg, M. (1985). 'The debate: a strategic technique'. *Family Process*, **24**, 259–271.

Singer, M.T. and Wynne, L.C. (1965). 'Thought disorder and family relations in schizophrenia. IV: results and implications'. *Archives of General Psychiatry*, **12**, 201–212.

Singer, M.T., Wynne, L.C. and Toohey, M.,. (1978). 'Communication disorders and the families of schizophrenics'. In *The Nature of Schizophrenia*, ed. Wynne, L.C., Cromwell R.L., and Matthysse, S. New York: Wiley.

Skynner, A.C.R. (1969a). 'Indications and contra-indications for conjoint family therapy'. *International Journal of Social Psychiatry*, **15**, 145–149.

Skynner A.C.R. (1969b). 'A group-analytic approach to conjoint family therapy'. *Journal of Child Psychology and Psychiatry*, **10**, 81–106.

Skynner, A.C.R. (1974). 'Boundaries'. *Social Work Today*, **5**, 290–294.

Skynner, A.C.R. (1976). *One Flesh: Separate Persons*. London: Constable. (Published in the USA as *Systems of Family and Marital Psychotherapy*. New York: Brunner/Mazel.)

Slipp, S. and Kressel, K. (1978). 'Difficulties in family therapy evaluation'. *Family Process*, **17**, 409–422.

Speck, R.V. and Attneave, C. (1971). 'Network therapy'. In *Changing Families*, ed. Haley, J. New York: Grune & Stratton.

Speck, R.V. and Ruevini, U. (1969). 'Network therapy: a developing concept'. *Family Process*, **8**, 182–191.

Sprenkle, D.H. and Olson, D.H. (1978). 'Circumplex model of marital systems. IV: empirical study of clinic and non-clinic couples'. *Journal of Marriage and Family Counselling*, **4**, 59–74.

Sprenkle, D.H. and Piercy, F.P. (1984). 'Research in family therapy: a graduate level course'. *Journal of Marital and Family Therapy*, **10**, 225–240.

Stanton, M.D. (1979). 'Family treatment approaches to drug abuse problems: a review'. *Family Process*, **18**, 251–280.

Steinberg, D. (1983). *The Clinical Psychiatry of Adolescence*. Chichester: John Wiley.

Steinglass, P. (1976). 'Experimenting with family treatment approaches to alcoholism, 1950–1975: a review'. *Family Process*, **15**, 97–123.

Steinglass, P., Tislenko, L. and Reiss, D. (1985). 'Stability/instability in the alcoholic marriage'. *Family Process*, **24**, 365–376.

Steinhauer, P.D., Santa-Barbara, J. and Skinner, H. (1984). 'The process model of family functioning'. *Canadian Journal of Psychiatry*, **29**, 77–88.

Steinmark, S.W. and Borkovec, T.D. (1974). 'Active and placebo treatment effects on moderate insomnia under counterdemand and positive demand instructions'. *Journal of Abnormal Psychology*, **83**, 157–163.

Stoller, F.H. (1968). 'The use of videotape (focused feedback) in group counselling and group therapy'. *Journal of Research and Development in Education*, **1**, 30–44.

Stuart, R.B. (1969). 'Operant-interpersonal treatment for marital discord'. *Journal of Consulting and Clinical Psychology*, **33**, 675–682.

Sturgeon, D., Kuipers, L., Berkowitz, R., Turpin, G. and Leff, J. (1981).

'Psychophysiological responses of schizophrenic patients to high and low expressed emotion relatives'. *British Journal of Psychiatry*, **138**, 40–45.

Sugarman, S. (1981). 'Family therapy training in selected general psychiatry residency programs'. *Family Process*, **20**, 147–154.

Sutcliffe, P., Lovell, J. and Walters, M. (1985). 'New directions for family therapy: rubbish removal as a task of choice'. *Journal of Family Therapy*, **7**, 175–182.

Tomm, K. (1980). 'Towards a cybernetic systems approach to family therapy at the University of Calgary'. In *Perspectives on Family Therapy*, ed. Freeman, D.S. Toronto: Butterworth.

Tomm, K. (1981). 'The Milan approach to family therapy: a tentative report'. In *Treating Families with Special Needs*, ed. Freeman, D.S. and Trute, B. Ottawa: Alberta & Canadian Associations of Social Workers.

Tomm, K. (1984a). 'One perspective on the Milan systemic approach: Part I. Overview of development, theory and practice'. *Journal of Marital and Family Therapy*, **10**, 113–125.

Tomm, K. (1984b). 'One perspective on the Milan systemic approach: Part II. Description of session format, interviewing style and interventions'. *Journal of Marital and Family Therapy*, **10**, 253–271.

Tomm, K. and Leahey, M. (1980). 'Training in family assessment: a comparison of three teaching methods'. *Journal of Marital and Family Therapy*, **6**, 453–458.

Tomm, K. and Wright, L. (1979). 'Training in family therapy: perceptual, conceptual and executive skills'. *Family Process*, **18**, 227–250.

Tonge, W.L., James, D.S. and Hillman, S.M. (1975). *Families Without Hope: A Controlled Study of 33 Problem Families*. British Journal of Psychiatry Special Publication No. 11. Ashford, Kent: Headley Bros.

Tseng, W.S. and McDermott, J.F. (1979). 'Triaxial family classification'. *Journal of the American Academy of Child Psychiatry*, **18**, 22–43.

Turner, R.M. and Ascher, L.M. (1979). 'A controlled comparison of progressive relaxation, stimulus control and paradoxical intention therapies for insomnia'. *Journal of Consulting and Clinical Psychology*, **47**, 500–508.

van der Hart, O. (1983). *Rituals in Psychotherapy: Transition and Continuity*. New York: Irvington.

van Trommel, M.J. (1984). 'A consultation method addressing the therapist–family system'. *Family Process*, **23**, 469–480.

Vaughn, C.E. and Leff, J.P. (1976). 'The influence of family and social factors on the course of psychiatric illness: a comparison of schizophrenic and depressed neurotic patients'. *British Journal of Psychiatry*, **129**,

125–137.

Vogel, E.F. and Bell, N.W. (1960). 'The emotionally disturbed child as the family scapegoat'. In *A Modern Introduction to the Family*, ed. Bell, N.W. and Vogel, E. New York: Glencoe: Free Press.

von Bertalanffy, L. (1968). *General Systems Theory: Foundations, Development Application*. New York: Braziller.

Wahler, R.G. (1976). 'Deviant child behaviour within the family developmental speculations and behaviour change strategies'. In *Handbook of Behaviour Modification and Therapy*, ed. Leitenberg H. Englewood Cliffs, New Jersey: Prentice-Hall.

Wallace, A.F.C. (1966). *Religion: An Anthropological View*. New York: Random House.

Walrond-Skinner, S. (1976). *Family Therapy: The Treatment of Family Systems*. London: Routledge & Kegan Paul.

Walrond-Skinner, S. (1978). 'Indications and contra-indications for the use of family therapy'. *Journal of Child Psychology and Psychiatry*, **19**, 57–62.

Walrond-Skinner, S. (1979). *Family and Marital Psychotherapy*. London: Routledge & Kegan Paul.

Walsh, F.(Ed.) (1982). *Normal Family Processes*. New York: Guildford.

Watzlawick, P. (1978). *The Language of Change*. New York: Basic Books.

Watzlawick, P. (1982). 'Hermetic pragmaesthetics or unkempt thoughts about an issue of *Family Process, Family Process*, **21**, 401–403.

Watzlawick, P. (1983). *The Situation Is Hopeless But Not Serious*. New York: Norton.

Watzlawick, P., Beavin, J.H. and Jackson, D.D. (1967). *Pragmatics of Human Communication*. New York: Norton.

Watzlawick, P., Weakland, J. and Fisch, R. (1974). *Change: Principles of Problem Formulation and Problem Resolution*. New York: Norton.

Weakland, J. (1977). 'OK – you've been a bad mother'. In *Family Therapy: Full Length Case Studies*, ed. Papp, P. New York: Gardner Press.

Weakland, J. (1979). 'The double-bind theory'. *Journal of the American Academy of Child Psychiatry*, **18**, 54–66.

Weeks, G.R. and L'Abate, L. (1982). *Paradoxical Psychotherapy: Theory and Practice with Individuals, Couples and Families*. New York: Brunner/Mazel.

Weiner, N. (1948). *Cybernetics, or Control and Communication in the Animal and the Machine*. Cambridge, Massachusetts: Technology Press.

Weiss, R.L., Birchler, G.R. and Vincent, J.P. (1974). 'Contractual models for negotiation in marital dyads'. *Journal of Marriage and the Family*, **36**, 321–331.

Wells, R.A. Dilkes, T.C. and Burckhard, N.T. (1972). 'The results of family therapy: a critical review of the literature'. *Family Process*, **11**, 189–207.

Wendorf, D.J. (1984). 'A model for training practising professionals in family therapy'. *Journal of Marital and Family Therapy*, **10**, 31–41.

Werry, J.S. (1979). 'Family therapy: behavioral approaches'. *Journal of the American Academy of Child Psychiatry*, **18**, 91–102.

Whitaker, C.A. (1958). 'Psychotherapy with couples'. *American Journal of Psychotherapy*, **12**, 18–23.

Whitaker, C.A. (1976). 'The hindrance of theory in clinical work'. In *Family Therapy: Theory and Practice*, ed. Guerin, P. New York: Gardner Press.

Whitaker, C.A. (1982). 'Comments on Keeney and Sprenkle's paper'. *Family Process*, **21**, 405–406.

Whitehead, A.N. and Russell, B. (1910). *Principia Mathematica*. Cambridge University Press.

Wilder, C. (1982). 'Muddles and metaphors: a response to Keeney and Sprenkle'. *Family Process*, **21**, 397–400.

Winnicott, D. (1960). *The Maturational Process and the Facilitating Environment*. London: Hogarth.

Winter, W. and Ferriera, A.J. (Eds.) (1969). *Research in Family Interaction: Readings and Commentary*. Palo Alto, California: Science and Behavior Books.

Wolin, S.J. and Bennett, L.A. (1984). 'Family rituals'. *Family Process*, **23**, 401–420.

Woods, M.D. and Martin D. (1984). 'The work of Virginia Satir: understanding her theory and technique'. *American Journal of Family Therapy*, **12** (4), 3–11.

Wright, L.M. and Leahey, M. (1984). *Nurses and Families: A Guide to Family Assessment and Intervention*. Philadelphia: F.A. Davis.

Wynne, L.C. (1961). 'The study of intrafamilial alignments and splits in exploratory family therapy'. In *Exploring the Base for Family Therapy*, ed. Ackerman, N., Beatman, F. and Sherman, S. New York: Family Service.

Wynne, L.C. (1981). 'Current concepts about schizophrenics and family relationships'. *Journal of Nervous and Mental Disease*, **167**, 144–158.

Wynne, L.C. (1983). 'Family research and family therapy: a reunion?' *Journal of Marital and Family Therapy*, **9**, 113–117.

Wynne, L.C., Cromwell, R.L. and Matthysse, S. (1978). *The Nature of Schizophrenia: new approaches to research and treatment*. New York: Wiley.

Wynne, L.C., Jones, J.E., and Al-Khayyal, M. (1982). 'Healthy family communication patterns: observations in families "at risk" for psychopathology'.In *Normal Family Processes*, ed. Walsh, F. New York: Guilford.

Wynne, L.C., Ryckoff, I., Day, J. and Hirsch, S. (1958). 'Pseudomutuality in the family relations of schizophrenics', *Psychiatry*, **21**, 205–220.

Appendix A

Family Therapy Journals

The American Journal of Family Therapy. Published quarterly by Brunner/ Mazel Inc., 19 Union Square, New York, NY 10003, USA. Includes summaries of articles from other journals. Special sections on continuing education and training, family measurement techniques, and 'research and clinical exchange' appear periodically.

The Australian and New Zealand Journal of Family Therapy. Lister House, 4/142 Ward Street, North Adelaide, 5006, South Australia, Australia. The main family therapy journal in the southern hemisphere.

The Family. Published twice a year by the Center for Family Learning, 10 Hanford Avenue, New Rochelle, NY 10805, USA. Deals principally with the application of Bowenian theory to family problems.

Family Process. Published quarterly by Family Process Inc., 149 East 78th Street, New York, NY 10021, USA. The longest- established journal in the field, and one of the best-known.

Family Relations Published quarterly by the National Council on Family Relations, 1910 W County Road B, Suite 147, St. Paul, Minnesota, 55113, USA.

Family Systems Medicine. Published quarterly by Brunner/Mazel Inc., 19 Union Square West, New York, NY 10003, USA. This is described as 'a journal at the confluence of family therapy, systems theory and modern medicine'. It contains much that is relevant to family therapy.

Family Therapy. Published three times per year by Libra Publishers Inc., 391 Willets Road, Roslyn Heights, New York, NY 11577, USA. This is the journal of the Family Institute of Marin, California.

The Family Therapy Networker. Published bi-monthly by the Family Therapy Network, 7703 13th Street NW, Washington, DC 20012, USA. An interesting journal which aims to promote contact between family therapy centres. Publishes news, interviews with prominent people in the field, and articles on various aspects of family therapy.

Family Therapy News. Published every two months by the American Association for Marital and Family Therapy, 1717 K Street, NW, Suite 407, Washington, DC 20006, USA. Contains news, interviews with leading therapists, information on legislative developments (mainly in the USA), and data on relevant current social trends.

The International Journal of Family Psychiatry. Published quarterly by International Universities Press Inc., 59 Boston Post Road, PO Box 1524, Madison, Connecticut 16443–1524, USA.

The International Journal of Family Therapy. Published quarterly by Human Sciences Press, 72 Fifth Avenue, New York, NY 10011, USA.

The Journal of Family Therapy. Published quarterly by Academic Press Inc. (London) Ltd, 24–28 Oval Road, London NW1 7DX England. The journal of the Association for Family Therapy; publishes mainly papers from British authors.

The Journal of Marital and Family Therapy. Published quarterly by the American Association for Marital and Family Therapy, 1717 K Street NW, Suite 407, Washington, DC 20006, USA. The academic journal of the National Council on Family Relations; a prestigious publication.

The Journal of Marriage and the Family. Published quarterly by the National Council on Family Relations, 1910 W County Road B, Suite 147, St. Paul, Minnesota 55113, USA.

Journal of Strategic and Systemic Therapies. Published quarterly by Donald E. Efron, Box 2484, Station A, London, Ontario N6A 4G7, Canada. Although not specifically a family therapy journal, it publishes many papers on family therapy and on therapy techniques suitable for use with families.

Marriage and Family Review. Published every two months by Haworth Press, 149 Fifth Avenue, New York, NY 10010, USA. A journal of abstracts drawn from a wide variety of sources.

Family Therapy Training Centres

A list of training centres in the USA and several other countries, compiled by Howard M. Weiss and D.A. Bloch, is available from Family Process, 149 East 78th Street, New York, NY 10021, USA.

In the United Kingdom, information can be obtained from: Association for Family Therapy, 6 Heol Seddon, Danescourt, Llandaff, Cardiff CF5 2QX.

Index of Authors

Subject Index